Sport in the Global Society

General Editor: J.A. Mangan

C'

LAW AND SPORT IN CONTEMPORARY SOCIETY

SPORT IN THE GLOBAL SOCIETY

General Editor: J.A. Mangan

The interest in sports studies around the world is growing and will continue to do so. This unique series combines aspects of the expanding study of *sport in the global society*, providing comprehensiveness and comparison under one editorial umbrella. It is particularly timely, with studies in the political, cultural, anthropological, ethnographic, social, economic, geographical and aesthetic elements of sport proliferating in institutions of higher education.

Eric Hobsbawm once called sport one of the most significant practices of the late nineteenth century. Its significance was even more marked in the late twentieth century and will continue to grow in importance into the new millennium as the world develops into a 'global village' sharing the English language, technology and sport.

Other Titles in the Series

Superman Supreme
Fascist Body as Political Icon
– Global Fascism
Edited by J.A. Mangan

Shaping the Superman
Fascist Body as Political Icon
– Aryan Fascism
Edited by J.A. Mangan

Scoring for Britain
International Football and International
Politics, 1900–1939
Peter J. Beck

Sporting Nationalisms
Identity, Ethnicity, Immigration and
Assimilation
Edited by Mike Cronin and David Mayall

Footbinding, Feminism and Freedom
The Liberation of Women's Bodies in
Modern China
Fan Hong

The Games Ethic and Imperialism
Aspects of the Diffusion of an Ideal
J.A. Mangan

The Race Game
Sport and Politics in South Africa
Douglas Booth

Rugby's Great Split
Class, Culture and the Origins of Rugby
League Football
Tony Collins

Making the Rugby World
Race, Gender, Commerce
Edited by Timothy J.L. Chandler and John
Nauright

The First Black Footballer
Arthur Wharton 1865–1930:
An Absence of Memory
Phil Vasili

Cricket and England
A Cultural and Social History of the
Inter-war Years
Jack Williams

France and the 1998 World Cup
The National Impact of a World Sporting
Event
Edited by Hugh Dauncey and Geoff Hare

LAW AND SPORT IN CONTEMPORARY SOCIETY

Editors
STEVE GREENFIELD
and
GUY OSBORN
University of Westminster

FRANK CASS
LONDON   PORTLAND, OR

First published in 2000 in Great Britain by
FRANK CASS PUBLISHERS
Newbury House, 900 Eastern Avenue
London, IG2 7HH

and in the United States of America by
FRANK CASS PUBLISHERS
c/o ISBS, 5804 N.E. Hassalo Street
Portland, Oregon 97213-3644

Copyright © 2000 Frank Cass & Co. Ltd.

Website: www.frankcass.com

British Library Cataloguing in Publication Data

Law and sport in contemporary society. - (Sport in the
  global society ; no. 22)
  1. Sports - Law and legislation
  I. Greenfield, Steve, 1960- II. Osborn, Guy, 1966-
  34'.099

ISBN 0-7146-5048-X (cloth)
ISBN 0-7146-8124-5 (paper)
ISSN 1368-9789

Library of Congress Cataloging-in-Publication Data

Law and sport in contemporary society / editors, Steve Greenfield
and Guy Osborn.
    p. cm. – (Sport in the global society, ISSN 1368-9789 ; no. 22)

  Includes bibliographical references and index.
  ISBN 0-7146-5048-X (cloth) – ISBN 0-7146-8124-5 (paper)
  1. Sports–Law and legislation. I. Greenfield, Steve, 1960– .
II. Osborn, Guy, 1966–   . III. Cass series–sport in the global
society ; 22.
  K3702.L39 2000
  344.73'099–dc21   00-012077

Printed in Great Britain by
MPG Books Ltd, Bodmin, Cornwall

This book is dedicated to the memory of

JOHN WILLIAM OSBORN

a fighter, gone too soon…

Contents

Part 3: Statutory Intervention

Part 4: Future Areas of Dispute

Series Editor's Foreword

In *A Man for All Seasons* Robert Bolt comments:

> The law is a causeway upon which so long as he keeps to it, a citizen may walk safely.

In contrast in the *Threepenny Opera*, Bertolt Brecht remarks:

> The law is simply and safely for the exploitation of those who do not understand it or of those who, for naked need, cannot obey it.

As the saying goes: you pays your money and you takes your choice!

In which camp do the editors of *Law and Sport in Contemporary Society* pitch their tent? In this ground-breaking (a not infrequently overused expression in academe but emphatically not so in this instance) book Steve Greenfield and Guy Osborn are firmly on the side of Robert Bolt while not quite so convinced as he seems to be of the reassuring security of the law.

With good timing the editors are also riding an academic wave as courses in sport and the law, sensibly, given the significance of the subject, now grace Sports Studies degrees in several universities, while law text books have emerged on the subject in recent years and there is even a journal on the subject for the legal profession.

Nor is this all. Specific sports, most noticeably soccer, which now contains a 'plethora of football-specific legislation' (p.xii) are increasingly involved directly in the law. In view of this and at least one striking paradox – boxing contradicts the specific legal principles covering the infliction of deliberately physical harm – Greenfield and Osborn have gathered together a set of arguments comprising a case for the adoption of a specific and independent concept: sports law. They postulate cautiously that perhaps sport (*per se*) is an area that has become ripe for legal regulation. The era of substantial, but not complete and certainly not wholly effective, freedom from the law may well be, and arguably should be, over – to overcome at least in part what Alfred Tennyson once noted, was

> The lawless science of our law,
> That codeless myriad of precedent
> That wilderness of single instances.

and, perhaps more to the point, the seemingly increasing ineffectiveness of sports bodies to regulate their own affairs satisfactorily. As Mihir Bose has recently remarked in *The Daily Telegraph* apropos of the transfer system: 'Football has always tried to be different to any other profession. As long as it was a cottage industry it did not matter, now it is a major multi-billion pounds industry it cannot get away with its arcane rules.'

As several of the chapters make abundantly clear, this is both a complicated and contentious area of debate and one that is far from resolution. In this regard what *Law and Sport in Contemporary Society* reveals all too clearly is that if Robert Bolt is to be proved right in the specific case of the law and modern sport, there is still some way yet to go. Few things no doubt will reveal this more clearly than the recent changes that FIFA and UEFA – prodded by the European Commission – are proposing to the European transfer system. An early indication of the troubles that lie ahead was the plunge in Manchester United shares that followed the FIFA and UEFA action.

In passing, I must confess that I have given way to the impulse to reveal a well-meaning bias – I warmed to the editor's statement that sports lawyers in their case-study work 'have an enormous amount to gain from the research of sports historians' (p.xiii)!

Law and Sport in Contemporary Society is a significant, important and welcome addition to sports studies and Sport in the Global Society.

J.A. Mangan
International Research Centre for Sport, Socialisation and Society
University of Strathclyde
October 2000

Introduction: Locating Law and Sport

Steve Greenfield and Guy Osborn

The thrust of this work concerns elements of the relationship between sport and the law. The breadth of the book, which encompasses elements of criminal, civil, public and European law, points towards an increasingly complex and extensive relationship, yet the very use of the phrase 'sport and law' is in itself contentious. There is a question mark as to whether sports law occupies any distinct identity. One view is that we are merely concerned with a coalescence of laws that impinge upon sport in a variety of areas. Within this model the subject matter might be dissected as instances of the application of traditionally classified legal areas to sport. For example, a negligence action rooted in a careless on field tackle or the tax implications of a cricketer's benefit. On this view, sports law has no independent identity but is only a subject area within which normal legal principles are to be applied. The alternative perspective is to consider sports' law as a readily identifiable discipline with its own characteristics, albeit one that draws upon other elements in addition to the unique features that set it aside.

The question remains as to what criteria are required to establish an independent area of both academic study and practice? On one level there needs to be the emergence of academic writing and this is now clearly occurring. Aside from the lone furrow previously ploughed by Edward Grayson with *Sport and the Law*, there are now other text books such as Gardiner and others, *Sports Law*. Heavyweight academic journals also feature articles on aspects of sport and the law, and there is a dedicated *Sport and the Law Journal* published under the auspices of the British Association of Sport and Law, which is primarily aimed at practitioners working within the field. Accompanying this has been the rise in academic courses dealing with sport and law that have recently developed in this country at Warwick University, Anglia Polytechnic University and Manchester Metropolitan University, as well as our own course at Westminster. Elsewhere, and particularly in the United States, this movement has a longer historical lineage with the acceptance of sports law and entertainment law as areas worthy of serious study. In this country we are now seeing the beginnings of a broader movement that embraces sports law – although the aims and objectives of the participants do not always coincide – and at the same time the legitimization of the area.

There is, in addition to academic study, the emergence of a specific body of legal rules that apply to sport; the plethora of football-specific legislation (see Chapter 10), both in relation to ground safety and the control of fans, are apposite examples. Within football, the reports of both Popplewell and Taylor dealt with the issue of specificity and came to the conclusion that specific measures were indeed required. The chapters by Edward Grayson and Guy Osborn provide further historical examples of sport-specific legislation which draw out the issue 'when did sports law start'? Any attempt to determine the birth of sport and law may be a rather futile exercise and depend entirely upon the subjective starting-point of what the discipline contains. In addition to statutes, we can see a body of rules developing where the common law has been applied. For example, restraint of trade actions that challenge the rules of governing bodies have developed from *Eastham* through *Greig* to *Watson*.[1] Boxing provides an apt illustration of the argument that sport is more than another area for the application of normal legal principles. As the House of Lords in *R*. v. *Brown* identified, the legal principles governing intentionally inflicted physical harm are in contradiction with boxing's very existence. Yet boxing continues. We would argue that this, in tandem with the increasing specialisms we note above, provides a coherent case for arguing in support of the identification of the concept of sports law.

On a broader level, 'sport and law' may be seen as an acceptance of the view that sport is an area that has become ripe for regulation, a terrain that, perhaps wrongly, has been seen as historically self-regulating or beyond the law, now subject to it. In fact, much of the debate that has centred around sports law's provenance has circled around this issue – should law cross the touchline? What is beyond debate is that there are a number of instances where the law intersects with sport and this book attempts to map some of these intersections by drawing upon key experts in the several fields. As we have indicated elsewhere, intervention may take a number of forms and levels, although we have previously argued that such interventions can broadly be classed as one of two forms:

> Sporting legal disputes take many forms and are perhaps most marked in that they tend to separate into two categories: *participatory* and *consumptive*. Participatory disputes tend to concern contractual and licensing disputes between players and clubs or governing bodies, contested disciplinary procedures and criminal and civil claims made between sporting participants. Consumptive relate to the regulatory powers that might affect how sports can be consumed – these may range from laws dealing with safety and public order when travelling to and attending sporting events, to the increasingly important areas of television rights, ownership and merchandising.[2]

While it is certainly the case that many of the chapters here fall into one or other of these categories, we have chosen not to group them in this way, nor indeed in any specific way. There are a number of themes and common elements in some of the chapters, yet the breadth and depth of the contributions point towards not only different methods of analysis but also to direct links to other disciplines.

The first chapter, by Edward Grayson, provides a personal account of the historical development of legal practice concerning sports issues. His role in the emergence of sport and the law relates not only to his involvement with some of the important cases, but also his academic commentary through his ground-breaking text *Sport and the Law*. His description of early examples of legal intervention in a number of fields is developed later by others, but his chapter firmly establishes the importance of considering the *history* of the discipline, in order to appreciate its modern form. Allied to this is the critical significance of the history of sport itself, or of individual sports, to appreciate the wider context. In fact, we would argue that sports lawyers have an enormous amount to gain from the research of sport historians.[3] The need for greater awareness of theory and context is the fulcrum of Steve Redhead's chapter, which approaches the subject from a different angle altogether. Redhead's method is a more theoretical one which tries to place the growth of sport and law in its broader position within the field of law and popular culture. He has written widely on the intersection of the two fields[4] and this chapter continues that theme. Redhead's piece is perhaps atypical in terms of what appears later in the text, as his ambit is broader than that of other contributors, arguing that all areas of popular culture should be treated seriously and not marginalized on some spurious 'classist' or 'New Right' grounds. Indeed, his point that areas such as law and sport (or law and popular culture, under the umbrella of which Redhead argues that the subject of law and sport needs to be understood) have been viewed with suspicion by academy is a well-made one, and one that books such as this aim to rectify.

Chapter 3 is the first thematic one in that it probes a particular area of (non-) intervention, boxing. Gunn and Ormerod analyse the complex relationship between boxing and the criminal law and this yields a pertinent example of how traditional legal principles fail in this field. This not only provides firm evidence of the specific nature of sports law that we have noted above, but also the importance of history in understanding the subject matter. It is boxing's long historical lineage that provides this protection from the criminal law for its participants.

Osborn, in Chapter 4, attempts to place the intersection of law and play within its broader context. The argument here is that, while often we are seduced by the sheer weight of contemporary legalization within sport to think that it is a recent phenomenon, in fact there is a long history of such intervention, although its focus may have changed. In fact, using historical examples with which we can draw current parallels, Osborn argues that a historical understanding is crucial in order to appreciate current legalization and future trends.

Parpworth's focus, in Chapter 5, is on the exercise of power by the governing bodies of sport. In particular, he centres upon the issue of judicial review, a device that can be utilized to challenge the decisions of public bodies. Parpworth provides a thorough dissection of the case law in the area. One crucial issue is what is denoted by 'public', and he charts the reticence of the courts to apply judicial review to sports bodies and their preference to leave intervention to issues of private law such as contractual remedies. Parpworth argues that perhaps a 'quantum leap' ought to be made to allow judicial review to embrace such areas.

Chapter 6 tackles the area of legal intervention with respect to behaviour on the field. Gardiner draws upon his previous extensive research into the issues of regulating sports field behaviour by examining the applicability of the criminal and the civil law to on-field violence and injury. Centring upon contact sports, the issue of innate aggression as part of the sport (playing to win, for instance) and the vexed one of consent to contact are covered in depth, with the suitability of the law as a mechanism for dealing with such instances being examined. Gardiner has long been a proponent of an antithetical approach to Edward Grayson, and has argued strongly that the law should cross the touchline only in more limited circumstances and that there are more efficient methods for such regulation outside of formal legal intervention. Here, Gardiner argues that the greater use of the law is indefensible in this context and that 'quasi-legal mediation and arbitration mechanisms', or, in a wider sense, internal ethical codes are the way forward for sporting regulation.

McCutcheon (Chapter 7) also deals with issues of behaviour, at least in terms of how the governing bodies, noted by Parpworth, deal with disciplinary issues. An interesting point is involved here – the internal rules of the sports being subject to external regulation. Interestingly, McCutcheon posits that the increasing willingness of the law to intercede in sporting disputes means that the laws of individual sports will need to become more formalized to counter this. He examines the tension that exists between the disciplinary procedures within sport (the internal ones) and the wider legal framework (the external ones) and the effects that the increasing reliance upon the external is having upon the internal machinery of sporting bodies.

Similarly, Greenfield in Chapter 8 examines intervention within the sphere of contract. He questions not only whether the law ought to intervene, but also whether the law can successfully enforce such contractual arrangements. However, case law has proved an effective method of altering restrictive terms and conditions for players, as the examples given demonstrate. What is apparent is that sportsmen, much like other entertainers, will freely sign agreements that may prove unenforceable. This is an area where the law has been a vehicle for change, but is largely impotent in the face of contractual breaches.

Weatherill, in Chapter 9, examines the impact of increasing commercialization upon the law's often uneasy relationship with sport. The case of *Bosman*, and the concomitant issue of 'when does a sport become a business', are covered within the penumbra of the role of European law in the sporting firmament. Going against the view that EC law is 'harming' sport, a line pursued by FIFA/UEFA after the *Bosman* ruling, for example, Weatherill in a well-argued chapter proposes that EC law could allow sport to be more autonomous.

While so far the chapters have in the main concerned the participants, Pearson in Chapter 10 looks into the regulation of the 'consumer', in this case the football fan.[5] He concentrates on a more historically rooted aspect of statutory intervention, the way in which football fans are regulated by legislation and the effect that such regulation has upon the civil liberties of supporters. Pearson's chapter provides in some ways an interesting bookend to Osborn's observations in Chapter 4, charting as it does the reaction and response to football-related disorder in a contemporary setting. Pearson analyses the efficacy of the football-specific legislation, and in particular the Football Supporters Act 1989, the Football Offences Act 1991 and the Football Offences and Disorder Act 1999, and also the wider effects of a government policy to police hooliganism that has curtailed the civil liberties of innocent supporters.

McArdle (Chapter 11) concentrates on internal issues and practices with regard to sports organizations, specifically analysing the contentious areas of harassment and discrimination. He provides an authoritative review of English case law, such as it is. His chapter includes the celebrated case involving Jane Couch ('the Fleetwood Assassin') and the British Board of Boxing Control, where the Board's failure to award a female boxer a licence on decidedly spurious grounds was challenged on the basis of sex discrimination, a case which is sure to be ground-breaking. McArdle also raises the related issue of the internal mechanisms for reporting workplace concerns and, in particular, the issue of whistle-blowing, with reference to the American experience, and argues that lessons can be learned from it.

Chapters 12 and 13 both deal with the future of football and the effects of the commercialization of the game. While both are football-specific, there are aspects of each which can be used to inform a wider sporting debate. The contribution by Toms (Chapter 12) centres upon the attempt by Rupert Murdoch's BSkyB to purchase Manchester United plc in September 1998. Toms assisted IMUSA in their representation to the Monopolies and xvi

Mergers Commission, and thus is in an informed position to write of both the bid itself and the wider commercial issues affecting football. Charting the shift of football clubs from small works' or church sides, via limited liability companies to the commercial, publicly-listed companies we see today, he illustrates why the bid for England's most famous club made good financial sense, given the game's importance in broadcasting terms. It also shows how campaigns on such issues can have a marked effect, that the fans are not just of economic importance to football,[6] and that in any area of sport they have a voice and can make a difference.[7]

One of the chief movers in the fans' campaign to prevent the Murdoch takeover, Adam Brown, contributes a chapter presenting a different stance on the challenges facing football. As he makes clear in his introduction to Chapter 13, his analysis of the government's Football Task Force (FTF) is conducted from the knowledge he gained from his membership of it. Brown's analysis provides both a fascinating insight into the workings and politics of such a body and the problems of reaching consensus within it. An optimistic note was sounded in the original remit of the FTF, which, instead of concentrating on the usual governmental concerns of law and order, embraced areas such as eliminating racism, disabled access to viewing facilities, commercial issues affecting fans, such as ticket prices, and merchandizing. Perhaps most interestingly, the wider issue of commercial conflicts between clubs, directors, owners and fans was covered in the final report in December 1999. Brown also deals with the crucial split that occurred during the preparation of this report, with the members of the FTF splitting into two camps on the issue of a football regulator, the Football Regulatory Authority. Unsurprisingly, this issue caused the splits in the FTF membership to become apparent, as the football authorities were antagonistic to such a proposal. This led to the publication of two reports; as we write no decision has yet been taken on which is to be followed.

Foster, in the final chapter, neatly dovetails many of the arguments and issues presented by Brown into a wider debate as to how, and whether, sport should be regulated. Foster presents a framework for debate, detailing a number of mechanisms that could potentially be used to regulate sport, analysing the applicability of each to the sporting terrain. In many ways Foster asks questions that are tackled, or hinted at, in all the preceding chapters – the tension between the law and the laws, the external and the internal, and the cultural and the economic.

When we originally put the idea for *Law and Sport in Contemporary Society* together, we wanted to make a statement that the area was a valid one and worthy of serious academic examination. To that end we sought to collect in one volume the views of those we considered to be the foremost academics in the field as a 'stick in the sand'. That said, there are always dangers in such an approach. One is that often a more critical and useful approach is fostered when one operates from the outside, and that the creation of a discipline, or its acceptance by what is rather grandly termed the academy, may blunt its effectiveness. Nevertheless, it remains our belief that the objective of the book is a valid one and outweighs any potential criticisms it may arouse.

Acknowledgements and Disclaimers

The existence of this book is part of this development of the subject matter and offers a broad contribution to it. It is certainly not intended to be definitive nor exhaustive in its coverage. The potential size of the area is indicated by the gaps that are present; for example, with respect to the legal dimensions to issues such as drug use and health and safety. Our attitude to sport and law was a necessarily subjective one, partly predicated by the expertise of the contributors we were keen to have and wider issues such as the available space and our general picture of what we wanted the book to be. Such gaps must be left to be filled another day.

As editors we would thank all the contributors to the book. We would also like to thank Frank Cass for agreeing to publish the text and for their enthusiasm for the project. In particular, Tony Mangan as series editor provided encouragement and Jon Manley provided much publishing expertise and guidance.

NOTES

1. *Eastham* v. *Newcastle United* [1963] 3 All ER 139, *Greig* v. *Insole* [1978] 1 WLR 302, *Watson* v. *Prager* [1993] EMLR 275.
2. S. Greenfield and G. Osborn, 'Law's Colonisation of Cricket', 13 *Soundings* (1999), 129–41.
3. Sports history is now a well-established field, with key journals such as *The International Journal of Sports History* and thriving national and international associations.
4. See, for example, S. Redhead, *Unpopular Cultures: The Birth of Law and Popular Culture*, Manchester, 1995.
5. It is, of course, contentious to talk of fans as consumers; however, there has been a marked move away from traditional ways of viewing people who consume football – this idea of consumption is one we raise earlier in the introduction. Similarly, it can be argued that the supporters and the crowd as an entity are, in fact, part of a participatory force, although again this perception has altered partly due to the regulation Pearson discusses and partly because of the internal dynamics of fan demographics and stadium construction.
6. See further on this campaign the insider view presented by Adam Brown and Andy Walsh, *Not for Sale! Manchester United, Murdoch and the Defeat of BSkyB*, Edinburgh, 1999.
7. Consider here also the position of fans within cricket mobilizing to protest against racism both in terms of the 'Stop the Seventy Tour' campaign (see Ch.4) and, in the 1990s, the 'Hit Racism for 6' campaign, both of which were based upon grassroots support.

PART 1

Perspectives

The Historical Development of Sport and Law

Edward Grayson

The modern history of sport and the law is divisible into three separate stages: 'reality', 'antiquity' and 'contemporaneity and the future'. Reality is traceable to the justifiable public accusation by the former Football Association Chief Executive, the late Ted (E.A.) Croker, that I had invented the subject.[1] Antiquity identifies legislative and structural sources from ancient Greece and Rome via medieval and early modern Europe, comparable to identifiable current circumstances and conditions. Contemporaneity explains the state of play today and its projection into the future.

Reality

'I don't approve of the police and the law's involvement with sport, and football in particular. We can look after our game ourselves, and it's all the fault of Edward Grayson, who invented sport and the law', protested Mr Croker in Birmingham's National Exhibition Centre on that occasion in 1988. He was on his feet declaiming this protest after Charles Woodhouse[2] had read a paper containing references to the common-law compensation remedies and criminal prosecutions for violent foul play, which had exploded to a degree and extent unknown before the Second World War, and progressively alarmingly during the 1960s and the 1970s.

While Croker was in full cry, I was just entering the Conference Hall accompanied by two long-standing and distinguished *Times* newspaper sources: David Miller (now with the *Daily Telegraph*) of association football renown with the Cambridge University Corinthian-Casuals, Pegasus and Britain's Olympic Games squad, and John Goodbody of English Channel swimming triumphs. As we walked in, Woodhouse drew attention to my arrival and invited me to respond. Accordingly, I pointed out to Mr Croker that, if he considered sport in general and football in particular, to be above the law he was out of order and that he should take care to be aware of this reality. Until that moment I had never thought of the accusation. On reflection, however, I realize that he was right; but for different reasons that I now recognize that he must have had in mind.

For on 7 February 1969, in the weekly *Police Review* journal under the heading of 'Crimes of soccer violence', I advocated police intervention for football pitch offences.[3] Ironically, this issue was floated once more while this chapter was in preparation in a news item on 10 March 2000, following a twenty-first-century echo of the events of the 1970s onwards, evidenced by televised fighting between Leeds United and Tottenham Hotspur players, and less public reportage of contemporaneous comparable fighting between Chelsea and Wimbledon in the players' tunnel. Two days after the publication of the *Police Review* piece, there appeared in the *News of the World* for 9 February a headline and text for Frank Butler's column: 'STARS BEHIND BARS, IT'S JUST CRAZY', followed by a text which began: 'I've read some crazy sporting gimmicks, but the silliest suggestion comes from a barrister who wants the police to have power to arrest footballers who commit dirty fouls.' It ended: 'the day the police take over from the referees will be the day the sport dies'.

This development had followed the arrival in court of football's first playing-field fatality since the two Leicester Assizes prosecutions in 1878 and 1898, respectively, of *R. v. Bradshaw*[4] and *R. v. Moore*.[5] Later, *R. v. Southby*[6] was transferred to Maidstone Assizes from Essex, and it was followed shortly afterwards towards the end of 1969 by the first traceable, personal-injury assault judgment for a foul football tackle during a minor local league Sussex match which later led to a £4,500 damages award, of which I wrote in the *New Law Journal*.[7] The judgment appeared on the eve of the notorious Chelsea v. Leeds United FA Cup final replay of 1970. Subsequently John Giles wrote of his club's progress in the 1970s:

> I get a rush of pride when I think of the great years with Leeds United.
> I also feel shame... now I can see clearly enough that we stretched the
> rules to breaking point... We went too far, too ruthless, I went too
> far...We did and we prospered. We never thought there might be a day
> when we would wonder if the price was too high.[8]

Giles wrote this while the first Butterworths' edition (1988) of *Sport and the Law* was being prepared for publication to coincide with Croker's accusation of my having invented the subject. Yet as all three Butterworths' editions have explained extensively, it all began much earlier than that, during the last fling of the traditional amateur during the 1950s.

A badly treated broken leg, from the Oxford University soccer trials, released my energies to prepare for the publication of my schoolboy's hero-worshipping Second World War correspondence with England's 21-times-capped England centre forward, G.O. Smith.[9] C.B. Fry, his great contemporary, contributed a foreword and it appeared as *Corinthians and Cricketers* on the eve of the Corinthian-Casuals FA Amateur Cup final appearance against Bishop Auckland before 80,000 at Wembley Stadium in 1955.[10] Corinthian-Casuals included Douglas Insole, of later *Greig* v. *Insole* 'Packer'[11] litigation fame, and Pegasus included Donald Carr, who had captained an England MCC team on tour in Pakistan.

At that period in sporting history, when winters and summers were clearly divisible into natural and traditional football and winter seasons, many such as Insole and Carr's contemporaries in the professional ranks, epitomized by Denis Compton of Arsenal and Middlesex, were eligible for benefit and testimonial payments. An anomalous distinction existed however; professional footballers' benefits were taxable, professional cricketers' were tax-free. It puzzled me, as it puzzled many others, until I examined the cases. The distinction was easily identifiable. The footballers' case contained a contractual element that the cricketers' did not. The solution was simple. With the players' blessing, eliminate the contractual element and follow the cricketers' House of Lords' precedent of *Reed* v. *Seymour*.[12]

There then appeared two articles in the then FA *Bulletin* for April 1953 and the then *Rating and Income Tax Journal* for 8 October 1953. Each is reproduced verbatim in Appendix 1 to the third edition of *Sport and the Law*. They brought to my chambers in Lincoln's Inn and later in the Temple, the chairman of the Professional Footballers' and Trainers' Union (now the Professional Footballers' Association), Jimmy Guthrie, who had captained Portsmouth when they beat Wolverhampton Wanderers in the last FA Cup Final before the war. In due course, a test case, with elimination of the contractual element, was mounted with players from Peterborough United, who were then outside the Football League, in the Midland Counties Football League. It was heard before the Special Commissioners of Income Tax, and the professional footballers' benefits were equated with those of professional cricketers, where they have remained until today.[13]

At about the same time, the restraint of trade flag was raised for the first time in the Aldershot County Court on behalf of Ralph Banks, who had been mesmerized by Stanley Matthews in the memorable FA Coronation Cup Final of 1953. When he was transferred from Bolton Wanderers to Aldershot and in due course wished to continue to Weymouth outside the Football League, he was trapped by the old retain-and-transfer system which was established later in the *Eastham* case, and in its turn a precursor to *Greig*, to be in restraint of trade in line ultimately with the *Bosman* principle. A Rent Restriction Acts possession action was counterclaimed with a declaratory plea for restraint of trade. A six-months' suspended possession was poised for appeal to the Court of Appeal when the restraint was removed before further arguments could be heard and a free transfer was effected to Weymouth.[14]

Finally, also during this period of preparation for *Corinthians and Cricketers*, the profits made by the joint Oxbridge Pegasus FA Amateur Cup winning team were clearly eligible for all the fiscal advantages of charitable status. The Inland Revenue would not agree: no funds existed to pursue the claim and, although the Sydney University Rugby Club was being approved by the New South Wales Equity Court in *Kearins* v. *Kearins*,[15] based upon the Aldenham School First World War decision in *Re Mariette*,[16] another 25 years had to await judicial acceptance of this advice to Pegasus in the FA Youth trust case of *IRC* v. *Macmullan*,[17] which also applied the *Marriette* principle of physical education's falling within the educational criteria of *IRC* v. *Pemsel*.[18]

During these days of sporting innocence, free from the current issues of drugs, violence and commercial corruption, the stimulus to activate the 1969 *Police Review* police prosecution concept and the 1970 *New Law Journal*'s recording damages for a soccer player's broken leg which had upset Croker in 1988 never entered my consciousness. But the anomaly of the imbalance between the Denis Compton differential benefit tax provisions, the restrictive practice, restraint-of-trade retain-and-transfer system, and educational charitable status were dominating my thoughts while preparing the first edition of *Corinthians and Cricketers* in 1955 (and transferring from Chancery Chambers in Lincoln's Inn to the wider territories of the Temple and the South-Eastern Circuit). These matters commanded my attention in applying easily identifiable, legal principles to sporting situations which had never been considered before in the manner that I developed, once I became aware of the need to remedy the then apparently insoluble problems. To that extent, and from that time, I am ready to plead guilty to having invented the subject of sport and the law, during that innovative gestation period in the early 1950s.

Two decades later the *Sunday Telegraph*'s 76-page booklet published in 1978, after a series of three articles in 1977, was the logical corollary for which the seeds had been sown in the 1950s. They were inspired by the breed of footballing-cricketers at both the Corinthians-Pegasus and the Denis Compton at Arsenal and Middlesex levels, which have now gone forever. Ian Botham, with his mixed footballing and cricketing experience, was one of the last to double at both games. His no less talented son Liam, who took five wickets for Hampshire on his county cricketing debut but ultimately switched to Rugby Union, first with West Hartlepool and more recently with Cardiff, illustrates vividly the inevitable choice to be made today. While the options remained for the Comptons, the Carrs and the Insoles at amateur and professional level, the opportunity came my way to link the law to sport – which was available to anyone else who might have been sufficiently motivated to take the action which appeared to me then to be appropriate. Yet even before my own discoveries, the sources and principles for what I uncovered and applied had existed since Greco-Roman times.

Antiquity

The antiquarian research student who may be concerned to trace the roots of modern sport and the law has ample material on which to draw. For the modern practitioner, and indeed the student concerned with active participation today, they have little practical benefit apart from creating an awareness of what Arsenal Football Club's most eminent and prestigious supporter, the Rt. Revd George Carey, Archbishop of Canterbury, said in a House of Lords debate on society's moral and spiritual well-being, on the eve of the Euro '96 competition: 'Rules do not get in the way of the game, they make it possible.'

Greco-Roman recreational activities, no less than those of our own era, had their own indigenous, competitive criteria, but beyond recognizing this basic existence, they would not concern the modern practitioner. More relevant to our own times, however, are the medieval legislative enactments for protecting archery and regulating gaming, hunting and other sporting demands which I have summarized by citing such authoritative sources as Blackstone and Holdsworth. The eighteenth-century commentaries of the English legal system's most traditional jurist and historian Blackstone identified gaming-laws sanctions as (Bk IV, Ch.13, p.174) 'constituted by a variety of acts of Parliament: which are so numerous and so confused and the crime itself [killing game even upon their own estates] of so questionable a nature, that I shall not detain the reader with many observations thereof'.

Nearer our own time, Sir William Holdsworth's monumental *History of English Law* traced back to Richard II a fragmentation comparable to our own period when he wrote under the head of 'Hunting and Game' (Vol.4, p.505):

> The legislation on this subject proceeded on many different principles. Sometimes it proceeded on the principle that assemblies for the purpose of hunting and sporting gave opportunities for riot and disorder; sometimes on the principle that hunting and sporting ought to be the privilege of landowners, and that other classes ought to employ themselves in a manner more suited to their condition in life; and sometimes on the principle that it resulted in the wanton destruction of game. We can see all these principles underlying Richard II's statute on the subject [13 Rich II, St 1, Ch 13] and they appear clearly enough in the various statutes of this period.

Those different principles' objectives have a common legal denominator which echoes today's legislative examples above and is rooted in realty and intellectual property law: the licence principle. It originated with the royal prerogative recognized by Blackstone from its creation after the Norman conquest and the parcelling out of the Forest Laws, and survives today in the New Forest. It has been perpetuated for centuries by Parliament, with an ebb and flow of restrictions and authorities for defining, preserving and killing different species of game; and it is structured to provide individual property ownership protection through the laws on civil trespass, criminal damage, poaching and the Public Order Act 1986.

Significantly, that fragmentation is replicated in our period with examples stretching from the Physical Recreation and Training Act 1937; introduced in anticipation of the Second World War's requirements for national fitness to fight, to the Olympic Symbol (Protection) Act 1995, with its creation of exclusive property rights in relation to the use of the five-rings symbol, consistent with current commercial requirements. In between, we have witnessed the cascade of safety legislation to fill the gaps created by the Ibrox (1971), Bradford City (1985) and Hillsborough (1989) stadium disasters, and litigation upon the application of known principles which has followed each of them. Thus one arrives at contemporaneity and the future.

Contemporaneity and the Future

The progression of the *Sunday Telegraph*'s 76-page booklet in 1978 to Butterworths' third edition of 631 pages in 2000 over 20 years later clearly identifies the subject's development without need for further comment. However, it is worth noting two fundamental assessments and developments which were not apparent at the time when I first became involved in the early 1950s days of innocence with tax-free benefits for footballers, laying the trail from *Banks* via *Eastham* and *Insole* to *Bosman*, with sporting educational charities awaiting approbation in the House of Lords with the FA Youth Trust deed in 1980.

One is the emergence of the contrasting cultures between show business, sport and recreation and their grass roots. The other is the true meaning of sport, if any meaning can be generally applied to it, and the arcane, arid and artificial argument about whether there is a law of sport or sports law.

So far as the first is concerned it is vividly illuminated by the antithesis between:

> *Manchester United Football Club plc*
> *proudly presents at its*
> *Old Trafford Theatre of Dreams,*
> *International All Stars Football Entertainment,*
> *including David Beckham (with Victoria*
> *Adams and Baby Brooklyn in the stands)*
> *under the management of*
> *Sir Alex Ferguson*

alongside
- Clayton playing fields at Oldham
- Foster's Field in Dorset
- New Milton Recreation Ground in Hampshire
- Town Moor, Newcastle-upon-Tyne
- Charterhouse vs Westminster, 1863 to date
- Oxford vs Cambridge, 1874 to date
- Corinthian-Casuals, 1882/83, at Tolworth, Surrey, 1989 to date

The second has been conveniently considered by the only public figure to demonstrate any realistic comprehension of what sport and the law comprise, who created the role of a government minister for sport, in addition to having been three times Lord Chancellor and also Editor-in-Chief of the fourth edition of *Halsbury's Laws of England*, Lord Hailsham of St. Marylebone. His grandfather, the first Quintin Hogg, is the subject of the only London statue with a football. The statue faces his own landmark foundation of the University of Westminster (originally, the Regent Street Polytechnic), outside the BBC in Portland Place, and he was the goalkeeper for the Old Etonians in the FA Cup Final of 1875/76, as well as initiator, with Lord Kinnaird, of the earlier Scotland vs England soccer matches. His father, the first Viscount Hailsham, was President of the MCC during the 1932/33 Jardine–Larwood bodyline bowling imbroglio. Thus his pedigree is at least consistent with an awareness of the subject.

As Minister for Science and Technology and Lord President of the Council in the Macmillan government, Lord Hailsham recalled during 1980 in *The Door Wherein I Went*:

It occurred during a Cabinet Meeting [in 1962] in which government responsibility for sport was being discussed. It was being said that, properly speaking, responsibility for sport was being shared between quite a number of departments and authorities, education, local government, universities, the services, and all the voluntary bodies dealing with athletics, from the Olympic and Commonwealth Games and League and Cup football at the top, to badminton, fives and even chess at the most refined and esoteric end of the spectrum. I pointed out that recreation generally presented a complex of problems out of which modern government was not wholly free to opt, and to which government funds were, in fact, and were likely to continue to be, committed in one way or another in coaching, in the provision of playing fields, in matters of safety at racecourses and football grounds. I waxed eloquent on this subject, talking of the fares for Olympic competitors and many other topics. I suggested that there was need, not for a Ministry but for a focal point under a Minister, for a coherent body of doctrine, perhaps even a philosophy of government encouragement. Paradoxically, I thought there was in fact a kind of analogy in the way in which I had tried to administer government science, making use of independent expertise, but not seeking to impose regulation or central administration. My eloquence had its effect on the Prime Minister and, before I knew where I was, I was left to organise the first government unit of this kind under Sir John Lang, who had been Secretary of the Admiralty when I was First Lord. As in most of the other things I have done in public life, except the Party Chairmanship, I always strive to work through other people with the minimum of fuss, as I find that this is the best way to get things done. This particular activity was a minor matter, and I thought comparatively little of it at the time since it occurred at a period when other things were occupying my mind [as a Cabinet Minister].

Nearly 30 years after what he had regarded in the context of the time to be 'a minor matter', he reflected further in *A Sparrow's Flight* published in 1990:

Sport, I believe... is an essential part of education. Years later, in my judicial capacity as Lord Chancellor, I was part-author of a judgment which authenticated the legal status of a fund for Association Football as a charitable trust [*IRC* v. *McMullan* [1980] AC 1]. Organised sport is undoubtedly part of our national culture. In mountain-climbing, cricket and most kinds of football, in hunting, fishing and game shooting, the British were the pioneers in the field of sport as it burgeoned in the nineteenth century.

From there, it was a logical step in the same work for him to claim, and as corroborated by the most authentic of sources identified hereafter: 'In a sense there is no such thing as sport. There is only a heterogeneous list of pastimes, with different governing bodies, different ethics and constantly varying needs.'

Four years later in 1994 he was corroborated from an unexpected legal source under a Treasury HM Customs and Excise notice, VAT 701/45/94. It gives a list of 113 British 'heterogeneous... pastimes with different governing bodies, different ethics and constantly varying needs' which qualify for exemption as non-profit-making activities for VAT purposes (see Appendix 1). The list was an arbitrarily Treasury-inspired document, which did not include chess or pigeon racing, the governing bodies of which are still protesting at their omission. Two years earlier, on 5 December 1992 in Cliff Morgan's never-to-be-forgotten BBC *Sport on Four* radio programme – axed contentiously by an unappreciative directorate in the face of strong public protests – the celebrated *Daily Mail* columnist and award-winning sports writer Ian Wooldridge illuminated all of this after the ejection of the four United Kingdom national soccer teams from the World Cup competition, when he posed and answered a question:

> Does sport still exist?
> Well it does, but you have to go out into the suburbs and shires to find it. Village cricket, soccer on Hackney Marshes, old boys' rugger teams getting legless afterwards, point-to-pointing, county golf, darts leagues in Dorset. What we have been watching in the frenetic World Cup soccer action this week was hardly about sport at all. It was all about [a] high performance branch of the entertainment industry.

He thereby crystallized the present public persona of whatever sport may mean; not a game of two halves, but a game of two conflicting and contrasting concepts: showbiz vs grass roots, and exercise for health and education within the rule of law on and off the playing field. That rule of law, on and off the playing field, is as essential for the future of sport in society, whatever sport may mean, as it is for society in general. For without the rule of law in society anarchy reigns. Without the rule of law in sport chaos exists.

The developments evidenced currently in the courts and Parliament demonstrate beyond a peradventure that sport cannot regulate itself, particularly as it is administered principally by non-professional, volunteer amateurs. Five years ago in an American journal Gardiner and Felix queried and, indeed, challenged my belief that 'the law will save sport from the violence of today', an argument they had consistently and perversely put forward in the face of what I would term overwhelming contrary evidence.[19] I am content to let the reader judge for him or herself. As Frank Butler wrote in the *News of the World* after my *Police Review* feature on crimes of soccer violence: 'The day the police take over from the referees will be the day sport dies.'

At the showbiz entertainment level it is arguable that it has died already as a concept of health and education within the rule of law. If the future for the grass roots is to have any value and benefit for society and those who take part in it, then it will survive only by the application of the rule of law, and at all dimensions in the words of Arsenal's No. 1 supporter as Primate of All England: 'Rules do not get in the way of the game, They make it possible.' For rules read laws; and at all levels (that is, of play and administration) statutory and judicial decisions, in the courts, are required to fill the gaps that appear daily with a horrendous and nauseating regularity, poisoned by an ill-informed media feeding on vast commercial chunks of the entertainment industry, as far removed from the true meaning of sport as Ian Wooldridge identified in the graphically illuminating image cited above.

APPENDIX 1

List of British sports activities which qualify for exemption as non-profit-making activities for VAT purposes (HM Customs and Excise, VAT 701/45/94).

Aikido	Gymnastics	Real tennis
American football	Handball	Roller hockey
Angling	Hang/para gliding	Rosser skating
Archery	Highland games	Rounders
Arm wrestling	Hockey	Rowing
Association football	Horse racing	Rugby League
Athletics	Hovering	Rugby Union
Badminton	Hurling	Sailing/yachting
Ballooning	Ice hockey	Sand/land yachting
Baseball	Ice skating	Shinty
Basketball	Ju jitsu	Shooting
Baton twirling	Judo	Skateboarding
Biathlon	Kabaddi	Skiing
Bicycle polo	Karate	Skipping
Billiards	Kendo	Snooker
Bobsleigh	Korfball	Snowboarding
Boccia	Lacrosse	Softball
Bowls	Lawn tennis	Squash
Boxing	Life saving	Street hockey
Camogie	Luge	Sumo wrestling
Canoeing	Modern pentathlon	Surf life saving
Caving	Motor cycling	Surfing
Chinese martial arts	Motor sports	Swimming
Cricket	Mountaineering	Table tennis
Croquet	Movement and dance	Taekwondo
Crossbow	sub-aqua	Tang soo do
Curling	Netball	Tenpin bowling
Cycling	Orienteering	Trampolining
Dragon boat racing	Parachuting	Triathlon
Equestrian	Petanque	Tug of war
Exercise and fitness	Polo	Unihoc
Fencing	Pony trekking	Volleyball
Field sports	Pool	Water skiing
Fives	Quoits	Weightlifting
Flying	Racketball	Wrestling
Gaelic football	Rackets	Yoga
Gliding	Racquetball	
Golf	Rambling	

NOTES

1. This was made at the 1988 annual conference of the Central Council of Physical Recreation on the eve of the publication by Butterworths of the first edition of *Sport and the Law*, London, 1988.
2. Charles Woodhouse, CVO, was my successor in 1993 as President of the British Association for Sport and the Law; he was at that time Honorary Legal Adviser to the Central Council of Physical Recreation.
3. 77 *Police Review* (1969) no.3969.
4. (1878) 14 Cox CC 83.
5. (1898) 14 TLR 229.
6. *The Times*, 21 Nov. 1968.
7. 120 *New Law Journal* (1970), 413.
8. *Daily Express*, 25 Aug. 1987, 30–1.
9. Smith had also scored a memorable Oxford University fourth innings century at Lord's in 1896 against Cambridge, three months after captaining England's pro–am soccer XI against Scotland from centre-forward at Glasgow as a true Corinthian and cricketer!
10. Two and four years, respectively, after the joint Oxbridge X1 Pegasus's two Wembley FA Amateur Cup triumphs before 100,000 crowds in 1953 and 1951, with three subsequent ones in 1957, 1983 and 1996.
11. See Greenfield, Ch.8 in this collection, for more detail of the Packer case.
12. [1927] AC 554.
13. *Rigby* v. *LRC, Peterborough Citizen and Advertiser*, 16 June, 24 July 1959. See also Grayson, *Sport and the Law*, 72–3, 148–9, App.1.
14. See *Aldershot* v. *Banks, Aldershot News*, 25 Nov. 1955; *Sport and the Law*, 3rd edn, London, 2000, 74–5.
15. [1957] SR NSW 286.
16. [1915] 2 Ch 284.
17. [1981] AC.
18. [1991] AC 531.
19. 5 *Marquette Sports Law Journal* (Spring 1995) no.2, 200.

2

Taking Law and Popular Culture Seriously: Theorizing Sport and Law

Steve Redhead

This chapter considers some aspects of the genesis of law and popular culture as a sub-discipline of socio-legal studies. In particular, it puts into context the fledgling area of sports law which, although present in the North America and the Australian law curriculum for some years, has only recently flourished more widely in the United Kingdom. This trend has complemented the international burgeoning of the sociology of sport, sport history and leisure studies since the late 1970s. The chapter highlights the theoretical impact, on such a disciplinary change, of cultural studies and related intellectual developments. The cultural study of popular culture, I want to argue, is the starting point for any analysis of sport and law in contemporary society. It is a necessary, if insufficient, condition for moving the subject forward.

Popular Culture: Dumbing Down or Growing Up?

In North America in the 1990s popular culture came under attack, just as American popular culture became global culture. Following tracts such as Michael Medved's attack on 'Hollywood',[1] the debate widened to become a culture war over the 'dumbing' of America. In 1996 two authors published a collection of essays about the process of 'dumbing down'. Katherine Washburn and John Thornton edited a collection of essays on the strip-mining of American culture,[2] including only one, by the *Rolling Stone* journalist Anthony de Curtis, explicitly 'in defense of popular culture'. The remainder of the contributions attempted to catch a national mood and blamed popular culture not merely for itself ('bad' films, television, music and so on) but for falling educational standards, professional incompetence and a disciplinary decline in ethics, jurisprudence, the social sciences and politics – 'bad' in general, or the dumbing of America as a whole culture.

In the United Kingdom the debate about popular culture has been manifest in different forms. The criticism of media, cultural and communication studies courses in further and higher education reflects a suspicion of the 'dumbing down' of the academy. The right-wing philosopher Roger Scruton, from a position of defending 'high' culture, has lambasted 'popular' culture.[3]

The *Independent* newspaper in Britain even coined the phrase 'Dumb Britannia',[4] itself an ironic play on the earlier media label 'Cool Britannia' first created by Viv Stanshall of the Bonzo Dog Doo Dah Band in the 1960s and revived by the press in the mid-1990s in debates about 'Britpop', Tony Blair, 'New Labour' and popular culture.

In the light of such debates there is a need to rehabilitate popular culture in the academy, placing it in the context of law and popular culture.[5] This task will not be achieved merely by celebrating something defined loosely as 'popular culture'. Several cultural studies texts[6] have at times been cited as celebrating popular culture from Madonna to Blue Jeans, Quentin Tarantino to Michael Jordan. On the other hand, Stuart Hall,[7] for many years the Director of the Centre for Contemporary Cultural Studies at the University of Birmingham, argued as Professor of Sociology at the Open University that:

> Popular culture is one of the sites where this struggle for and against a culture of the powerful is engaged. It is also the stake to be won or lost IN that struggle. It is the arena of consent and resistance. It is partly where hegemony arises, and where it is secured ... that is why 'popular culture' matters. Otherwise, to tell you the truth, I don't give a damn about it.

In Hall's view, at least in the early 1980s, 'popular culture' had to do with politics, the possibility of socialism and the undermining of capitalism. In fact, Colin MacCabe[8] has pointed out that in much of this academic/political enterprise 'there is no definition of popular culture as such' and notions of popular culture are taken from 'a series of overlapping cultural debates' with 'no effort to arrive at a precise definition'. For MacCabe 'the Left's interest in popular culture has always had' the element in it 'that battles lost economically and politically can be turned into cultural victories'. Fast forward to the late 1990s, when, due to the massive shift to the right over two decades, terms such as 'left' and 'right' had become much less tangible, and it could be claimed that 'the story of our times is that the right has won economically and politically but the left has won culturally'. Certainly the spectacle of right-wing philosophers such as Roger Scruton so venomously attacking contemporary 'popular culture' (and 'youth culture') suggests that there must, after all, be something interesting going on in the terrain of the 'popular' in culture.

In the area of popular music studies[9] the aesthetic value of the popular has come under sustained discussion. What makes Keats better then Bob Dylan? Or vice versa? Or mid-1960s Dylan better than mid-1980s? Or REM better than Boyzone? Or Hip-Hop better than Speed Garage? What is noticeable about rightist responses by writers such as Scruton is that their dismissive judgements are so obviously based on limited knowledge or familiarity with the subject matter. The attempt to put a 'value' on low culture (as has always been done on 'high') is an important enterprise and also brings into play the question of constituting popular culture in general as a (serious) academic object,[10] made all the more difficult when the object of desire in question is all about having 'fun'.

To take popular music, and popular culture, seriously means, too, an emphasis on the 'production' of such culture, not merely its consumption by 'fans', 'subcultures' or 'ordinary' consumers. The roots of 'cultural populism'[11] – the uncritical celebration of popular culture, especially in the academy – have been located in this excessive leaning on the consumption rather than the production of cultural commodities. However, any proper historical examination of popular culture over the last two decades – the era of the emergence and eventual decline of the New Right – would inevitably highlight the free 'enterprise culture', market-oriented, corporate-production model as much as 'Keynesian' state intervention in the making of the 'pop' and popular culture which was being archived for posterity at the end of the century. A return to an emphasis on 'cultural production' – the concentration on cultural *industry* – alone will not solve the dilemma I drew attention to earlier. Does the academy, uncritically or otherwise, celebrate popular culture, or does it regard it as an arena of struggle, as politics by other means? To say whether one is for or against popular culture is not an easy question to answer.

For Law and Popular Culture: Putting Sports Law in Context

One way to take popular culture seriously has been to draw on cultural studies – to 'take in' cultural studies wherever and whenever necessary. This, though, has occurred against a backdrop of 'cultural studies', as a discipline with academic boundaries, appearing to be in some sort of permanent crisis in the last decade.[12] As a result of this uncertainty regarding the terrain of the cultural, the way in which the sub-discipline of law and popular culture has developed has often been in terms of additions to the law curriculum – law and the media, law and sport, entertainment law (including law and film, law and literature), law and medical ethics, and gender and law, and so on. The issue often raised in the validation of such subject areas is 'what has LAW got to do with it?', and the response tends to be to pack the courses with more or less conventional black letter, positivistic approaches to a mass of legal rules, leaving little space for theoretical reflections of any kind. Indeed, an empiricist legal positivism, for so long hunted down by the sociological movement in law in the twentieth century, has been resurrected in some of the approaches to sport and the law in

Britain. A publication such as *Sport and the Law Journal*, begun in 1993 as the house journal of the British Association for Sport and the Law and based at the Manchester Metropolitan University, is a case in point. Emerging essentially as a practitioners' guide to the recent practice of sports law in the English, and to some extent, the European courts, the articles published in it show little reflection beyond the 'anecdotal' evidence of solicitors or barristers from their day, or week, in court. 'Sport' here is not a theorized domain which might be subject to different kinds of legal and social regulation, and subsequent explanation and criticism. It is similar to the object of desire of the 'fan' in other contexts of popular culture – popular music, film, video, television, pulp fiction, the internet – where the commodity is simply plucked out of the air and the legal issue added to it on an *ad hoc* basis.

Taking law and popular culture seriously means doing more than this. It means taking in socio-legal studies[13] perspectives and expanding the legal[14] imagination to take in the 'cultural' and the 'popular'. It may also mean 'taking on' socio-legal studies in so far as this field too has become atrophied. In many ways the study of law and popular culture currently represents the best hope of reinvigorating socio-legal studies. Positivistic entrenchment, as seen in many interpretations of the area covered by sports law, is well on the way to eclipsing some of socio-legal studies' earlier gains in the 1970s and the 1980s. The idea that law is simply the taken-for-granted 'rules' in statute and case law, and that legal education – including sports law where it is on the curriculum – is basically about the understanding and exposition of these rules is extremely widespread in the contemporary higher education world.

Current models for socio-legal studies will certainly include the 'juridic' and the 'disciplinary', though these are far from satisfactory in themselves. The 'juridic' model has tended to conceive of law as an instrument of power, itself conceptualized as a 'thing' to be owned or controlled. As far as popular culture is concerned this model of socio-legal studies has tended to view it as a realm fit for regulation – or 'repression' – by legal means. Debate in this area has been over whether the form of popular culture being regulated should, or should not, be so regulated.

This 'juridic' model has been subject to a form of 'Foucauldian' critique. Michel Foucault, theorizing law and sexuality, dismissed the 'repressive hypothesis' in favour of an emphasis on 'incitement to discourse'. The 'disciplinary' model conceives power no longer as a thing or an instrument but as an interlocking network of discourses and practices themselves producing counter-resistances. Popular culture, like sexuality in Foucault's work, functions as a 'domain'.

The disciplinary model conceives popular culture as a domain whose contours are policed or 'disciplined' by laws or other means of regulation. I developed this notion myself in relation to the legal regulation of 'pop' and 'youth' culture in *The End Of The Century Party: Youth and Pop Towards 2000* first published back in 1990.[15] It proposed a possible framework for the socio-legal understanding of the regulation of youth and popular culture. These contours, however ,'disappeared' before our eyes as mediatization and globalization grew apace. In a decade which Jean Baudrillard had told us to write off before it had begun, the rate of change – 'acceleration' – in popular culture left boundaries and domains such as the popular and the cultural looking far from certain and predictable. Law, and other forms of regulation, which might 'police' or 'discipline' such boundaries, were also subject to this acceleration and 'disappearance'.

Looking Back on the End of the Century: A Way Forward

As we look back at the end of the millennium, the century itself looks somewhat different. For Paul Virilio[16] we are looking back on the end of a 'century of hyperviolence'. For Jean Baudrillard,[17] 'Everthing Must Go!' in the 'End of the Century Sale', where the party, and the orgy, are over, and the wars, ethnic conflicts and armed insurrections of the twentieth century were being replayed backwards as we (slowly) counted down into the twenty-first century and the third millennium. In some of my work I have explored the implications of some of the writings of Baudrillard and, more especially, of Virilio which teach us to 'forget Foucault' and the disciplinary model. In this work[18] an alternative to the juridic and disciplinary models arises, by virtue of seeing legal and other regulation of popular culture being complemented – through the tendency for law to 'disappear' into popular culture – by the popular cultural regulation of law. I take Austin Sarat's[19] point that a cultural explanation of law neglects at its peril the materiality of law, especially its inscription on bodies, and its association with violence, pain and death. However, I want to maintain an allegiance to the 'disappearance' model. It is important to distinguish this from so-called 'post-modern' theory, which in any case is better seen as emanating from 'post-structuralist' debates. Recent useful books from within art history, on Baudrillard by Rex Butler[20] and Christopher Horrocks,[21] for instance, make no reference to the 'post-modern' in explications of Baudrillard's anti-modernist and anti-post-modernist outpourings. Virilio, as a theorist of accelerated (and decelerated) culture,[22] is in turn capable of a close reading, and use, without situating it in any post-modern context.

It is in its current potential theoretical development of socio-legal studies that law and popular culture lays claim to being the 'new pretender'[23] in the twenty-first century. As far as sports law is concerned, the conceptual object 'sport' is not a pre-given, ungendered, pre-theoretical field which law (pre-given, ungendered, pre-theoretical) acts upon, or refuses to act upon. The constituting of the conceptual object is extremely important. As with other spheres or domains where the public/private divide is called into question (the family, the sexual) law is a means for constituting the sphere or domain. But in the highly reflexive, mediatized, accelerated culture of today what passed for the separate sphere of 'sport' (where, mostly, law feared to tread, towing a *laissez-faire* line), even as short a time ago as the 1950s, is now fully integrated into popular culture.

Sport, in legal terms, is part of the entertainment and media industries which are globalized and subject to an ever increasing rapidity of change. Sport and the law in contemporary society will only ever be understood in the more general context of law and popular culture.

NOTES

This essay builds on a paper given to the Law and Society Association Annual Conference in Chicago in May 1999, 'Taking on Cultural Studies', and I am grateful for comments from the audience at that meeting which have contributed to the present version.

1. M. Medved, *Hollywood Versus America*, London, 1993.
2. K. Washburn and J. Thornton (eds.), *Dumbing Down: Essays on the Strip-Mining of American Culture*, New York, 1996.
3. R. Scruton, *An Intelligent Person's Guide to Modern Culture*, London, 1998. Scruton has elsewhere written in defence of the culture of 'the hunt' in British society: see *On Hunting*, London, 1998.
4. See J. Sutherland's essay 'Dumb Britannia' in the *Independent*, 2 March 1999 and in subsequent days of the same week, especially J. Walsh, 'How Low Can We Go' and B. Hoskyns, 'The Day the Music Died'. The following weekend the magazine *LM* (formerly *Living Marxism*) ran a conference entitled 'Culture Wars: Dumbing Down, Wising Up?' on 'standards in the arts, education and the media'. One of the discussion sessions was on 'the forward march of cultural studies'. The Centre for Corporate and Public Affairs in the Faculty of Business and Management at the Manchester Metropolitan University invited Alan Rusbridger, editor of the *Guardian*, to give its annual Cobden Lecture in 1999 – his title was 'Ethics Man: Is The Media Really Dumbing Down?'
5. For an overview of the field see my *Unpopular Cultures*, Manchester, 1995, and my 'Editorial Introduction' to the *International Journal of Sociology of Law* special issue on law and popular culture [24 (1996) no.2, 85–87].
6. For instance, J. Fiske, *Understanding Popular Culture*, London, 1989, has been cited in this way. Some of my own work in the late 1980s has been criticized for 'celebrating' its focus – football, music, drugs, 'madchester' – but I would want to argue that the fleeting 'carnivalesque' that it sought to expose, or uncover, is not capable of being grasped by being 'for' or 'against' it.
7. S. Hall, 'Notes on Deconstructing the Popular', in R. Samuel (ed.), *People's History and Socialist Theory*, London, 1981.
8. C. MacCabe, 'Defining Popular Culture', in MacCabe, *The Eloquence of the Vulgar*, London, 1999.
9. See S. Frith, *Performing Rites: On the Value of Popular Music*, Oxford, 1996. For debate on Frith's sociology of popular music in general, see M. Pickering and K. Negus, 'The Value of Value: Simon Frith and the Aesthetics of the Popular', and Frith, 'A Note on the Value of Value', 34 *New Formations* (1998).

10. See S. Frith, *Pearls and Swine: Instituting Popular Culture* (Manchester, forthcoming).

11. For an attack on 'cultural populism' see S. Frith and J. Savage, 'Pearls and Swine' in my edited book with D. Wynne and J. O'Connor, *The Clubcultures Reader: Readings in Popular Cultural Studies*, Oxford, 1997. The label of 'popular cultural studies' was designed to counter the proliferation of 'populist' cultural studies but also to draw attention to the importance of the 'popular' in law and popular culture.

12. See 12 *Cultural Studies* (1998) no. 4, special issue on cultural studies.

13. See P.A. Thomas (ed.), *Socio-Legal Studies*, Aldershot, 1997, an interesting collection of socio-legal essays, which, even in the late 1990s, nevertheless contained no reference to law and popular culture or to communications, media or cultural studies in general.

14. In Britain the Unit for Law and Popular Culture at the Manchester Metropolitan University, instituted in 1990 and the Centre for the Study of Law, Society and Popular Culture at the University of Westminster in 1994, developed within Law Schools with a certain amount of interest in socio-legal studies, though there was interaction with other disciplinary areas in both of these universities. MA/LLM courses in sports law and entertainment law, respectively, are being taught there. Anglia Polytechnic University's Sports Law Unit has been developing for a number of years, again with socio-legal input, and at the University of Warwick School of Law a law-in-context undergraduate sport and law course has run for over a decade.

15. Manchester University Press.

16. 'A Century of Hyperviolence: an Interview with Nicholas Zurbrugg', 25 *Economy and Society* (1996) no.1.

17. J. Baudrillard, 'The End of the Millennium, or the Countdown', 15 *Theory, Culture and Society* (1998) no.1.

18. For instance, see my *Post-Fandom and the Millennial Blues*, London, 1997. See also my 'Post-Fandom and the Millennial Boos', a review of R. Giulianotti, *Football: A Sociology of the World Game*, Cambridge, 1999, and other works, *International Review for the Sociology of Sport* (forthcoming).

19. A. Sarat, Review of *Unpopular Cultures*, 4 *Social and Legal Studies* (1995) no.4.

20. R. Butler, *Jean Baudrillard: the Defence of the Real*, London, 1999.

21. C. Horrocks, *Jean Baudrillard and the Millennium*, New York, 1999; the book is included in a series called 'Postmodern Encounters'.

22. See my forthcoming *Paul Virilio: Theorist for an Accelerated Culture* (Cambridge), which looks at Virilio's potential contribution to such ventures as a 'rhythmology' and an 'aesthetics of disappearance'.

23. To echo the phrase in Thomas, n.13.

3

Despite the Law: Prize-fighting and Professional Boxing

Michael Gunn and David Ormerod

Introduction

Boxing, and in particular professional boxing, has been bedevilled in recent years by a number of highly publicized tragedies in the ring.[1] Despite these tragedies, the Law Commission in its recent Consultation Papers[2] declined the opportunity to review the legality of professional boxing. In 1994 the Law Commission concluded that

> boxing, if it is to remain lawful, can only do so by the application of public policy considerations that are particular to that sport. Since that is a matter of pure policy, divorced from the more general considerations addressed in this chapter, we do not think it would be useful for us to add to the already formidable public debate on the issues.[3]

In 1995 the Commission continued to 'take the view ... that the continuing legality of boxing, amateur or professional, is a matter for Parliament to decide'.[4] The Law Commission does not deny that a review of the legality of boxing may be necessary, and several of their Lordships alluded to the questionable nature of its legality in the leading case on consent and offences against the person, *Brown*.[5] It is our aim to provide a reassessment of the legality of the sport.

Our approach is to consider the strengths and weaknesses of the arguments for making boxing illegal. In considering whether a form of behaviour should be criminal, it is important to begin with a recognition of the normal philosophical stance adopted by the decision-maker and to assess the proposal against that stance. There are a number of stances which may be taken, though it has to be said that Parliament does not consistently adopt a single one, tending instead to be pragmatic in its approach to criminalization, endeavouring to assess the strengths and weaknesses of the proposal without reference to a driving philosophical stance. It is necessary to provide a brief explanation of the most pertinent philosophical approaches so that the public policy arguments discussed later may be better assessed.

Most present-day criminal law jurists, at least those writing in Western democracies, favour liberalism as the basis for criminalization. The traditional liberal viewpoint is that the imposition of a criminal sanction represents the most severe infringement of a person's liberty, and, as such, should be available only where there is a clear social justification. Autonomy is then the touchstone of liberalism. The most detailed exposition of liberal theory in criminal law is provided by Feinberg. He summarizes the central tenet – the Harm Principle – as: 'It is always a good reason in support of penal legislation that it would be effective in preventing (eliminating, reducing) harm to persons other than the actor (the one prohibited from acting) *and* there is no other means that is equally effective at no greater cost to other values.'[6] Boxing could properly be made unlawful on either the harm to others principle or the offence to others principle, but not the harm to self principle. The arguments which we shall review are unlikely to satisfy anybody who takes such an approach to criminalization. The liberal approach, as proposed by Feinberg, will also, however, allow for 'soft paternalism'. By adopting a soft paternalist approach to criminalization 'the State has the right to prevent self-regarding harmful conduct … *when but only when* that conduct is substantially non-voluntary, or when temporary intervention is necessary to establish whether it is voluntary or not'.[7] In the context of boxing, this would necessitate having the means to ensure that boxers are capable of deciding whether to box (and it might be accepted that the nature and degree of the harm caused to boxers is so great that it is not possible to accept that any boxer could be regarded as competent to make such a decision) and that they have sufficient relevant information upon which to base such a decision.[8] Towards the end of our argument we identify some areas where the soft paternalist might be convinced, for example, not only of the need for increased information to boxers so that they are fully aware of the risks they run in pursuing their chosen career, but also of the need for greater medical support at fights, the elimination of certain aspects of boxing (such as outlawing the head punch), and a reduction of the length of bouts in terms of both the time of a round and the number of rounds in a fight.

For boxing to be made illegal it would be necessary, therefore, to adopt a paternalist approach. This chapter does not advocate such an approach. However, as has been said, Parliament will not necessarily legislate according to the adoption of a particular philosophical approach to criminalization. As such, the strength of the several arguments must be carefully assessed. Viewed through the pragmatic Parliamentary lens, one might say that if the harm to the individual sufficiently outweighs the benefits to be gained by that individual, then that might well convince the legislators to criminalize boxing.[9]

Our reassessment of the legality of boxing involves discussion of the following issues:

 i. the procedures by which the legality of boxing might be questioned in a court

ii. the criminal offences which boxing might involve

iii. whether the boxer's factual consent is legally significant in the light of the public interest arguments about boxing

iv. the practical reality of criminal proceedings being instituted

v. the likely response of the courts, and

vi. an examination of the arguments for stricter safeguards and for the banning of boxing.

History

Boxing has a very long history[10] and there is no doubt that at present the sport of professional boxing is lawful in England.[11] It is worth noting that boxing as we now know it came to be recognized in law by default rather than design.[12] In the nineteenth century the courts were anxious to outlaw prize-fighting, and in order to do so successfully they permitted what then appeared to be the relatively tame version conducted with padded gloves in private. As the Law Commission stated in 1994,

> Boxing originally appears to have been regarded as lawful not through any application of principle, or by reference to the legal rules applying to other sports, but simply because it was not the prize-fighting that had been declared unlawful, on grounds as much related to public order as to the law of offences against the person, in *Coney*.[13]

The eighteenth and the nineteenth century saw the advent of the prize-fight or bare-knuckle fight.[14] These fights became popular in the developing urban areas. Originally the bouts were without any rules or restrictions. By 1743 the then champion of England – James Brougham – introduced a new set of rules. Under these, rounds lasted until a man went down, hitting was prohibited when a man was on the floor, the below-the-belt punch was outlawed, and fighters were given 30 seconds to 'come up to scratch' (the mark in the centre of the fighting area) if they had been knocked down. Finally, and perhaps most significantly, a referee whose decision was final was introduced.[15] These rules were so effective that they survived for almost a century, being superseded by the London Prize Ring Rules of 1839, which also regulated the ring size to a 24-ft square ring.

The next development came with the famous Queensberry Rules being drawn up in 1865 by John Graham Chambers. These banned wrestling, required padded gloves, three-minute rounds with one-minute intervals, seconds to assist the combatants, and the ten-second knock-out rule. Despite initial reluctance, following their acceptance by influential people such as the World Bare-Knuckle fight champion John Sullivan,[16] the rules were soon adopted throughout the boxing world.

The courts became involved in the world of prize-fights in an attempt to regulate the degree of harm to which people could consent.[17] They distinguished between the sparring match and the prize-fight[18] on the basis of the likelihood of one of the combatants becoming seriously injured.[19] This was a difficult distinction to make, especially since, as the rules developed, the combatants in prize-fights began to wear gloves of a fashion. The courts finally arrived at what appeared to them to be a reasonable solution: they left the issue to the jury. In *R. v. Orton*[20] the Court for Crown Cases Reserved confirmed this jury direction:

> if it were a mere exhibition of skill in sparring [it was not unlawful]; but that if the parties met intending to fight till one gave in from exhaustion or injury received it was a breach of the law and a prize-fight, whether the combatants fought in gloves or not.[21]

This direction was partly based upon the decision in *R. v. Young*[22] in which Bramwell B held that a death resulting from a gloved fight in a private place was not unlawful. He stated:

> if a death ensued from a fight, independently of it taking place for money, it would be manslaughter, because a fight was a dangerous thing and likely to kill; but the medical witness here stated that this sparring was not dangerous, and not a thing likely to kill.[23]

The matter was further considered by the Court for Crown Cases Reserved in *R. v. Coney,*[24] which is still regarded today as a leading authority on the issue of consent.[25] The case was primarily concerned with a charge of aiding and abetting a prize-fight. There was no doubt that prize-fighting was illegal, but the courts were anxious to clarify the sparring/prize-fight distinction. A sparring match is legal because, according to Cave J, there is no blow struck in anger nor is a blow struck which is 'likely or intended to do corporal hurt, but... a blow struck in sport, and not likely, nor intended to cause bodily harm, is not an assault...'[26] It is legal according to Mathew J because it is not dangerous.[27] Similarly, Stephen J took the view that

> where life and limb are exposed to no serious danger in the common course of things, ... consent is a defence to a charge of assault, even where considerable force is used as, for instance, in cases of wrestling..., sparring with gloves, football, and the like; but in all cases the question whether consent does or does not take the form of the application of force to another, its illegal character is a question of degree depending upon the circumstances.[28]

Hawkins J also took into account the likelihood of a breach of the peace consequent upon a fight.[29]

One academic gleaned from the dicta in *Coney* that: 'The tests therefore of legality in a boxing match are (i) is it a breach of the peace or does it tend to it, and (ii) does it endanger life or health. If it does either of these it is unlawful and no consent can make it otherwise.'[30]

As Glanville Williams has since pointed out, the more satisfactory of these two reasons for the nineteenth-century decisions relates 'to the possible injury to the combatants'.[31] He concludes elsewhere that these decisions leave open the possibility that fighting is unlawful 'where the circumstances make it likely that injury, or (at least) some kind of serious injury, will be caused'.[32]

It has been presumed, since *Coney*, that a boxing match is more like a sparring match than a prize-fight and is, therefore, legal. It is not the intention of the combatants in a boxing match to fight until one of them is exhausted, although the nature of many fights is that the parties do exhaust themselves.[33] The brief consideration that we have given to the history of pugilism shows the development in the interest in it. It is important to emphasize that this meant that the prize-fight was by the mid-nineteenth century looking much like a bare-knuckle version of boxing. The finishing touches were added by the Queensberry Rules. By this time 'sparring' had become accepted as a respectable pastime, with even the nobility, including the monarchy, being involved.

The law's attitude to these developments was to recognize that it was no longer legitimate to outlaw all such organized fighting, and the distinction between boxing and sparring became crucial to the law. It can be argued that the present-day acceptance of the legality of boxing stems from this early distinction. There are two main difficulties with this view. First, the professional boxing bout of today certainly looks like a closer descendant of the prize-fight, while the amateur boxing contest is more akin to the sparring of the mid-nineteenth century. Although the professional fight follows the Queensberry rules, there are other traits bearing resemblance to the prize-fight: the fighters receive payment and fight to (near) exhaustion. The second difficulty is that the early distinction between sparring and prize-fighting was far from clear, and it would be most unsatisfactory if that formed the basis of the present law. While claiming to be distinguishing between the unlawful prize-fight and the lawful sparring match on the basis of the risk of serious injury, the courts were, in reality, interested in a wider range of factors. These included whether payment was made to the fighters, whether the rules were observed and gloves worn, what degree of regulation existed, and whether there was a danger of public disorder at the event. Often the courts seemed to be abdicating responsibility for the decision by leaving the matter to the jury, as in *Orton*.[34]

The Procedures for Raising the Question of Legality

There are three obvious procedures whereby the question of the legality of boxing might be raised. First, a boxer might be prosecuted for an offence, either on the basis of an allegation that he clearly acted outside the rules of the sport[35] or merely for being involved in a boxing match. In the former, the question of the legality of boxing would arise indirectly, since the focus would be on a particular incident. The question would be of direct relevance in the latter, since the focus would be on the sport as an entity rather than on any given incident(s). Secondly, the Attorney-General might wish to seek a declaration as to the legal status of boxing. A court would have to be prepared to entertain the application and, before granting a declaration, it would have to be convinced that boxing necessarily involves the commission of one or more criminal offences.[36] Thirdly, a boxer might sue his opponent in negligence or trespass to the person for injuries suffered as a consequence of a particular fight. A boxer who has suffered injuries might sue the British Boxing Board of Control (BBBC),[37] the owners of the stadium in which the fight took place, the organizers of the fight or the referee.[38] The basis of his claim would be that boxing is unlawful where injury is likely or is intended to be caused and that the defendant's responsibility for the fight meant that he had a duty of care to prevent injuries from being sustained.[39] In the course of such civil actions, it might be necessary to consider whether boxing involves the commission of a criminal offence, as did McInerney J in the Australian case *Pallante* v. *Stadium Pty Ltd*.[40]

The Possible Criminal Charges

The relevant criminal offences which would be considered in the legal actions identified above are those under the Offences against the Person Act 1861 concerned with the causing of bodily harm, that is ss.47, 20 and 18 and common assault and battery, now summary offences under s.39 of the Criminal Justice Act 1988.[41]

All that is required for 'actual bodily harm' is some degree of pain or discomfort.[42] All boxing matches (except those which count technically as matches but where no boxing takes place; for instance, because an opponent does not turn up) involve the causing of such harm by each boxer to the other, as they cannot be won without one boxer punching the other. The nature of a punch is that it must inflict the necessary bodily harm, even if the particular boxer in question does not have a particularly hard punch. Thus, the *actus reus* of the s.47 offence is satisfied in any boxing match. It could be that all boxing matches involve not only actual bodily harm, but also grievous bodily harm, as required by ss.20 and 18. Certainly, grievous bodily harm is caused in some fights. It is well known that a professional boxer's punch is extremely powerful[43] and can result in grievous bodily harm.[44] Grievous bodily harm means 'really serious harm'[45] and could be satisfied, for example, by a broken nose.[46] It would seem that this form of harm is caused in most, if not all, fights, whether they end quickly with a knockout or go the distance, leaving each party close to exhaustion. However, it is possible that grievous bodily harm will not occur in every fight, especially if two defensive boxers are involved. If so, the legality of boxing generally cannot be challenged on the basis that all bouts necessarily involve the commission of an offence contrary to s.20 or 18.

All that need be established for the *mens rea* of a s.47 offence is that a boxer foresaw the risk of assaulting his opponent.[47] Since the object of a fight is to score points against the opponent by hitting him, that *mens rea* is always satisfied, even if any particular boxer does not have a knockout punch and would not use it if he had. It is probable that the *mens rea* for a s.20 offence would also always be satisfied. The boxer must foresee the risk of causing some, albeit minor, physical harm. He does not have to foresee the kind of harm which actually eventuates, that is grievous bodily harm.[48] Thus the *mens rea* for both s.47 and s.20 would appear to be satisfied in all boxing matches.

It is possible that the *mens rea* for a s.18 offence is also necessarily present. A boxer must intend to cause grievous bodily harm. 'Intention' in this context carries the same meaning as in the law of murder.[49] It exists where the consequence, grievous bodily harm, is the purpose of the boxer or is foreseen as virtually certain by him and then it may be found that he intended it.[50] Any boxer must be aware of the power of a punch, and that grievous bodily harm is very likely in any fight. Thus it is possible that it would be inferred that all boxers have the intention to cause grievous bodily harm. That a boxer does not desire such consequences is irrelevant. The terrorist who plants a bomb on an aeroplane, not wanting to kill but knowing that all the occupants will die if the bomb explodes at altitude, intends the death of the occupants.[51] The boxer is an analogous case. If, however, he claims that he did not expect the consequence of serious harm and if such a view can be taken seriously, it is possible to argue that the *mens rea* is not present. If such an argument is plausible, it is not possible to argue that a boxing match *necessarily* involves the commission of an offence contrary to s.18. This was recognized by the Law Commission when it stated that:

> The ultimate objective of every boxer is to knock his opponent out, conduct that almost inevitably involves the infliction of grievous bodily harm on the opponent, contrary to section 18 of the Offences against the Person Act 1861. That this conduct is inherently hostile is

reinforced by the aggressive posture that appears often to be adopted before contests. And the rules of the sport, or at least the way in which they are administered, do not appear to guarantee against the infliction of gratuitous injury. The point goes further than merely non-fatal injury to the person, because under the present law it is murder to cause death by an attack intended to cause grievous bodily harm. That is not merely a theoretical observation, since the British Medical Association reports that worldwide since 1945, 561 deaths have occurred during boxing, most of them caused by a single or multiple concussive blow.[52]

The BBBC took exception to this view claiming that 'the essence of boxing is not the ultimate infliction of serious injury.... Nor is it ... the ultimate objective of every boxer to knock his opponent out.'[53]

What is clearly the objective of any boxer is to score points – which cannot be achieved without hitting the opponent. This will amount to the infliction of sufficient harm to amount to the *actus reus* for s.47, as argued above. Subject to the relevance of consent, it would appear, therefore, that all fights, not just some, necessarily involve at least the commission of an offence contrary to s.47 of the Offences against the Person Act 1861.

Any fight involves the commission not only of a s.47 offence, but also of an attempt to commit it, contrary to s.1(1) of the Criminal Attempts Act 1981. Squaring up to punch is an act more than merely preparatory to the commission of an assault, that is, the throwing of a punch. The necessary intent is present for an attempt. Thus if only one boxer throws a punch which knocks the other out, both have committed offences: one the full offence (s.47) and the other an attempt. If it were argued that there are fights in which no bodily harm is actually caused, the availability of the attempt charge defeats the argument that some boxing matches do not involve the commission of an offence.

Finally it is worth noting that, although the courts have occasionally discussed the requirement of 'hostility' prior to there being a provable offence,[54] it is not an element in any of the crimes considered here. At most it means that there must be *mens rea* for an assault or battery, and, therefore, adds nothing to the elements of the various offences already considered.[55] It would not have to be established that a boxer was hostile or felt ill-will to his opponent.

Consent

Where harm is caused to others, this is not, in itself, a sufficient argument to criminalize that activity as, at least under a liberal approach, competent adults may consent to that harm. This is a recognition of the central tenet of respect for the autonomy of individuals. The question is whether boxers may validly consent to a boxing match. This requires consideration of two things: (1) whether there is factual consent, (2) whether the law recognizes that factual consent as valid.

Undoubtedly both boxers do in fact consent before a fight, although it is not clear to what degree of harm or risk of harm each consents. The amount of information that each boxer possesses before the fight might be questioned, but it is unlikely that a serious challenge to consent can be made on this basis. Similarly, a claim that adult boxers lacked the capacity to consent would not, ordinarily, have any foundation. The question becomes whether the law recognizes this factual consent.

Anyone may legally consent to battery and assault. The doubt is whether boxers may consent to the infliction of bodily harm. This is a question of public policy. The courts are empowered to impose limits on the bodily harm to which people may consent.[56]

The nineteenth-century cases mentioned earlier indicate that some account must be taken of the degree of harm to be inflicted. In the *Attorney-General's Reference (No.6 of 1980)*[57] the Court of Appeal developed this approach:

> It is not in the public interest that people should try to cause, or should cause, each other actual bodily harm for no good reason. Minor struggles are another matter. So, in our judgment, it is immaterial whether the act occurs in private or in public; it is an assault if actual bodily harm is intended and/or caused. This means that most fights will be unlawful regardless of consent.
>
> Nothing which we have said is intended to cast doubt upon the accepted legality of properly conducted games and sports, lawful chastisement or correction, reasonable surgical interference, dangerous exhibitions, etc. These apparent exceptions can be justified as involving the exercise of a legal right, in the case of chastisement or correction, or as needed in the public interest, in other cases.[58]

Fighting is unlawful despite consent. It appears to follow that all activity involving the infliction of actual bodily harm involves the commission of an offence except where it occurs within, for example, a properly conducted sport. The consent of participants in properly conducted sports is accepted by the courts because these sports are 'needed in the public interest'. Applying this test, boxing appears to be lawful. This not to suggest, of course, that all activity within the rules of boxing, or any other sport, is lawful just because it is within the rules. However, it is necessary to ask a more fundamental question: can it be said that professional boxing is needed in the public interest, particularly in the light of the existing medical evidence?

The decision of the Court of Appeal in *Attorney-General's Reference (No.6 of 1980)* was followed, by the House of Lords, in *R.* v. *Brown* which was concerned with sado-masochistic activities.[59] Their Lordships decided, by a bare majority, that the laying of charges under the Offences against the Person Act 1861 was proper where either wounding or actual bodily harm was inflicted. Considerations of policy and public interest, such as the protection of society against a cult of violence, the possibility of the corruption of young men and the danger of serious injuries, required that consensual sado-masochistic activities in private between homosexuals involving the infliction of actual bodily harm should constitute offences under ss.20 and 47 of the Offences against the Person Act 1861. Although that case was not concerned with boxing, several of their Lordships expressed opinions on the legal position of boxing and it is valuable to consider these in more detail.

The Decision of the House of Lords in *Brown*

Lord Templeman, in the majority, stated that 'Ritual circumcision, tattooing, ear-piercing and violent sports including boxing are lawful activities.'[60] However, Lord Jauncey, also in the majority, concluded that

> [*Coney*] is authority for the proposition that the public interest limits the extent to which an individual may consent to infliction upon himself by another of bodily harm and that such public interest does not intervene in the case of sports where any infliction of injury is merely incidental to the purpose of the main activity.[61]

The infliction of injury is not, it is submitted, 'merely incidental to' boxing.

The discussion of boxing in the House of Lords in *Brown* is not conclusive: all the comments were *obiter*. Furthermore, it would appear that at least some of their Lordships were unhappy with professional boxing as an exception to the unlawfulness of assaults intended to cause actual bodily harm. Lord Templeman commented that *'Rightly or wrongly* the courts accepted that boxing is a lawful activity.'[62] Lord Slynn of Hadley, dissenting, stated that:

> It seems to me that the notion of 'consent' fits ill into the situation where there is a fight. It is also very strange that a fight in private between two youths where one may, at most, get a bloody nose should be unlawful, whereas a boxing match where one heavyweight fighter seeks to knock out his opponent and possibly do him very serious damage should be lawful.[63]

In examining the distinction which grew up between the lawful sparring match and the unlawful prize-fight, Lord Mustill, dissenting, stated that

> although consent is present in both cases the risks of serious violence and public disorder make prize-fighting something which 'the law says shall not be done' whereas the lesser risk of injury, the absence of public disorder, the improvement of the health and skills of the participants and the consequent benefit to the public at large combine to place sparring into a different category, which the law says 'may be done'.[64]

His Lordship continued:

> That the court is in such cases making a value judgment, not dependent upon any general theory of consent, is exposed by the failure of any attempt to deduce why professional boxing appears to be immune from prosecution. For money, not recreation or personal improvement, each boxer tries to hurt the opponent more than he is hurt himself and aims to end the contest prematurely by inflicting a brain injury serious enough to make the opponent unconscious, or temporarily by impairing his central nervous system through a blow to the midriff, or cutting his skin to a degree which would ordinarily be well within the scope of s.20. The boxers display skill, strength and courage, but nobody pretends that they do good to themselves or others. The onlookers derive entertainment, but none of the physical and moral benefits which have been seen as the fruits of engagement in manly sports. I intend no disrespect to the valuable judgment of McInerney J, in *Pallante v. Stadiums Pty.* when I say that the heroic efforts of that learned judge to arrive at an intellectually satisfying account of the apparent immunity of professional boxing from the criminal process have convinced me that the task is impossible. It is in my judgment best to regard this as another special situation which for the time being stands outside the ordinary law of violence because society chooses to tolerate it.[65]

The decision of the House of Lords in *Brown* was challenged before the European Court of Human Rights. It was claimed that the prosecution was a breach of the right to respect for private and family life under Article 8 of the Convention. That challenged failed.[66] It was presumed that Article 8(1) was applicable, though the Court questioned 'whether the sexual activities of the applicants fell entirely within the notion of "private life" in the particular circumstances of the case'. Those circumstances were, in particular, the 'considerable number of people involved in the activities'.[67]

Thus the central issue was whether the restriction upon private life satisfied Article 8(2), and the Court took the view that 'the whole issue of the role of consent in the criminal law is of great complexity and the contracting states should enjoy a wide margin of appreciation to consider all the public-policy options'. States are entitled to 'regulate, through the operation of the criminal law, activities which involve the infliction of physical harm'. It is a matter for each state to determine the level of harm to be tolerated and, in so doing, it will balance 'public health considerations' and the 'general deterrent effect of the criminal law' against 'the personal autonomy of the individual'. The degree of injury, which could not be characterized as 'trifling or transient', was sufficient to distinguish this case from those earlier ones that concerned consensual homosexual behaviour. There was no evidence that there was bias against homosexuals, as the case was predicated on the 'extreme nature of the practices involved and not the sexual proclivities of the applicants'. Furthermore, the case was easily distinguishable, on the severity of injury involved, from that later English case where a prosecution for mere buttock-branding had failed: *Wilson*.[68]

An Article 8 challenge would not be permissible against boxing, because the activity is too public. If a boxing ban were imposed and challenged, the European Court would be faced with numerous public policy arguments which are discussed below. The crucial issue would, indeed, be the degree of injury suffered and the interference with personal autonomy that would flow from any banning of the sport.

The Public Interest and Boxing

The present legality of professional boxing is based solely on grounds of policy. In this section we identify the major policy elements in an attempt to consider the question: is professional boxing needed in the public interest? When these policy factors are studied, and the medical evidence is considered, we believe that it is time for the appellate courts to consider whether public policy is still in favour of the 'sport'. This approach is open to the appellate courts on the basis that the comments in *Brown* about boxing are *obiter* and so a full and careful consideration of the medical evidence was not undertaken. We take the view that the courts are likely to conclude that it is lawful, and consistent with public policy. We see no reason to distinguish boxing by men from boxing by women. The nature of the arguments that follow apply to both groups. Any argument to ban women boxing as an issue separate from banning boxing also for men appears simply to be discriminatory.[69]

An Assessment of the Public Interest Arguments for Boxing

Boxing Is a Sport

It might be argued on the sole ground that, as boxing is a sport, it is in the public interest and is therefore legal. The Court of Appeal and the House of Lords do not doubt the 'accepted legality of properly conducted sports and games'.[70] However, simply to call something a sport would be unlikely to be adequate. The futuristic 'sport' of rollerball, as depicted in *Rollerball* (1975), would not be legal just because it was described as a sport. There is no Parliamentary recognition of what constitutes a 'sport'. The Sports Council does not declare activities to be recognized sports, but does recognize some as eligible for funding – including boxing.[71]

Boxing Promotes a Fit and Healthy Society

The training undertaken by participants in boxing increases their general level of fitness and health. Training for boxing discourages drinking, smoking and drug-taking.[72] Fit and healthy people are conducive to a healthy society and such an objective is in the public interest. However, boxing is a dangerous sport.[73] It is quite clear that there are many safer ways of ensuring a fit population, particularly if people are advised as to the most suitable and sensible activities for them to undertake.[74]

Boxing Training Instils Discipline

The training necessary to be a boxer is carried out in a disciplined manner and, when combined with the ethos of boxing, tends to instil self-discipline.[75] Some boxers claim that they would have led lives of crime without the self-discipline instilled in them by boxing.[76] However, boxing is not the only sport promoting self-discipline. Many of the oriental martial arts are regarded as the paradigm sports in which self-discipline is essential. Those martial arts not involving full-contact[77] are not inherently dangerous. Any full-contact martial art may be regarded in the same light as boxing.[78]

Boxing Offers an Opportunity for Self-advancement

The sport attracts boys from poorer backgrounds and gives them an opportunity to work their way out of poverty.[79] 'Boxing today, and boxing always, belongs to the poor.'[80] The most successful professional boxers make themselves financially secure for life. But poverty and other social disadvantages could be addressed directly by appropriate focused government social-welfare policies. Further, it has been suggested that attracting people from poorer backgrounds means that they are thereby exploited by being encouraged to be involved in a dangerous sport for the amusement of the less disadvantaged.[81] It is also alleged that boxing careers are lengthened solely to earn more money, without due regard to the dangers of the sport.[82] Finally, the 'lure of boxing [being] quite simply money: fighting for gain' was itself sufficient for Lord Cochrane of Cutts to call for an end to boxing.[83] This is a weak argument, even though it was part of the basis for the abolition of prize-fighting. Some would say it becomes a class issue. As one commentator explained, 'I smell pomposity and condescension in every word of the anti-boxing campaign...'[84] The purport of this argument is that the opposition is class-based in objecting to an activity primarily involving working-class, often poor, people, but being objected to by middle- and upper-middle-class, usually financially well-off, people.

Boxing Is Popular

The sport is undoubtedly popular. In 1987 it was estimated that there were 5,000 licensed professional boxers in the United States.[85] Boxing is also a popular sport with ring-side spectators and television and cinema audiences. For example, the Watson–Eubank fight attracted an audience of 12.8 million.[86] This figure compares favourably with the most popular television programmes. The 'Rocky' films were box-office hits. The first time that Mike Tyson boxed in Britain in January 2000 produced an incredible response both in the speed with which the tickets for the fight sold and the media attention heaped upon him. Yet it should not be forgotten that popularity, or being of interest to the public, is not equivalent to being in the 'public interest'.

The Public Interest Arguments against Boxing

Boxing Is Dangerous

Boxing is dangerous.[87] In any given match acute injuries may occur. In addition, a boxer may suffer chronic injuries as a result of his boxing career. A significant number of deaths result from boxing matches.[88] Concussion is a frequent acute injury, and the consequences are surprisingly severe. Studies have shown a high rate of morbidity and unemployment in concussed patients three months after what appeared to be insignificant head injuries.[89] 'The implications for boxers, who frequently suffer many more concussions, are obvious.'[90] Among other acute injuries,[91] the most frequent are eye injuries.[92] The most common one is detachment of the retina.[93] Although 'few of the injuries give rise to symptoms of immediate visual loss... in a sample of active professional boxers 58 per cent had at least one sight threatening injury to the angle, lens, or retina (half had bilateral damage)'.[94]

While the acute injuries are in themselves sufficient to give rise to considerable concern, the chronic injuries consequent on boxing, that is brain damage, are of greater legal and policy significance. It is the nature of the chronic injuries and the fact that they are caused by the very nature of the sport that distinguishes boxing from other sports in which, admittedly, there may be greater acute injury and death.

There are numerous studies establishing that chronic brain damage is a likely consequence of a boxing career.[95] One survey discovered brain damage in the form of organic cerebral dysfunction in 87 per cent of a group of professional boxers who had had many fights.[96] Studies undertaken in the 1960s discovered a lower incidence of brain damage, but still found: 'slowed motor performance clumsiness, dysarthia, ataxia of gait, tremors, rigidity, spasticity, memory deficit, slowness of thought, and personality change form the full-blown picture, occurring in 17 per cent to 55 per cent of professional boxers'.[97] The explanation for the apparent discrepancy between the results of these studies lies in the greater range of tests used in later surveys, in particular through neuropathological observations,[98] and the longer careers of the boxers in the later study producing the higher incidence of brain injury.

Somewhat surprisingly, the main danger is not a knockout or a heavy punch, but the effect of numerous, individual injuries, each producing minimal or unobservable effects which mount up to produce chronic brain damage.[99] The term 'punch drunk' was used by Martland as early as 1928 to describe a person displaying the relevant symptoms.[100] Millspaugh coined the phrase 'dementia pugilistica' in 1937 to describe the same thing.[101]

The evidence that boxing is dangerous might be challenged. The number of deaths has decreased significantly in recent times, but this is most likely to be a product of the dramatic reduction in the number of bouts any given boxer fights as well as the safety measures introduced at the ring-side and between bouts.[102] It has been suggested that the evidence establishing the dangerous nature of boxing is biased.[103] It is difficult to accept this, given the vast literature and numerous studies from many countries on the subject, though Brayne, Sargeant and Brayne do point out that, after a survey of studies obtained through a Medline search, 'in none of these studies did the design allow more than measures of association to be inferred. They measured different outcomes ranging from radiological appearances and neuropsychological tests to biochemical measures of blood brain barrier integrity.'[104] There is also some evidence for a genetic predisposition to dementia pugilistica in high-exposure boxers, which, if established, would have a significant impact upon the boxing debate.[105]

A further counter-argument is that, although boxing is dangerous, there are many other dangerous sports in which harm occurs to participants.[106] So, for example, Lord Brooks of Tremorfa in the House of Lords debate on the Boxing Bill 1991 drew attention to statistics which showed that, of the 480 deaths in sport between 1969 and 1980, only two occurred in professional boxing, whereas there were 93 in mountaineering and rock climbing, 85 in motorcycling, 66 in football, 53 in horse riding, 34 in parachuting and hang gliding, 28 in motor racing, 32 in rugby, 28 in scuba diving, 16 in canoeing, nine in both cricket and hunting, six in golf, four in rowing, and three in both karate and judo.[107] While there are fewer fatalities than in some other sports,[108] there are nevertheless a significant number of fatalities and, further, it is only in boxing in which there is a high incidence of chronic, rather than acute, serious injury: chronic brain damage.[109] In spite of this fact, it is argued by some that boxing is unfairly singled out in the debate on dangerous sports. There is, however, a further factor which distinguishes boxing from other contact sports such as Rugby Union and Rugby League. Only in boxing is the object of the exercise to inflict bodily harm on the opponent. In other dangerous sports injury is an incidental and non-necessary element of participation.

Boxing has three principal distinguishing features from all other sports. First, it is the aim of the boxer to strike blows upon his opponent, indeed, this is a prerequisite of winning a bout. Secondly, medical evidence suggests a far higher incidence of serious chronic injury in boxing than in any other sport. Thirdly, since many of the other dangerous sports involve sole participants, there are no potential defendants to prosecute. These features lend considerable force to the argument in favour of the criminalization of boxing. However, they do not necessarily meet the philosophical objection that it is for the participants, as autonomous agents, to decide whether they wish to undertake the risks, and not for society to prevent such a choice.[110] It is this point that is critical for the liberal approach to criminalization. Nevertheless, it might be thought that the argument is circular, since the whole point is whether society should prevent boxers from having the choice because of the inherent dangers of the sport. Although autonomy is a fundamental principle in the English law of consent, the question is whether it can be subordinate to other principles, here the public interest, as supported by scientific evidence.[111] The paternalist would agree, but not the liberal.

Violence Begets Violence

First, it is said that the sport of boxing encourages the use of violence in other circumstances. Secondly, boxing presents a poor image to children and others, especially when participants become celebrity figures, such as Muhammad Ali, Chris Eubank, Frank Bruno and Henry Cooper. The argument is similar to that with regard to the effect of violent television upon children. Even though television is far more pervasive, invasive and influential, there is still considerable debate as to its effects. How, therefore, can this argument be credibly sustained when applied to boxing *per se*? In the United States an experimental study by Celozzi, Kazelskis and Gutsch[112] found support for the basic premises in the work of Bandura[113] and Berkowitz[114] which suggests that exposure to violent programming tends to make observers more aggressive. It was found that aggression levels increased in male high school students upon viewing televised violence in ice hockey. This must support the argument that watching intentionally violent activity in the boxing ring will lead to aggression. Moreover, the argument may take yet another form: even if people do not resort to similar activity, the coverage by the media of the excitement of seeing boxers fighting, cutting one another, knocking each other down and ending a fight exhausted is repulsive and unacceptable.[115] The answer to such an argument is, of course, for those repulsed to avoid watching and reading about boxing. More significantly, it is not conclusively proven that there is a causal link between violence portrayed by the media and violent action by its watchers, hearers, readers or other users.

Boxing Encourages Gambling

Boxing is said to encourage gambling. This argument is, however, unpersuasive. It is taken from the nineteenth-century cases and, while the evils of gambling are significant, it is not a serious argument against the public interest in maintaining boxing. The argument could be applied with much greater force to horse-racing, but few would even dream of arguing for the abolition of the 'Sport of Kings' on this ground.

The Practical Likelihood of Successful Proceedings

Despite our argument as to the legality of boxing and its availability for review by the appellate courts, it must be recognized that the likelihood of the matter arising before the courts is slim, particularly in view of the statements in *Brown* that the Crown Prosecution Service would or could not countenance a prosecution of a boxer simply for boxing. On the other hand, Lord Lane in the Court of Appeal in *Brown* said that 'where ... there has admittedly been inflicted either wounding or actual bodily harm, it was in our judgment both permissible and correct to lay charges under the 1861 Act'.[116] The infliction of actual bodily harm, therefore, would not *per se* be sufficient to justify the laying of charges, but if there was evidence of ill-will on the part of a boxer, prosecution could not be ruled out.

There is only a remote possibility that the Attorney-General would contemplate instituting proceedings for a declaration or that a boxer would institute proceedings involving an allegation that boxing itself is illegal. Even if the Attorney-General were to contemplate seeking a declaration the numerous obstacles in his path indicate that the proceedings would probably fail.[117]

In the unlikely event that a head-on challenge to boxing were to be raised before the courts, it is submitted that there is reason to doubt the currently accepted legality of boxing. However, boxing has been a recognized sport for a considerable time. To declare that it was illegal would be a major step for the courts to take. Even if the judges believe in the declaratory theory of the common law, it is unlikely that a court would wish to interfere so fundamentally with the way a section of society has chosen to organize itself over a considerable period of time.[118] The fact that the numerous supporting activities might consequently face criminal liability for aiding and abetting also militates against the courts' declaring boxing to be illegal.[119] However, the courts might just be persuaded by the compelling medical evidence suggesting that boxing is not in the public interest, and take a radical view. The courts are entitled to do so, and will grasp the opportunity if they are convinced of the need to develop the law in this way.[120]

Reform and Prohibition

We concur with the conclusion of the Law Commission that it is 'for Parliament to take an entirely separate decision, in the light of the material seriously put before it by the British Medical Association and others, as to whether boxing should continue to be lawful'.[121]

It is in the public interest for the future of boxing to be debated. The debate may take two forms. First, a debate about banning boxing or banning professional boxing. Secondly, a debate about improving the safety standards associated with boxing.

Banning Boxing

A complete ban on boxing would lead to the eradication of the brain damage and other injuries currently suffered by pugilists. The British, the Canadian, the Australian and the American Medical Associations have all called for such a ban in the last two decades, as has the World Medical Association.[122]

Many of the calls for the banning of boxing extend only to the banning of professional boxing.[123] The available evidence suggests that amateur boxing is safer than professional.[124] Professional boxing has been banned in Sweden since 1969 and in Norway since 1982.[125] Maintaining the sport in its amateur form would maintain many of the advantages of the sport and reduce the inherent dangers.[126]

But boxing is unlikely to be banned. Even after the Watson–Eubank fight, the government refused to set up an inquiry into professional boxing or to establish a study to ascertain the long-term effects of the sport. Further, it made clear that it is the sole responsibility of the sport's governing bodies to monitor brain-stem injuries as a result of boxing accidents.[127] The House of Lords has three times refused a second reading to a bill aimed at banning professional boxing, on the third occasion at the end of a poorly-attended debate.[128]

Boxing has probably been accepted as a sport of interest to too many people for too long for a ban realistically to be contemplated.[129] Boxing's supporters have a strong hand in terms of the popularity of the sport and some have considerable influence. Moreover, no ban would prevent boxing for reward. Either participants would leave the country in which boxing was banned or only where amateur boxing was permitted, or boxing would go underground.[130] Currently, the strict regulations of the BBBC are avoided by some boxers, for example, those whose licensed career has been ended on medical grounds such as retinal or brain damage, by entering into unlicensed, illegal fights.[131] If boxing were banned, the number of such fights would increase. Finally, the argument that boxing participants are autonomous agents is likely to be extremely influential in rejecting a ban. Many hold to the view that intervention in autonomous activity can be permitted only where harm to others is caused or risked, and if other participants are also autonomous, consenting agents there is no justification for intervention.[132]

Improving Safety Standards in Boxing

The liberal, accepting soft paternalism as discussed above, would be happy to see the introduction of measures to improve the information for potential boxers, to ensure that boxers were capable of making the decision to box and also measures to ensure, in so far as is possible, the safety of boxers.

Ensuring boxers are capable. Measuring capacity is not easy.[133] However, where there is doubt about the ability of any given individual to make a properly informed decision whether to box, that assessment must be an extremely thorough one. There is a strong argument for banning boxing by children under 16 on the grounds of a lack of capacity fully to appreciate the (long-term) medical dangers involved in the activity.[134]

As regards adult boxers, there is an obligation to ensure that they have the necessary information, in an appropriately digestible format, upon which a rational decision can be made. So, it might be worth considering following the lead of Canadian neurosurgeons, who have recommended... that boxers should sign a form of informed consent, similar to that given to patients prior to major brain surgery. It would spell out the risks of acute and chronic brain damage. Only then could it be truly said that boxers were choosing to continue to fight in the full understanding of the risks that they were running.[135]

In this way, respect for the principle of autonomy is satisfied. Allowing decisions to be made on no, or incomplete, information does not respect that principle.[136]

Making boxing more safe. Boxing is now much safer in Britain than it used to be, for which the BBBC is to be congratulated. The BBBC implemented new standards for improving safety yet further in the light of the Eubank–Watson fight.[137] A new Regulation 8 was passed on 23 May 1992, which requires advanced warning to the accident and emergency department of the local hospital and to the nearest neurosurgical unit, and the facilities to communicate with them by telephone throughout the fight. In addition, there must be a trained team of paramedics and an ambulance available with the necessary resuscitation equipment at the venue. While the Board continues to review safety procedures, it can do more, which is one of the lessons to be learned from the *Watson* case.[138]

A number of additional proposals have been made, in particular, by medical commentators, in order to make boxing safer. First, there is the somewhat startling suggestion that boxers should stop wearing gloves. One medical opinion is that 'this would decrease damage to the brain, since the boxing glove absorbs sweat and then acts like a club, delivering heavier blows, and since the increased pain and injury to an ungloved boxer's hands would decrease the number and force of punches thrown'.[139] As this may appear, in the absence of overwhelming medical evidence, to represent a return to the barbarism of bare-knuckle prize-fights, it would probably be less favourably viewed by the general public than the present gloved fights.

Secondly, an elementary suggestion for minimizing injury to the head is the introduction of headgear in all boxing matches. Currently, headgear is compulsory only in amateur boxing, having been first introduced into Britain by the Olympic movement. Medical opinion on this matter is divided. Headgear would certainly decrease the force of a punch to the head by as much as 50 per cent.[140] It is equally clear that the introduction of headgear would reduce the number of facial lacerations suffered.[141] Although the evidence suggests that there is no reduction in the number of knock-outs when headgear is worn, this is not a strong argument against the introduction of headgear since knock-outs are not the real cause for concern. The real cause is the repeated, sub-concussive blows to the head which cause brain damage.[142] A different concern is that the wearing of headgear may cause the boxer to have too much confidence about personal safety and so not take the proper avoidance action that he would have done if he were not wearing a headguard. More problematic for the argument in favour of headgear is the claim that, 'by adding weight and surface irregularity to the head, blows could rotate the head more effectively, which would result in *more* brain damage'.[143] If this claim is true, there can be no greater public interest in boxing with headgear than without it.

Thirdly, there is the suggestion of reducing the number of rounds per contest. Since brain damage in boxers is caused by the repetition of blows to the head, fewer rounds would reduce the opportunity for this to happen, thus making the sport safer.[144] Jordan doubts this: 'Instinctively one would suspect that reducing the number of rounds might decrease the chances of brain injury in boxing; however this has not been scientifically confirmed.'[145] Since that article was written, there has been a reduction in the number of rounds for professional boxing bouts from 15 to 12. It should be noted that amateur boxers fight only three rounds,[146] and that many professional, non-championship fights are shorter than 12 rounds, most frequently eight or ten. Perhaps the number of rounds should be reduced further. It is difficult to see how the scientific evidence could be clearer and yet the boxing fraternity remains to be convinced that the number of rounds per fight should be reduced.

The suggestion for reducing the number is also based on a claim that it would also decrease the risk of exhaustion and its associated dangers. On the other hand, shorter contests would almost certainly lead to an increase in frenetic activity and more speedy scoring by hitting an opponent, as is the case in amateur boxing, and perhaps place a higher premium on the hard puncher. If this were so the goal of improving safety might well be defeated.

Finally, there is some support in the medical profession for a proposal to outlaw head punches altogether.[147] This degree of change in the nature of the sport would be so radical, however, that it might be as unacceptable to the boxing community as a total ban. The government has rejected calls for 'steps to reduce the potential damage caused by blows to the head', content that the BBBC was well-equipped to review safety standards.[148]

Conclusion

The Law Commission has stated that:

> The only explanation of injury and death continuing to be caused in boxing with complete impunity, at least as far as the criminal law is

concerned, is that the immunity of boxing from the reach of the criminal law is now so firmly embedded in the law that only special legislation can change the position.[149]

There is a strong argument that boxing is contrary to the public interest and therefore illegal since all fights involve the infliction or attempted infliction of actual bodily harm. But an argument that boxing is illegal is unlikely to get to court and would be unlikely to succeed in any event. There is a strong philosophical objection to banning boxing, and there is no apparent Parliamentary interest in doing so, as evidenced by the succinct Parliamentary response by the Health spokesman Tom Sackville, MP, when asked what proposals the government had to discourage people from engaging in the dangerous activity of boxing: 'None. Individuals should have the freedom to participate in the activities of their choice so long as they are within the law and are fully aware of the risks involved.'[150]

Since a ban is unlikely, despite the weight of medical evidence, improvements in safety standards need to be introduced, even if these make dramatic changes to the current nature of the 'sport'.[151]

NOTES

This chapter appeared first as an article, M. Gunn and D. Ormerod, 'The Legality of Boxing', 15 *Legal Studies* (1995), 181. We are grateful to the editors Derek Morgan and Celia Wells for permission to use it as the basis for the present chapter. We have benefited from many discussions with others over the points made, but we are entirely responsible for what appears here.

1. For example, the death on 28 April 1994 of Bradley Stone following his defeat in a British super-bantamweight fight and the death in 1998 of Felix Bwalya, who died nine days after fighting Paul Burke. The serious brain injuries sustained by Michael Watson after fighting Chris Eubank on 26 September 1991 for the World Boxing Organization's Super-Middleweight Championship of the World provides another famous example. It led to litigation, by Watson, about the ring-side medical assistance which he claimed exacerbated the injuries suffered during the fight: *Watson* v. *British Boxing Board of Control* [1999] All ER (D) 1031. The dangers of amateur boxing were also driven home by the injuries suffered by an amateur boxer, Kian Kwok Lee, on 12 November 1991, resulting in his being placed on a life-support machine: *The Independent*, 14 November 1991, 39. See also E. Grayson, 'Boxing Clever', 142 *New Law Journal* (1992), 48, and M. Seabrooke, 'Going to Hell in Your Own Way', ibid., 438.

2. Law Commission, Consultation Paper No.134, *Consent and Offences against the Person*, London, 1994 and Consultation Paper No.139, *Consent in the Criminal Law*, London, 1995, at paras.12.32–12.38. See R. Leng, 'Consent and Offences against the Person: Law Commission Consultation Paper No.134', *Criminal Law Review* (1994), 480; D. Ormerod, 'Consent and Offences against the Person: Law Commission Consultation Paper No.134', 57 *Modern Law Review* (1994), 928; S. Shute, 'The Second Law Commission Consultation Paper on Consent (1) Something Old, Something New, Something Borrowed: Three Aspects of the Project', *Criminal Law*

Review (1996), 684; D.C. Ormerod and M.J. Gunn, 'The Second Law Commission Consultation Paper on Consent (2) Consent – a Second Bash', *Criminal Law Review* (1996), 694.

3. Law Commission Consultation Paper No.134, para.2.9.
4. Law Commission Consultation Paper No.139, para.12.38.
5. [1994] 1 AC 212; [1993] 2 WLR 556, at 561 *per* Lord Templeman, at 592 *per* Lord Mustill and at 605 *per* Lord Slynn of Hadley.
6. J. Feinberg, *The Moral Limits of the Criminal Law*, 4 vols, New York, 1986–90, Vol.1, 26. For a critique of Feinberg and the harm principle, see A. Brudner, 'Agency and Welfare in the Penal Law', in S. Shute, J. Gardner and J. Horder (eds), *Action and Value in Criminal Law*, Oxford, 1993.
7. Feinberg, *Moral Limits*, Vol.3, 12.
8. Ibid., 3–26 and Ch.22.
9. See G. Williams, 'Consent and Public Policy', *Criminal Law Review* (1962), 74 and 154 esp. 159. See also the discussion of this point in the context of the European Convention on Human Rights at 31–2 below.
10. There is evidence that boxing was taking place in the Aegean as early as 1500 BC. The sport was popular with the Greeks as a method of training young men for battle – it enhanced their strength, stamina and it was introduced as a sport at the 23rd Olympiad in 688 BC. The sport conducted by the ancient Greeks was very different from the highly organized bouts of today, but nevertheless there were similarities in that the Greeks did wear some leather thongs on their hands. The Romans transformed the sport into a gladiatorial combat to the death, involving spiked gloves. See M.B. Poliakoff, *Combat Sports in the Ancient World*, New Haven, 1987.
11. See *Brown. A fortiori*, amateur boxing.
12. See also Law Commission Consultation Paper No.139, para.12.36.
13. Law Commission Consultation Paper No.134, para.10.19. There was no challenge, on consultation, to that view: Consultation Paper No.139, para.12.36.
14. See generally E.J. Gorn, *The Manly Art: Bare-Knuckle Prize-fighting in America*, Ithaca, 1986.
15. Ibid., 24.
16. Sullivan won the last World Championship bare-knuckle fight on 8 August 1889. See Gorn, *The Manly Art*.
17. The decision in the Australian case, *Pallante* v. *Stadiums Pty. Ltd (No.1)* [1976] VR 331 refers to the attitudes of the nineteenth-century courts and the distinction they attempted to draw between the prize-fighter and the boxer. See also N. Parpworth, 'Boxing and Prize-fighting: the Indistinguishable Distinguished', 2 *Sport and the Law Journal* (1994), 5.
18. A prize-fight is a fight with bare fists fought for money and until one party is exhausted, see, e.g., the Earl of Balfour in the debate on the Boxing Bill, Lords Hansard, 4 December 1991, col.293, cp. McInerney J. in *Pallante*, at 335.
19. See British Medical Association, *Report of the Working Party on Boxing* (1984), 3. The writing of the Queensberry Rules and the creation of organizing bodies such as the Amateur Boxing Association reduced the chances of serious injury, see also *Pallante*, at 336.
20. (1878) 14 Cox CC 226.
21. Ibid., at 294.
22. (1866) 10 Cox CC 371.
23. Ibid., at 373.
24. (1882) 8 QBD 534.
25. See *R.* v. *Brown* [1994] 1 AC 212.
26. *Coney*, at 539.
27. Ibid., at 547.
28. Ibid., at 549.

29. Ibid., at 553.
30. E. Manson, 'Notes', 6 *Law Quarterly Review* (1890), 110.
31. Williams, *Consent.*
32. G. Williams, *Textbook of Criminal Law*, London, 1978, 536.
33. Not only was Michael Watson seriously injured in their 1991 fight, but also the 'victor', Chris Eubank, was so exhausted at the end of the fight that he had to spend the night in hospital.
34. (1878) 14 Cox CC 226. See also Parpworth, n.17.
35. Limits are imposed on the actions of the boxers, as in other sports, so that the attitudes of the players will not be determinative of the violence which is legally permitted in the sport; see, in the context of rugby union, *R.* v. *Billinghurst* [1978] Crim LR 553, Newport Crown Court. See generally E. Grayson, *Sport and the Law*, London, 1994. See also the comments of the Law Commission in its Consultation Paper No.134, para. 42.3.
36. The general approach is that established by Woolf J. in *Attorney-General* v. *Able* [1984] 1 All ER 277 when considering the legality of a booklet about suicide.
37. This is the action taken by Michael Watson against the British Boxing Board of Control, successfully alleging negligence in the provision of ring-side medical assistance. The legality of the sport was not, though, in issue.
38. In *Smoldon* v. *Whitworth* [1997] PIQR 133 a referee was successfully sued in consequence of his refereeing of a colts Rugby Union game.
39. This was the cause of action in *Pallante* v. *Stadiums Pty Ltd (No. 1)* [1976] VR 331, McInerney J. in the Supreme Court of Victoria.
40. Ibid.
41. Under the Law Commission's proposed Criminal Law Bill (see Law Commission Report No.128, *Legislating the Criminal Code: Offences against the Person and General Principles*, London, 1993), the new offences of violence will be intentionally causing serious injury (cl.2), recklessly causing serious injury (cl.3), and intentionally or recklessly causing injury (cl.4).
42. *R.* v. *Reigate JJ, ex parte Counsell* (1984) 148 JP 193, DC.
43. For example, the peak force of Frank Bruno's punch, measured scientifically was 'in excess of that required to fracture facial bones.... An equivalent could have been delivered by a padded wooden mallet with a mass of 6kg (13lb) if swung at 20 mph.': J. Atha, M.R. Yeadon, J. Sandover and K.C. Parsons, 'The Damaging Punch', 291 *British Medical Journal* (1985), 1756, at 1757.
44. If it is necessary to take account of the brain damage caused, see text at p.34.
45. *D.P.P.* v. *Smith* [1961] AC 290, HL.
46. *R.* v. *Saunders* [1985] Crim LR 230, CA; *R.* v. *Chan-Fook* [1994] 1 WLR 689.
47. *R.* v. *Savage; R.* v. *Parmenter* [1992] 1 AC 699, HL and *R.* v. *Roberts* (1972) 56 Cr App R 95, CA.
48. *R.* v. *Mowatt* [1968] QB 421, CA, approved by the House of Lords in *Savage, Parmenter.*
49. This follows from the decision of the House of Lords in *R.* v. *Moloney* [1985] AC 905; *R.* v. *Woollin* [1999] AC 82.
50. As required by the guidelines established by the Court of Appeal in *R.* v. *Nedrick* [1986] 3 All ER 1, applying *Moloney* and *R.* v. *Hancock and Shankland* [1986] AC 455, HL, as amended by the House of Lords in *Woollin.*
51. See *Moloney.*
52. Law Commission Consultation Paper No.134, para.10.20.
53. Law Commission Consultation Paper No.139, para.12.35.
54. See, e.g., *Fairclough* v. *Whipp* (1951) 35 Cr App R 138; *Wilson* v. *Pringle* [1987] 1 QB 237; and *Brown.*
55. See *T.* v. *T.* [1988] Fam 52; *Re F* [1990] 2 AC 1; *Brown.*
56. See Williams, *Consent;* ibid., *Textbook;* J.C. Smith, *Smith and Hogan: Criminal Law,*

9th edn, London, 1999, 408–13; *R.* v. *Donovan* [1934] 2 KB 498, CCA; *Attorney-General's Reference (No. 6 of 1980)* [1981] QB 715, CA; *Brown; R.* v. *Wilson* [1996] 3 WLR 125; *Jaggard, Laskey and Brown* v. *United Kingdom* (1997) at <www.dhcour.coe.fr>.

57. [1981] QB 715.
58. Ibid., 719.
59. [1994] 1 AC 212. See Law Commission Consultation Paper No.139, paras.10.16–10.41, which are particularly illuminating on the importance, when examining policy and legal issues in relation to sado-masochistic sex, of identifying most participants' interest in power rather than violence.
60. Ibid., 231F.
61. Ibid., 241G.
62. Ibid., 232B (emphasis added).
63. Ibid., 278G–H.
64. Ibid., 265D.
65. Ibid., 265D–G.
66. *Laskey, Jaggard and Brown* v. *United Kingdom* (1997); see n.56.
67. Ibid., para.36.
68. Ibid., paras.40–47. *Wilson.*
69. The government has no plans to take any action on women's boxing; see answers to Parliamentary questions by the then Minister for Sport, Tony Banks, MP, on 21 April and 30 November 1998. Jane Couch has been successful in gaining a licence, from the British Boxing Board of Control, to fight professionally in Britain, but only after taking a claim for sexual discrimination against it (Electronic Telegraph, 31 March 1998 at <www.telegraph.co.uk>). In 1998 the Department of Health confirmed that it had not conducted research into the medical dangers particular to women's boxing; see Tessa Jowell, MP, Commons Hansard, written answer, 1 December 1998, col.165.
70. *Attorney-General's Reference (No. 6 of 1980)* [1981] QB 715, at 719 and *Brown*, at 231F (per Lord Templeman), at 241H (per Lord Jauncey), at 265–6 (per Lord Mustill), and at 277D (per Lord Slynn).
71. Kate Hoey, MP, Commons Hansard, written answer, 30 November 1999, col.86W.
72. See British Medical Association, *Boxing*, 3.
73. For the medical evidence see below.
74. The British Medical Association points out that all sports have the relevant beneficial effects: British Medical Association, *Boxing*, 3.
75. See, e.g., Lord Brooks of Tremorfa, the Earl of Shrewsbury and Lord Metson, in the Boxing Bill debate, cols.300, 303 and 308, respectively.
76. See, e.g., R.G. Morrison, 'Medical and Public Health Aspects of Boxing', 255 *Journal of the American Medical Association* (1986), 2475.
77. See, e.g., Lord Addington, Boxing Bill debate, col.294.
78. Ibid.; and see Law Commission Consultation Paper No.139, paras.12.39–12.50 and Appendix D. This covers, e.g., kick boxing, which the government refused to regulate after the death of Sean McBride, see T. Banks, Commons Hansard, written answer, 25 June 1997, col.529. It is, perhaps, more likely that the new sport of total fighting might be banned. In this sport 'anything goes – bar eye gouging, biting, striking to the groin or throat, or bending back the fingers', S. Hall, 'Opposition Grows to New Sport of Total Fighting', *Guardian*, 28 Feb. 2000.
79. See, e.g., Earl of Shrewsbury, Boxing Bill debate, col.303.
80. T. Hauser, *The Black Lights*, London, 1987, 13.
81. Morrison. Boxers have formed the Professional Boxers Association to safeguard their interests and avoid such exploitation.
82. See, e.g., Lord Metson, Boxing Bill debate, col.309. The temptation to resurrect a career for financial gain is best indicated by the resumption of boxing, when in their 40s, by George Foreman (who became a world champion in 1994) and Larry Holmes.

83. Boxing Bill debate, col.307.
84. A.D. McLean, 'Letter: Freedom of Risk', *e-British Medical Journal* (1998), 19 June.
85. A.J. Ryan, 'Intracranial Injuries Resulting from Boxing: a Review (1918–1985), 6 *Clinics in Sports Medicine* (1987), 31, at 42.
86. See, e.g., Lord Cavendish of Furness, Boxing Bill debate, col.316.
87. This factor was a major element in the 1991 debate in the House of Lords, see, in particular, the speeches of Lord Taylor of Gryfe, Lord Walton of Detchant and Lord Rea, Boxing Bill debate, cols.291, 294–6 and 304–7, respectively.
88. 645 fatalities were recorded from January 1918 to June 1983. From 1979 to 1985 28 fatalities were identified: Ryan, 31. See also L.D. Jordan, 'Neurological Aspects of Boxing', 44 *Archive Neurologica* (1987), 453 and P.W. Lampert and J.M. Hardman, 'Morphological Changes in Brains of Boxers', 251 *Journal of the American Medical Association* (1984), 2676. In Australia it has been estimated that there is one death per 10,000 contests; see R.J. Burns, 'Boxing and the Brain', 16 *Australia and New Zealand Journal of Medicine* (1986), 439. See also J.A.N. Corsellis, 'Boxing and the Brain', 298 *British Medical Journal* (1989), 105.
89. Ryan, 33–4.
90. Ibid., 34.
91. Further injuries which may result include fractures of various bones, damage to the liver, spleen and kidney, fractured ribs, and skin wounds (e.g. the 'boxer's nose' and the 'cauliflower ear'), see R.J. Ross, I.R. Casson, O. Siegel and M. Cole, 'Boxing Injuries: Neurologic, Radiologic and Neuropsychologic Evaluation', 6 *Clinics in Sports Medicine* (1987), 41, at 44.
92. Ibid., 44.
93. Ibid. See also J.I. Maguire and W.E. Benson, 'Retinal Injury and Detachment in Boxers', 255 *Journal of the American Medical Association* (1986), 2451; D.J. Smith, 'Ocular Injuries in Boxing', 28 *International Ophthalmology Clinics* (1988), 242; A. Leach, J. McGalliard, M.H. Dwyer and D. Wong, 'Ocular Injuries from Boxing', 304 *British Medical Journal* (1992), 839; D. McLeod, 'Ocular Injuries from Boxing: Reply', 304 *British Medical Journal* (1992), 840; J. Toczolowski, M. Gerkowicz, I. Jankowska, S. Misztal and J. Kowalewski, 'Badania ukladu wzrokowego zawodnikow klubow bokserskich [Examination of the Visual System in Boxers]', 93 *Klin-Oczna* (1991), 63; G. Vadala, M. Mollo, S. Roberto and A. Fea, 'Boxing and the Eyes: Morphological Aspects of the Ocular System in Boxers', 7 *European Journal of Opthalmology* (1997), 174. Some of the most famous boxers have suffered this injury, for example, Maurice Hope, Gary Mason, Sugar Ray Leonard and Frank Bruno; the injury ended the career of the first two. As to the dangers in amateur boxing, see A. Wedrich, M. Velikay, S. Binder, U. Radax, U. Stolba and P. Datlinger, 'Ocular Findings in Asymptomatic Amateur Boxers', 13 *Retina* (1993), 114, whose findings suggest that there is still a significant risk of eye injury in amateur boxing.
94. McLeod, 197.
95. See, for example, J.A.N. Corsellis, C.J. Bruton and D. Freeman-Browne, 'The Aftermath of Boxing', 3 *Psychological Medicine* (1973), 27; M. Kaste, T. Kuurne, J. Villki, K. Katevuo, K. Sainio and H. Meurala, 'Is Chronic Brain Damage in Boxing a Hazard of the Past?', *Lancet* (1982), 1186; R.J. Ross, M. Cole, J.S. Thompson and K.H. Kim, 'Boxers – Computed Tomography, EEG, and Neurological Evaluation', 249 *Journal of the American Medical Association* (1983), 211; Lampert and Hardman; I.R. Casson, O. Siegel, R. Sham, E.A. Campbell, M. Tarlau and A. DiDomenico, 'Brain Damage in Modern Boxers', 252 *Journal of the American Medical Association* (1984), 2663; Morrison; Burns; Jordan, 'Neurological Aspects'; Ross, 'Boxing Injuries'; R.W. Enzenauer and R.J. Enzenauer, 'Boxing-Related Injuries in the US Army, 1980 through 1985', 261 *Journal of the American Medical Association* (1989), 1463; Corsellis, 'Boxing and the Brain'; S. Sawauchi, T. Terao, S. Tani, T. Ogawa and T. Abe, 'Traumatic Middle Cerebral Artery Occlusion from Boxing', 6 *Journal of*

Clinical Neuroscience (1999), 63. For a research review, see Ryan, 'Intracranial Injuries' (1987) and A.J. Ryan, 'Intracranial Injuries Resulting from Boxing', 17 *Clinics in Sports Medicine* (1998), 155.

96. Casson, 'Brain Damage' and Editorial, 255 *Journal of the American Medical Association* (1986), 2483. Cf. the comments of R. Atkins, MP, 'It does nothing but good for a young boy. You rarely see anything other than a bloody nose.' *Sunday Times*, 29 Sept. 1991, sect.2, p.3.

97. Ross, 'Boxers – Computed Tomography', 212.

98. Corsellis, 'Boxing and the Brain'.

99. Ross, 'Boxers – Computed Tomography', Casson, 'Brain Damage', 2666, Lampert and Hardman.

100. H.S. Martland, 'Punch Drunk', 91 *Journal of the American Medical Association* (1928), 1103.

101. J.A. Millspaugh, 'Dementia pugilistica', 35 *United States Naval Bulletin* (1937), 297.

102. See Ryan, 'Intracranial Injuries' (1987) and Burns.

103. An allegation made by L. Adams, see *The Times Higher Education Supplement*, 27 Sept. 1991, 5.

104. H. Brayne, L. Sargeant and C. Brayne, 'Could Boxing Be Banned? A Legal and Epidemiological Perspective', 316 *British Medical Journal* (1998), 1813, at 1814.

105. B.D. Jordan, N.R. Relkin, L.D. Ravdin, A.R. Jacobs, A. Bennett S. Gandy, 'Apolipoprotein E epsilon 4 Associated with Chronic Traumatic Brain Injury in Boxing', 278 *Journal of the American Medical Association* (1997), 136.

106. See, e.g., G.J. Annas, 'Boxing: Atavistic Spectacle or Artistic Sport?', 73 *American Journal of Public Health* (1983), 811.

107. Boxing Bill debate, col.302.

108. The fatality rate for boxing has been calculated as 0.13 deaths per 1,000. The fatality rate for sky diving is 12.3; hang-gliding 5.6 and mountaineering 5.1: Council Report on Injury in Boxing, 249 *Journal of the American Medical Association* (1983), 254, at 255. See also Corsellis, 'Boxing and the Brain'.

109. 'An unpublished survey of 165 British neurologists in 1974 about their encounters with the punch drunk syndrome associated with various sports yielded: 12 jockeys; 5 soccer players; 2 rugby players; 2 professional wrestlers; 1 parachutist; and 290 boxers', British Medical Association, *Boxing*, 15.

110. See, for example, A.L. Whiteson, 'Injuries in Professional Boxing: Their Treatment and Prevention', 225 *Practitioner* (1981), 225.

111. See also Lord Taylor of Gryfe and Lord Soper, Boxing Bill debate, cols.292 and 296–8, respectively.

112. 'The Relationship between Viewing Televised Violence in Ice Hockey and Subsequent Levels of Personal Aggression', 4 *Journal of Sport Behaviour* (1981), 157, see also G.W. Russell, 'Response of the Macho Male to Viewing a Combatant Sport', 7 *Journal of Social Behavior and Personality* (1992), 631.

113. 'Social Learning Theory of Aggression', in J.F. Knutson (ed.), *The Control of Aggression: Implications from Basic Research*, Chicago, 1973.

114. L. Berkowitz, *The Roots of Aggression*, Atherton, 1969.

115. See Burns and Corsellis, 'Boxing and the Brain', 109.

116. [1992] 2 QB 491, at 497G.

117. See *Attorney-General* v *Able* [1984 1 All ER 277, where Woolf J. made it clear that a civil court has to be careful not to usurp the jurisdiction of the criminal courts, in particular the jury. See Professor Sir John Smith's commentary in *Criminal Law Review* (1984), 34 and J. Jaconelli, 'Hypothetical Disputes and Moot Points', 101 *Law Quarterly Review* (1985), 587.

118. There is a similarity with the approach of Lord Edmund Davies in *D.P.P.* v. *Morgan* [1976] AC 182, where, although singularly disliking the rule established by the Court

for Crown Cases Reserved in *R.* v. *Tolson* (1889) 23 QBD 168, he felt constrained by the passage of time to regard the matter as one with which it was inappropriate for the courts to deal.

119. The argument is similar to that to be found in the Practice Statement of the House of Lords indicating the self-imposed restraints on overruling their own earlier decisions in the criminal law, see *Practice Statement (Judicial Precedent)* [1966] 1 WLR 1234 and S.H. Bailey and M.J. Gunn, *Smith and Bailey on the Modern English Legal System*, 3rd edn, London, 1996, 438–43.

120. See, e.g., the decision of the House of Lords to declare that a husband may commit rape upon his wife: *R.* v. *R* [1991] 4 All ER 481.

121. Law Commission Consultation Paper No.134, at para.10.22.

122. Morrison.

123. See, e.g., the Boxing Bill 1991 proposed in the House of Lords, Boxing Bill, Lords Hansard, cols.290–320.

124. The evidence comes from Swedish research: Y. Haglund, G. Edman, O. Murelius, L. Oreland and C. Sachs, 'Does Swedish Amateur Boxing Lead to Chronic Brain Damage? 1. A Retrospective Medical, Neurological and Personality Trait Study', 82 *Acta Neurologica Scandinavia* (1990), 245; Y. Haglund and G. Bergstrand, 'Does Swedish Amateur Boxing Lead to Chronic Brain Damage? 2. A Retrospective Study with Cerebral Computed Tomography and Magnetic Resonance Imaging', 82 *Acta Neurologica Scandinavia* (1990), 312; Y. Haglund and H.E. Persson, 'Does Swedish Amateur Boxing Lead to Chronic Brain Damage? 3. A Retrospective Clinical Neurophysiological Study', 82 *Acta Scandinavia Neurologica* (1990), 353; O. Murelius and Y. Haglund, 'Does Swedish Amateur Boxing Lead to Chronic Brain Damage? 4. A Retrospective Neuropsychological Study', 83 *Acta Neurologica Scandinavia* (1991), 9. The research concludes that modern Swedish amateur boxing does not seem to lead to significant signs of neuropsychological impairment or 'punch drunkenness', nor does it seem to differ in this respect from soccer playing or track and field sports. See also R.L. Heilbronner, G.K. Henry and M. Carson-Brewer, 'Neuropsychologic Test Performance in Amateur Boxers', 19 *American Journal of Sports Medicine* (1991), 376.

125. British Medical Association, *Boxing*, 2.

126. The British Medical Association, however, points out that 'brain damage is a likely consequence whether in amateur or professional fighting', see ibid., 17. R.J. Butler, W.I. Forsythe, D.W. Beverly and L.M. Adams, 'A Prospective Controlled Investigation of the Cognitive Effects of Amateur Boxing', 56 *Journal of Neurology, Neurosurgery and Psychiatry* (1993), 1055, examined 86 amateur boxers in relation to their neuropsychological state on three occasions: pre-bout, immediate post-bout and follow-up within two years; 31 water polo players and 47 Rugby Union players acted as controls. 'No evidence of neuropsychological dysfunction due to boxing was found, either following a bout or a series of bouts at follow up. None of a range of parameters including number of previous contests, recovery from an earlier bout, number of head blows received during a bout and number of bouts between initial assessment and follow up, were found to be related to changes in cognitive functioning.' See also Y. Haglund and E. Eriksson, 'Does Amateur Boxing Lead to Chronic Brain Damage? A Review of Some Recent Investigations', 21 *American Journal of Sports Medicine* (1993), 97. 'Fifty former amateur boxers were examined and compared with two control groups of soccer players and track and field athletes. All subjects were interviewed regarding their sports career, medical history, and social variables. They underwent a physical and a neurologic examination... No signs of serious chronic brain damage were found among any of the groups studied. However, the electroencephalography and finger-tapping differences between the groups might indicate slight brain dysfunction in some of the amateur boxers.'

127. Written answer from the Secretary of State for Education and Science, Commons Hansard, 16 Oct. 1991, col.173–4.
128. The House voted against Lord Taylor of Gryfe's Bill in 1991 by 20 to 17.
129. See, e.g., Lord Bellhaven and Stanton, Boxing Bill debate, col.298.
130. See, e.g., the Earl of Balfour, Lord Brooks of Tremorfa and the Earl of Shrewsbury, Boxing Bill debate, cols.293, 302 and 304, respectively. The fact that boxing has not been driven underground in Sweden, Norway and Iceland is not likely to be relevant in view of the differences in boxing cultures between those countries and Britain.
131. Earl of Balfour, Boxing Bill debate, col.293.
132. See, e.g., R.H. Patterson, 'On Boxing and Liberty', 255 *Journal of the American Medical Association* (1986), 2481, Whiteson. See also, e.g., Lord Metson, Boxing Bill debate, col.310.
133. See Law Commission Consultation Paper No.139, Part V and, in the health law context, M.J. Gunn, J.G. Wong, I.C.H. Clare and A.J. Holland, 'Decision-making Capacity', 7 *Medical Law Review* (1999), 261.
134. J. Pearn, 'Boxing, Youth and Children', 34 *Journal of Paediatrics and Child Health* (1998), 311. Boxing will not be part of the national curriculum: E. Forth, MP, Commons Hansard, 2 March 1995, col.648, T. Banks, MP, ibid., written answer, 18 May 1999, col.326.
135. British Medical Association, *Boxing*, 18.
136. It seems that many boxers may have sufficient information, as is indicated in *Watson* v. *British Boxing Board of Control* [1999] All ER (D) 1031, where Kennedy J held that 'there was no doubt that W consented to accept the risk of an injury such as that he in fact sustained. He had not, however, accepted, by agreeing to fight under the Board's rules, any risk that followed from those rules not having been properly worked out.'
137. In the subsequent litigation by Watson against the BBBC, it was held, on the facts, that 'the practice in regard to the number and expertise of medical advisers that was followed by the Board was unacceptable. The Board's doctors were not chosen because of their special experience in any relevant areas, and there was no evidence to suggest that the Board considered and balanced the difficulty of providing any adequate response to the risks of head injury against the frequency of occurrence and severity of outcome. The alternative protocol suggested by other doctors, and adopted in Wales, was clearly more appropriate:' *Watson, per* Kennedy J.
138. T. Banks, MP, Commons Hansard, written answer, 14 July 1998, col.115. For the *Watson* case, see n.136.
139. Morrison.
140. Jordan, 'Neurological Aspects', 454 and see S. Schmidt-Olsen, S.K. Jensen and V. Mortensen, 'Amateur Boxing in Denmark', 18 *American Journal of Sports Medicine* (1990), 98.
141. Ibid.
142. See text above at p.35.
143. Morrison. But the research into eye injuries counters this argument against headgear, see Toczolowski.
144. '... the longer one's professional boxing career, the greater is the likelihood of brain damage': Casson, 'Brain Damage'.
145. Jordan, 'Neurological Aspects', 458.
146. Amateur boxing carries a reduced risk of brain damage since the combatants fight for shorter periods and consequently suffer fewer blows to the head, see Kaste.
147. Ibid. See also Morrison, 2479, Smith, 'Ocular Injuries', Schmidt-Olsen and J. Pearn, 'Letter: Reducing Brain Damage in Boxers', 168 *Medical Journal of Australia* (1998), 418.
148. T. Banks, MP, Commons Hansard, written answer, 14 July 1998, col.115.
149. Law Commission Consultation Paper No.134, para.10.21.

150. Commons Hansard, 2 March 1995, col.246.
151. Elements of this argument could apply to other sports. While it would not be possible
      to argue, for example, that cricket as a whole could be affected, it is possible to
      consider whether permitting leg theory fast bowling might not involve the necessary
      commission of the same crimes as examined in this chapter, see M. Gunn, 'The
      Impact of the Law on Sport with Specific Reference to the Way Sport Is Played', 3
      Contemporary Issues in Law (1998), 221, at 236–8.

4

Football's Legal Legacy: Recreation, Protest and Disorder

Guy Osborn

> It has often been recognised that the experience of play and festivity gives rise to a distinctive world of culture and consciousness. Play has the power to create a coherent sense of experience which is radically different from that of everyday life. It can oppose a new and temporary order to the order of conventional routine; it is able to dissolve normal restraints, sanction what would on other occasions be impermissible, and sometimes allow for fantasies which seem but madness to be actually realised. Play can temporarily overpower the sense of the reality of the everyday world of labour, suffering and responsibility. It permits the sense of excitement to flourish, offsetting those feelings of boredom and weariness. The experience of gaiety and play is not an ordinary experience: it is extra-ordinary; it involves relief from care, a momentary liberation from those burdens and tribulations which are all too real.[1]

Recreation, or play, has a key role within society. Forms of recreation can provide a chance to escape from mundanity, or may provide an arena to let off steam; they may act as a sort of 'social glue' that encourages a communal sense of identity and belonging, or be purely a form of relaxation, of losing oneself. Historically, recreation has embraced many forms such as sport, music and dancing, and has often focused on community, or at least communal, events. This chapter concentrates on one particular form of recreation: football.[2]

Football as we know it in the twenty-first century is a heavily media-controlled, and arguably media-constructed, commodity, at least at the professional level.[3] At the same time, the role of law in terms of the regulation of the sport has contemporaneously taken centre stage; other chapters in this book deal with how the law has increasingly intervened within the sporting terrain. For example, Pearson (Chapter 10) illustrates the use of legislation by the Thatcher, Major and Blair administrations to tackle what was perceived as the 'hooligan problem', McArdle (Chapter 11) looks at issues of discrimination and responsibility within sport, all underpinned by both British and European legislation, while Grayson (Chapter 1), Redhead (Chapter 2) and Foster (Chapter 14) all continue the debate about the location of the law within sport or play, and hint at the regimes that govern it. This chapter serves a number of functions, the first and prime one of which is to impart a sense of history and illustrate some instances both of the evolution of a sport (football) and its social importance, and how the sport has been perceived, and regulated, historically. In fact, while the debate about how sport and law interrelate has risen to some prominence in recent years,[4] there is a long history of censure and intervention that casts light upon more recent developments. To put the more recent developments within context, this chapter looks at the regulation of sport by concentrating on football, and, in particular, having examined its origins, analyses the ways in which football has been regulated, on a number of fronts and through a number of devices, since its birth. One particular area – of the use of football (and sport generally) as a political vehicle will be examined – drawing contemporary parallels where appropriate. It is crucial to appreciate that when we talk of regulation, regulation embraces a number of forms and it is not merely the law which regulates 'play'.

The Origins of Football

> The folk-football of ancient times has interest for the historian and the psychologist. It has wider interest, however, for what it represents is what, as ardent followers of the game, we are. In more than a thousand years the nature of football has not changed: its forms have ... British football is a mirror in which is reflected the British people; not the best people, nor the worst people, but the whole lot. That is why it infuriates while it pleases.[5]

To try to chart the historical development of association football as we know it today is notoriously difficult. This is partly because games that involved a ball or type of ball have been played throughout history in some form or another by several cultures, but to see a direct lineage between these games and football is not always obvious as the way in which the ball was used is not always clear:

> From Anglo-Saxon or pre-conquest England only scanty records of the sports and pastimes of the people have survived, but from scattered allusions, however, we know that dicing, hawking, and hunting were indulged in. But ball play is passed over in silence. There is, nevertheless, at least one exception, apparently overlooked, and that is in connection with the story of Merlin (Ambrosius) in the ninth-century Nennian *Historia Britonum*. King Vortigern had sent messengers throughout his realm in search of a boy born without a father. These ambassadors finally found such a one among a party of boys who were playing a game of ball (*pilae ludus*) and had fallen to quarrelling. The nature of the game is not defined, and though it might have been football, so specific an interpretation cannot be pressed upon the text of this passage ...[6]

So while there are several mentions and recollections of what might purport to be football, or a precursor of what we now know as football, it is difficult to chart this with accuracy as references to games in literature tend to be general rather than specific. Marples gives a number of potential origins of the game.[7] The Romans have been credited with introducing football to England, an argument that Marples suggests may be traced to Merculari who linked the Roman game *harpastum* as a precursor of Italian football.[8] However, as Young notes, while it is undoubtedly the case that the Romans occupied Britain and it may be assumed that there would be some indigenous involvement in the game of *harpastum*, 'at the same time it may safely be assumed that the native population had evolved their own kind of ball-play, just as when English colonists desirous of exporting football to America found that the indigenous Indians had a football game of their own already firmly established'.[9] At the same time, other games that can be seen as related to what we now know as football have been practised in cultures such as China (Tsu-Chu). The Japanese had developed a game known as *kemari*, possibly based upon the Chinese model, during the early Christian era and ball games were part of the athletic aesthetic of classical Greece.[10]

There was, however, no standardization between games, and certainly nothing like the highly formalized and systemized structures that now exist. To a large degree the peculiarity of individual communities dictated the ways in which such 'diversions' were generally played, and football in particular was consumed. In some games kicking was *de rigueur*, in others throwing was allowed; the types of 'ball' used could vary considerably from one region to another; the 'rules' could be fairly well documented and enforced in some areas, a high degree of discretion being allowed in others.[11] In a similar way, the games could be highly ritualized and organized or far more impromptu and casual. Even the forum for the games could vary considerably: 'A contest might be over an extensive stretch of countryside, with one goal perhaps the village well and the other a church a mile or two distant in an adjacent parish ... or it could be in a convenient enclosed field, the goals a pair of stakes, or any other handy markers, a few yards apart.'[12]

Bale[13] provides an interesting exposition of the spatial limits and focus of football over the ages, putting forward a four-stage model of development of the space upon which football is played and consumed. His first stage exhibits 'flexible boundaries and weak rules of exclusion', where there are no spatial limits and the relationship between players and spectators is blurred; his second he terms 'enclosure', where the limits of the pitch are defined and players and spectators are segregated. This stage of enclosure would broadly correspond in a formal sense to the codification of pitch size and dimensions by the creation of the Football Association[14] and the creation of standardized rules for the game.[15] The first model is the one that persists during the era of folk football, as described below.

One of the most famous expositions of the history of sports is Joseph Strutt's *Sport and Pastimes*.[16] In a survey of all ball games, Strutt notes that football is distinguished from many of the other games he analyses because of the use of the foot, and, while he cannot put a date on its origin, points out that it was not a popular exercise before the reign of Edward II. From around this time, a variety of entertainments such as cock-fighting were practised on Shrove Tuesday, and, indeed, in many parts of the country the main football match of the year was held on this date.[17] These events persisted and were still widely practised in the nineteenth century. Some practices even endure today although their form may have been altered or amended to provide for higher levels of safety. Not all games took place on this date; for example, in some areas games took place on other important dates such as Good Friday and even Christmas Day.

Perhaps the most renowned Shrove Tuesday football games are those at Derby and Ashbourne. There are differing views on the origins of the game in Derby, where it may be as a commemoration of Danish invaders or a remembrance of a local tribe of legend, the Coritani. The Shrove Tuesday game became intimately bound up into part of the ritual surrounding the day, where a match took place between the parishes of All Saints' and St. Peter's (although not all the participants were actually members of the two parishes), with the respective 'goals' being a waterwheel, which had to be knocked three times, and a nursery gate over a mile away. There were no formalized rules, the ball was merely dropped into the mass of players and 'survival of the fittest' ensued with a variety of tactics being employed. For example, a classic St Peter's tactic was to get the ball into the River Derwent, taking the ball a long route to their goal but crucially in the opposite direction from the All Saint's watermill. At other times the ball was hidden and then later smuggled to the opposing goal under the cover of night; occasionally real cunning could be employed: 'New ploys for attack or defence were warmly received: on one occasion, for instance, an enterprising fellow was reputed to have escaped with the ball into a sewer and passed under the town, only to be surprised as he surfaced by a party of opponents.'[18]

There are many other instances of such games taking place, be they local derivatives such as 'camping' in Norfolk and hurling in Cornwall. Similarly, a game also took place at Ashbourne on the same day:

> The game was played in a very rough fashion, and many injuries were the result, besides the public being driven out of the main street and the windows having to be shuttered up. Frequently the ball was pursued along the meadows, crossing and re-crossing the dividing stream; but no amount of ducking was sufficient to dampen the ardour of the contestants.[19]

While these were fairly structured and tied into local custom and ritual, there were also, of course, a great many spontaneous, recreational games of football, along with other forms of play, that would have been part and parcel of everyday life. It is undoubtedly the case that football was an important and integral part of society. Strutt does note, however, that while football was well established up until the seventeenth century, with much evidence in places such as *The Spectator* of games on village greens and the annual matches (such as the Shrovetide ones above), football's popularity did, in fact, begin to die out until it was revived by the public schools.

By the eighteenth century these schools certainly practised some forms of football. It was at this point still without any fixed rules, and the way in which it was played owed much to oral histories and spatial constraints. The crucial difference from folk football such as the Shrove Tuesday games was the social background of the participants. The game they played was still rough until a period of reform began during the 1830s when the practice of the game in schools began to be informed by muscular Christian values, exemplified by the efforts of Thomas Arnold at Rugby School and the 'cult of athleticism'.[20] The game was primarily practised at seven public schools who had all written their own rules, all distinct but with some common characteristics. Once these young men left school and wanted to continue playing the game, a body of rules eventually began to evolve with a broadly common acceptance by the early 1880s. The Football Association itself was formed in 1863, although agreement between the mainly southern clubs who had joined the nascent Association on the exact form of the rules was not reached until a compromise was arrived at in 1877 between the northern and the southern clubs, and one set of rules not accepted nationwide until 1882.[21] At this point the game began to be highly systemized and internally regulated, and the commercial opportunities for its exploitation were beginning to be appreciated. While the game itself was becoming more formalized, and while, as Pearson shows, the *external* regulation of the game became prominent a century later, it is important to appreciate that throughout this period football had been perceived as worthy of regulation and that this was often translated into outright prohibition.

The Early Regulation of Football

While football is the prime focus of this chapter, it was, of course, not the only sport that has historically been subject to prohibition. Wigglesworth notes that there was a range of designated unlawful sports and a plethora of recreational activities that were pursued, so much so that 'a Royal Declaration of 1618 sought to define which sports were and were not socially and legally acceptable'.[22] There were, indeed, laws prohibiting sports such as hunting, quoits and other sports as well as football, and these instances of regulation have persisted for centuries. As noted below, this was often couched in terms of detracting from more noble or useful pursuits such as archery which could help any war effort and was deemed socially useful:

> Acts to promote the practice of archery while proscribing other activities had been passed in the reigns of Edward II, Edward III, Richard II, Henry IV, VII and VIII particularly and specifically at times of perceived national weakness to outside threat or internal disorder, and in 1477 the Commons petitioned Edward IV to execute these laws effectively for the first time.[23]

Attempts were made to enforce Acts promoting archery at the expense of games such as football and hockey, with fines being levied for playing proscribed sports. Football was still, however, the most popular form of popular recreation and, notwithstanding the many pronouncements and edicts made against it (Wigglesworth notes that 23 edicts were issued against football between the fourteenth and the seventeenth century), it continued to be played throughout the country, although it was still subjected to periodic prohibition. Strutt notes a number of instances of prohibition, including Edward II's issuing of a proclamation in 1314 'forbidding the hustling of over-large balls within the city under pain of imprisonment',[24] Edward III's forbidding games in 1349, Richard II's forbidding it by statute in 1389 and this statute being re-enacted in 1401. The justification for these prohibitions Strutt puts firmly down to the violence of the practice, with some examples given of injuries and even fatalities. He notes that Sir Thomas Elyot described football as 'nothyng but beastely fury and extreme violence', and that Stubbes described it as 'a develishe pastime ... and hereof groweth envy, rancour, and malice, and sometimes brawling, murther, homicide and great effusion of blood, as experience daily teacheth' in his *Anatomie of Abuses*.[25] This negative response to sport was, to a degree, part of a desire for people to improve themselves and not indulge in idle pastimes of no value. The other side of this argument was that it would be better for society as a whole if more worthwhile pursuits were practised.

By the nineteenth century many of the traditional recreations were in seemingly terminal decline, and this was seen by many commentators to be a sign of progress within society, with customs that had once been tolerated being systematically denigrated. Perhaps the prime rationale for the hostility to popular recreation was the quest for labour discipline in an era of increasing industrialization, and the concomitant view that 'many of the traditional diversions were apt to appear scandalously self-indulgent and dissipated – wasteful of time, energy and money'.[26] This view was fostered to a large extent by Puritan dogma with its emphasis on social discipline:

Although religious enthusiasms in England subsided after 1660, many of the Puritans' social values persisted, at first with diminished strength and diluted by the revived traditionalism of the Restoration, but by the next century in a consolidated, more rigorous, and more widely accepted form; the Charity School movement, proposals for the reform of poor relief, the campaign for the reformation of manners, many of the influential writings on social matters – these were some of the later expressions, though more secular in tone, of the social morality of seventeenth-century Puritanism.[27]

This, as Malcomson notes, not surprisingly posed a serious threat to traditional distractions and forms of recreation. With the onset of industrializaton, this threat was exacerbated as industry itself was seen as being a sign of progress and as a virtue, while idleness was considered an abrogation of one's 'duty' to society. Because of this, many popular traditions were frowned upon, especially if the pursuit of such idle pleasure altered the efficacy of industrial output:

> ... the first Thing commonly thought on by Youth is Recreation and Pleasure: A Degree of which (if the Recreation be lawful) cannot reasonably be objected to; but Care must be taken that the Pursuit of Pleasure may not too much contract, or quite exclude any necessary Duty, and that it indispose not for the Returns of Labour.[28]

In this way work and recreation could be seen to represent opposite ends of a spectrum of social usefulness, and that often the pursuit of recreation would act to impede the progress that industrialization had fostered, primarily because of the loss of working time and other problems that might ensue as a by-product of popular recreation. The best way to enforce such labour discipline was by the law. One of the legal ways in which industrial efficiency could be protected was by a proactive police and a strict legislative programme, although some commentators noted that such legal devices should be applied in a subtle way and by stealth, lest the work force react negatively. However, if this were to prove successful, the national economy would reap the benefits of such a regime. Suppressing such activities would, of course, prove problematic in that these events had become part of public life, were part of custom and tradition, and therefore to curtail them would meet with resistance.

A further challenge to such tradition was seen in the form of the evangelical movement concerned, as it was with self-discipline and moral reform although it centred more upon the individual and his own private life than the community as a whole. The underpinning of evangelicalism was the politics of sin and the threat to the individual of temptation. Events such as holiday celebrations and other popular recreations such as football provided an obvious outlet for this temptation and thus was 'a dangerous fruit'. Under evangelicalism, recreation should be undertaken only in extremely small doses as it pandered to the inherent depravity of man, and if it were partaken at all, its form should be morally worthwhile and 'sought only in order to refresh the spirits for higher tasks'.[29] A further aspect of recreational restraint was fostered by strict observance of the sabbath; non-observance was seen as profligate and a precursor of a life of vice. Methodists, too, had strong views on the role of recreation and would sometimes organize events to counteract certain activities:

> They frequently conducted camp meetings at the times of wakes in order to counteract, and hopefully to undermine, the influence of profane festivity; in August 1820 a camp meeting was held on the Sunday of the annual football contest between Preston and Hedon in the East Riding, and at Ashbourne in 1845 the local congregation organized a tea party as a counter-attraction to the Shrovetide football match.[30]

Apart from the religious attacks detailed above, and the actions of the legislature and local magistrates, there were other ways in which the ability to practise sports and recreations were curtailed. While football is now seen as the world game – and part of the reason for this is simple: the materials needed to play the game are limited in nature – one thing that is crucial is a space to play the game in. The enclosure movement, where fields were enclosed and lost to the community, meant that it became more difficult to find somewhere to play. Some claimed that sports such as football had almost ceased to be played as a result of enclosure, as fields that previously were open to all fell into the hands of private landowners, although some owners did call for alternative provisions to be made. Indeed, the Enclosure Act 1845 did provide for the preservation of village greens to this end, a belated recognition of the effects of previous enclosures. Examples of areas where enclosure led direct to the curtailment of football include Hornsea, Coventry and Portsmouth. In addition to this, with increased urbanization and public space at a premium, even the use of public thoroughfares for games became contentious and no alternatives for such 'games spaces/places' were proposed until the late nineteenth century with the rise in public parkland.

Often, in enclosure disputes[31] the whole issue of the importance of 'custom' to the people was illustrated. Part of the popular view of custom was that people in authority, or higher up the social hierarchy, would make concessions to allow the labouring people some form of privilege in the form of holiday or recreation: 'Whatever their legal standing may have been, all customs had the same basic social significance: they imposed certain requirements on the more powerful people to patronize or tolerate specific activities which were of especial benefit to popular interests.'[32] Shrovetide football matches, for example, were seen as part of this process: an act, a tradition that was somehow validated and legitimized over hundreds of years. Indeed, sometimes such 'customary rights' were posited as possible defences or justifications to legal transgressions.[33] With football in particular, land that had been earmarked for use in the sport came increasingly under attack. There were a number of places that were historically known as football grounds such as 'camping close' in East Anglia ('camping' being the playing of football), Baldock, Skelton and Kirkleatham, and others where it was permitted to play the game. However, whether it was on economic, social or other grounds, many of such practices and the places upon which they were practised tended to fall into abeyance or be abrogated.

Football's condemnation also took the form of outright prohibitions from influential quarters. Rather than on the basis of its distracting from the war effort, as archery in particular had been in previous centuries, it began to centre upon inconvenience and nuisance, particularly when played in public thoroughfares. One instance, in Manchester in 1608, shows a court order prohibiting the playing of football in the streets because of the damage that had previously occurred, and specific officers were appointed between 1610 and 1618 to ensure that this order was complied with. Similar orders date from 1615 in the City of London and in Maidstone some 40 years later. This continued into the next century, with a number of documented attempts to prevent football being played, including even the famous Shrovetide match in Derby. Magistrates in Kingston even wrote to the Home Secretary in 1799 detailing the difficulties they encountered in attempting to suppress their own Shrove Tuesday game:

> It having been a practice for the populace to kick foot ball in the Market Place and Streets of this Town on Shrove Tuesday to the great nuisance of the Inhabitants and of persons travelling through the Town and complaints having been made by several Gentlemen of the County to the Magistrates of the Town they previous to Shrove Tuesday 1797 gave public Notice by the distribution of hand bills of their determination to suppress the Practice which not having the desired effect several of the offenders were Indicted and at the last Assizes convicted but sentence was respited ...[34]

These were public order concerns, often based around issues of nuisance and disturbance to the ordinary life of the community – the Highways Act 1835 even made reference to the sport and provided for a fine of up to 40 shillings for playing football on the highway. Street football, in fact, was prohibited in many parts of the country in the late nineteenth century.[35] Similarly, attempts were also made to regulate the Shrovetide game in

Derby. Delves gives an illuminating account of the suppression of street football there during this period,[36] partly predicated as part of a wider attempt to eradicate working-class popular culture, of which the suppression of street football was the most obvious manifestation. Delves notes that attempts to suppress football had been made in 1731, 1746 and 1797, before opposition became more pronounced in the early nineteenth century. His analysis centres on the period 1800–50 and he gives telling examples of anti-football action towards the end of this period. The *Derby Mercury* claimed in 1845, perhaps somewhat melodramatically, that football caused:

> ... the assembling of a lawless rabble, suspending business to the loss of the industrious, creating terror and alarm to the timid and peaceable, committing violence on the persons and damage to the properties of the defenceless and poor, and producing in those who play moral degradation and in many extreme poverty, injury to health, fractured limbs and (not infrequently) loss of life; rendering their homes desolate, their wives widows and their children fatherless.[37]

These strong words produced the desired response, as the mayor banned the game, and other games and inducements were offered in its place to placate the players and townspeople. Some of the footballers disregarded this edict and were later prosecuted and fined for participating in the 'illegal game'. The suppressors continued their quest with vigour in the following years. In 1846 magistrates had warned potential players against participating, and this was backed up with the swearing in of hundreds of special constables in readiness for any potential transgression. A tense Shrove Tuesday ensued, culminating in the reading of the Riot Act and the football game was later resumed outside the boundary of the borough, an incident that led to five prosecutions. The following years saw public houses shut and troops mobilized, although any disorder was minor in comparison to that in 1846. The suppression of football during this period could be seen as a response to its incompatibility with industrial efficiency as noted above, and also a reflection of the social tensions that existed during this time; football was policed in much the same way as demonstrations such as those enacted by the Chartists had been policed – football was seen as a *political* issue. This aspect of sport being used as a political issue, and often as a vehicle for protest, is analysed below.

Sport and Protest

The links between sport and politics are contentious and intertwined, as Cashmore puts it: 'This is the reason why sport and politics mix so well –

because people think they shouldn't.'[38] There have been many examples in the twentieth century of sports being used for political ends, from Hitler's usurpation of the 1936 Olympics, to the several Olympic boycotts in the 1970s and 1980s. Similarly, sporting events can be a vehicle for resistance or sporting protest, as may be seen by the formation of the Olympic Project for Human Rights (OPHR). This included the actions of Tommie Smith and John Carlos, who, after coming first and third, respectively in the 200m at the Mexico Olympics, bowed their heads and raised clenched fists on the winners' podium:

> I wore a black right-hand glove and Carlos wore the left-hand glove of the same pair. My raised right hand stood for the power in black America. Carlos' raised left-hand stood for the unity of black America. Together they formed an arch of unity and power. The black scarf around my neck stood for black pride. The black socks with no shoes stood for black poverty in racist America. The totality of our effort was the regaining of black dignity.[39]

On a related level, sport could be used as a focus for protest, or at least a camouflage for it. Again, this is nothing new. Sporting events throughout the twentieth century have provided a vehicle for both sporting and wider political protest. An example of this is the anti-apartheid protest of the Stop the Seventy Tour campaign (STST) orchestrated by Peter Hain. Here the high media profile of sport, and particularly the place which sport occupied in the psyche of South Africans, meant that sport was used as a vehicle for the anti-apartheid movement. A number of boycotts had been attempted in protest at the policy of apartheid, including the avoidance of fruit and other South African products. In sport, the Campaign against Race Discrimination was founded in 1958 and in 1962 the South African Non-Racial Olympic (SANROC) committee followed. SANROC followed the African National Congress (ANC) into exile when the leaders and organizers were targeted. A number of victories occurred, such as the abandonment of a New Zealand Rugby Union tour in protest at the South African policy of not accepting the selection of any Maoris. Similarly, the 1968 MCC tour was cancelled when Pretoria refused to accept the selection of a 'Cape Coloured' for the English test side. However, shortly after this victory it was announced that the scheduled South African cricket tour of England would go ahead in 1970; the reaction to this was that Hain, then of the Young Liberals, drafted a motion to their own subgroup (South Africa Commission) which advocated direct action to prevent tour matches from taking place. This was a crucial shift for the sporting anti-apartheid movement:

> Sports apartheid protests in Britain up until that time had been

symbolic: holding up banners outside sports grounds and the like. These had been impressive and vital stages in the process of mobilizing awareness. Indeed, they still had an important role to play. But the new dimension was *direct action*: physically disrupting the very events themselves and thereby posing both a threat and a challenge which could not be ignored by the sports elites who had been impervious to moral appeals and symbolic protest.[40]

The campaign was hugely successful. Focusing on the Springbok rugby tour that preceded the planned cricket tour, the activists included trade unions, student bodies and local Anti-Apartheid Movement groups, and their direct action took a number of forms.[41] The first match, due to take place at Oxford University, was switched through pressure from the student union, weedkiller being sprayed on the ground and threats made to disrupt the match. However, even the switch to the higher profile ground at Twickenham played to the STST strength as they were able to utilize this in the press. Other disruption throughout the tour included demonstrations at all the matches, although the tactics adopted included the gluing of the hotel-room door locks of the players to hinder them in leaving for a match, one demonstrator chained himself to the steering wheel of the team coach, while others evaded the heavy security cordon and chained themselves to the goalposts at Twickenham before a game. The players voted to go home in the face of this protest, but this was vetoed by the management and the tour meandered to an end against a constant background of protest and disquiet. While the cricket tour was still scheduled to take place, further action at all the county grounds before the season started and cumulative and concerted political pressure eventually led to the tour being called off.[42] A well-thought-out and supported sporting protest had effectively boosted the whole Anti-Apartheid Movement, and Olympic expulsion and exclusion from competition in other sports followed.[43]

However, that sport could be used in such a way is by no means a recent construct. In the seventeenth century a policy of enclosure was being carried out as described above. This was something that E.P. Thompson classed as ' ... a plain enough case of class robbery, played according to fair rules of property and law laid down by a parliament of property-owners and lawyers'.[44] The process of enclosure basically foisted a capitalistic property-owning ethos upon the traditional entity of the village, undermining historical means of agrarian production and creating a sense of displacement on the labourers and villages affected. Enclosure, in fact, took a number of forms. While initially, beginning in the fourteenth century, enclosure involved the commandeering of land by the rich and powerful, this process later began to achieve a veneer, at best, of respectability; 'influence was more subtly applied and the resulting agreement might well be enshrined in a decree entered upon the record of the Court of Chancery'.[45] The process became further formalized with the involvement of Parliament and, by the eighteenth century, legislation was the chief means of enclosure.

This process would begin with a petition which named both the petitioners and the land concerned. This would then be presented in Parliament by a friendly Member, it would then be examined in committee and reported upon, before, after a cursory examination by the House of Lords, it would become law. Such a petition could not be presented until it had been posted in the parish for a certain period of time, ostensibly for any objections to it to be raised. Parliament's role then became:

> ... eliciting whatever opposition there was and confining [the process] to the issue of principle, before the business of actual division got under way. Parliament's most delicate role was to judge whether opposition could safely be ignored. This it was mostly prepared to do if the objectors amounted to no more than a fifth or a quarter of the landowners by value (not number).[46]

Tate notes that these Enclosure Acts were strongly criticized by commentators, pointing out that these have seen the parliamentary process as 'mere mockery' and a purely formal and mechanical confiscation of land, echoing Thompson's description of 'class robbery'.[47] Protests against enclosure were strong. Thompson cites the example, culled from Home Office papers, of a group of parishioners from Cheshunt who petitioned Parliament with the end result that their 'common rights' were taken into account when the enclosure award was made.[48] However, the point is strongly made that this was unusual, given the lack of education and articulation that would have existed at the time, in tandem with the fact that to petition in this way would involve the embracing of an 'alien culture' and would necessitate the help of educated accomplices. It is then perhaps unsurprising that forms of protest were seen by the victims of enclosure as a potential method of attacking this 'class robbery'; 'Enclosure-riots, the breaking of fences, threatening letters, arson, were more common than some agrarian historians suppose'.[49] Given that football was a widespread phenomenon, it is perhaps unsurprising that it was used as a cloak for political action in this area. Some methods of protest, for example against the enclosure of the fenland, were organized under the guise of a football match, such as when in June 1638 a game of 'camping' allowed hundreds of men to convene and proceed to destroy a series of drainage ditches. Malcomson notes a letter in March 1699 from the Privy Council to the Lord-Lieutenants of Cambridgeshire, Norfolk, Huntingdonshire and Northamptonshire detailing that football had been used as a pretence to destroy drainage and other works associated with enclosure, and going on to state that:

Wee have thought fit to acquaint your Grace therewith, and that wee have sent directions to the High Sheriff and Justices of the Peace to hinder and obstruct all Riotous or Tumultuous meetings in or near Bedford Levell upon account of football Play or otherwise and to suppress and disperse the Same, Recommending to your Graces particular Care to sue all proper means for the preventing and Suppressing any Such Riotous or Tumultuous assembly whereby the Publick Peace may be disturbed or Endangered.[50]

Sometimes football may have been a symbolic form of protest at enclosure, rather than as a Trojan horse, but there are also other examples of football and protest, such as those during the food riots in 1740, when a game was cover for the pulling down of a mill. In a similar vein, Malcomson notes a game in West Haddon in 1765, which was advertised in the local paper. The advertisement was couched in positive and optimistic terms, it was to be for a prize, and gentlemen who wished to play were instructed to congregate at a number of public houses in the area. However, its report the next day was somewhat less effusive, noting that, in fact, the large assembly formed themselves into a mob, burned fences and caused other damage:

Football play, it would seem, was a convenient and sometimes effective pretence for gathering together a large assemblage of local dissidents; and it could only have functioned in this way, as a convincing shield for rebellious intentions, if it were a familiar, accepted, and relatively ordinary reason for drawing together a considerable crowd.[51]

So football has been used as a focus for direct action and, given this historical use, it is unsurprising that the crowds have been used as recruiting grounds by political groups, and football or other sports grounds could still be used in this way. However, agitation and organization have become more difficult in this way since both the topography of the stadium has changed in the wake of the Taylor Report[52] and the legislative programme that has been enacted by successive administrations over the past decades. However, in tandem with the growing trend towards issue politics rather than party politics, we have seen the mobilization of some football fans on particular issues, particularly with the rise of fan interest groups and protest groups such as the Football Supporters Association, Football Fans against the Criminal Justice Act, and Libero!, with different levels of success.

Conclusion

The foregoing has illustrated both the genesis of football and how football has been policed and regulated. In addition, examples of sporting protest were outlined, with particular emphasis being placed upon the example of the Stop the Seventy Tour campaign. When considering the mass of legislation throughout the 1980s and 1990s (as detailed by Pearson, for example, in Chapter 10), the process of creeping legalization and regulation perhaps becomes less surprising when an appreciation of sporting, and particularly football, history is considered. It is interesting to compare some particular aspects of this with how it would be regulated today, and in certain instances to consider current practices which echo previous policy. Previous work[53] has illustrated that, in fact, the highly successful Stop the Seventy Tour campaign would have fared less well under the heavily regulated public order regime of the 1990s. In fact, many of the actions of disruption and peaceful protest had become highly regulated in the intervening years, and a later campaign, also attacking racism (Hit Racism for Six), would be unable to use the tactics that had been so successful during the Springbok tour in 1969.

A mass of legislative provisions have been passed, with laws enacted strengthening police powers generally,[54] as well as in more specific areas such as football, a game which once more had been perceived as undesirable and unwanted, a folk-devil once again.[55] Particularly, in terms of protest, one of the chief ways in which fans would have historically have made their feelings public would have been by congregating on the pitch after a game and protesting, sometimes sitting down in the centre circle, sometimes merely calling for the resignation of the object of their ire. However, since the Football Offences Act 1991, to go on to a football pitch has become criminalized and now to go on to the pitch may end in a criminal conviction, removing one potential way in which the fans' anger could be vented. Similarly, we have argued elsewhere that football fans' civil liberties have been much curtailed by a series of legislative provisions. Even within cricket, the ground has become 'sacred space', with Lord Avebury, commenting during the passage of the Criminal Justice and Public Order Act 1994, that the new provisions on aggravated trespass would have had a marked effect if they had been in place during the 1970 protests against racist South Africa: 'If the Bill had applied at the time of the Stop the '70 Tour Peter Hain would have been liable to three months' imprisonment. I do not see that we want to extend the scope of imprisonment in this way.'[56]

The legislation was passed and this now has implications for sporting protest with these types of protest now being potentially covered by criminal sanctions and penalties: the legal terrain potentially affecting the ability to protest peacefully. Similarly, while it could not be compared with the process of enclosure, local authorities prohibiting ball games in certain public spaces,[57] a tightening of the laws of nuisance and trespass, and the continuing erosion of places to play – both by developers and the sale of school playing fields – have further regulated the ability to play games such as football. However, as other chapters here illustrate, regulation of sport has now moved on from public order and other issues to embrace private and commercial issues. This, of course, is a sign that the nature of sport has changed and the people who consume sport have changed. Greenfield (Chapter 8) shows that the private relationships that bond players and clubs have become highly regulated, although he argues strongly that they may be unenforceable, and Weatherill (Chapter 9) well illustrates the most recent manifestations of where such regulation might go. This chapter shows that such regulation is historically rooted, and that, while the form of the regulation might change and the emphasis shift, sport is an area that has become heavily colonized and regulated by the law. Other chapters hint at the contemporary situation and likely future developments within sporting regulation; this chapter has tried to demonstrate that a sense of the past helps us in our understanding of the present.

NOTES

1. R. Malcomson, *Popular Recreations in English Society*, Cambridge, 1973.
2. Hereafter I use the term 'football' to denote association football unless otherwise indicated in the text.
3. Of course, it would be trite to argue that football generally is so mediatized.
4. This embraces many areas, for example see Gunn and Ormerod (Ch.3) on how the law deals with some of the problems created by the sport of boxing, especially in terms of questions of consent and potential serious physical injuries.
5. P. Young, *A History of British Football*, London, 1969, 9.
6. F. Magoun, 'Football in Medieval England and in Middle-English Literature', 35 *American Historical Review* (1929) no.1, 33 is excellent and well written; in addition Magoun has written on the origins of Scottish football, 'Scottish Popular Football', 37 *American Historical Review* (1931) no.1, 1.
7. M. Marples, *A History of Football*, London, 1954.
8. Ibid., 2.
9. Young.
10. Ibid., 2.
11. See generally on this Malcomson, 34ff.
12. Ibid., 35.
13. J. Bale, *Sport, Space and the City*, London, 1991.
14. The reference here is to the formation of the English Football Association. This notion of the English inventing football, something that was exploited during EURO '96 and the coda of 'Football's coming home', turned into a hit song and terrace anthem by Ian Broudie, David Baddiel and Frank Skinner, has been criticized on a number of grounds, see B. Carrington, '"Football's Coming Home". But Whose Home? And Do We Want It? Nation, Football and the Politics of Exclusion', *Fanatics*, 1998, 10–23.
15. The later models of 'partitioning' and 'surveillance' are not relevant for our purposes at this point but are higher levels of regulation that occur after the FA codification.
16. J. Strutt, *The Sports and Pastimes of the People of England* (1801; 1903 edn, ed. J. Charles Cox, London).
17. Malcomson gives examples of games taking place at Alnwick, Chester-le-Street, Sedgefield, Derby, Ashbourne, Nuneaton, Corfe Castle, Twickenham, Teddington, Bushey Park, Dorking, Richmond, Kingston-upon-Thames, Hampton Wick, East Molesey, Hampton and Thames Ditton.

18. Malcomson, 37.
19. Young, 4.
20. See generally on the development of football from around this period, the excellent T. Mason, *Association Football and English Society 1863–1915*, Sussex, 1980.
21. Ibid., 15.
22. N. Wigglesworth, *The Evolution of English Sport*, London, 1996, 1.
23. Ibid., 14.
24. Strutt, 95.
25. Ibid., 96.
26. Malcomson, 89.
27. Ibid., 90.
28. Quotation taken from *The Servant's Calling: With some advice to the apprentice* (1725), noted in Malcomson, 93.
29. Ibid., 103.
30. Ibid., 107.
31. See below for a more detailed analysis of the process of enclosure and one of the ways in which football was used to protest against this.
32. Malcomson, 111.
33. For example, Malcomson notes a case heard in the King's Bench in 1665 where, against a charge of trespassing in a field for the purposes of having a dance, the defendant pleaded that the whole village had used the field in this way since time immemorial. He also notes a case in Great Tey in 1728. Here some parishioners were indicted for breaking on to land to play games – their defence centred upon the fact that 'The young people of Tey and the neighbouring parishes have been known to play at football and other games there constantly from time to time and particularly on every Trinity Monday which is the Time of the fair at Tey – and we prove this for upwards of 70 years and the old witnesses who prove the Same which boys say they have heard their fathers say they did play there ... ', ibid., 112.
34. Ibid., 139.
35. Ibid., 141.
36. A. Delves, 'Popular Recreation and Social Conflict in Derby, 1800–1850', in E. Yeo and J. Yeo, *Popular Culture and Class Conflict 1590–1914*, Sussex, 1973.
37. Ibid., 90.
38. E. Cashmore, *Making Sense of Sports*, London, 1996, 235.
39. See M. Marqusee, 'Sport and Stereotype: from Role Model to Muhammed Ali', 36 *Race and Class* (1995), 20–1.
40. P. Hain, *Sing the Beloved Country*, London, 1996, 50.
41. Ibid. Hain's book gives a thoroughly readable, insider account of the action and events which this section draws heavily upon.
42. Apart from Hain, see further on this S. Greenfield and G. Osborn, 'Enough is Enough: Race, Cricket and Protest in the UK', 30 *Sociological Focus* (1997) no.4, 373.
43. That the legal terrain in England and Wales has changed, and that such a campaign would be difficult to mount now is discussed in the conclusion.
44. E. Thompson, *The Making of the English Working Class*, London, 1991 (originally published 1963), 237–8.
45. W. Cornish and G. Clark, *Law and Society in Modern England*, London, 1989, 138.
46. Ibid., 138. Cornish and Clark provide some interesting background to both the Parliamentary process and the role of enclosure commissions. For the role of influence and friendship in the process of allocation see 137–41.
47. W. Tate, *The English Village Community and the Enclosure Movements*, London, 1967. Tate gives a scholarly review of the erosion of the English village by enclosure and an excellent analysis of the organization of both society and the agrarian village. It also provides an excellent historical trawl through the Parliamentary process and the forms of enclosure award.

48. Thompson, 240.
49. Ibid., 241.
50. Malcomson, 40, from material in the Public Record Office.
51. Ibid.
52. Taylor chaired the inquiry into the Hillsborough disaster; *The Hillsborough Stadium Disaster. Inquiry by the Rt. Hon. Lord Justice Taylor. Final Report*, Cm 962, London, 1990.
53. See Greenfield and Osborn.
54. See, for example, the Public Order Act 1986 and the Police and Criminal Evidence Act 1984.
55. See generally here S. Greenfield and G. Osborn, 'When The Writ Hits the Fan. Panic Law and Football Fandom', in A. Brown (ed.), *Fanatics! Power, Race, Nationality and Fandom in European Football*, London, 1998.
56. Hansard House of Lords, May 1994, col.714 .
57. There were reports in the media in early 2000 that the place where Paul Gascoigne learned to play now bears signs stating 'No ball games'.

PART 2

Judicial Intervention

5

Guarding the Game: Governing Bodies and Legal Intervention

Neil Parpworth

The bodies responsible for the governance of sport in the United Kingdom exercise considerable powers. The decisions which they make may have a profound effect upon those who fall under their jurisdiction. At a time, therefore, when the courts have shown themselves increasingly willing to rule on the legality of the exercise of administrative power in accordance with the procedure known as judicial review, it is noteworthy that sports governing bodies have been held by the courts not to be susceptible to their supervisory jurisdiction. In this chapter, therefore, the intention is to focus upon the key decisions of the courts in an attempt to explain why it is that judicial review is not available to those who wish to challenge the decisions of such bodies.

The Rule in *O'Reilly* v. *Mackman*

The procedure known as an application for judicial review is set out in Order 53 of the Rules of the Supreme Court and s.31 of the Supreme Court Act 1981. These provisions are broadly similar, although they are capable of being distinguished in several quite important ways. For example, with regard to the time limit for making an application for leave to apply for judicial review, rule 4 of Order 53 requires that the application 'shall be made promptly and in any event within three months from the date when the grounds for the application first arose', whereas s.31(6) entitles the High Court to refuse to grant leave where it considers that there has been 'undue delay' in making the application. For present purposes, it is important to note that neither Order 53 nor the 1981 Act declares judicial review to be an exclusive procedure for obtaining a declaration or an injunction where an individual's rights under public law have been infringed. However, in the leading case of *O'Reilly* v. *Mackman*,[1] the practical effect of the House of Lords ruling was the establishment of procedural exclusivity.

In *O'Reilly*, four prisoners challenged by originating summons or writ decisions made by the Board of Visitors of Hull Prison relating to forfeiture of remission of sentence. They claimed that the decisions were null and void because the Board had failed to observe the principles of natural justice in reaching their decisions. The Board's application to strike out the actions was refused at first instance but granted on appeal. The issue for the House of Lords to determine was, therefore, whether it amounted to an abuse of the process of the court to allow the enforcement of rights arising under public law by a means other than the reformed Order 53 procedure. The House of Lords concluded unanimously that it was. In the often quoted words of Lord Diplock:

> ... it would in my view as a general rule be contrary to public policy, and as such an abuse of the process of the court, to permit a person seeking to establish that a decision of a public authority infringed rights to which he was entitled to protection under public law to proceed by way of an ordinary action and by this means evade the provisions of Order 53 for the protection of such authorities.[2]

This 'general rule' of procedural exclusivity means that, in practice, those who wish to bring proceedings need to ensure that they do so in accordance with the correct procedure. Simply stated, this means that public law matters are to be challenged by way of Order 53 and private law matters by way of an ordinary action. However, Lord Diplock declared in *O'Reilly* v. *Mackman* that the rule was of general application. In other words, there are exceptions to the rule to be determined on a case by case basis. For example, in addition to the two exceptions which Lord Diplock outlined,[3] it has been held by the House of Lords that the rule has not removed the right of the individual to rely upon a public law matter as a defence to civil or criminal proceedings brought against him:[4] *Wandsworth London Borough Council* v. *Winder*[5] and *Boddington* v. *British Transport Police*.[6]

O'Reilly v. *Mackman* is thus an example of the failure to pursue the appropriate legal procedure. The prisoners failed to 'opt in' to Order 53 as they ought to have done. In *R.* v. *East Berkshire Area Health Authority ex p Walsh*,[7] the respondent authority sought to establish what Sir John Donaldson MR referred to as the 'obverse' of *O'Reilly*. In other words, rather than claiming that the impugned decision was a public law matter which should therefore have been challenged by way of Order 53, the authority argued that, despite its status as a public body, the applicant's dismissal from a nursing post was a private law matter for which the appropriate remedy was a complaint to an industrial tribunal rather than an application for judicial review. That this argument succeeded demonstrates that public bodies do not operate exclusively in the public law domain; they may also operate in the realms of private law. However, for present purposes, the case is of interest because the authority's argument that judicial review was the incorrect procedure has subsequently been advanced by several sports governing bodies faced with applications for the review of decisions that they have made.

The Authorities

A leading case on the reviewability of the decisions of sports governing bodies is the decision of the Court of Appeal in *Law* v. *National Greyhound Racing Club Ltd*.[8] In this case, the plaintiff, a greyhound trainer, had his licence suspended for six months after stewards of the club found that he had in his charge a dog which had failed a 'dope test'. The plaintiff sought by way of an originating summons a declaration that the stewards' decision was void and *ultra vires*. For their part, the defendants sought to have the proceedings struck out as an abuse of the process of the court. It was their contention that any challenge to their decision ought to have been by way of judicial review. Thus, rather than being an example of its 'obverse', *Law* has much in common with *O'Reilly* v. *Mackman*.

During the course of his judgment in *Law*, Lawton LJ noted that in *Fisher* v. *Director General of Fair Trading*.[9] Waller LJ had described the National Greyhound Racing Club (NGRC) as 'a limited company whose objects include acting as the judicial body for the discipline and conduct of greyhound racing in England, Wales and Scotland'.[10] For the purpose of achieving these objects, the NGRC had drawn up the 'Rules of Racing'. Any person who wished to take part in greyhound racing in stadiums licensed by the NGRC was 'deemed under rule 2 to have read the rules and to have submitted themselves to such rules and to the defendant's jurisdiction'. In other words, the powers of the stewards to suspend the plaintiff were derived from a contract between the two parties. He had consensually submitted to their jurisdiction. Accordingly, since it was a well-established principle that private or domestic tribunals were outside the scope of *certiorari*,[11] it followed that judicial review would not have been the appropriate procedure for challenging the stewards' decision.

Law is an important case in the context of the present discussion. Evidently there was some confusion as to the status of the NGRC, at least on the part of the defendants if not the plaintiff or the court. Rather than contending that it was a private body, and hence beyond the supervisory jurisdiction of the courts, the NGRC sought to argue the reverse. In the opinion of Slade LJ, it was 'easy to understand' why it would want a challenge to one of its decisions brought by way of an application for judicial review. This would enable it to benefit from the procedural safeguards for respondents inherent in judicial review proceedings, that is, the leave requirement and the three-months' time limit for the making of an application.[12] The existence of such safeguards has caused at least one commentator to argue that sports governing bodies should not be brought within the scope of judicial review. In Professor Oliver's opinion: 'Unlike politically accountable bodies such as the Crown, ministers, and local authorities, they are not subject to election and other political controls, which to an extent counterbalance the procedural privileges enjoyed by many respondents in judicial review.'[13]

The decision in *Law* has subsequently been followed in what may collectively be called 'the Jockey Club cases'. In the first of these, *R. v. Jockey Club, ex p Massingberd-Mundy*,[14] the applicant sought judicial review of a decision by the Disciplinary Committee of the Jockey Club not to allow him to continue to act as a chairman of a panel of stewards. Events arising out of a race at Doncaster had caused the Committee to conclude that the applicant was no longer qualified to act as a chairman, although it was happy for him to continue to act as a steward. The applicant sought an order of *certiorari* to quash the decision and an order requiring the Disciplinary Committee to reconsider the matter. Whether such relief could be granted depended upon whether the Jockey Club was a body which was susceptible to judicial review. The Divisional Court concluded that it was not.

In reaching such a conclusion, both judges felt the constraints placed upon them by the decision in *Law*. Thus Neill LJ observed that

> ... an examination of the Charter [the Royal Charter under which the Jockey Club was established] and of the powers conferred on the Jockey Club strongly suggest that in some aspects of its work it operates in the public domain and that its functions are at least in part public or quasi-public functions. Accordingly, if the matter were free from authority I might have been disposed to conclude that some decisions at any rate of the Jockey Club were capable of being reviewed by the process of judicial review.[15]

It ought to be noted, however, that this opinion was immediately qualified by the observation that in any future case 'it would be necessary to bear in mind that owners, trainers and riders of horses as well as executives of the various racecourses have a contractual relationship with the Jockey Club and have agreed to be bound by the Rules of Racing'.[16] The other judge in *ex p Massingberd-Mundy*, Roch J, in fact went rather further than Neill LJ when he observed that, in the absence of authority, he 'would have reached the conclusion'[17] that the Jockey Club was a body whose decisions were subject to judicial review. In his judgment, such a conclusion would not have resulted in the Jockey Club's being inundated with applications because, in each case, '... it would be for the applicant to show that he had sufficient interest in the decision before leave could be granted, as well as having to show a *prima facie* case that there existed grounds on which the court could exercise its supervisory jurisdiction'.[18]

Nevertheless, due to their inability to make a distinction of any real substance between the organization, the objectives, the rules and functions of the Jockey Club and the NGRC, both judges had little alternative but to conclude that the Disciplinary Committee was a domestic tribunal. Accordingly, Mr Massingberd-Mundy's application was dismissed.

However, Roch J left the door open for the future when he observed that

> There may be cases where the authority of the stewards of the Jockey
> Club will not be derived from a contract between them and the person
> aggrieved by their act or decision or alternatively may not be derived
> wholly from contract. It seems to me that if such a case were to arise,
> then the question 'is such an act or decision of the Jockey Club
> susceptible to judicial review?' may receive an answer different from
> that given by the Court in *Law's* case.[19]

The next 'Jockey Club' case to be decided, *R.* v. *Jockey Club, ex p RAM
Racecourses Ltd*,[20] involved a challenge brought by way of judicial review
against a decision by the respondent to refuse to allocate to the applicant
company a minimum of 15 fixtures at its proposed new racecourse on a
greenfield site at Telford in Shropshire. The applicant claimed that a report
published by the Jockey Club, in which it was stated that an additional 60
fixtures ought to be allocated in the 1990 and the 1991 season and that an
unspecified number of these should be made available to any new licensed
racecourse, had created a legitimate expectation that its new racecourse
would be allocated fixtures. The Divisional Court's conclusion on this point,
that no such legitimate expectation had been created, is of secondary interest
to the present discussion. Of primary interest, however, are the observations
that were made on the question of jurisdiction.

Before the Divisional Court in *ex p RAM Racecourses*, counsel for the
applicant submitted that the decision in *ex p Massingberd-Mundy* was
wrong.[21] The basis for this assertion was that the Divisional Court in that
case had erroneously considered itself bound by the earlier decision in *Law*.
It was argued by counsel that, in fact, *Law* was distinguishable from *ex p
Massingberd-Mundy* for the reason that the NGRC derived its power and
authority from contract whereas there was no contractual relationship
between Mr Massingberd-Mundy and the Jockey Club. This distinction was
accepted by both judges in *ex p RAM Racecourses*.[22] However, if *ex p
Massingberd-Mundy* is indeed a case unconnected with contract, then this
fact is difficult to reconcile with the concluding remarks of Roch J quoted
above. The case before him seems to have fallen squarely within the
exception to which he alluded. This apparent paradox casts some doubt upon
the correctness of that decision. Nevertheless, the Divisional Court in *ex p
RAM Racecourses* was not prepared to depart from the earlier ruling. Stuart-
Smith LJ, who gave the first judgment, observed that

> ... at the end of the day I am unable to say that I am convinced that the
> decision of this court in *R.* v. *Disciplinary Committee of the Jockey
> Club, ex p Massingberd-Mundy* ... was wrong. It is quite clear that it

was not in any way *per incuriam*, the court having given careful consideration to *Law*'s case and, we are told, other extensive citations of authority. But for this authority I should have held that the decisions of the Jockey Club in this case were amenable to judicial review.[23]

The doctrine of *stare decisis* requires that a court exercising the supervisory jurisdiction is bound to follow the rulings of those courts equal to it in status, unless it is 'convinced' that the earlier judgment was wrong.[24] Despite their evident misgivings about the decision in *ex p Massingberd-Mundy*, neither judge in *ex p RAM Racecourses* was convinced of the incorrectness of the decision. Indeed, Simon Brown J explained the limited extent of his disagreement with the earlier decision in the following manner:

> The substantive decision there subject to challenge was that of the disciplinary committee to remove the applicant's name from the list of those eligible to sit as chairmen of local panels of stewards. All that the applicant had therefore enjoyed was a non-renewable privilege. I have no difficulty in regarding that particular decision as one taken within an essentially domestic context lacking any significant public dimension and as non-reviewable on that ground. It is only in so far as the court's decision rested upon the wider ground – that the Jockey Club can never be reviewable in regard to any of their decision-making functions that I would respectfully question its correctness.[25]

While it may be possible to make such a distinction in respect of *ex p Massingberd-Mundy*, to accept the correctness of the decision but to doubt the correctness of any wider principle that the case sought to establish, it was rather unfortunate that the wider principle was then cited as the reason for holding that a decision of the Jockey Club when exercising a 'quasi-licensing power'[26] was not subject to judicial review. In short, *ex p RAM Racecourses* represented a second occasion on which it is clear that had the Divisional Court been free from authority, it would have held that the Jockey Club was a body susceptible to judicial review. The irony lies in the fact that it was erroneous to believe that it was bound by *Law*.

It might be argued, therefore, that the net effect of *ex p RAM Racecourses* was that the law on this issue was placed in some doubt despite the observations made by Simon Brown J in that case to the contrary.[27] However, as he readily acknowledged, this was an issue which 'will not go away' since 'sooner or later the Court of Appeal will have to resolve it'.[28] The opportunity to do just that presented itself in *R. v. Disciplinary Committee of the Jockey Club, ex p Aga Khan*.[29]

The Aga Khan was the owner of a racehorse which won the 1989 Oaks, a classic race for three-year-old fillies, run at Epsom. The horse was subsequently disqualified by the Disciplinary Committee of the Jockey Club after traces of a banned substance were found in a routine urine sample. The Aga Khan sought judicial review of the committee's decision. For its part, the Jockey Club contended that it was a private and domestic body which derived its authority from the contractual relationship between itself and those who agreed to be bound by the 'Rules of Racing'. Since the applicant fell within this category of persons, it followed that any remedies which might be available to him in respect of the committee's decision were private law remedies. Ruling on the preliminary issue of whether the court had jurisdiction to hear the application, the Divisional Court concluded that it did not.[30] The Aga Khan appealed against that decision.

All three judges who heard the appeal in *ex p Aga Khan* agreed that the Jockey Club was not a body that was susceptible to judicial review. They did so in accordance with *Law* on the basis that the club's authority derived from the agreement of the parties, that is, a consensual submission to jurisdiction. In giving judgment, Sir Thomas Bingham MR readily accepted that 'those who agree to be bound by the Rules of Racing have no effective alternative to doing so if they want to take part in racing in this country'.[31] Similarly, Farquharson LJ referred to the fact that 'the invitation to consent is very much on a take it or leave it basis'.[32] Sentiments such as these suggest that the 'consent' in cases such as *Law* and the present one might be described as being a 'legal fiction'. Can it really be said that the submission to jurisdiction is 'consensual' when, in truth, an individual has no other alternative if he wishes to ride, own or train racehorses in the United Kingdom?

Fredman and Morris[33] have argued that there are a number of drawbacks in relying upon contract as the determining factor when considering the availability of judicial review. Chief amongst these is that 'the equation of contract with private law is based upon the misguided belief in the voluntary, consensual nature of contract, obscuring the reality of underlying power relations'.[34] In the authors' opinion, where the governing body exercises monopoly powers, 'the voluntary nature of submission is highly questionable'.[35] The unreality of the contract between the parties has been raised in argument before the courts. Thus in *Aga Khan* itself, counsel for the applicant questioned the reality of describing the relationship between the parties as consensual. The point was countered by Farquharson LJ with the rather unconvincing observation that 'nobody is obliged to race his horses in this country and it does not destroy the element of consensuality'.[36] While it is indeed the case that nobody is obliged to take up racing horses as his livelihood, for those that do, the consensual basis for their submission to the Jockey Club's jurisdiction does seem doubtful. As a matter of fact they may be said to have consented, but to describe the relationship as genuinely 'consensual' may be to deny the true meaning of that particular word.[37]

Accordingly, there may be a case for arguing that as a matter of principle:

> Judicial review should not be excluded for reasons of 'consensual submission' where the relevant body has *de facto* monopolistic powers which the complainant has no practical choice but to acknowledge, whether by contract or otherwise, if he wishes to participate in the area of life governed by the body in question.[38]

The influence of the decision in *Law* extends beyond the 'Jockey Club cases'. In *R.* v. *Football Association of Wales, ex p Flint Town United Football Club*,[39] the applicant, a member of the Welsh FA, wished to join the Bass Northwest Counties League for the 1990–91 season in the hope that a better standard of football would prevent the further loss of players. However, Welsh FA and FIFA rules prevented a club from participating in a competition or becoming a member of another national association without the permission of its then current association. The applicant accordingly applied for permission to play in the Bass League. It was confident that permission would be granted since other clubs had previously received a favourable reply. However, the Welsh FA's intermediate committee rejected the application at a meeting at which it had resolved to establish a Cymru Alliance League in order to improve playing standards in North Wales. On appeal, the committee's decision was upheld by a commission of the Welsh FA. The applicant sought judicial review of both decisions. On examining the rules of the respondent association, Farquharson LJ concluded that they evidenced a contract between the applicant and the respondent. Accordingly, the Divisional Court was bound by the earlier Court of Appeal decision in *Law*. Moreover, the court in *ex p Flint Town* was not prepared to accept the argument that, despite the contractual relationship, there was a sufficient public element in the respondent's decision to justify judicial intervention under Order 53. In the words of Farquharson LJ, with which Nolan J agreed, 'consequences affecting the public generally can flow from the decisions of many domestic tribunals'.

　　The decision in *ex p Flint Town* is but one further example of a court's declining an invitation to 'act boldly to extend the frontiers of judicial review'.[40] The contractual nature of the relationship between the parties was recognized by the court, but, if it was a reality, it was a contract which favoured the respondent rather than the applicant. Although Flint Town were clearly at liberty to join a league run direct by the Welsh FA or by an association affiliated to it, their liberty to remove themselves from that league and join another run by a different national association was severely restricted by FIFA rules. In other words, their liberty to enter into a contractual relationship with the Welsh FA was not matched by their liberty to bring that relationship to an end. This 'injustice' was further compounded by the fact that their appeal against the intermediate committee's decision was heard by a Welsh FA commission rather than by an independent panel or tribunal. The decision in *Law* was also followed in *R.* v. *Eastern Counties Rugby Union, ex p Basildon Rugby Club*,[41] where the applicant sought an order of mandamus to compel the respondent (a constituent body of the Rugby Football Union) to place it in a higher division. In dismissing the application, Macpherson J stressed the domestic, contractual nature of the dispute and observed that 'if this is a matter of public law, then so could be any dispute about fixtures and perhaps even team selection and so on in many sports'. In his opinion, 'such a possibility seems ... to be outlandish'.[42]

The Public Law Element

Judicial review is principally concerned with the lawfulness of public law decisions made by public bodies. Whether or not a particular body is in fact a public body is therefore an important issue to determine. The customary way of deciding the matter is to establish the source of the body's power or authority. If that source is statutory or the prerogative, then the body in question will be a public body. Accordingly, government departments, local authorities and the police are but several examples of public bodies. Where, however, the source of the power is based on a contract between the parties then the relevant body will be a private or domestic body. Clubs and associations are therefore examples of this latter type of body in that they derive their power from the agreement of their members. The 'source of the power' test will normally provide the answer to the question 'is this body susceptible to judicial review?' However, there may be occasions when the test is not decisive. If this is indeed the case, then it is necessary to turn to 'a landmark decision in respect of the true scope and extent of this court's supervisory jurisdiction'[43]: *R.* v. *Panel on Takeovers and Mergers, ex p Datafin plc.*[44]

The facts of *Datafin* need not detain us further, suffice to say that the case was concerned with the jurisdictional issue of whether or not a self-regulatory panel without statutory, prerogative or common law powers, or a contract between itself and those who dealt in the market, was a body that was susceptible to judicial review. In holding that the decisions of the Panel could be subject to review, Lloyd LJ stressed that 'in between the extremes' which can be identified by applying the source of the power test:

> ... there is one area in which it is helpful to look not just at the source of the power but at the nature of the power. If the body in question is exercising public law functions, or if the exercise of its functions have public law consequences, then that may ... be sufficient to bring the body within the reach of judicial review.[45]

Thus *Datafin* is authority for the proposition that whether or not a body is susceptible to judicial review may be determined by looking at the nature of the function performed by that body. In the later case of *R. v. Chief Rabbi of the United Hebrew Congregations of Great Britain and the Commonwealth, ex p Wachmann*,[46] Simon Brown J used the expression 'governmental interest' to explain why it was that certain non-governmental bodies have been held to be subject to the supervisory jurisdiction of the courts. In effect, the body in question is deemed to be performing a function which is of such importance that, if it did not exist, the government would feel the need to create a body to perform the same function.

Given the scope of their powers and the popularity of the activities which they regulate, it is perhaps not very surprising that post *Datafin*, several attempts have been made to apply the 'governmental interest' argument to sports governing bodies. In *ex p Aga Khan*, the Court of Appeal was, in fact, divided on this issue. Sir Thomas Bingham MR was 'willing to accept that if the Jockey Club did not regulate this activity the government would probably be driven to create a public body to do so'.[47] However, neither of the other two judges who heard the appeal agreed with him on this point. Farquharson LJ observed that

> The courts have always been reluctant to interfere with the control of sporting bodies over their own sports and I do not detect in the material available to us any grounds for supposing that, if the Jockey Club was dissolved, any governmental body would assume control of racing. Neither in its framework or its rules or its function does the Jockey Club fulfil a governmental role.[48]

This difference of opinion is perhaps not so very surprising if it is accepted that there is a 'lack of consensus as to the proper functions of government' and that this therefore makes the 'governmental interest' test 'singularly difficult to apply with any degree of certainty'.[49] In *R. v. Football Association Ltd, ex p The Football League Ltd*,[50] where the Football League sought judicial review of decisions made by the Football Association relating to, among other things, the creation of a Premier League for the 1992–93 season, it was argued that if the FA did not exist, the government would have had to intervene to create a body to run football. In rejecting this submission, Rose J observed that

> ... the evidence of commercial interest in the professional game is such as to suggest that a far more likely intervener to run football would be a television or similar company rooted in the entertainment business or a commercial company seeking advertising benefits such as presently provides sponsorship in one form or another.[51]

It is clear, therefore, from the foregoing examples that English courts have displayed a marked reluctance to extend the scope of judicial review to cover sports governing bodies. Professor Craig has argued that there are three main strands in the courts' reasoning: that not all power is public power; the suitability of public-law controls being applied to the body in question; and, that if such bodies were held to be susceptible to judicial review, where would the line be drawn?[52] To these three might be added a fourth: that, despite recognizing that certain sports are industries and that their controlling bodies exercise considerable power, there is an inherent belief in the Corinthian nature of sport which justifies judicial non-intervention. In support of this latter point it is worth remembering that, although private domestic tribunals are subject to the rules of natural justice in the same way as public bodies, it was observed by Sir Robert Meggary VC in *McInnes* v. *Onslow-Fane*[53] that

> ... the courts must be slow to allow an implied obligation to be fair to be used as a means of bringing before the Courts for review honest decisions of bodies exercising jurisdiction over sporting and other activities which those bodies are far better fitted to judge than the Courts.[54]

Returning to Craig's third strand, this implicitly involves a 'floodgates' argument. The judiciary appear to be acutely aware that, if they were to hold that a particular sports governing body was subject to review (assuming that it did not have statutory powers), then other sports governing bodies would also be likely to fall within their supervisory jurisdiction. In *R.* v. *Football Association, ex p The Football League Ltd*, Rose J considered that arguments for making the FA subject to review based upon the popularity and revenue generated by football could be applied 'in relation to cricket, golf, tennis, racing and other sports'.[55] Although, as he himself acknowledged, this does not amount to a jurisprudential reason for refusing judicial review, it does afford a practical explanation of the judicial reluctance to intervene. Nevertheless, in the later case of *Stevenage Borough Football Club Ltd* v. *The Football League Ltd*,[56] where the club sought to challenge the validity of ground admission and financial criteria which effectively prevented it from being promoted from the GM Vauxhall Conference to the Football League, Carnwath J took a rather different view on the question whether the extension of judicial review to sports governing bodies such as the FA would result in excessive pressure on judicial time. Having regard to the case before him, he observed that

> In spite of the efforts of the parties, and the economy of the presentation, the writ procedure with pleadings, discovery, and oral

evidence, inevitably is more elaborate, time consuming and expensive than judicial review. Most of the facts in the present case were uncontentious, and little emerged in the process of oral evidence which could not have been adequately dealt with by affidavit and examination of documents. Under the judicial review procedure, if properly conducted, the case for each party can generally be set out in one main affidavit on each side, supported only by relevant documents, rather than, as in this case, in some sixteen witness statements, fifteen files of documents, and transcripts of five days of oral evidence.[57]

'Floodgates' arguments by no means always provide a satisfactory explanation as to why the law should not be allowed to develop in a particular way.[58] Indeed, there is a danger that they may sometimes be invoked in the absence of a more principled reason for opposing legal change. In the present context it is at least arguable that 'if an expanding jurisdiction threatens further to increase waiting lists ... then the remedy is the appointment of more judges to the Crown Office list, not self-imposed fetters on what cases will be heard'.[59]

Lessons from Other Jurisdictions

Given that the English common law system has taken root in other jurisdictions across the world, most notably in the Commonwealth, it is perhaps instructive to examine whether the approach of the courts in some of these countries to the issue of the amenability of sports governing bodies to judicial review accords with the British experience.

The closest common law system, at least in terms of geography, is Ireland. In *Murphy* v. *Turf Club*,[60] the applicant sought judicial review of a decision by the Turf Club to revoke his licence to train horses, following an inspection of his stables which revealed that they were in an unsatisfactory condition. In refusing the application for judicial review, Barr J had regard to the way in which the scope of judicial review has been extended in English law by the decision in *Datafin*. However, in his opinion, the Panel on Takeovers and Mergers was a body which was distinguishable from the Turf Club on the basis that the authority of the latter derived from the contractual relationship between itself and the applicant. Moreover, although there was a public dimension to the regulation of horseracing in Ireland, the Turf Club was not performing a public law function when it revoked the applicant's licence. Thus applying *Law*, the applicant was not entitled to relief by way of judicial review. An action for breach of contract would have been the appropriate means of redress.

Since *Murphy* was decided, the Irish Horseracing Industry Act 1994 has put certain of the Turf Club's regulatory functions on a statutory footing.[61] The conferment of statutory powers thus means that the club will be susceptible to judicial review in respect of decisions taken in the exercise of these powers, but not in respect of decisions based on a contractual relationship between itself and the relevant party. It would appear, however, that the decision in *Murphy* is 'still applicable to most other sports bodies which do not enjoy statutory powers'.[62]

In the New Zealand case *Finnigan* v. *New Zealand Rugby Football Union*,[63] two members of local rugby clubs in Auckland sought to challenge a decision made by the Council of the New Zealand Rugby Football Union to accept an invitation for a New Zealand representative side to tour South Africa. In holding that the plaintiffs did have standing to challenge the decision, Cooke J observed that

> While technically a private and voluntary sporting association, the Rugby Union is in relation to this decision in a position of major national importance ... In this particular case, therefore, we are not willing to apply to the question of standing the narrowest of criteria that might be drawn from private law fields. In truth the case has some analogy with public law issues. This is not to be pressed too far. We are not holding that, nor even discussing whether the decision is the exercise of a statutory power – although that was argued. We are simply saying that it falls into a special area where, in the New Zealand context, a sharp boundary between public and private law cannot realistically be drawn.[64]

In an article[65] in which they review the Commonwealth jurisprudence on the judicial control of sporting bodies, Beloff and Kerr draw attention to a case which is of particular interest in the present discussion. In *Jockey Club of South Africa* v. *Forbes*,[66] the Club sought to appeal against an order granted by a lower court which quashed a fine that it had imposed upon a jockey for an alleged breach of the rules relating to the doping of horses. It was the Club's contention that the relationship between the two parties was contractual and that, therefore, any challenge to their decision ought to have been brought by a private law action. Although the Appellate Division accepted that the relationship was indeed contractual, it was nevertheless of the opinion that the judicial review procedure in South Africa (coincidentally known as Rule 53 of the Uniform Rules of Court) 'extends to decisions of domestic tribunals and does not apply only to breaches by officials of duties imposed on them by public law'.[67] South African administrative law therefore differs from its English counterpart in that it does not place anything like the same emphasis upon the public law/private law distinction. The rule in *O'Reilly* v. *Mackman* was thus of no avail to the South African Jockey Club in this case.

Beloff and Kerr have argued that the Appellate Division in *Jockey Club of South Africa* v. *Forbes* acted with 'refreshing common sense'[68] when determining that the South African equivalent of Order 53 did not establish a rule of procedural exclusivity. In their opinion, the court 'commented sagely' when it observed that 'Rules are not an end in themselves to be observed for their own sake. They are provided to secure the inexpensive and expeditious completion of litigation before the courts ... '[69]

If we were to recall the remarks of Carnwath J in *Stevenage Borough Football Club Ltd* v. *The Football League Ltd* quoted above, we can see that they echo the pragmatism shown by the South African Appellate Division in the present case.

The Common Law

It is clear from the relevant authorities that sports governing bodies have considerable power and that they are as able to 'throw their weight around'[70] as much as many public bodies. As a matter of principle, therefore, there is a strong case for arguing that 'it is becoming increasingly desirable that private bodies be generally subject to some means of judicial supervision'.[71] It is equally clear that to extend the scope of judicial review so as to encompass such bodies is one way in which this might be achieved. To date, the attempts to encourage the courts to apply the Order 53 procedure to sports governing bodies have foundered on the rock of 'contract'. However, 'judicial supervision' might be achieved in practice were the courts to recognize and apply the common-law principle of the control of monopolies. This principle, which has been discussed by both Craig[72] and Forsyth,[73] 'imposed a duty to act reasonably on those who exercised monopoly power even where that power simply existed *de facto*'.[74] It is reflected in several nineteenth-century authorities such as *Allnutt* v. *Inglis*,[75] where it was held that the London Dock Company, as owners of the only warehouses in which wine importers could bond their wine, could not exploit their monopoly position. They were under a duty to charge only a reasonable sum for their hire. Applying this principle to non-statutory bodies, Forsyth wonders 'why should the common law not impose on those who exercise monopoly power, whether that power derives from the ownership of property or otherwise, a more general duty to act reasonably, for instance, to heed the rules of natural justice, not to act irrationally and not to abuse their powers'.[76]

If we were to recall the decision in *ex p Datafin*, it is worth noting that the self-regulatory nature of the Panel and the 'enormous power' that it wielded caused Lloyd LJ to observe that it was 'not less but more appropriate that it should be subject to judicial review by the courts'.[77] The case itself was, of course, decided upon the basis of the public-law nature of the function performed by the Panel. However, the words quoted from the judgment of Lloyd LJ suggest there were also public-policy reasons for holding that the Panel was subject to review based on the need to control its power. In the 'Jockey Club cases' it is worth noting that the monopolistic powers of that body have been referred to on a number of occasions. Thus in *Nagle* v. *Fielden*,[78] where the plaintiff sought to challenge the decision of the Jockey Club to refuse her a training licence on the ground of her sex, Lord Denning described the club as 'an association which exercises a virtual monopoly in an important field of human activity'.[79] Similarly in *R.* v. *Jockey Club, ex p Massingberd-Mundy*, Roch J remarked that the Jockey Club 'has near monopolistic powers in an area in which the public generally have an interest and in which many persons earn their livelihoods'.[80] The language of the monopoly was perhaps most vividly employed by Sir Thomas Bingham MR when he observed that

> There is in effect no alternative market in which those not accepted by the Jockey Club can find a place or to which racegoers may resort. Thus by means of the rules and its market domination the Jockey Club can effectively control not only those who agree to abide by its rules but also those – such as disqualified or excluded persons seeking to participate in racing activities in any capacity – who do not.[81]

The use of the term 'monopoly' has also been used to describe the powers of other sports governing bodies. Thus in *R.* v. *Football Association, ex p Football League*, Rose J observed that the FA had 'virtually monopolistic powers'[82] in respect of the control of English football. In *R.* v. *British Basketball Association, ex p Mickan*,[83] the term 'monopoly' was not applied to the powers exercised by the British Basketball Association. However, the manner in which Cumming-Bruce LJ described the association's control of basketball suggests that it would not have been out of place to say that it had monopolistic power. Interestingly in *Law*, although the NGRC had monopolistic control of greyhound racing south of Bedford but operated on a non-monopolistic basis north of it, neither of the judgments in that case made mention of 'monopoly'.

It might be argued, therefore, that the common law principle of the control of monopolies provides what Forsyth terms 'the juristic basis for an extension of judicial review'[84] to bodies such as the Jockey Club. In his opinion, if the principle is recognized by the courts, 'then it should make no difference whether that principle is vindicated by action or by judicial review proceedings provided that the form of proceedings chosen is otherwise appropriate'.[85] From a practical point of view, however, the choice of proceedings is important. As has previously been noted, there are those who consider that sports governing bodies ought not to be allowed to benefit from the procedural safeguards in Order 53 which are designed to protect public bodies from unmeritorious claims. Thus, rather than allowing the common law to be used to extend the scope of judicial review, it may be that it can be used to provide remedies outside the Order 53 procedure for those subject to the jurisdiction of private bodies not exercising governmental functions.

In an important contribution to this debate,[86] Professor Oliver has argued that there are certain common values underlying both public and private law. She contends that these values, which she refers to as 'autonomy', 'dignity', 'respect', 'status' and 'security',[87] are enforced by the courts so as to ensure that the weak are not oppressed by the exercise of power by the strong. Judicial enforcement crosses the public/private law divide, so that while judicial review 'strongly reflects these key values', it also 'underlie[s] the law of defamation and other torts, contract, property, company law and so on'.[88] In effect, therefore, Oliver argues in favour of what she terms a 'common law duty of considerate decision-making'.[89] A person aggrieved by a decision of a private body, such as a sports governing body, could thus be granted declaratory or injunctive relief via the private law on essentially the same basis as the grounds for judicial review. The imposition of such a duty would, as Oliver acknowledges, undermine the public/private law distinction. However, in her opinion this would be 'no bad thing'.[90] In support of this, she draws attention to the fact that Scottish administrative law does not make the same distinction.[91] We have already seen in *Jockey Club of South Africa* v. *Forbes* that the same is true of South Africa.

Forsyth has argued that a general duty to act reasonably, that is, to heed the rules of natural justice, not to act irrationally and not to abuse power, is implicit in the restraint of trade case of *Fielden*.[92] Oliver clearly shares this view since she has contended that the Court of Appeal was exercising a 'supervisory jurisdiction', in the sense that it was examining the facts of the case on the basis of the judicial review grounds of illegality, irrationality and procedural impropriety.[93] Moreover, she regards the decision in *McInnes* v. *Onslow-Fane*[94] as a further example of a case where 'the court was providing protection for a plaintiff's enjoyment of the five key values'.[95] In *R.* v. *Jockey Club, ex p RAM Racecourses*, Simon Brown J observed that *Fielden*, *Eastham* v. *Newcastle United Football Club Ltd*,[96] *McInnes* v. *Onslow-Fane* and *Breen* v. *Amalgamated Engineering Union*[97] were all examples of cases which 'had they arisen today and not some years ago, would have found a natural home in judicial review proceedings'.[98] However, Oliver is of the opinion that to argue that they would 'cannot stand with the decisions in *Law*, *Aga Khan* and other cases to the effect that such decisions by such bodies are not subject to judicial review'.[99] It is respectfully submitted that this must be the correct view. The creativity which the courts exhibited in those cases in developing a cause of action does not extend to subjecting sports governing bodies to the Order 53 procedure.

Conclusion

It is clear from the authorities that, when faced with an application for judicial review of a decision made by a sports governing body, English courts have adopted an 'abstentionist stance'.[100] They have regarded the relations between such bodies and those subject to their separate jurisdictions as primarily matters of contract, even where the facts would appear to indicate otherwise.[101] It may be that the reluctance to bring sports governing bodies within the scope of Order 53 is in part based upon a desire not to place extra burdens upon already stretched judicial resources.[102] If this is indeed the case, it might be considered unfortunate that pragmatism has been allowed to stand in the way of principle. If judicial review is 'a dynamic area of law, well able to embrace new situations as justice requires',[103] then perhaps justice requires that a 'quantum leap'[104] is made and that sports governing bodies are brought within the Order 53 procedure. However, the omens are not especially encouraging. As Beloff has pointed out, 'no less than three Vice-Chancellors of different generations have taken the view that the courts should abstain where possible from interfering with the decisions of bodies controlling sporting spheres'.[105] If the Order 53 procedure is to be extended to sports governing bodies, perhaps through the recognition of the common law principle of the control of monopolies, then such a development may have to come from the House of Lords. Free from the authority of *Law* and the 'Jockey Club cases', perhaps their Lordships would be prepared to effect a further extension to their supervisory jurisdiction. Whether or not they will have the opportunity to consider the matter remains to be seen.

NOTES

1. [1982] 3 All ER 1124.
2. Ibid., at 1134.
3. These were: where the parties have agreed that civil proceedings were the most appropriate action; and, where a public law issue arose as a collateral issue to a private law claim; see [1982] 3 All ER 1124 at 1134.
4. See C. Emery, 'The Vires Defence – Ultra Vires as Defence to Civil or Criminal Proceedings' [1992] CLJ 308.
5. [1985] AC 461; [1984] 3 WLR 1254; [1984] 3 All ER 976.
6. [1998] 2 WLR 639; [1998] 2 All ER 203.
7. [1985] QB 152; [1984] 3 All ER 425.
8. [1983] 1 WLR 1302; [1983] 3 All ER 300.

9. [1982] ICR 71.
10. Ibid., at 73.
11. See, for example, *R.* v. *Criminal Injuries Compensation Board, ex p Lain* [1967] 2 QB 864.
12. [1983] 1 WLR 1302 at 1311.
13. D. Oliver, 'Common Values in Public and Private Law and the Public/Private Divide' [1997] PL 630 at 644.
14. (1990) 2 Admin. LR 609.
15. Ibid., at 625–6.
16. Ibid.
17. Ibid., at 629.
18. Ibid., at 631.
19. Ibid., at 633.
20. (1990) [1993] 2 All ER 225.
21. Ibid., at 241.
22. Ibid., at 241 and 245, respectively.
23. Ibid., at 244.
24. This proposition is based on the test formulated in *R.* v. *Greater Manchester Coroner, ex p Tal* [1984] 3 All ER 240 which was cited in *ex p RAM Racecourses.*
25. Ibid. at 245.
26. Per Simon Brown J, ibid., at 248.
27. Ibid.
28. Ibid.
29. [1993] 2 All ER 853.
30. Unreported, 3 July 1991.
31. [1993] 2 All ER 853 at 867.
32. Ibid., at 873.
33. S. Fredman and G. Morris, 'The Costs of Exclusivity: Public and Private Re-examined' [1994] PL 69.
34. Ibid., at 74.
35. Ibid.
36. [1993] 2 All ER 853 at 871.
37. The *Oxford English Dictionary* defines 'consensual' as 'relating to or involving consent'. 'Consent' is defined as a 'voluntary agreement to or acquiescence in what another proposes or desires'.
38. D. Pannick, 'Who Is Subject to Judicial Review and in Respect of What?' [1992] PL 1 at 4.
39. CO/1033/90, 11 July 1990.
40. Ibid., per Farquharson LJ.
41. CO/1554/87.
42. Ibid.
43. *Ex p Datafin* was described in these terms by Simon Brown J in *R.* v. *Jockey Club, ex p RAM Racecourses Ltd* [1993] 2 All ER 225 at 246.
44. [1987] 1 All ER 564.
45. Ibid., at 583.
46. [1993] 2 All ER 249.
47. [1993] 2 All ER 853 at 866.
48. Ibid., at 872.
49. Fredman and Morris, at 72.
50. (1991) [1993] 2 All ER 833.
51. Ibid., at 848-849.
52. P.P. Craig, *Administrative Law*, 4th edn, London, 1999, 777–8.
53. [1978] 3 All ER 211.
54. Ibid., at 223.
55. [1993] 2 All ER 833 at 849.

56. *The Times*, 23 July 1996. The decision was later upheld by the Court of Appeal; see (1997) 9 Admin. LR 109.
57. Ibid.
58. See, for example, the remarks of Lord Bridge in *Leech* v. *Deputy Governor of Parkhurst Prison* [1988] AC 533 at 566 cited in Pannick, at 7 n.37.
59. Pannick, at 7.
60. [1989] IR 171. This case along with a number of other Irish cases is considered by J.P. McCutcheon, 'Judicial Control of Sporting Bodies: Recent Irish Experiences', 3(2) *Sport and the Law Journal* (1995), 20.
61. Ibid., at 25 n.12.
62. Ibid.
63. [1985] 2 NZLR 159.
64. Ibid., at 179.
65. M. Beloff and T. Kerr, 'Judicial Control of Sporting Bodies: the Commonwealth Jurisprudence', 3(1) *Sport and the Law Journal* (1995), 5.
66. (1993) (1) SA 649.
67. Ibid., at 659.
68. 'Judicial Control of Sporting Bodies: the Commonwealth Jurisprudence', at 5.
69. (1993) (1) SA 649 at 661.
70. See Sir G. Borrie, 'The Regulation of Public and Private Power' [1989] PL 552 at 561. These remarks were of general application to private bodies. For present purposes, they have been confined to sports governing bodies.
71. Ibid.
72. P.P. Craig, *Administrative Law*, 340–2.
73. C. Forsyth, 'Of Fig Leaves and Fairy Tales: the Ultra Vires Doctrine, the Sovereignty of Parliament and Judicial Review' [1996] CLJ 122.
74. Ibid., at 124.
75. (1810) 12 East 527.
76. 'Of Fig Leaves' at 125.
77. [1987] 1 All ER 564 at 582.
78. [1966] 1 All ER 689.
79. Ibid., at 693.
80. (1990) 2 Admin LR 609 at 630. In *R.* v. *Disciplinary Committee of the Jockey Club, ex p Aga Khan* [1993] 2 All ER 853, Sir Thomas Bingham MR noted that at the end of 1990, it had 'been estimated that over 100,000 people depend for their livelihood on racing and betting' (at 856).
81. *R.* v. *Disciplinary Committee of the Jockey Club, ex p Aga Khan* [1993] 2 All ER 853 at 859. See also the remarks of Stuart-Smith LJ and Simon Brown J in *R.* v. *Jockey Club, ex p RAM Racecourses* (1990) [1993] 2 All ER 225 at 229 and 247, respectively.
82. [1993] 2 All ER 833 at 848.
83. Unreported, 17 March 1981.
84. 'Of Fig Leaves' at 126.
85. Ibid., at 125, n.14.
86. D. Oliver, 'Common Values in Public and Private Law and the Public/Private Divide' [1997] PL 630.
87. Ibid., at 631.
88. Ibid.
89. Ibid., at 643.
90. Ibid., at 632.
91. Ibid., at 632–3. For a discussion of this point, see Lord Clyde, 'The Nature of the Supervisory Jurisdiction and the Public/Private Distinction in Scots Administrative Law', in W. Finnie, C. Himsworth and N. Walker (eds.), *Edinburgh Essays in Public Law*, Edinburgh, 1991; W.J. Wolffe, 'The Scope of Judicial Review in Scots Law' [1992] PL 625. Both cited in Oliver, at 633, n.20.

92. [1966] 1 All ER 689.
93. These are the chapter headings which Lord Diplock used to describe the grounds for review in *Council of Civil Service Unions* v. *Minister for the Civil Service* (the GCHQ case) [1984] 3 All ER 935 at 950–1.
94. [1978] 3 All ER 211.
95. 'Common Values' at 636.
96. [1963] 3 All ER 139; [1963] 3 WLR 574.
97. [1971] 1 All ER 1148; [1971] 2 WLR 742.
98. [1993] 2 All ER 225 at 247–8.
99. 'Common Values' at 636.
100. This expression was used by P. Morris and G. Little in 'Challenging Sports Bodies' Determinations' [1998] 17 CJQ 128.
101. The decision in *R.* v. *Jockey Club, ex p Massingberd-Mundy* is perhaps the best example of this having occurred.
102. This thesis is advanced by Morris and Little at 131.
103. Per Simon Brown J in *R.* v. *Jockey Club, ex p RAM Racecourses Ltd* (1991) [1993] 2 All ER 225 at 248.
104. This was what Rose J thought would be necessary if the courts were to apply 'principles honed from the abuse of power' to sports governing bodies; see *R.* v. *Football Association, ex p Football League* [1993] 2 All ER 833 at 849.
105. M. Beloff, 'Pitch, Pool, Rink, ... Court? Judicial Review in the Sporting World' [1989] PL 95. The three Vice-Chancellors of whom he speaks are Sir Robert Megarry V-C in *McInnes* v. *Onslow-Fane*; Sir Nicholas Browne-Wilkinson V-C in *Cowley* v. *Heatley, The Times Law Report*, 24 July 1986; and Scott J in *Gasser* v. *Stinson* unreported, 15 June 1988.

6

Tackling from Behind: Interventions on the Playing Field

Simon Gardiner

> Much of sports appeal comes from its unrestrained qualities, the delight of its unpredictability, the exploitation of human error, and the thrill of its sheer physicalness.[1]
>
> Ronald Di Nicola and Scott Mendeloff

Introduction

One of the major issues involved in the burgeoning development of sports law in Britain during the last decade has questioned the degree to which the law should get involved in regulating behaviour on the sports field. The debate has revolved around the opposing contentions that 'the law does not stop at the touchline' on the one hand and that the law's intervention is highly problematic on the other. The debate has moved on to attempt to proscribe when and where the law should regulate violent and unacceptable play with a recognition that, due to the competitive nature of contact sports, and especially team sports where physical interaction is pervasive, some test needs to be developed to systemize the law's intervention. Essentially the question is how should violent play be regulated on the sports field when if it occurred in other areas of social life it would not be legally tolerated.

Recent cases in the United Kingdom both in the criminal and the civil law have seen legal regulation used in substitution of the internal mechanisms of the relevant sporting supervisory bodies. The use of the civil law as a remedy to obtain compensation for injuries that have suspended or ended careers is a recent development in professional sport that seems to be becoming more attractive to injured players.[2] The criminal law, however, has a longer history of intervention. It has been recognized since the late nineteenth century that sports participants who use intentional or reckless force which is likely to cause bodily injury to another will be acting illegally.[3] In recent years two Law Commission Consultation Papers concerning the law of consent for assault offences have been published that have proposed modifications in how consent should operate concerning physical contact in sports, suggesting a clearer regulatory role by the criminal law.[4]

This chapter will focus on the appropriateness of this developing legal regulatory framework and, ignoring the obvious issues surrounding the fighting sport of boxing, the variety of martial arts and the plethora of extreme sports, will formally focus on team contact sports. A central contention supporting such intervention is that sport has become increasingly violent and that the law is the appropriate mechanism to restore peace. Economic arguments suggest that there are significant costs in terms of lost working days and disability caused by sports-related injuries.[5] Moral arguments equate the use of excessive violence in sports participation as a form of cheating.[6]

It is therefore vital to determine how sports violence should best be understood. The developing legal doctrine in the relevant areas in the civil law of negligence and the criminal law of assaults will be examined and specific issues analysed. The issue of how consent operates as far as the sports athlete is concerned will be critically evaluated. An attempt to lay down the parameters of this legal intervention will be made and encouragement given to international and national sports governing bodies and other relevant parties to develop more appropriate mechanisms to respond to this phenomenon.

Sports Violence: What Is It?

The support for the greater involvement of the law in regulating conduct on the sports field is often predicated on the belief that the game has become increasingly violent. This supports the law's greater involvement as being legitimate on the basis 'of the state's entitlement to guard against the dangers of uncontrolled brutality and excessive violence'.[7] This may be a popular perception, but is sport really any more violent than in the past? The study of violence in sport in Britain has been focused most specifically on spectator violence and most notably in the context of football hooliganism.[8] However, the phenomenon of violence on the sports field and between participants in sport has also been the concern of extensive sociological examination.

Violence is generally embedded in all post-industrial societies. It is found in the streets, on the media and in the home. It is therefore a pervasive social phenomenon. Sports-participation violence both reflects wider societal violence and also reproduces and embodies it. So the questions of whether we should regulate it, and if so how, are not completely separate from wider debates about the regulation of violence, for example, on television. What we culturally mean when we talk of violence is problematic. Determining what is sports-participation violence has been a major definitional problem.

Should it be restricted to physical force or does it encompass sexual, racial and homophobic insults? Within the sociology of sport, three conceptual explanations are commonly found in the literature on sports violence that assist in this problem of definition. Behaviour can be characterized as assertive and defined as goal-directed behaviour, involving the use of legitimate verbal or physical force, perhaps best understood in the term of 'playing the game hard'. In comparison, aggression is seen as an overt physical or verbal act that can physically or psychologically injure another. This aggression, first, may either be an essentially instrumental, intentional infliction of injury as a means towards a goal such as the gaining of money or victory, and, secondly hostile, where the behaviour has the primary intention of inflicting pain or injury. This latter understanding of physical aggression is that which best matches 'sports-participation violence'.

Whether this attempt to distinguish types of behaviour is of any use in the world of contemporary sport is questionable. Where explicit professionalization, a 'winning is all mentality', with its consequential commercial rewards, and the role of sport in the construction of masculinity are pervasive values of contemporary sport, violence is a reflection of a complex amalgam of values. For example, in which part of this typology of sport-participation violence should the following explanation of violence in Rugby League be understood: 'Within the game's confrontational philosophy players and coaches are accustomed to indulge in the practice of "psyching out" the opposition by means of running in or tackling somewhat harder than is entirely necessary in order to intimidate and therefore to give themselves a psychological advantage.'[9]

A major problem is that, of course, competitive sport is necessarily aggressve. As Dunning says, 'all sports are inherently competitive and hence conducive to the arousal of aggression'.[10] As a biological reality of the human condition, many forms of sport (rugby, boxing, martial arts and hockey) have become forums where legitimate, socially acceptable and often ritualized physical force is displayed. This may be termed sports violence, but of a kind that is legitimate. As Dunning again states, 'in some sports ... violence in the form of "play fight" or "mock battle" between two individuals is a central and legitimate ingredient'.[11] Too often though the support for aggression is used rhetorically to describe what is in 'reality violence pure and simple'.[12] Perhaps a reasonably general definition will suffice. As Smith suggests, sports violence is 'Physical assault that is designed to, or does, injure another person or persons physically or the intent to injure another.'[13]

However, James, first acknowledging the problems of different degrees of harm and injury resulting from physical contact, secondly delineating what acts and injuries can be consented to by victims, and thirdly the different states of mind that the perpetrator may have, presents a wide working definition of participator violence as being: 'The intentional, reckless or negligent touching by one sports participant of a co-participant, which causes personal injury to that other and occurs during the course of participation in a sport.'[14]

The role of the law and its intervention into this social field reifies the notion of illegitimacy and aids the construction of violence. Where any physical force is plainly not a part of the game in relation to the rules of a particular sport or exceeds what is seen as acceptable, it is constructed clearly in terms of violence – it is not legitimate. A primary role for the law is the protection of the person, the prohibition of the use of violence. One of the major problems, however, is that violence or violent conduct are not defined in English law. The terminology is of psychic assault (technically an assault) and physical assaults (technically batteries) and is used both in the civil and the criminal law. In the latter, consequential, incremental degrees of harm such as actual bodily harm and grievous bodily harm denote the severity of the criminal charge.

If the premise is that sport is an occasion for the display of legitimate aggression, the normative rule structure regulating this type of human interaction is an important determinant of where the line between the legitimate and the illegitimate is to be drawn. This normative order is complex and consists of the informal and unwritten conventions and working (playing) cultures within sport, the formal safety and playing rules of the sport, and the express provisions of the law. The reality is that violence pervades many sports and, as Young comments, is 'taken for granted, considered legitimate, natural and even desirable, not just by those responsible for organizing sport but also in dominant ideology'.[15] Working cultures legitimize acts of gratuitous violence as being 'part of the game'. On the whole, this is supported by a complex interaction of the main actors in this sphere – coaches, owners, sponsors and, perhaps crucially, the media. The player has been increasingly socialized into the specific sports setting that is dominated by an ideology dictated by other actors, most notably the coach. They are socialized out of taking individual responsibility.[16] However, there are dissident voices. Players' unions have, for example, increasingly become concerned about practices that put their members at undue risk[17] and some sports bodies have formally challenged the ethical basis of violent play.[18]

This 'turf war' between competing types of rule for the right to regulate has an important impact on the construction and understanding of violence. The more violent sport is seen, the greater the need for the law to intervene. Of course, there are other major issues as far as the causation of sports violence is concerned, ranging from the view that sport offers a socially acceptable context in which aggression is expressed, to the view that sports violence is socially-constructed behaviour that serves to legitimize other forms of social violence. The issue of sex has also become increasingly important, with sports violence being seen as a practice which helps to construct contemporary forms of masculinity.[19] There is no opportunity in this chapter to explore these issues in detail, but a note of caution needs to be aired. At a time when a social problem is identified as needing more stringent legal intervention, the terminology used and the form of that social problem need to be carefully considered.

The Media

Television primarily but the media as a whole have a crucial role in defining violence for sports consumers.[20] The amount of televised sport has increased exponentially in recent years and most play in elite sport is under the gaze of the video camera and subject to far more analysis and inspection.[21] Incidents are repeatedly replayed and contradictory attitudes are often displayed. Television can be particularly censorial when it plays the role of judge and jury concerning violent play, but conversely it can use violence to 'sell sport', for example, in promotional trailers for up-coming events. The advent of 'super slo-mo' can transform incidents that are bloody and violent into artistic and sensual moments of beauty. In some sports a symbiotic relationship has developed between television companies and sporting bodies, such as in Canadian ice hockey where extreme physical brutality is commonly condoned.[22] It is recognized as having major problems of violence and fighting, comparatively greater than in British sports. The use of the hockey stick is potentially fatal and fistfights are common. As Horrow says, 'in no other sport are the risks to health subordinated to victory and accepted as an inherent part of the game'.[23] It is claimed that the National Hockey League ignores the violence since it sees it as an integral part of the game's support and commercial success.[24] Television companies exhibit a schizophrenic approach: they will support the game's construction in terms of violence and a style of play that best maximizes the television audience and maximizes advertising revenue.

Injuries

Perhaps the best measure of the changing nature of sports-participation violence is the statistics concerning injuries. There are about 19 million sports injuries in England and Wales each year, about half of them in people aged between 16 and 25 years of age. As many as three-fifths of new injuries are caused by collisions between players.[25] Focusing on professional sport, Young argues: 'by any measure professional sport is a violent and hazardous workplace replete with its own unique forms of "industrial diseases"'.[26]

Even when compared with recognizably dangerous occupational groups such as coal miners and building workers, Young clearly equates the sports field as the workplace for professional sportsmen and women, with its regularity of routine injuries in team sports and, as such, it is a significantly dangerous place. Sports athletes need to be understood as victims with their informal acceptance and internalization of sports violence.[27] It has become increasingly apparent that professional team sportsmen have been subject to consistent physical and medical exploitation. This is not only in terms of physical force, but it is identified too in inappropriate coaching practices, over-training, playing while injured and potentially negligent medical supervision.

In professional football a recent research report focusing on the role of club doctors and physiotherapists concluded that a number of doctors were inexperienced in sports medicine and were often appointed not on ability and experience but as a result of whom they knew and being part of a pre-existing network.[28] Many physiotherapists do not possess the relevant qualifications and are often ex-players. Essentially the report sees that cultural values dominantly found within football had adversely impacted upon the medical management of injuries to players, which manifests itself, for example, in players often playing while unfit and aggravating their injuries. The overtly masculinized working culture found within football creates the scenario where the need to keep on playing while injured is equated with being a 'good professional'.

Although, clubs in the Premier League now need to employ qualified physiotherapists, this continues not to be the case in the Nationwide League. In 1998 an action against Sunderland Town FC by a player was based on a claim that an injury was negligently diagnosed and treated by the club's physiotherapist.[29] The action failed, but it clearly indicated that the qualifications, experience and working practices of such staff are issues of importance. Professional players are major assets to clubs, and it has become apparent that greater care needs to be exhibited. Although there have been a number of problems in terms of characterizing cumulative injuries in sport as industrial diseases,[30] there is significant evidence emerging of the long-term harm that may result from certain types of play or medical treatment.[31]

A recent case involving boxing in England has for the first time ruled that a governing body owes a duty of care to boxers participating in a bout organized within its auspices and may become liable for failing to provide effective medical treatment.[32] This decision has wide implications as to the promoting and securing of safety in sports events. However, it is not easy in Britain to find detailed data in any particular team sport as regards either actual playing injures or the long-term effects on a playing career. But it does seem that the nature of injuries has changed in recent times. For example, in rugby there is evidence that there has been a decrease in life-threatening injuries, including spinal injuries, but an increase in chronic complaints.[33] This can be attributed to rule changes that have promoted safety, coaching practices and better playing equipment and protection.

Is Sport More Violent Today?

The argument that sport is more violent now than in the past is one that is contested. There is substantial evidence that, in general, contemporary sport is no more violent than in the past. Modern sport tends to be played at a quicker pace, with greater reliance on physical fitness and stamina. The media play a key role in highlighting and analysing incidents much more than in the past. This has contributed to a moral panic[34] concerning the amount and degree of violence on the sports field. Where is the line to be drawn to curb such activity? Focusing on football, the modern game has grown out of unregulated and mass participatory games where high levels of violence were customarily tolerated. In Italy in the Middle Ages an antecedent of football, the game *gioca della pugna* is described by Guttmann as: 'often little better than a pitched battle ... a thousand or more men and women joined in the annual stone fight, which became so violent that the authorities attempted to moderate the bloodshed in 1273 by threatening that those who killed their opponents would henceforth be tried for murder'.[35]

In comparison, the modern game of football is highly regulated and controlled, both by a set of official rules external to players and self-control by the players themselves.[36] Similarly, cricket, a game with little physical contact, is often now portrayed as becoming more intimidatory, especially as regards fast bowling.[37] However, there have been occasions in the past, as in the 'bodyline' test series in the 1930s, involving greater levels of violence.[38] In North America, with its differing cultural perspectives on sport, violence has been more widely perceived. In the USA, with a greater propensity to physical contact, often in a gratuitous and retaliatory form, there has been awareness for many years of the prevalence of violence in the national sports of basketball, baseball, American 'gridiron' football and ice hockey. As Neilson prophesies:

> Each of the four major American sports has its own brand of senseless violence. As far as criminal law is concerned ... given the major role that professional sports plays in American culture, the sports violence problem must be controlled; without some type of restraint, the future of sport may hold grave possibilities for our society.[39]

Our understanding of how we should define sports violence and its relative level is determined by a complex interaction between the construction of and changes in the playing and safety rules, styles of play,[40] the tension between working cultures[41] that challenge the boundaries of legitimate play and codes of ethics that promote concepts such as fair play,[42] the role of officials and administrators in the way they police the rules, all within a milieu of a 'winning is all' mentality. This presents a complex and problematic explanation of violence in contemporary sport.

Legal Doctrine

In Britain the debate has developed through the work of Edward Grayson, in a series of books and articles.[43] He has consistently argued that the 'law does not stop at the touchline', and that it is axiomatic that both the civil and the criminal law should be involved in incidents of violence. For Grayson the only way to deliver contemporary sport back to a halcyon era of Corinthianism is through the rule of law: 'without adherence to the rules of play on the field and the Rule of Law off it anarchy would prevail for sport as well as society'.[44]

The accuracy of Grayson's historical analysis has been questioned.[45] His argument is crude – he largely ignores the problematic issue of consent and ignores the specificity of sports field violence in the context of general violence – and, as James, argues, 'he fails to develop the law, in the tradition of the common law, to confront a relatively new phenomenon, by the incremental change of existing principles'.[46] There is surely at least a clear distinction to be made between the punitive nature of the criminal law and the compensatory character of the civil law. The criminal law's involvement is more contentious. Grayson emphatically believes that all law should be actively involved in the regulation of violence on the field and should be prioritized over the intervention of the appropriate supervisory body of the sport in question.[47]

The Role of Law: Civil Law

Over the last few years athletes have increasingly resorted to civil law actions to seek financial compensation for loss caused through injury, both in professional and in amateur sport. This has involved actions against other players,[48] the referee,[49] medical personnel,[50] sports clubs[51] and sports governing bodies.[52] 'Tort law is the best way to deter violent conduct among athletes and provide them an adequate remedy for their injuries. Tort law imposes financial liability on the athlete ... and this will hit him where it hurts most – in his pocket.'[53]

Civil actions available for injuries suffered during the course of a game are either trespass to the person or, more specifically, a battery or, alternatively, negligence. It is the latter action that is, in practice, employed due to the need to prove that the defendant intended the contact for an actionable battery, together with the court's view that there cannot be a negligent trespass to the person.[54] Reflecting the wider trends involving the development of liability based on negligence, the tripartite test as established in *Donoghue* v. *Stevenson*[55] has been applied to potential liability on the sports field.[56] A major issue has been what is the relevant standard of care that must be exercised so that a defendant who falls below it renders himself liable to an action in negligence? In Britain, the main view has been that the standard is that which is reasonable in all the circumstances. Such a test allows particular factual circumstances to be considered. However, it has also been argued that ordinary negligence standards cannot be applied in the sporting context. In *Wooldridge* v. *Sumner*[57] it was stated that the appropriate standard should be reckless disregard, a test that has been adopted in certain states in America.[58]

Perhaps the most significant case in recent years has been *Smoldon* v. *Whitworth and Nolan*.[59] For the first time liability for causing personal injury was established against an official in a contact team sport. In 1991, during the course of a game of rugby being played between two teams at colts level, Ben Smoldon, the hooker for one of the teams, suffered a broken neck when a scrum collapsed. Proceedings were issued against one of the opposing players, Whitworth, and the match referee, Nolan. The action against Whitworth failed since no one player could be identified as being singularly responsible for the critical collapse. The case against Nolan was successful at first instance in the High Court and was subsequently the subject of an unsuccessful appeal. The significance of the case lies in the fact that it was the first time in the jurisprudence of major rugby-playing nations that such liability had been established in court.

Something notable about the case is the limitation placed by the judgment on liability, that is, the breach of duty. The judge went as far as to say that it could not be stressed 'too strongly' that the decision was based upon special considerations, namely, the particular facts of the case; the vital fact that this was a colts game; the law of rugby as modified for colts; and the laws and customs of rugby in the 1991/92 season.

It was held that it was 'fair, just and reasonable' to impose a duty on the referee. Curtis J held that the duty of referees was to exercise that degree of care for the safety of players which would be appropriate in the circumstances. The judge felt it appropriate to accept the test of a higher degree of foreseeability stipulated in the Lord Chancellor's speech in *Smith* v. *Littlewoods*.[60] It was with this background that the special considerations that applied in the context of colts' matches, in particular the duty to enforce the crouch–touch–pause–engage phased sequence (CTPE) that was introduced before the plaintiff's accident occurred to cover matches at colts level, was analysed.

At the appeal, the defendant accepted that a duty of care was owed. However, it was argued that the appropriate standard of care was not merely that which was reasonable in all the circumstances, but there was a need to show a reckless disregard for the safety of the person injured. This was the degree of duty of care for both players and officials. The defendant had relied on the argument that, for liability to arise, the damage must be a highly foreseeable consequence and not merely a possibility. The Lord Chief

Justice, however, ruled that the standard test should be applied, the circumstances of the incident in the game being crucial.

National Governing Bodies' Duty of Care

Two other recent cases have shifted the focus of injured participants looking to sue their assailants towards sports governing bodies and their duty to provide a safe working environment. Of course, in terms of civil liability anyone may potentially be liable as long as he owes a legally-recognizable duty of care to the aggrieved party. It is often a very pragmatic decision: sue the party who has the deepest pockets.

In England, the case of *Watson* v. *BBBC*,[61] saw the British boxer Michael Watson win his case for compensation against the sport's governing body, the British Boxing Board of Control (BBBC) after he suffered brain damage in a world title fight in 1991. Watson suffered the irreparable damage after a punishing super-middleweight contest against the world champion and fellow Briton Chris Eubank. He collapsed in the ring at the end of the fight and later underwent emergency surgery to remove a blood clot from his brain. He was left paralysed down his left side and has never worked again after losing half his brain function.

Mr Justice Kennedy ruled that the board owed him a duty of care to provide medical staff in attendance on the night with the 'training and equipment to resuscitate a fighter in his condition'. He believed that the BBBC and its medical advisers were rather complacent and had not instituted what he called the 'medical protocol' concerning the need for the early resuscitation of those with serious head injuries that had been accepted in medical circles since the 1970s. He believed that the BBBC medical advisers had not 'looked outside their own personal expertise'. They had failed to be 'prospective in their thinking and seek competent advice as to how a recognised danger could best be combated'. In making the safety arrangements for a professional boxing contest held under its aegis, the defendant owed a duty of care to the claimant, a participant in that contest, to ensure that adequate resuscitation equipment and medical assistance were available at the ringside in the event of the claimant's suffering a serious head injury in the course of the bout. Watson is considered to be the first case in which a regulatory body authority has been held liable for the negligent failure to regulate, resulting in damages.

In Australia, a case has resulted in an opposing decision as far as the liability of a governing body. The High Court of Australia has reversed the decision of the NSW Supreme Court[62] in *Agar* v. *Hyde*; *Agar* v. *Worsley*.[63] The plaintiffs both claimed for injuries suffered in the same colts rugby match. Hyde alleged that a scrum was directed to be formed by the referee of the match. The front row of the scrum, which comprised Hyde, and the two props supporting him had not formed into position when the players from the opposing team scrum, which had then formed, charged into him. Hyde's neck was positioned at such an angle that when the force exerted by the opposing players struck it, it was broken resulting in severe spinal injuries. The plaintiffs sued nine different defendants including the Australian and New Zealand Rugby Unions, the match referee and the International Rugby Football Board (IRFB), which at the time of the commencement of the action was an unincorporated association.

The IRFB were named as defendants for their failure, as the body responsible for promulgating the Laws of the Game, to ensure that the rules of rugby union prevented or reduced the risk of injury, in this case to hookers, that befell the appellants. The High Court concluded that a decision to compete in a game is made freely and with that decision comes responsibility and in these particular circumstances, no relevant duty of care arose.

> Rugby union is notoriously a dangerous game. It is a game, often of quite violent bodily contact. Everyone who plays it is vulnerable ... The respondents here could not possibly have been ignorant of any of these matters ... Sport, particularly amateur sport, stands in an entirely different position from the workplace, the roads, the marketplace, and other areas into which people must venture. When adults voluntarily participate in sport they may be assumed to know the rules and to have an appreciation of the risks of the game. In practically every sport safer rules could be adopted. Should the international body controlling cricket have been held liable for not prescribing the wearing of helmets by batsmen before the West Indian cricket selectors unleased upon the cricketing world their aggressive fast attack of the 1970s? Should cricket be played with a soft, rather than a hard ball?[64]

The Role of Law: Should Foul Play Be a Crime?

Over the last few years in Britain the criminal law has intervened more in sports field violence, but the incidence of players, particularly from professional sports, appearing in court is still rare. There are a number of offences that individuals may be charged with. The offence of breach of the peace has been used against sportsmen on a number of occasions. In football, for example, in 1980 Charlie George, the then Southampton Town football player, was convicted of behaving in a way that was likely to cause a breach of the peace for his conduct during a match. In 1988 during the Glasgow Derby, a number of Rangers and Celtic players were charged with breach of the peace following a goalmouth 'scrum'. Two players were convicted, one was found not guilty and another had his case 'not proven'.

Additionally, police have cautioned professional players for swearing by intervening during the actual commission of the game.

These incidents have led to concern about who is in charge of a game, the police or the referee? As far as the law of assault and battery is concerned, there have been a number of cases over the last 15 years with only a few of these in major club rugby union and professional football.[65] There have been a larger number of prosecutions in amateur rugby and football, which reflects a greater likelihood that offences are reported to the police and that the Crown Prosecution Service will prosecute when compared with professional incidents.[66]

In 1992 a criminal prosecution ended in acquittal.[67] It involved the Brentford footballer Gary Blisset, who was charged with causing grievous bodily harm, under s.20 of the Offences against the Person Act 1861, to the former Torquay United player John Uzzell. This is a rare prosecution in professional sport – most have been for the lesser offence of assault occasioning actual bodily harm under s.47. Blisset was involved in a flying collision when both he and Uzzell were challenging to get possession of the ball. Uzzell suffered a fractured eye socket and cheekbone and subsequently retired. The referee saw the incident and Blisset was sent off. The Crown Prosecution Service commenced a prosecution after the police reported the case. Blisset said at his trial that what had occurred was an accident, as the two players had jumped for a fifty-fifty ball. He had tried to avoid colliding with Uzzell when he realized that he was not going to avoid the ball. The most controversial comment in the trial was by Graham Kelly, the Football Association's chief executive, who said it was an 'ordinary aerial challenge', which he would see 200 times a week if he attended four matches.

In 1995 Duncan Ferguson was convicted and imprisoned for an off-the-ball head butt against John McStay during a match between Glasgow Rangers and Raith Rovers.[68] This case reflected an increased tendency of the Glasgow region procurator-fiscal to embark on sports-participation criminal prosecutions, which led to the Lord Advocate's drawing up guidelines for criminal prosecutions for sports-field violence in Scotland.[69] Spasmodic incidents of violent behaviour on the field (often little more than scuffles) periodically stimulate calls for greater police intervention.[70]

The Issue of Consent

In contact sports a crucial issue is what sports athletes are consenting to as their participation. What some of the preceding commentary has clearly questioned is whether they are even able to provide an informed consent?[71] Legal issues surrounding consent to physical force both in the civil law and the criminal law are not unproblematic. When this is within the context of sporting endeavour the issues become increasingly complex.

Civil Law

The issue of consent in the civil law is constructed upon the consent of *volenti non fit injuria* – no injury is done to one who consents. A terminological distinction can be drawn. First, the use of the term 'consent' is often used as a defence to intentional harms. This is based on the principle 'that no man can enforce a right that he has voluntarily waived or abandoned'.[72] Secondly, the term 'assumption of risk' is used as a defence to negligent harms. The courts have constructed this as meaning agreement on the part of the plaintiff to exempt the defendant from the duty that he would otherwise owe. The courts have also ruled that it is a question of fact whether a real consent to the assumption of risk without compensation can be deduced from all the circumstances of the case in question.[73]

In a number of sporting cases this question has been examined. A series of cases has indicated that sports spectators assume the risk of any harm caused by a player unless it results from intentional or reckless conduct.[74] However, as far as participants are concerned, *Condon* v. *Basi*[75] indicates that it is a question of fact whether the plaintiff had consented to the risk. So, for example, in *Smoldon*, the defendant argued the principle of *volenti*. It was found that the plaintiff could not be held to have consented to the referee's breaches of his duty of the kind that were found. In *Watson* it was held that, although the claimant clearly consented to the risk of injury at the hands of his opponent, he did not consent to the risk of injury flowing from the BBBC's failure to ensure that its safety arrangements were as carefully worked out as they might have been. Mr Justice Kennedy stated that 'before the point could even arguably be raised by the defendant, it would have to be shown that the claimant knew that the case on safety was not as the Board [the BBBC] claimed it was'.

Criminal Law

In the criminal law the issue of consent has proved significantly more problematic to determine and there seems to have been some inconsistency in the development of a doctrinal approach to consent to assault on the sporting field. Historically, English common law has allowed consensual force between individuals. The use to others of violence short of permanent maiming has been justified in the past.[76] Until the nineteenth century duelling leading to death was untouched by the criminal law. In the eighteenth century there were contrary views as to the effect of the consensual use of force in sporting situations. Hale argued that death occurring in a mutually consensual activity, such as wrestling, would result in a liability for manslaughter because the participants in such a sport intend to harm each other.[77] Conversely, Foster stated that two individuals who 'engage by mutual consent' in such activities have no intention to harm one another, and therefore there could be no liability for manslaughter on the death of the other player.[78]

Two nineteenth-century cases indicate that, in football, players who used intentional or reckless force that is likely to cause bodily harm to another would be acting illegally.[79] Neither of the cases specifically considered the issue of what effect the victim's consent to involvement in the game would have on the defendant's liability. However, there was an inference that, if the defendant were playing within the rules and practices of the sport, the player would not be acting in a manner likely to cause bodily harm. As stated in *Bradshaw*:

> if a man is playing according to the rules and practices of the game and not going beyond it, it may be reasonable to infer that he is not actuated by any malicious motive or intention, and that he is not acting in a manner which he knows will be likely to be productive of death or injury.[80]

This suggests that players consent to the risk of incurring a particular type of injury during a game. This was the view taken by Lord Mustill in *Brown*,[81] where the position of consent in the law of assaults was given a comprehensive review. A player in a contact sport: 'by taking part ... also assumes the risk that the deliberate contact may have unintended effects, conceivably of sufficient severity to amount to grievous bodily harm. But he does not agree that this more serious kind of injury may be inflicted deliberately'.[82]

Similarly, in *Billinghurst*[83] the judge directed the jury that players were only deemed to consent to the force of a kind which could reasonably be expected to happen during the game. He went on to say that 'there must be cases which cross the line of that to which a player is deemed to consent'.[84] If the game is carried out within established guidelines, there seems to be a presumption that serious injury is not foreseeable. The rules of the sport have therefore been seen as a crucial guide to the type of contact and injury that players consent to, and therefore a clear determining role as to the criminal law's intervention. They are designed to avoid the serious danger of injury. Participants who cause injury to others within the reasonable application of the rules of the sport can rely on the victims' consent to potential harm within the rules. However, the reality is that in contact sports there is a continued risk of injury. If consent is limited only to the operation of the specific rules of the sport it will be overly restrictive.

Consent works within a wider test than the sport's rules alone. In football, for example, the commission of fouls due to 'illegal tackles' and the consequential injuries have inevitability, and, although being outside the legalistic interpretation of the rules, are inside 'the code of conduct', 'playing or working culture'[85] of the game. This provides a wider area in which consent will be operative. Glanville Williams similarly states; 'the consent by the players to the use of moderate force is clearly valid, and the players are even deemed to consent to an application of force that is in breach of the rules of the game, if it is the sort of thing that may be expected to happen during the game'.[86]

This has produced a largely subjective test for consent based on the expectations of players regarding their involvement within the game regulated by the rules and working culture of the sport. Players consent to injuries that are incidental to physical contact within this sphere and immunity from criminal liability should exist. However, as stated above, any intentional or reckless infliction of injury will not attract the immunity. In *Bradshaw* it was stated that liability would occur where the defendant 'knew that, in charging as he did, he might produce serious injury and was indifferent and reckless as to whether he would produce serious injury or not'.[87]

Subjective vs Objective Constructions

A useful way to analyse the problems surrounding the question of how consent to criminal assault should be understood in sport is to examine the review of law and proposals made by the Law Commission in the context of the House of Lords' decision in *Brown,* concerning the criminalization of factually-consensual, sado-masochistic sexual activity.[88] Although focusing on issues of how consent is formulated and what threshold of harm can be consented to, the Law Commission has had two attempts at formulating how consent should be constructed. In the first Consultation Paper in 1993,[89] the Commission argued that the subjective construction of consent should be replaced by an objective test.[90] It argued that it is artificial to talk of participants' (subjectively) consenting to risk of injury, as opposed to consenting to take part in the game.[91] The approach in a number of Canadian cases to the legal regulation of violence in ice hockey matches was used by the Commission to support this move to an objective construction of consent. This was first articulated in the case of *Cey*[92] and has been supported in later cases.[93] This case concerned an assault in an amateur ice hockey match where the accused used his stick to push the victim into the boards surrounding the rink. It was held that, although consent by the player inevitably involves an assessment of the player's subjective view as to the victim's consent, the scope of it should be determined by objective criteria. These were seen as: first, the conditions under which the game in question is played; secondly, the nature of the act which forms the charge; thirdly, the extent of the force employed; fourthly, the degree of risk of injury; and fifthly, the state of mind of the accused.[94]

In *Cey*, Gerwing JA for the majority, considered that the trial judge had been wrong in giving a direction only on the issue of whether the accused had intended to cause serious injury and thereby to exceed the standards by which the game of hockey should be played. She stated that the subjective state of mind of the accused is only one element, and, in fact, 'not particularly significant',[95] in determining whether actions fall within the scope of activity to which the victim implicitly consents. She considered that the objective criteria discussed should be used to determine whether the actions of the accused were so 'violent and inherently dangerous as to be excluded from the implied consent'.[96]

It is strongly argued that this *objectivizing* of the concept of consent would lead to an unworkable approach.[97] The dissenting judgment in *Cey* by Wakeling JA, however, presents a more appropriate way to construct criminal liability. As has already been suggested, consent to bodily contact and to violence is implied from participation. That is on the basis of play subject to the rules and also the working culture within the game. Penalties exist within the rules of the game to penalize infringement. As Wakeling JA argues:

> The player also expects that in the heat of the action some contact will take place which is dangerous and will therefore occasionally cause injury, even severe injury, but no injury is intended. This conduct will as well call for a penalty, but not criminal charges, for it is such an integral part of the game that a player cannot expect to avoid it and therefore must have given his consent. On the other hand, conduct which is perhaps motivated by retaliation and, in any event, is intended to do bodily harm, could not be taken as within the scope of implied consent. In fact, it may be that a player cannot legally give consent to such a standard of behaviour.[98]

This argument supports the subjective view of the participant's being an important determining factor concerning the operation of consent.[99] It enables the criminal law to have a legitimate role to intervene in incidents where there is clear intentional or reckless retaliation, often, but not exclusively, in off-the-ball incidents.[100] There is a strong argument, however, that this should ideally occur only after internal regulatory mechanisms have failed to control and penalize such acts effectively.[101] By adopting an essentially subjective construction of consent, the intervention of the law in physical contact during the 'working culture' of the game can be seen as outside the ambit of the law.

The second Consultation Paper in 1995[102] provides a less doctrinal analysis of consent and suggests a more practical development, stating that the 'law must compromise between treating the victim's consent as a complete defence and regarding it as wholly immaterial'.[103] This, therefore, creates a continuum within which the intervention of the law needs to be determined. The one essential factor in the Law Commission's most recent proposals is the need for the consequential harm to amount to a 'serious disabling injury' before any potential liability can be incurred, where the players have consented to the risk of or to actual injury.[104] This is defined as: 'an injury or injuries which cause distress, and involve the loss of a bodily member or organ or permanent bodily injury or permanent functional impairment, or serious permanent disfigurement, or severe prolonged pain, or serious impairment of mental health, or prolonged unconsciousness'.[105]

In addition, the second Law Commission paper, modifying its approach in the first, presents the rules of the sport as the determining issue of when the criminal law can intervene. Injury, including serious disabling injury, caused within the rules of the sport will not be subject to a prosecution. The Commission proposes the 'special exception' to be, 'that a person should not be guilty of an offence of causing injury if he or she caused the relevant injury in the course of playing or practising a recognised sport in accordance with its rules'.[106]

A major question is whether actions within and without the rules are an appropriate demarcation to determine criminal liability. The problem of making specific distinctions between the playing rules of the sport and its working culture have already been alluded to. As with the first Consultation Paper, there is general acceptance that the intentional infliction of injury should lead to criminal liability and not be the subject of any exception. This is predicated on the premise that such intentional infliction will inevitably be outside the rules of the sport. The clearest examples are 'off-the-ball' acts of retaliation. However, this may not be so straightforward a distinction to make. As Gunn argues in the context of boxing, 'the sport itself, and its rules, require the participants to act with the intention of inflicting harm to others'.[107]

He concludes that this reality allows us to argue that the sport of boxing is illegal. Within the context of this latest proposal by the Law Commission, this provides us with an interesting perspective and perhaps with a useful example of the conundrum that the issue of consent and violence in sport presents: are there some sports where physical contact straddles the fine line between legal and legitimate activity and illegal activity that should be subject to the gaze of the law? Both Gunn and the second Law Commission Consultation paper use cricket as an example. Gunn suggests that short-pitched, intimidatory bowling ('bouncers') amounts at least to an assault; if there is physical contact it could lead to a more serious offence.

It could be argued that cricket is perhaps a not particularly helpful example to use with no English criminal prosecutions having been brought for resulting injury. However, the regulation of short-pitched bowling within the rules is useful to illustrate the problems of constructing the test of liability around the playing rules. The rules concerning the evaluation of what is intimidatory, short-pitched bowling and the frequency with which it may be used by an individual bowler have been modified a number of times and can be problematic for the umpires. Using the above test proposed by the Law Commission, what would be the position if a 'bouncer' not ruled an intimidatory delivery injured a batsmen, but was ruled illegal as a no-ball owing to the bowler's front foot being beyond the batting crease? If a 'serious disabling injury' resulted, could criminal liability apply?

Conclusion

This chapter has posed more questions than it has provided answers. There has been an attempt to explain a developing area of legal regulation within the context of a complex sporting phenomenon. What best-practice model should develop to regulate sports-participation violence? A major contention is that law and an emphasis on constructing legal liability are not the appropriate mechanisms to challenge excessive sports field violence. The danger of arbitrary legal enforcement – the vagaries and lottery of establishing liability in the tort of negligence and the complexity and enigma of criminal consent – makes the support of a greater use of the law indefensible. Of course, there is the ironic contention that the use of legal intervention in certain social fields such as sport is a form of violence itself: 'Even when we realise the way law itself often exaggerates the threat of violence outside law, we can never ourselves imagine that law could ever finally conquer and undo force, coercion and disorder: its promise is a promise to substitute one kind of force – legitimate force for another.'[108]

The spectre of the law regulating excessive bodily contact on the sports field creates the danger of inconsistent and oppressive decisions that will adversely impact upon the very nature of sport itself. But if not the law, what other forms of intervention are appropriate? Officials adjudicating on the playing field can have greater powers to stamp out 'unnecessary roughness' that may lead to more excessive and violent conduct.[109] Sports national and international governing bodies should attempt to deal with sports violence in-house through effective compensatory mechanisms[110] and improved disciplinary procedures.[111] It has to be acknowledged, however, that sports bodies do not have a good track record in this respect. Disciplinary tribunals are not able to be subject to judicial review and there are clear potential restraint-of-trade issues.[112] Quasi-legal mediation and arbitration mechanisms independent of governing bodies may be appropriate developments that prioritize the dynamics of sport over those of the law.[113]

Ethical codes are also increasingly being used to engage with excessive conduct, whether it be exploitation of child athletes, drug abuse or sports violence. These can be used to challenge the working cultures that promote illegitimate, violent play and deliberate injury to opponents. In addition, sports organizations are beginning to take a proactive approach in eliminating potential risks by developing risk-management plans.[114] The idea behind such plans is to analyse where and why accidents may occur, how such accidents might be prevented and to determine which types of risk are acceptable. Besides safety and accident prevention, a good risk-management plan should also include provisions for insurance coverage and the regular inspection of facilities and equipment. It is important to understand that it is almost impossible to make any physical activity or sport risk-free. Only the banning of the activity would have this goal. This has happened in the United States with such high-risk sports as javelin throwing and pole vaulting. If athletic and recreational activities are to remain exciting, challenging and creative, then a degree of controlled danger and risk must exist.[115]

What seems clear is that there is an urgent need for a systemized study to evaluate more accurately the extent and causes of sports participation violence in Britain. In the context of the increased legal regulation of this problem, the dangers are only too real of excessive juridification of sports participation on the playing field. It is the law's involvement that needs to be tackled – if not, the cost may be that the unrestrained competitive essence and inherent physical qualities of contact sports will be irreversibly damaged.

NOTES

1. R. Di Nicola and S. Mendeloff, 'Controlling Violence in Professional Sport: Rules Reform and the Federal Sports Violence Commission', 21 *Dusquesne Law Review* (1983), 845.
2. Perhaps the most significant case in recent years has been *Condon* v. *Basi* [1985] 2 All ER 453, which held that a duty of care is owed by one sports participant against another.
3. *R.* v. *Bradshaw* (1878) 14 Cox Crim. Cases 83 and *R.* v. *Moore* (1898) 14 TLR 229.
4. Law Commission Consultation Paper No.134, *Criminal Law: Consent and Offences Against the Person*, London, 1994 (LCCP 134) and Law Commission Consultation Paper No.139, *Criminal Law: Consent in the Criminal Law*, London, 1995 (LCCP 139).
5. S. Moore, Special Report No.24, *Sports Insurance*, Health and Safety Commision, 1995, put the cost to the British economy at around £400m.
6. See S. Gardiner, A. Felix, M. James, R. Welch and J. O'Leary, *Sports Law*, London, 1998, 57–66.
7. LCCP 139, para.12.3.
8. See T. Mason, *Sport in Britain*, London, 1988, 22–35.
9. Submission to LCCP 139, n.4 para. 12.15.

10. E. Dunning, 'Sport as a Male Preserve: Notes on the Social Sources of Masculine Identity and its Transformations', 3 *Theory Culture and Society* (1986) no.1, 80.
11. Ibid., 81.
12. S. Jackson, 'Beauty and the Beast: a Critical Look at Sports Violence', 26 *Journal of Physical Education of New Zealand* (Dec. 1993) no.4.
13. M. Smith, *Violence and Sport*, Toronto, 1983, 7.
14. M. James, 'Legal Regulation of the Sportsfield', unpublished PhD thesis, Anglia Polytechnic University, 2000.
15. K. Young, 'Violence in the Workplace of Professional Sport', 26 *International Review for the Sociology of Sport* (1991), 6.
16. J. Pooley, 'Player Violence in Sport: Consequences for Youth Cross-nationally', 25 *ICHPER Journal* (1989) no.3, 6.
17. For example, the English Professional Footballers' Association has displayed posters in changing rooms showing the horrendous injuries that can result especially from the use of elbows.
18. See n.41.
19. L. Bryson, 'Sport and the Maintenance of Masculine Hegemony', 10 *Women's Studies International Forum* (1987) no.4, 349–60; M. Messner, 'When Bodies Are Weapons: Masculinity and Violence in Sport', 25 *International Review for the Sociology of Sport* (1990), 203–20; ibid., *Power at Play: Sports and the Problems of Masculinity* (1992) no.3.
20. K. Weis, 'How the Print Media Affect Sports and Violence: the Problem of Sports Journalism', 21 *International Review for the Sociology of Sport* (1986) nos.2/3.
21. Video evidence is systematically used in governing bodies disciplinary tribunals and has been used in judicial proceedings, see S. Gardiner, 'The Third Eye: Video Adjudication in Sport', 7 *Sport and the Law Journal* (1999) no.1.
22. D. Whitson and R. Gruneau, *Hockey Nights in Canada*, Toronto, 1993; also see M. Smith, 'Violence and Injuries in Ice Hockey', 2 *Clinical Journal of Sports Medicine* (1991), 104.
23. R. Horrow, *Sports Violence: The Interaction between Private Law Making and the Criminal Law*, Arlington, VA, 1980, 176.
24. G. Russell, 'Does Sports Violence Increase Box Office Receipts?', 17 *International Journal of Sports Psychology* (1986) no.3.
25. L. Smith, 'Sports Injuries Are Badly Managed in Britain', *British Medical Journal* (1996), 1499–500.
26. K. Young, 'Violence, Risk and Liability in Male Sports Culture', 10 *Sociology of Sport Journal* (1993) 373.
27. Young, 'Violence in the Workplace', 3.
28. I. Waddington, M. Roderick and G. Parker, *Managing Injuries in Professional Football: a Study of the Roles of the Club Doctor and Physiotherapist*, Centre for Research into Sport and Society, 1999.
29. *Brady* v. *Sunderland Football Club* (1998), unreported case, see 1 *Sports Law Bulletin* (1998) no.5, 4.
30. See the unsuccessful attempts by Billy Mcphail, the ex-Glasgow Celtic player to claim industrial disability for medical conditions including pre-senile dementia which he argues were caused by persistent heading of old-style leather footballs during the 1950s, see 1, no.4 and 2, no.3 *Sports Law Bulletin*. Also see on relationship with heading footballs and injury, R.C. Schwartz, 'Heading the Ball in Soccer: What's the Risk of Brain Injury?', 26 *Physician and Sports Medicine* (1998) no.11.
31. The long-term disabling consequences of pain-killing Cortisone injections especially, for example, have recently been acknowledged, see *Daily Mail*, 14 Feb. 2000.
32. *Watson* v. *British Boxing Board of Control* (1999) unreported, see 2 *Sports Law Bulletin* (1999) no.6.
33. B. Wilson, K. Quarrie, P. Milburn and D. Chalmers, 'The Nature and Circumstances

of Tackle Injuries in Rugby Union', 2(2) *Journal of Science and Medicine in Sport* (1998), 153.

34. See S. Cohen for an explanation and analysis of moral panics in *Folk Devils and Moral Panics: The Creation of Mod Rockers*, London, 1972.

35. A. Guttmann, *Sports Spectators*, New York, 1986.

36. See S. Gardiner and A. Felix, 'Juridification of the Football Field: Strategies for Giving Law the Elbow', 5 *Marquette Sports Law Journal* (1995) no.2, 189, for a fuller account of changes of rules and styles of play in football.

37. See later, pages 107–8.

38. See Gardiner *et al.*, 59–61.

39. B. Neilsen, 'Controlling Sports Violence: Too Late for the Carrots – Bring on the Big Stick', *Iowa Law Review* (1989), 681. Also see P. Anderson, 'When Violence Is not Part of the Game: Regulating Sports Violence in Professional Team Sports', 3 *Contemporary Issues in Law* (1998) no.4, 240.

40. C. Critcher, 'Putting on the Style: Aspects of Recent English Football', in J. Williams and S. Wagg (eds), *British Football and Social Change: Getting into Europe*, Leicester, 1991.

41. See S. Gardiner, 'The Law and the Sportsfield', *Criminal Law Review* (1994), 513.

42. See Council of Europe, *Code of Sports Ethics, Fair Play – the Winning Way*, Strasbourg, 1995.

43. *Police Review* (19 Nov. 1969), 'On the Field of Play', *New Law Journal* (1971) 413, 'The Day Sport Dies', *New Law Journal* (1988) 9, 'Keeping Sport Alive', *New Law Journal* (1990) 12, 'Foul Play' *New Law Journal* (1991) 742, 'Making Foul Play a Crime' (with Catherine Bond), *Solicitors Journal* (1993) 693, 'Drake's Drum Beat for Sporting Remedies/Injuries', *New Law Journal* (1994) 1094, *Sport and the Law*, 3rd edn, London, 1999.

44. E. Grayson, *All England Annual Report* (1989), 286.

45. Gardiner *et al.*, 42–7.

46. James, 2000, p.60.

47. E. Grayson and C. Bond, 'Making Foul Play a Crime', *Solicitors Journal* (1993), 693.

48. *Elliot* v. *Saunders* (1994) unreported. See A. Felix and S. Gardiner, 'Drama in Court 14: *Elliot* v. *Saunders*', 2 *Sport and the Law Journal* (1994) no.2; *Watson and Bradford City FC* v. *Gray and Huddersfield Town FC*, unreported (1998), see 1 *Sports Law Bulletin* (1998) no.6.

49. Successful actions in the last few years include *Smoldon* v. *Whitworth and Nolan* (*The Times*, 18 Dec. 1996).

50. *Brady* v. *Sunderland Football Club* (1998), unreported, see 1 *Sports Law Bulletin* (1988) no.5, 4.

51. Ibid. Also see J. Gardiner, 'Should Coaches Take Care?', *New Law Journal* (1993), 1598, concerning potential liability of sports coaches, and S. Greenfield and G. Osborn, 'Aesthetics, Injury and Liability in Cricket', 13 *Professional Negligence* (1997), 9, concerning potential liability of groundsmen.

52. *Watson* v. *British Boxing Board of Control* (1999), *The Law Times*, 24 Sept. 1999, see 2 *Sports Law Bulletin* (1999) no.6.

53. G. Jahn, 'Civil Liability: an Alternative to Violence in Sporting Events', 15 *Ohio University Law Review* (1994), 243.

54. *Letang* v. *Cooper* [1964] 2 All ER 929.

55. [1932] AC 562.

56. *Condon* v. *Basi* [1985] 2 All ER 453.

57. [1963] 2 QB 43.

58. See *Nabozny* v. *Barnhill,* 334 NE 2d 258 (Ill. App.Ct. 1975), see M. Narol, 'Sports Torts: Emerging Standards of Care', *Trial* (June 1990), 20. Also see *Lestini* v. *West Bend Mutual Insurance Co.,* 176 Wis 2d 901, 501 NW 2d 28 (1993).

59. *Smoldon* v. *Whitworth and Nolan* (*The Times*, 18 Dec. 1996). See A. Felix and T. Lee,

'Sports Injuries: *Smoldon* v. *Whitworth and Nolan* – the Liability of Officials' (Pt 1), 1 *Sports Law Bulletin* (1998) no.2; 'Sports Injuries: *Smoldon* v. *Whitworth and Nolan* – the Liability of Officials' (Pt 2), 1 *Sports Law Bulletin* (1998) no.3.

60. [1987] 1 AC 241.
61. *Watson* v. *British Boxing Board of Control.*
62. See A. Gibson, 'World Digest: Australian Sporting Law Highlights in 1999', 3 *Sports Law Bulletin* (2000), no.2, 16, for details of NSW Supreme Court decision.
63. *Agar* v. *Hyde*; *Agar* v. *Worsley* [2000] HCA 41.
64. Ibid., paras. 126 and 127.
65. In professional football there have been few successful prosecutions for assault. In 1988 Kamara admitted causing grievous bodily harm to the Shrewsbury Town player Jim Melrose while playing for Swindon Town. In 1993 Mark Stein of Stoke City was convicted of assault occasioning actual bodily harm for injury caused to Jim Gannon of Stockport County. In rugby union reported cases primarily concerning appeals against sentence include, *Billinghurst* [1978] Crim LR 553; *Gingell* (1980) 2 Cr.App.R (S) 198, who was convicted of inflicting grievous bodily harm when his assault during a rugby match led to a fractured cheekbone, jaw and nose. A sentence of six months reduced to two on appeal. In *Johnson* (1986) 8 Cr.App.R (S) 343 was convicted of s.18 OAPA for biting off part of an opposing player's ear during a rugby match and received a six-months' sentence. Also see *Bishop* (1986 unreported); *Lloyd* (1989) 11 Cr.App.R (S) 36; *Chapman* (1989) 11 Cr.App.R.(S) 93, *Calton* (1998) unreported, see 1 *Sports Law Bulletin* (1998) no.5, 3.
66. In football convictions include *Birkin* [1988] Crim LR; *Shervill* (1989) 11 Cr.App.R (S) 284; *Lincoln* (1990) 12 Cr.App.R.(S) 250; *Davies* (1991) Crim LR 70, McHugh (1998) unreported, see 1 *Sports Law Bulletin* (1998) no.2, Moss (1999) unreported; see 2 *Sports Law Bulletin* (1999) no.4, 2.
67. See S. Gardiner, 'Not Playing the Game: Is It a Crime?', *Solicitors Journal* (1993), 628.
68. One leading example was the conviction and imprisonment of the then Glasgow Rangers player Duncan Ferguson; see *Duncan Cowan Ferguson* v. *Andrew Christie Normand*, Scottish Criminal Case Reports, 1995.
69. Lord Advocate's *Instructions* to the Chief Constables in Scotland [under s.12 Criminal Procedure (Scotland) Act 1995]. For commentary see M. James and S. Gardiner, 'Touchlines and Guidelines: the Lord Advocate's Response to Sportsfield Violence', *Criminal Law Review* (Jan. 1997), 41 and S. Miller, 'Criminal Law and Sport in Scotland', 4 *Sport and the Law Journal* (1996) no.2, 40.
70. See 'Shorts', 3 *Sports Law Bulletin* (2000) no.2, 7.
71. See earlier pages 95–6.
72. *Chapman* v. *Ellesmere* [1932] 2 KB 431.
73. *Chatterton* v. *Gerson* [1980] 3 WLR 1003.
74. *Woolridge* v. *Sumner* [1963] 2 QB 43.
75. [1985] 2 All ER 453.
76. Hawkins, *Pleas of the Crown*, 8th edn, Vol.1. Also see Stephen's, *A Digest of the Criminal Law*, 1894.
77. M. Hale, *History of Pleas of the Crown*, 1778.
78. M. Foster, *Crown Cases and Crown Law* (1763) 260.
79. *R.* v. *Bradshaw* (1878) 14 Cox Crim. Cas. 83 (football player killed when charged by one opponent with a protruding knee); *R.* v. *Moore* (1898) 14 TLR 229 (football player killed when violent push from behind caused his head to strike another player's knee).
80. Ibid. *Bradshaw* at 85.
81. [1993] 2 WLR 556.
82. Ibid., at 592H–593A.
83. [1978] Crim LR 553.
84. Ibid., at 554.

85. See Gardiner (1994). The American Model Penal Code, s.2.11(2)(b), also provides this approach, which states that players consent to 'reasonably foreseeable hazards of joint participation in a lawful athletic contest or competitive sport'.
86. G. Williams, 'Consent and Public Policy', *Criminal Law Review* (1962), 74.
87. (1878) 1 Cox CC 83 at 85. The position in *Bradshaw* has gained support in *Venna* [1975] 3 All ER 788.
88. See L. Bibbings and P. Alldridge, 'Sexual Expression, Body Alteration and the Defence of Consent', *Journal of Law and Society* (1993), 356 and M. Weait, 'Fleshing It Out', in L. Bently and L. Flynn (eds), *Law and the Senses*, London, 1996.
89. For a general analysis see D. Ormerod, 'Consent and Offences against the Person (1994)', 57 *Modern Law Review* (1994), 931.
90. LCCP 134.
91. Ibid., para.41.3.
92. (1989) 48 CCC (3d) 480.
93. These were followed in *Ciccarelli* (1989) 54 CCC (3d) 121, *Leclerc* (1991) 67 CCC (3d) and *Jobidon* (1991) 2SCR 714.
94. (1989) 48 CCC (3d) 480 at 490–1.
95. Ibid., at p.481.
96. Ibid.
97. See Gardiner and Felix (1995), 203–4.
98. CEY (1989), at p.482.
99. For further analysis see Gardiner (1994).
100. The conviction of Scott McMillan for assault after chasing an opponent and head-butting him during a Scottish rugby match is an example of a clear act of retaliation (*The Times*, May 1994). Another Scottish head-butting incident involving the Glasgow Rangers player Duncan Ferguson has been the subject of a criminal prosecution, see n.68.
101. For details of improved internal disciplinary mechanisms see Gardiner and Felix (1995), 189.
102. LCCP 139.
103. Ibid., para.4.21.
104. For general analysis of LCCP 139 see S. Shute, 'Something Old, Something New, Something Borrowed: Three Aspects of the Project', *Criminal Law Review* (1996), 684 and D. Ormerod and M. Gunn, 'Consent – a Second Bash', *Criminal Law Review* (1996), 694.
105. LCCP 139, para.4.51. This definition is acknowledged as having some inspiration in the views of Glanville Williams in 'Force, Injury and Serious Injury', *New Law Journal* (1990), 1227–9.
106. LCCP 139, para.12.68.
107. M. Gunn, 'Impact of the Law on Sport with Specific reference to the Way Sport Is Played', 3 *Contemporary Legal Issues* (1998) no.4.
108. A. Sarat, 'Speaking of Death: Narratives of Violence in Capital Trials', 27 *Law and Society Review* (1993) no.1.
109. For example, 'sin bins' are being used in a greater variety of team contact sports, e.g., their recent introduction into international rugby union; see 3 *Sports Law Bulletin* (2000) no.2,7.
110. See D. Gendell, 'No-fault Compensation in New Zealand Sport', 3 *Sports Law Bulletin* (2000) no.2.
111. See P. McCutcheon, 'Sports Discipline, Natural Justice and Strict Liability', 28 *Anglo-American Law Review* (1999), 37.
112. See A. Felix, in Gardiner *et al.*, *Sports Law*, 1998, Ch. 4; D. Pannick, 'Judicial Review of Sports Bodies', 2 *Judicial Review* (1997) no.3, 150; and P. Morris and G. Little, 'Challenging Sports Bodies' Determinations', 17 *Civil Justice Quarterly* (1998), 128.

113. See for example the Laussanne-based Court of Arbitration for Sport [see M. Beloff, 'The Court of Arbitration for Sport at the Olympics', 4 *Sport and the Law Journal* (1996) no.3, 5] and the UK-based Sports Dispute Resolution Panel [see K. Vleck, 'The Sports Dispute Resolution Panel', 5 *Sports Law Administration and Practice* (1998) no.2, 1]. For an Australasian perspective also see B. Doyle, 'The ANZSLA Dispute Resolution Service', 3 *Sport and the Law Journal* (1995) no.3, 38.

114. See J. Wolohan, 'Sports Injuries: Risk Management Developments in the United States', 1 *Sports Law Bulletin* (1998) no.6, 10 and D. Cotton and T. Wilde (eds), *Sports Law for Sports Managers*, Dubuque, 1997.

115. A balance needs to be struck; for example, the compulsory introduction by the England and Wales Cricket Board of helmets for under-18 players in competitive matches; see 3 *Sports Law Bulletin* (2000) no.2.

7

Sports Discipline and the Rule of Law

J. Paul McCutcheon

Introduction

The rule of law demands adherence to a number of fundamental precepts of justice. In most legal systems broad principles are generally endorsed and incorporated into a variety of national and international legal instruments. The considerations of justice involved extend beyond constitutional matters and are apt to arise in any circumstance where a body is invested with the authority to make determinations that are adverse to the interests of individuals. The bodies in question include courts and statutory tribunals as well as the broad range of disciplinary bodies and decision-makers that exist in the private sphere. In this chapter a number of issues that might be involved in the exercise of its disciplinary jurisdiction by a sports body are identified and considered. In particular, I take the view that, as that jurisdiction expands and as sports bodies seek to regulate and impose sanctions in respect of a wider range of conduct, these matters are likely to have a greater impact.

A starting point is the observation of Lord Denning in *Enderby Town Football Club Ltd* v. *The Football Association Ltd*[1] that

> Justice can often be done in them [that is, domestic tribunals] better by a good layman than by a bad lawyer. This is especially so in activities like football and other sports, where no points of law are likely to arise, and it is all part of the proper regulation of the game.

That observation is taken to express the general judicial attitude to domestic tribunals and it has been cited with frequent approval. Nevertheless, his Lordship was sufficiently perspicacious to qualify his remarks with the important rider 'where no points of law are likely to arise'. It is my view that nowadays issues of law, both substantive and procedural, are more likely to arise and that the demands of justice are liable to become more onerous and increasingly legalistic. The point might be taken further: in especially serious cases the law could properly require adherence to procedural standards that approximate to those that operate in courts and, to this extent, a further juridification of sports discipline is likely to result. Signs of this trend are already evident in the increasing number of legal challenges to the decisions of disciplinary bodies and the response by governing bodies to the greater prospects of success in such cases. One reaction has been the drafting of disciplinary codes in more legalistic terms, sometimes prompted by judicial utterances,[2] together with guarantees of procedural protection congruent with due process demands. The latter include entitlements to legal representation and the requirement that the case against an athlete be established to a certain standard of proof, with the standard in some cases being proof beyond reasonable doubt. At this stage dicta to the effect that association rules should not be construed as if they were contained in a statute[3] are matched by observations that such measures are quasi-statutory and ought to be interpreted accordingly.[4] To the traditionalist who espouses a non-interventionist approach this development might be regrettable, but I suggest that it is both inevitable and welcome. Where serious disciplinary matters are involved the fundamental dictates of justice demand scrupulous adherence to the highest standards of procedural and substantive fairness.

Sports Discipline Is Distinctive

A number of characteristics make sports discipline distinctive. First, sport by its nature is a rule-based activity that readily facilitates a disciplinary function. A myriad of rules – playing rules, eligibility rules, competition rules and the like – governs the regular conduct of sport and, in consequence, it is necessary to establish an apparatus to ensure the interpretation and enforcement of those rules. An inevitable result of the organization and codification of sports rules is the corresponding development of an adjudicative and interpretative function, thus, in effect, sports have developed their own internal 'legal systems'. In the past disciplinary standards were flexible and informal with external judicial intervention being the rare exception. In recent years we have witnessed a greater willingness on the part of participants to invoke the aid of external authorities, such as courts and independent arbitrators, in the resolution of sports disputes. It is almost inevitable that increased external involvement will result in a more legalistic regulatory and disciplinary environment. To an extent the development of sports legal systems matches that of any other legal system and is characterized by a metamorphosis from customary, unwritten informal standards to a more formal and less flexible regime.

A second feature of sports discipline in the modern era is the increased willingness of participants to invoke the assistance of the courts. Athletes and others who are dissatisfied with the resolution of disputes by the internal decision-making machinery are more likely now than in the past to litigate. This phenomenon may be attributed to several causes. One is the increased commercialization of sport to the point that it is now perceived as being a business rather than a leisure or recreational activity. The financial stakes involved at the level of elite sport are so great that the business conventions of the marketplace rather than the conviviality of the clubhouse are liable to govern relationships. And just as 'ordinary' commercial disputes are likely to be resolved in the courts, so too are sports disputes that have a commercial dimension. However, this does not explain the increase in sports litigation where the commercial aspect is negligible, as is the case with poorly funded minority sports and amateur activities. In this respect I believe that there are other causes at work. Society has in general become more litigious, citizens are more aware of and more willing to seek the enforcement of their rights, and disputes are more likely to end up in the courts. And when the competitive nature of sport and, more importantly, of athletes is taken into account it is not difficult to understand why sports disputes are liable to be fought to the bitter end.

A third distinctive feature is the social prominence that is attached to sport. It cannot be doubted that sport is 'a vitally important social force'.[5] Sport seems to occupy a greater portion of the national agenda: sport as a news item has migrated from the back pages to all parts of the newspaper – the front page, the opinion pages, the style section. At the same time it has assumed a greater political significance. This is evident in the fact that many countries have a ministry for sport and governmental involvement in sport at a variety of levels is normal. Bids to host the Olympic Games or the World Cup are enthusiastically endorsed by governments and now are not likely to succeed without such support. And, in some societies, it is noted that sporting success is a typical route to political office. More generally, the level of media attention that sport attracts has reached saturation levels and prominent athletes are attributed a status that often exceeds their sporting excellence. In these times sports stars are celebrities whose lives, both professional and personal, are subject to intense scrutiny. This is as true, if not more so, of disciplinary matters as of other aspects of their lives. The misdeeds of athletes are liable to attract greater media coverage than in the past and the disciplinary function is equally exposed to publicity. What previously would have been resolved in the committee room is now managed in the full glare of media scrutiny. Given the tendency of certain elements of the media to exaggerate, there is a danger that the exercise of the disciplinary function will be distorted: the fear is that the governance of sport will be shaped by a desire to protect its image rather than a concern to ensure justice to participants.

The disciplinary jurisdiction of sports bodies has expanded. Hitherto sports discipline principally concerned matters that could be said clearly to relate to the conduct of the sport. However, in recent years demands that sports bodies should discipline athletes for an ever-widening range of misconduct are discernible. These demands, which are no doubt driven by the greater publicity that sport attracts and the celebrity of prominent athletes, are commonplace in North America but are becoming increasingly vocal on this side of the Atlantic. Sports bodies are expected to take action against their athletes in respect of lifestyle matters – such as recreational drug use,[6] public drunkenness and gambling[7] – the expression of unpopular political or religious beliefs, and conduct in their private lives – such as child neglect and spousal abuse.[8] The contention is that misconduct of this sort adversely affects the image and integrity of the sport and that as such it properly falls within the jurisdiction of the relevant disciplinary authority. In this respect athletes are to be held to higher standards of conduct than other celebrities or high earners: there are few demands that rock musicians or film actors be held to account for similar misdeeds by their own industries or employers. There is something of an irony here: as athletes have become the 'new rock stars' they are to be punished for the conduct that is often celebrated in rock stars. The view of athletes as role models is often cited as justifying a higher standard of behaviour, but the same might be argued with varying degrees of conviction with respect to musicians and actors. A more compelling factor probably is that society expects sport to reflect the higher virtues of honesty and moral integrity. This demand is uniquely strong in the case of sport and is not made in respect of many other aspects of human activity.

A consequence of the commercialism of sport and its public prominence is that athletes who now face disciplinary charges by their governing bodies are placed in considerable jeopardy. At stake are the rights to earn a livelihood, to property and to reputation, interests that have long merited legal protection. The sanctions liable to be imposed in the event of the charge being established – expulsion, suspension and fines – directly affect athletes' earning capacity and property interests. At the same time, an athlete's reputation is placed in jeopardy, since the effect of an adverse finding is to label or stigmatize him as a miscreant. The extensive publicity that disciplinary matters can attract and the expansion of disciplinary jurisdiction beyond purely sporting conduct exacerbates matters. It is one thing for a sports tribunal to conclude that a footballer who committed a foul tackle was guilty of violent conduct; it is quite another for the same body to conclude that he is a wife-beater, a drug-taker or a drunkard.

A Criminal Dimension to Sports Discipline

The overlap between sports discipline and the criminal law must be noted. Many serious breaches of disciplinary rules are also criminal acts. Violent conduct in a contact sport often amounts to an assault and in some cases an aggravated assault. The making of 'unwarranted gestures' to spectators can attract liability for public-order offences. An athlete who accepts bribes is potentially guilty of offences against prevention of corruption legislation, while the receipt of irregular payments (so-called 'bungs') might involve the commission of revenue offences. And, of course, involvement in doping also attracts possible liability under drugs legislation. In these cases the disciplinary issues are difficult to divorce from the criminal matters. In some instances the alleged wrongdoing might be the subject of separate criminal investigation and proceedings. However, as often as not, the criminal law is not invoked, the view being that the public interest is satisfied if the sanctioning of the athlete is handled by his or her governing body. In this respect sports discipline is apt to become a surrogate for the criminal law.

But even if there is no question of possible criminal liability the consequences of an adverse disciplinary finding are potentially as great. In addition to losing the opportunity to compete and, where relevant, to pursue a livelihood, a sanctioned athlete will be exposed to enduring moral obloquy. This was recognized by the Irish High Court in *Quirke* v. *Bord Luthchleas na hÉireann* where Barr J focused on the consequences for an athlete of a suspension for disciplinary reasons:[9]

> ... where a suspension is imposed by way of punishment, it follows that the body in question has found its member guilty of significant misconduct or breach of rules. The gravity of that finding is proportionate to the length of the suspension imposed and the effect of it on the person suspended. There can be no doubt that an international athlete who is suspended by way of punishment from all major competition for as long as eighteen months, which includes a particular Olympic Games, has had a substantial penalty imposed on him. Furthermore, *even after the period of suspension expires*, the moral implications of its imposition remain.

These remarks acknowledge that an adverse disciplinary finding involves a moral judgment and serves to stigmatize the athlete in question.[10] In this regard similar concerns of justice can be identified in the criminal law and sports discipline alike, at least where the substance of the charge involves an allegation of violence, drug-taking or fraudulent conduct. The criminal dimension to disciplinary matters was also central to another Irish High Court decision, *Flanagan* v. *University College Dublin*,[11] a case that involved a disciplinary charge of plagiarism against a student. Barron J explained the connection between criminal justice and domestic discipline:[12]

> Once a lay tribunal is required to act judicially, the procedures to be adopted by it must be reasonable having regard to this requirement and to the consequences for the person concerned in the event of an adverse

decision. Accordingly, procedures which might afford a sufficient protection to the person concerned in one case, and so be acceptable, might not be acceptable in a more serious case ... Clearly matters of a criminal nature must be treated more seriously than matters of a civil nature, but ultimately the criterion must be the consequence for the person concerned of an adverse verdict... the charge of plagiarism is a charge of cheating and as such the most serious breach of academic discipline possible. *It is also criminal in nature.* In my view the procedures must approach those of a court hearing.

Barron J also outlined the procedural protections that were demanded by the requirements of natural justice. *Inter alia*, the applicant should have received written details of the precise charge being made against her and of the basic facts alleged to have constituted the offence; she was entitled to representation by the lawyer of her choice[13] and was not confined to being represented by the officials nominated in the University's disciplinary code; she should have been informed of these rights and of any others afforded by the code; she should have been allowed to hear the evidence against her, to challenge that evidence on cross-examination and to adduce her own evidence. In all this comes close to requiring a process that mirrors that in a criminal trial and it might be taken to impose too great a burden on the disciplinary body. However, Barron J dismissed as 'irrelevant' the submission that the respondents would face considerable difficulty were they required to adopt a procedure that came close to a criminal trial. In his view it was incumbent upon them to put in place a disciplinary mechanism that is capable of dealing with the contested issues of fact and opinion. While *Flanagan* concerned the question of a university's disciplinary authority, I suggest that the principles involved are applicable in any context, including the sporting, where a body is charged with the task of investigating and determining serious disciplinary charges.

The Duty of Fairness

The applicability of the duty of fairness in sports discipline is beyond question and the real issue concerns the degree of flexibility that may be allowed to disciplinary bodies. The philosophy underlying the decision in *Flanagan* is that, where serious charges are faced, a domestic tribunal is expected to adopt procedures that come close to those that would operate in ordinary court proceedings. This state of affairs entails a diminution in the flexibility that has traditionally characterized sports discipline, which to some was seen as a cardinal virtue, and its replacement by a more rule-bound regime. For the reasons already alluded to, this is a proper and welcome development. Thus an athlete who faces serious charges can rightly expect a hearing before an impartial body, the right to independent legal representation, prior notice of the charge and disclosure of its material particulars, clearly defined evidentiary rules (both as to burden and standard of proof) and a right of appeal. In fact, many of the better-regulated sports have altered their procedures, especially in relation to doping, to effect a change to a more legalistic disciplinary environment. This may be taken variously to represent a concern for the issues of justice involved, a recognition of the consequences of depriving an athlete of his or her livelihood and reputation, or a fear of being overturned in successful legal proceedings. A detailed analysis of the new disciplinary dispensation is beyond the scope of this chapter, but a number of general issues can be identified and merit brief comment.

The principle *nulla poena sine lege* invokes several issues of concern. One is that disciplinary offences should be defined in advance and with sufficient clarity so as to put athletes on notice of the conduct that is prohibited and of the associated sanctions. In this context the broad, open-ended offences such as 'bringing the game into disrepute' or 'misconduct' that are contained in many sports codes are open to criticism.[14] The open-ended terms in which such offences are drafted do not readily facilitate reasonable notice of what is proscribed and are liable to place too much discretion in the hands of the decision-maker. On the other hand, it might well be that those offences have been confined within acceptable limits by the decisions of the relevant disciplinary tribunals and thus their interpretation should assuage any fears in this regard. This raises the related concern of accessibility. In as much as the meaning of a disciplinary code depends on its interpretation, it is important that the relevant decisions are publicized so that athletes might be properly informed and, probably more importantly, that their legal advisers are in a position to mount a full defence. In other words, what may be called the 'common law' of sport, in the form of its authoritative rulings, should be accessible to those who are potentially affected by it. In this latter context some recent improvement is discernible through the reporting of important decisions in reasonably accessible sources such as *Sport and the Law Journal* and the recent publication by the Court of Arbitration for Sport of its decisions.[15]

The interpretation of both the substantive and the procedural provisions of a disciplinary code is a matter of some importance. The power to interpret vests the decision-maker with a discretion, and, as we observed in the preceding paragraph, this is particularly acute where broad, vaguely defined provisions are concerned. The difficulty is that a disciplinary tribunal may face the dilemma of having to choose between irreconcilable interests, namely the rights of the athlete and the image and good governance of the sport. Of course, courts and arbitrators face this type of dilemma daily and like them a sports tribunal should be morally and intellectually equipped to manage its adjudicative function. Accordingly it is crucial that disciplinary codes be interpreted strictly and *contra proferens* mirroring the similar principles of construing penal provisions.

The law of evidence does not bind domestic tribunals, but increasingly disciplinary codes provide for questions of evidence, in a sense creating a domestic law of evidence. Such provisions typically allocate the burden of proof, allow the drawing of inferences, impose reverse onuses, specify the standard of proof and regulate the reception of particular species of evidence such as videotape. As with many other aspects of sports discipline, a trend towards a more legalistic regime is noticeable.[16] Tribunals are now likely to be called upon to decide upon a variety of questions of evidence. Where the relevant disciplinary code contains evidentiary provisions the principles of strict construction outlined in the preceding paragraph should be adopted. Where the code is silent on such matters the application of evidentiary standards that are consistent with an athlete's presumed innocence can be expected, at least in serious cases. It is difficult to imagine a modern disciplinary code that places the entire burden of proof on the athlete, in effect operating a presumption of guilt until innocence is established, and no doubt such a code would receive a hostile reception in the courts. The question of reverse onuses is somewhat different. Some codes place a burden on the athlete once certain primary facts have been established. For example, a typical provision is that a positive laboratory analysis is prima facie proof of doping unless the athlete proves the contrary. A court has yet to determine the issue conclusively, but it is noteworthy that the reverse onus provisions in the International Tennis Federation's doping rules caused the greatest concern for the Court of Appeal in *Wilander* v. *Tobin*,[17] although that court concluded that it was acceptable 'in the context of a code of this kind' to expect an athlete to rebut the prima facie scientific case.

A frequent feature of disciplinary codes is the imposition of mandatory sanctions for serious offences, especially where doping is involved. Once a disciplinary tribunal has found that the relevant offence has been committed the sanction applies without further ado. This is designed to ensure that all offenders face the same penalty, but it does so at the expense of taking the individual characteristics of the offence and of the offender into account. To date, mandatory sanctions in sports codes have survived judicial scrutiny where the importance of combating doping was emphasized.[18] On the other hand, it might be contended that a system of mandatory sentencing is too blunt an instrument and that some allowance ought to be made for individual circumstances. This works in two ways: in some cases the culpability of the offender might merit a more severe sanction, while in others a lesser penalty will properly reflect the athlete's guilt. In respect of the latter there is evidence that disciplinary bodies and appellate tribunals at times adopt a more flexible approach than that which a literal application of the rules would require in order to relax the mandated penalty.[19] This is consistent with the principle that the punishment should fit the crime and the requirement of natural justice that a person should be allowed to address a tribunal on the question of penalty. These considerations militate against a regime of automatic or fixed penalties and it is not beyond the bounds of possibility that current mandatory sanction provisions will face further external challenge.[20]

The intersection of sports justice and the criminal law must also be noted. In some cases an alleged breach of discipline will also be the subject of a separate criminal investigation. In such cases the holding of a disciplinary hearing before the criminal matter has been disposed of could pose difficulties: a full defence in a disciplinary hearing might require the disclosure of material that could be used in criminal proceedings, thus undermining the athlete's privilege against self-incrimination. In such circumstances the prudent course would be to postpone the disciplinary hearing pending the conclusion of any criminal case.[21] Given the delays that are frequently associated with the criminal process, the governing body might in the meantime wish to suspend the athlete, especially where a serious breach is alleged. In *Quirke* v. *Bord Luthchleas na hÉireann* the Irish High Court drew a distinction between a suspension that is imposed following a full disciplinary enquiry and one that is imposed pending a hearing.[22] The former is the sanction for a breach of discipline while the latter is a 'holding operation'; the suggestion in *Quirke* is that the latter is permitted pending inquiries.[23] On the other hand, it is conceivable that the delay in criminal proceedings would be of such lengthy duration that any interim suspension would be unduly onerous: in particular, an athlete might end by serving a temporary suspension for a longer period than the full suspension he or she would receive in the event of being found guilty of the disciplinary charges.

The Question of Waiver

Although some commentators would prefer to view the issue as one of public law,[24] the dominant judicial view in the British Isles is that the authority of a disciplinary body is based either on contract[25] or consensual submission to its jurisdiction.[26] It follows that the rights an athlete enjoys are determined by the terms of that contract or consensual submission. Where the contract is silent the courts typically construe the requirements of natural justice as implied terms. As far as the substance of natural justice is concerned, it is probably immaterial whether the duty of fairness is imposed as a matter of public law or private law, as it is evident that the same standards are demanded irrespective of the legal category into which that duty is placed.[27] To this extent the migration of the principles of natural justice from public law to private law is virtually complete. However, given that sports discipline is classified as a private law matter, it would seem that it is possible to exclude the requirements of natural justice, or of any particular requirement, by express terms to that effect.

General contract theory supports the view that the various requirements of natural justice could be excluded by a suitably phrased term or set of terms. Such terms are improbable in the modern era and we have noted that, if anything, the tendency is to provide express due process guarantees in disciplinary codes. Nevertheless, the theoretical issue remains: to what extent would a purported waiver by an athlete of his or her natural justice entitlements be considered legally effective? Several legal doctrines are likely to intrude here.

The first is the principle of strict construction and its adjunct, the *contra proferentum* rule. A document that purports to exclude what would otherwise be enjoyed as normal due process entitlements would inevitably be construed strictly, with the benefit of any doubt and ambiguity being resolved in favour of the athlete. Moreover, experience in other areas of the law has shown that, when required, the courts can be imaginative in combating the ingenuity of legal drafting; their capacity to develop rules and doctrines to circumvent the best efforts of lawyers should not be underestimated. This is particularly so where there is a perceived abuse of power, where a dominant party seeks to limit or exclude the rights of those in a weaker bargaining position. In this context reference may be made to the efforts of the courts to limit the effect of exemption clauses in consumer contracts in the decades before the enactment of consumer protection legislation. While legislation was ultimately necessary to protect consumer rights, the courts played their part in attempting to limit the abuses of power in this area. In short, I suggest that it is highly improbable that one could draft an effective, comprehensive clause excluding all due process requirements that the courts would be unable to circumnavigate. It might be that less draconian clauses that dilute some of the normal natural justice requirements would survive judicial scrutiny, but this remains to be seen. For example, a term in a disciplinary code might seek to exclude legal representation from certain hearings. This might be acceptable where minor breaches are alleged, where, in Lord Denning's words, 'no points of law are likely to arise', but it may be doubted whether such exclusion in the case of serious charges would be judicially endorsed.

Secondly, the doctrine of restraint of trade might be invoked to nullify a purported exclusion of natural justice. Aside from any question of construction, the rule would fall to be evaluated by restraint of trade criteria: does it go no further than is reasonably necessary to protect a legitimate interest of the governing body? Is it in the interests of the athlete? And can it be justified in terms of the public interest? So far the Court of Appeal has upheld the lawfulness of doping rules that impose strict liability, that provide for mandatory penalties and that place a reverse onus on an athlete who has tested positive.[28] On the other hand, it is fair to suppose that the exclusion of standard elements of natural justice, such as a denial of professional representation or the imposition of a presumption of guilt, would be found to be unreasonable restraints of trade. It is difficult to see how such measures could be justified in the interests of the governing body or in the public interest. But while restraint of trade may be invoked in cases where an athlete's livelihood is in jeopardy, it will be of little assistance in amateur or recreational sport where there is no question of the restriction affecting a person's earning power.

Thirdly, aside from any question of contract, the right to fairness might be guaranteed by another legal instrument that is capable of being applied to the relationship in question – the European Convention on Human Rights, national constitutions and human-rights legislation spring to mind. In this context, the exclusion of natural justice assumes a different dimension and the question is whether, or more accurately to what extent, a private agreement is capable of restricting the application of human rights. This will be ultimately resolved in the United Kingdom through the interpretation of the Human Rights Act and the comparative experience of Irish law might prove instructive. The right to fair procedures has been recognized by the Irish courts as being constitutionally protected, despite its not being specifically enumerated in the fundamental rights provisions of the Constitution. Moreover, the courts have held that the obligation to respect constitutional rights is not confined to public bodies – constitutional rights can be asserted in private law. Here the requirement to observe fair procedures has, where relevant, been implied into contracts.[29] While the courts have yet to rule definitively on the issue, the better view is that for a waiver of a constitutional right to be effective it must be done with 'clear knowledge'.[30] At the very least this would have to be brought to the attention of the person who is said to have waived his or her right and it is probable that attempts to secure the waiver of rights in standard form contracts or similar documents would be resisted by the courts.

Conclusion

It is now unlikely that disciplinary codes would be drafted in draconian terms that are designed to deny athletes the basic tenets of justice and, in any event, such efforts are liable to receive a hostile judicial reception. Thus, the question of waiver is unlikely to arise and instead the relevant issue concerns the extent to which disciplinary standards in sport should approximate those of a court. The continuing transformation towards a more legalistic regime is driven by a combination of the internal amendment of disciplinary codes and by external judicial and arbitral scrutiny. The contention in this chapter is not that legalism ought to dominate sports discipline for its own sake. Indeed, a judicial attitude of non-interventionism that facilitates and encourages flexibility and informality is consistent with the general tenor of natural justice and the rule of law. At the same time, where vital interests such as livelihood, property and reputation are involved, the requirements of justice are more demanding and call for more definite substantive and procedural protection. This is especially the case where prominent athletes are concerned whose cases are attended by extensive media interest and publicity and where the temptation to act according to the moral precepts of the boulevard press is likely to be felt most strongly. Moreover, as the disciplinary jurisdiction of sports expands, matters that might otherwise have been dealt with by the criminal or civil law are likely to be resolved domestically. This pertains to conduct that occurs in the course of the sport – for example, violent play, doping, irregular payments – and to that that hitherto was considered to be beyond the scope of the sport, such as matters of lifestyle and private conduct. Where sports discipline applies to serious misconduct and involves potentially onerous consequences, a legalistic regime informed by the fundamental dictates of justice is necessary and desirable.

NOTES

1. [1971] 1 Ch.591 at 605.
2. See *Wilander* v. *Tobin*, *The Times*, 8 April 1996 (CA, 26 March 1996) *per* Neill LJ: ' ... it is important that, in the case of international bodies of the standing of the [International Tennis Federation] who are responsible for major international sports, the rules which govern their affairs should be most carefully drafted so that the possibility of confusion and doubt is removed ... it is therefore incumbent on those responsible to make sure that the rules are absolutely clear, and drafted so that the possibility of confusion is avoided.' The Rugby Football Union amended its disciplinary procedures in the light of the decision in *Jones* v. *Welsh Rugby Union*, *The Times*, 6 March 1997 (QBD, 27 Feb. 1997), *The Times*, 6 Jan. 1998 (CA, 19 Dec. 1997).
3. E.g., *Fisher* v. *National Greyhound Racing Club* unreported, CA, 31 July 1985 *per* Purchas LJ; *Heatons Transport* v. *Transport and General Workers Union* [1973] AC 15 at 100–1 *per* Lord Wilberforce; see also M. Beloff, T. Kerr and M. Demetriou, *Sports Law*, Oxford, 1999, 31.
4. E.g., *Enderby Town Football Club Ltd* v. *Football Association Ltd* [1971] 1 Ch 591 at 606 *per* Lord Denning; also *Bonsor* v. *Musicians' Union* [1954] Ch 479 at 485; *McCord* v. *Electricity Supply Board* [1980] ILRM 153 at 161.
5. Beloff *et al.*, 2.
6. See, e.g., D. Sisson and B. Trexell, 'The National Football League's Substance Abuse Policy: Is Further Conflict between Players and Management Inevitable?', 1 *Marq.*

Sports LJ (1991), 1; E. Rippey, 'Contractual Freedom over Substance-related Issues in Major League Baseball' 1 *Sports Lawyers Journal* (1994), 143.

7. See *Molinas* v. *National Basketball Association* (1961) 190 F. Supp. 241, in which a lifetime suspension for betting was upheld. A number of prominent baseball personalities have been banned for their association with gambling including Willie Mays and Mickey Mantel, who had taken public relations positions with casinos after retirement (both were reinstated in 1985), and Pete Rose who had bet on baseball games, including some involving his own team, the Cincinnati Reds; Rose has not been reinstated with the result that, *inter alia*, he cannot be admitted to Baseball's Hall of Fame; this ruling was challenged in *Rose* v. *Giametti* (1989) 721 F. Supp. 906, but Rose eventually withdrew the action and accepted the Commissioner's jurisdiction and penalty; see generally T. Ostertag, 'From Shoeless Joe to Charley Hustle: Major League Baseball's Continuing Crusade against Sports Gambling', 2 *Seton Hall J. of Sport Law* (1992), 19.

8. See 'Out of Bounds: Professional Sports Leagues and Domestic Violence', 109 *Harv. L. Rev.* (1996), 1048; for a more journalistic account see J. Benedict, *Public Heroes, Private Felons*, Boston, MA, 1997.

9. [1988] IR 83 at 87–8 (emphasis added).

10. See also *Wright* v. *The Jockey Club* QBD, unreported, 15 May 1995; *Cowley* v. *Heatley, The Times*, 24 July 1986 (CD, 22 July 1986). The question of stigma was alluded to in *McInnes* v. *Onslow-Fane* [1978] 3 All ER 211 at 223, where Megarry VC noted that 'this is not a case in which there has been any suggestion of the board considering any alleged dishonesty or morally culpable conduct of the plaintiff ... the refusal of the plaintiff's application by no means necessarily puts any slur on his character ...'

11. [1988] IR 724.

12. Ibid., at 730–1 (emphasis added).

13. See also *Clancy* v. *Irish Rugby Football Union* [1995] 1 ILRM 193, stating that the plaintiff and his advisers were entitled to present his case (to transfer from one rugby club to another) verbally to the defendants.

14. See Bitel, 'Disciplinary Procedures from the Point of View of the Individual', 3 *Sport and the Law Journal* (1995), no.3, 7 at 8.

15. See M. Reeb (ed.), *Digest of CAS Awards 1986–1998*, Berne, 1998.

16. See, e.g., IAAF Rule 59.5, which states that 'the IAAF or the [national federation] (as the case may be) shall have the burden of proving, *beyond reasonable doubt*, that a doping offence has been committed' (emphasis added).

17. *The Times*, 8 April 1996 (CA 26 March 1996).

18. *Gasser* v. *Stinson* QBD, unreported, 15 June 1988; *Wilander* v. *Tobin, The Times*, 8 April 1996 (CA 26 March 1996).

19. See Beloff *et al.*, 208–10.

20. *Student A and Student B* v. *A Secondary School* Irish Times Law Report, 31 Jan. 2000, is an interesting example of the judicial resistance to mandatory sanctions; while generally deferring to the defendant school's authority on the matter, the Irish High Court construed its 'zero tolerance' drug policy which provided for automatic expulsion as stipulating a disposal option rather than mandating the school authorities; a student who acknowledged his or her guilt would still be entitled to make representations on the question of penalty.

21. This would appear to be the practice adopted by, *inter alia*, the Football Association; see Parker, 'Disciplinary Proceedings from the Governing Body Point of View', 3 *Sport and the Law Journal* (1995), no.3, 3 at 6.

22. [1988] IR 83 at 87.

23. American authority, however, suggests that even in the case of a suspension pending a full disciplinary hearing (a 'holding operation') there is, in general, an obligation to afford the athlete a fair and meaningful hearing; see *Harding* v. *United States Figure*

Skating Association (1994) 851 F. Supp. 1476; *Lindemann* v. *American Horse Shows Association Inc.* (1994) 624 NYS 2d 723.

24. Beloff *et al.*, 194; M. Beloff, 'Pitch, Pool, Rink, ... Court? Judicial Review in the Sporting World' [1989] PL 95; see also S. Gardiner *et al.*, *Sports Law*, London, 1998, 240–1.

25. See, e.g., *Baker* v. *Jones* [1954] 2 All ER 553; *Law* v. *National Greyhound Racing Association* [1983] 1 WLR 1302; *R.* v. *Disciplinary Committee of the Jockey Club, ex parte Aga Khan* [1993] 1 WLR 909; *Wilander* v. *Tobin, The Times*, 8 April 1996 (CA, 26 March 1996); *Jones* v. *Welsh Rugby Union, The Times*, 6 Jan. 1998 (CA, 19 Dec. 1997); *Murphy* v. *Turf Club* [1989] IR 171; *Bolger* v. *Osborne* [2000] 1 ILRM 250. Similar views have been expressed by Australian courts: see *Beale* v. *South Australian Trotting League* [1963] SASR 209; *Trivett* v. *Nivison* [1976] 1 NSWLR 312; *Stolley* v. *Greyhound Racing Control Board* (1972) 128 CLR 509.

26. See, e.g., *Calvin* v. *Carr* [1980] AC 574; *Gasser* v. *Stinson*, QBD, unreported, 15 June 1988.

27. See *Modahl* v. *British Athletic Federation*, QBD, unreported 28 June 1996, CA unreported 28 July 1997, equating public law and private law standards in this regard; also *Cowley* v. *Heatley, The Times*, 24 July 1986 (CD, 22 July 1986) referring to the *Wednesbury* principles in private law proceedings; and *Stininato* v. *Auckland Boxing Association Inc.* [1978] 1 NZLR 1. Nevertheless, the differences between public law and private law proceedings in relation to form of proceedings, remedy, *locus standi* and limitation period should be noted.

28. *Gasser* v. *Stinson*, QBD, unreported, 15 June 1988; *Wilander* v. *Tobin, The Times*, 8 April 1996 (CA, 26 March 1996).

29. See *Becton Dickenson Ltd* v. *Lee* [1973] IR 1; *Meskell v CIE* [1973] IR 121; *Glover* v. *BLN Ltd* [1973] IR 388.

30. See *Murphy* v. *Stewart* [1973] IR 97. See generally J.M. Kelly, *The Irish Constitution*, 3rd edn, ed. Hogan and Whyte, Dublin, 1994, 687–9. J.C. Casey, *Constitutional Law in Ireland*, 2nd edn, London, 1992, 529, considered it arguable that in some cases a contract of employment might impliedly constitute a waiver of a particular right; e.g., in relation to *Flynn* v. *Power* [1985] ILRM 336 he suggested that a teacher in a Roman Catholic school might be held to waive her right to privacy to the extent that she could be dismissed on the basis of her adopting a lifestyle which conflicted with the school's ethos.

8

The Ties that Bind: Charting Contemporary Sporting Contractual Relations

Steve Greenfield

A few days after my seventeenth birthday I became a bondsman, a serf, a slave. And, more than willingly. Because I was below the then age of consent my widowed mother also had to sign the form that made me a professional footballer with Dundee.[1]

Introduction

The theoretical law of contract often fits uneasily into the relationship of employer and employee. Classical contract theory, particularly with respect to the idea of a free negotiation of the terms of the agreement, seems largely inapplicable when the bargaining power of the parties is often markedly unequal. A key feature of British industrial relations for a large part of the twentieth century was the doctrine of collective *laissez-faire* and the absence of significant legislative regulation of contracts of employment. Common law actions remained, but without any of the contemporary legislative protection such as the redundancy and unfair dismissal provisions. The reliance on trade unions to provide bargaining weight against employers provided the collective dimension to negotiations across numerous industries and workplaces. Professional sportsmen, indeed, entertainers more generally, have an additional dimension to their contractual position, a relationship with a paying public and a vocation that the spectators may view enviously. Those that pay to watch may have a vicarious relationship with those 'privileged' enough to play for the club.[2] An often heard complaint about players who are not performing to the right level is that they are 'not fit to wear the shirt', the donning of the club's colours is seen as a privilege denied to the fan through lack of ability or opportunity. This public dimension to this extraordinary employment relationship will often focus on the terms and conditions enjoyed by the players. Not only are the spectators drawn into discussions over a private contractual matter of the player's terms of employment, but newspapers and other media maintain a constant speculative approach towards such contracts. The speculation applies not just to wage levels at times of (re)negotiation, but also whether contracts will be completed, for instance, whether a player will be transferred. This trend of reporting has developed apace as the cost of wages has risen, although given that hard details of such terms are inevitably scarce the media-contrived figures ought to be treated with some scepticism.[3] The spiral of higher wages has led to continuous allegations that player-power dominates the higher levels of the games. This term, 'player power', is often used in a pejorative fashion to indicate that the balance of power has somehow shifted in a way that is contrary to the interests of the game as a whole. The reaction of the cricket authorities, and indeed parts of the media, to the development of World Series Cricket in the late 1970s often shared this perspective. It seemed as if players were to blame for seeking to improve their living standards and consequently betraying the traditions of the sport, whatever these might be.

Much of the blame for the ills in the contemporary game of association football is laid at the feet of Jean-Marc Bosman, who, through his action in the European Court, seems to be held entirely responsible for any number of problems.[4] For example, the amount of income that top sportsmen can earn is one contractual issue that is often highlighted and is closely connected with the freedom of a player to transfer at the end of his existing contractual commitments, which is a consequence of the *Bosman* decision. This 'right to move' at the end of the contractual period, without any transfer fee, is a relatively recent phenomenon and not many governing bodies have embraced 'free' movement with much relish. Indeed, it has taken a number of landmark legal decisions to move to a situation where non-contracted players enjoy the right to find a new employer without financial penalty to the new employer. In both the *Eastham* and the *Bosman* case the authorities stressed the need to maintain the status quo of restrictive contractual regimes in order to preserve the game.[5] This extremely conservative (re)action is not borne out by subsequent events and the game is able to adapt and develop within a new climate.

Legal cases are, of course, only one part of the equation and much that has happened to alter the position of professional players has been through more traditional industrial-relations methods. Particularly in the area of professional football, the role and function of the Professional Footballers' Association (PFA) have been crucial in developing a new contractual regime.[6] The PFA has a history dating back to the early part of the twentieth century and has been forceful in both negotiations and also in supporting the legal challenges.[7] This has been less important in the other major English team sports, such as cricket and rugby union, whose players unions have proved far less influential. Both organizations have a limited history both in terms of their creation and of effective negotiation. The Professional Cricketers' Association was formed only in 1967, described by Marqusee as the point when 'trade unionism made its belated entry into commercial cricket'.[8] It has had to deal with two particularly controversial issues that have divided the membership. First, the question of South Africa and player involvement in rebel tours and, secondly, the Packer affair which bitterly split cricket from top to bottom.[9] Rugby union players have been fully professional only since 1995 and a players' association has developed alongside this switch.

What is clear is that in a relatively short period the contractual position and status of leading players within some sports has altered radically. While acknowledging the role of collective action, particularly with respect to the case of professional football, the question that dominates this chapter is what role the law has played in this transformation. It also seeks to explore whether traditional contractual principles are now appropriate within this relationship that buys and sells sporting talent. A logical starting point is the initial change from the recreational to the professional game.

Towards Professionalism

The shift away from amateurism towards professional sport took place at different times in particular sports. There was always the question of the extent to which payments were being received, by players, and ignored by the relevant authorities. The more widespread this degree of 'shamateurism' exists the harder it is to confront it and rugby union provides a most pertinent example of this. Mason cites rowing as an early example of where a distinction was drawn between those who were strictly amateurs and those who were not.[10] Bound up with the question of payment for playing are a number of issues such as class, geography and economic change, and not all factors are relevant to the same degree in all sports.[11]

Within association football professionalism emerged in the northern clubs which imported skilful Scottish players and were an alternative power base to the previously dominant southern-based sides. It was this latter group that had formed the Football Association in 1863 to provide a body to administer the game and standardize rules.[12] As the number of spectators began to increase, more money became available to the clubs which looked to recruit the best players from wherever they could. In 1879 Darwen, with two Scottish players in the ranks, reached the quarter-finals of the FA Cup before finally losing to the Old Etonians.[13] The movement of players between clubs inevitably fuelled suspicions that the strict amateur rules were being ignored. The authorities overlooked such breaches, as Young has observed, 'as this transition took place polite eyes were averted'.[14] Attempting to stem the tide towards full professionalism both the FA, in 1882, and the nascent county associations altered their rules to outlaw payments.[15] There were examples of clubs expelled from both the FA and the Cup competition.[16] However, pressure for change built up, mainly through the northern clubs, and eventually in 1885 a degree of professionalism was legitimized in England. This overt acceptance of professional players could only encourage their spread. This led to the need for organized matches to generate income through gate money and the formation of the Football League in 1888. Although there had been some indignant reaction, notably from Sheffield and Scotland, to the sacrifice of pure amateurism, within 25 years of the formation of the FA the question was largely settled and a league with professional players in place.[17]

As the matter was being settled within association football, it was causing problems within rugby football. A major problem would be that players, certainly in Lancashire, could switch to play association football for clubs which could legitimately pay them. Collins attributes the question of payments becoming a live issue to the increasing participation of the working class as both players and spectators:

> Consequently as working-class men took up the rugby game, they brought with them a range of cultural practices which were based on the necessity of selling their labour power in whichever way was the most lucrative, including the utilisation of sporting prowess. 'Spoort's gooid lads, but brass is better', was how a dialect story of the time summed up this attitude. A greater clash with the ideals of public school sport could not be imagined, especially for those who sought to utilise football as a medium for moral improvement. The centrality of the cash nexus in working-class sport also gave rise to the apparently paradoxical situation of working-class players supporting the operation of market forces in rugby and capitalist mill owners opposing them.[18]

The pressure for payment for 'broken time' and the attempts by the middle classes to retain control of the game led to the schism in 1895 and the eventual emergence of two differently constituted codes.

Cricket provides a fascinating example of the gulf between the unpaid and the paid, the gentlemen and the players, and was a long-running sore within the game. There was an open acknowledgement of payment, hence the different descriptions, so cricket did not experience the same problem as football in coming to terms with payment. The history of the game is bound up with the use of paid players. The formal distinction between the two groups was ended only in 1962 and had been a distinction that had considerable significance. The two groups could have separate changing rooms and gates to enter the field, as well as being described differently on the score cards. John Snow, who went on to become one of England's premier fast bowlers, tells how, at the start of his career in 1961 with Sussex, he was not allowed to change with the professional players but given a spot in the amateurs' changing room. He assigns this attitude of the professional players to 'reverse snobbery, if you like. Getting their own back Silly?

Perhaps, but understandable on the part of the older players who had suffered under the feudal system that existed in earlier years.'[19] Professionalism has a long history within cricket, with servants being employed to play for their patrons in games which were designed essentially for gambling. Brookes draws out the distinction between the retained and the independent paid players.[20] The former being those who had other occupations for their patron. The other group, of independent players, were able to ply their (cricketing) trade for whichever team was prepared to pay for them. The structure, and indeed the nature of the game at the time, with the emphasis on paid players employed on an *ad hoc* basis for patrons encouraged the formation of travelling professional sides. For example, William Clarke developed the All-England XI whose avowed aim was not only to spread the game but essentially to exploit the commercial opportunities that such games provided.

It is clear that the move towards professionalism in all the sports discussed here was intimately linked, not only to the history of the sport, but most importantly to the changing social and economic conditions. Changes in the type of work, working patterns and increased opportunities to travel allowed sport to develop as a commercial enterprise out of local origins. Professionalism would not have been economically possible, other than through the type of patronage that existed within cricket, without the commercial opportunities that the new era of sport brought with it. However, the concessions over payments could also bring restrictive contractual regimes both in terms of movement and income.[21]

Restraint of Trade and Contractual Freedom

In both cricket and football a strict contractual regime for the professional players developed based firmly on the principle of wage control. The Football League adopted the maximum wage principle in 1910–11 and restricted freedom of movement. Wages could be curbed because the movement of players between clubs was so limited, thus preventing a free market arising. Without a free market in wages it was left to the individual and the collective bargaining process to improve terms and conditions. However, this is more difficult when employers are also organized in a collective group. This renders the fundamental principles of contract law even more obsolete. The law is rooted within the historical period of *laissez-faire* economics with the emphasis firmly fixed upon the individual. Consequently the collective dimension is difficult to incorporate within this individualistic legal framework. This has caused problems where terms from collective agreements need to be incorporated into an individual contract in order for the term to be enforceable. Courts have taken a view that a trade union does not act as an agent for the member in the negotiation, *Burton Group Limited* v. *Smith* [1977] IRLR 351, so terms cannot be incorporated this way. An alternative approach, in the absence of an express incorporation, is to use the mechanism of implication to give the term effect.[22] The other key feature of contractual theory that has significant impact is the concept of the sanctity of agreements that have the correct form. What has assisted sportsmen and other entertainers has been the development and subsequent application of the doctrine of restraint of trade which has been used to deal with the issue of contractual enforceability. The legitimacy of restricting free trade came to be recognized within two distinct areas, competition by ex-employees and the sale of businesses, and for partial rather than general restraints.[23] The case of *Nordenfelt* extended the principle to permissible general restraints, but it is the case of *Esso* that is credited with broadening the approach of the courts, as Lord Reid observed, 'It is much too late now to say that this rather anomalous doctrine of restraint of trade can be confined to the two classes of case to which it was originally applied. But the cases outside these two classes afford little guidance as to the circumstances in which it should be applied.'[24] It has been this apparent judicial blessing to apply the doctrine more broadly that has assisted a number of sportsmen to free themselves from rigid contractual or administrative regulation. The first example of this involved the international footballer George Eastham.

Association Football

Eastham was not the first challenge to the contractual regime that bound professional footballers, there had been the earlier cases of *Kingaby* and *Banks*.[25] According to Harding, the Players' Union was actively seeking a case, involving the transfer system, to bring to court and picked Kingaby after selecting a short list. Harding outlines the background to the case and, in particular, the apparently strained relationship between the Union and the player. He attributes the failure of the case to the tactics adopted by counsel for Kingaby:

> In court, Mr Rawlinson, KC, acting for Kingaby, immediately made what was to be a fundamental error. He set out to attack Aston Villa's *motives* in setting a prohibitive fee on Kingaby's head, rather than attacking the transfer system itself.
>   The subsequent debate, therefore, took for granted the 'legality' of the system. Rawlinson made no attempt to prove that it was an unreasonable restraint of trade. Rather, he claimed that Aston Villa had acted 'maliciously' when using it.[26]

The court held that the plaintiff had no cause of action even if the fee charged was excessive, because it was within the terms of the employment. It would seem that a chance had been lost and it would be a further 40 years before the Union would be able to launch the next challenge. Guthrie indicates that in the late 1950s the PFA was looking for a dispute between player and club to adopt to challenge the retain and transfer system.[27] The *Banks* case, which involved a possession claim and consequent counterclaim over the retain and transfer system, had been heard in the Aldershot County Court, with the possession order being granted.[28] The Union was actively pursuing an appeal when Banks was given a free transfer.[29] The background to the Eastham dispute was a longstanding quarrel between the League and the PFA over terms and conditions. At issue were the major bones of contention, the retain and transfer system and the maximum wage, while there were also claims over items such as the raising of wage levels and fees for televised matches. After three players' meetings to discuss the failure of negotiations, the PFA was instructed to negotiate on four points:

- A drastic alteration of the present form of contract with its restrictions and injustices.
- A situation leading to a successful negotiation for a minimum wage with the abolition of the maximum.
- A player's right to a percentage of transfer fees.
- The setting up of a joint committee of the League and the PFA with the FA, if thought necessary, to deal with problems of transfers and other disputes.[30]

The dispute between the employers and the PFA led to the brink of strike action. Following mass meetings of the players, a strike notice was issued. It then seemed that an agreement had been reached though the League Clubs rejected the deal that had been agreed by its Management Committee.[31] The final offer of the League was rejected by the Union and Harding neatly sums up the outcome: 'Thus it had taken a year of meetings, arguments and brinkmanship, not to mention the expenditure of valuable nervous energy on the part of Cliff Lloyd, George Davies, Jimmy Hill and the ageing Joe Richards to return – almost – to square one.' The agreement had led to the removal of the maximum wage which clearly diluted the desire of the leading players to maintain the fight against the retain and transfer system. The challenge to the system was to be launched, not through negotiation and further threats of industrial action, but by legal action.

The retain and transfer system combined to provide a strict contractual regime without any long-term security for the players. Contracts ran annually, ending on 30 June and the club had to decide, between 1 May and the first Saturday in June, whether it wished to offer the player a new contract. This inevitably provided an incentive for players to make it clear to the club, through their performance, that they were worthy of a new deal. The club had to offer at least the minimum annual wage of £418.00. If the club wished to retain a player it would inform the League and the Association accordingly. A player would be placed either on the retained list, those players that the club wished to keep, or the transfer list, those players that the club was willing to sell. If a player was unhappy with either the terms on which the club wished to retain him or the fee that the club was asking for him there was a right of appeal to the League's Management Committee. If a player did not wish to re-sign he was still bound to the club unless it agreed to transfer him. It was the failure to allow him the transfer that he wanted and the retention of his services by Newcastle that led Eastham to challenge the entire retain and transfer system.

Eastham had joined Newcastle United from the Ards club in Northern Ireland in 1956 and signed annual contracts, the last one in 1959/60. Eastham wished to transfer to a club in the south of England but his request was refused by Newcastle. Eastham sought to use the appeal procedures but when this did not produce the required response he started his legal action. He was fully supported by the PFA who were looking for such an opportunity and he continued with the action even when the transfer he had sought was eventually granted. The club had presumably hoped that once the transfer, to Arsenal for a fee of £47,500, was permitted, he would drop the action, as had happened with Ralph Banks, who was granted a free transfer by Aldershot.

Wilberforce J criticized the combined operation of both the retain and the transfer system. As he pointed out, clubs would retain players who they were actually willing to transfer, and should therefore be on the transfer list, in order to prevent the player getting the fee reduced or a free transfer on appeal.[32] A player who did not wish to continue with his previous club was not able freely to join another; should he be retained his only hope was that the club would transfer him. Clearly the rules affected the ability of a player who was out of contract to find new employment and operated in restraint of trade. Given this finding, the question moved on to whether such restraints could be justified. Wilberforce was more concerned with the retention system and thought that a transfer system without the retention system or a modified retention system was 'another matter'. Indeed, he thought that the transfer system 'might be said to be in the interests of the players themselves'.[33] It is perhaps this observation that contributed to the maintenance of the post-contract transfer system until *Bosman*.

This point, that Eastham had already got the transfer he had sought, was a potentially awkward one for the Union and drew comparisons with the *Banks* case. The defendants argued that the court had no jurisdiction to grant a declaration, given that the matter had been settled and that in any event he could not obtain this remedy against the Football Association and the Football League. Wilberforce J conceded that this latter point was without 'decisive authority'. Wilberforce J was prepared to exercise judicial discretion to grant a declaration against Newcastle United, but also, considering the restrictions imposed by the governing bodies, went further and declared 'that the rules of the Association and the regulations of the League relating to retention and transfer of players of professional football, including the plaintiff, are not binding on the plaintiff and are in unreasonable restraint of trade and *ultra vires*' (*Eastham* at 160).

The *Eastham* case was heard before the expansion of restraint of trade, introduced by *Esso*, and so the issue was treated, by Wilberforce, as an example of post-contractual restraint on ex-employees. The defendants had argued that the retention system was merely a series of options and relied on dicta in *Warner Bros* v. *Nelson*, that such terms were not required to be justified.[34] Fortunately for Eastham, the retention rules required him to re-sign in order to be paid and so there was no automatic continuation of the relationship. If this had been a contractual option exercised at the behest of the employers, then, given the then conditions surrounding restraint of trade, it is likely that Wilberforce J would have considered these to be a restraint within a contract and therefore outside any challenge. The post-*Esso* expansion has now seen the development of challenges to existing contracts.[35]

The question was how the football industry would adapt to encompass the *Eastham* decision. Clearly the retention system could not survive, but what would be put in its place? This provided the PFA with an awkward dilemma: should it step up its action and try to push for much greater freedom of players on the back of the *Eastham* decision or attempt to negotiate a new compromise with a hostile Football League? Guthrie argues that the PFA missed a golden opportunity: 'With the goal wide open and the opposing defence in ruins, the Professional Footballers Association put the ball wide.'[36] Harding's view is rather more benevolent and points out that the PFA was not a strong trade union but with a limited number of members it had only a limited income. Additionally the lifting of the maximum wage provisions and the subsequent increase in wages for the best players had removed the common denominator that had existed. This explains the conciliatory approach adopted by the PFA. The main change was the introduction of an independent tribunal which was a stage beyond the appeal to the League Management Committee. This system, plus amendments to the options granted to the club, did provide a freer regime.

The Chester Report, as part of its wider brief, examined the nature and form of the contractual relationships within professional football.[37] It concluded that the changes post-*Eastham* had led to some significant differences, particularly the number of free transfers being given, especially in the lower divisions.[38] The reason for this was that, if a fee was requested, until the transfer was made the club would have to continue to pay wages according to the existing contract. However, if a free transfer was granted, at the end of the contract wages would be paid only until the end of the contract on 30 June. A further factor at work was the abolition of the maximum wage which also contributed to a decline in the number of professional players. Chester was still rather scathing about the contractual changes after *Eastham*: 'a contract which is renewable indefinitely on a year to year basis at the option of one of the parties seems to us to go beyond the normal contractual relationship and to be more one-sided than the situation demands. In general we are against one-way options unless freely negotiated'.[39] Despite the recommendations of Chester and pressure from the PFA, negotiations to alter the transfer system and the basics of the contract were not fundamentally altered until the late 1970s. The final blow to post-contractual restraints was dealt by the *Bosman* case in 1995. A consequence of *Bosman* has been increased contractual security, with longer contracts being offered and renegotiations well before their end, for those players in demand, to avoid the situation where a valuable player can leave without payment. It has taken over 30 years since *Eastham* to develop a more balanced contractual regime for clubs and players, though a frequently heard complaint within the media is that this regime hands too much leverage to the leading group of players. It remains to be seen what will happen when transfer fees within contracts are abolished. Clearly, there will be less need for clubs to always offer such long contracts; at the moment the length is required to protect the player's transfer value. The absence of any fees may also reduce the money available to players by the clubs. At present clubs will be prepared to offer a free-transfer player payments that reflect the saving in any transfer fee that the club is not having to pay. If there are no fees, the distinction will be abolished and the free-transfer player will have no perceived advantage. However, the buying clubs will have more money to spend since it will not be paid on fees at all. The abolition of any fees might also have significant effects on those clubs which sell to survive. What is clear, from looking at the history of the development of professional footballers' contracts, is the pivotal role played by Wilberforce's judgment in *Eastham*. Harding outlines the inherent structural weaknesses within the PFA that limited its ability to make even more fundamental changes than it achieved, and in a sense it was *Eastham* that filled this power vacuum.

Cricket

Cricket's history and development shaped the contractual relationships that emerged as the game became fully professionalized. When the history of cricket is analysed what stands out is the quite extraordinarily dominant role and position of a private club, the Marylebone Cricket Club (MCC). The club was formed in 1787 and quickly became the dominant force, replacing Hambledon, which had been an early leader in the game. The MCC developed not only as the premier club but as the guardian of the laws of the game. It occupied a central role within the game's administration for nearly 200 years, and it was only changing political pressures that led to a diminution of its role.[40]

One of the major differences between the professional cricketers and the footballers was the absence, until 1968, of a professional representative body. Interestingly enough, when the PCA was formed it was welcomed by both the MCC and the employers; indeed, the MCC secretary addressed the first AGM in 1968.[41] This is no doubt a reflection on the conservative nature of the body which was also, during its formative years, receiving funding from the Test and County Cricket Board (TCCB), the employers.[42] This situation of an employer financing the employees' body would very likely debar the 'union' from obtaining a Certificate of Independence from the Certification Officer.[43] One of the first steps taken by the PCA was to provide accident and illness insurance for members, though it has proved more difficult to raise wages to levels comparable with those of other sports. Even in 1995 the newly appointed general secretary David Graveney indicated the nature of the problem: 'An uncapped player earns between £5,500 and £8,500 depending on age; while for a capped player the minimum wage is £14,500. I am embarrassed saying that.'[44] The conservative approach of the PCA, and ultimately of its members, was indicated by the response to the Packer affair in the late 1970s.[45]

The 'Packer affair' split the game of cricket. Some opponents of Kerry Packer's attempts to create an alternative to the official game drew apocalyptic visions of the outcome. It seemed that the national game was under threat and, what was worse, from an Australian with assistance from the English captain at the time, who was a South African! The background to the issue was Packer's hope of obtaining broadcasting rights from the Australian Cricket Board for his own television channel. When the ACB indicated that it was going to sign a contract with the Australian Broadcasting Commission, Packer developed an alternative series of matches under the umbrella title of World Series Cricket (WSC). In a short space of time a rival game to that organized by the established governing bodies was set up. Given that the starting point was no players, grounds nor infrastructure, this was an extraordinary achievement. The key point was the recruitment of players. In order to have a spectacle suitable for television WSC needed to have the best players in the world, otherwise 'official' cricket would clearly be more attractive. Initially 35 players were signed up, 18 Australians and 17 overseas players.[46] Packer was seemingly able to recruit with ease and, as he pointed out, cricket was 'the easiest sport in the world to take over. Nobody bothered to pay the players what they were worth'.[47] The first response of the English authorities was to sack the England captain Tony Greig, who had been a leading figure in recruiting to WSC. The International Cricket Conference (ICC) took action in July which would have led to the banning of players who played in any of the rival matches; 1 October was set as the cut-off date in order, no doubt, to give players the opportunity to reconsider their position.[48] The TCCB had already taken a similar stance at its meeting in July, but made any action dependent on the ICC's position. The cumulative effect of the action by the ICC and the TCCB was a ban from both county and test cricket, effectively preventing the players from earning a living from 'official cricket'. The proposed ban from county cricket was for a two-year period from the date of the last 'disapproved' match played in. Packer and three of the players sought injunctions preventing the authorities from banning them; these were refused by the judge since the TCCB had given an undertaking that no players would be banned until the outcome of the trial.[49] In addition to the action of the players, WSC sought injunctions restraining the authorities from inducing breaches of the players' contracts with WSC. The case, *Greig and Others* v. *Insole and Others* was heard between September and early November 1977.[50]

The Packer affair divided the cricket world and provoked outraged reactions by establishment figures. The editorial director of *The Cricketer* E.W. Swanton, in an article during the height of the crisis, concluded passionately:

> Throughout cricket history the hour has generally found the man, and the game has always proved stronger than the individual. That cricket has suffered, and will continue to suffer, grave damage brooks no argument. But it is still possible to believe that out of evil good may come, that from the winter of our discontent may yet come a glorious summer.[51]

Not all commentators were as hostile to Packer's concept and some other countries adopted a more relaxed attitude.[52] What was clear was the importance of the court action to determine the ability of the governing bodies to exert such strict control over the game. As Slade J observed at the outset, 'these issues have already produced an acute division of opinion throughout the cricketing world and may perhaps continue to be debated so long as the game is played'.[53] Slade J was also surprised, given the organization of international cricket and the rewards earned by the players, that a rival promoter had not previously emerged.

The essential question that Slade J had to determine was the validity of the ban imposed by the ICC and that proposed by the TCCB, and though this was a seemingly straightforward restraint of trade issue, it was clouded by a number of other points.[54] At the heart of the restraint question was the financial structure of international and county cricket and the consequent threat to the game posed by WSC. Professional cricket is in many ways a distinctly odd phenomenon: anyone who has had the pleasure of attending a run-of-the-mill county match will be struck by the absence of spectators. Even at the large test match grounds there will often not be any significant crowd. Local derbies will attract larger crowds, but it is the one-day game which has generated spectator interest. Professional domestic cricket is, as one of the witnesses in *Greig* observed, 'basically a player's sport'. The absence of significant spectator income at this level of the game means that the counties largely depend on the income generated from test matches to survive. Test match cricket, particularly with the advent of one-day internationals, is a profitable business; Slade J pointed out that the 1977 Australian tour of England would realize a net profit of almost £1m. If the ICC could demonstrate that WSC threatened the finances of the international game, the action to protect it could be lawful.[55] The nature of county cricket also meant that professional cricketers were relatively, to other sportsmen, poorly paid.[56]

Slade J drew on Wilberforce's judgment in *Eastham* to deal with several pertinent points. First, for the plaintiffs there was the question of *locus standi* given the absence of any contractual relationship in this case with either the TCCB or the ICC, which Wilberforce had determined in Eastham's favour. Secondly, there was the notion that the governing bodies of sport, the Football League and the Football Association in *Eastham*, had legitimate interests, as 'custodians of the public interest', that they were entitled to take reasonable steps to protect. The problem for the authorities was that, when the position was subject to rigorous analysis, it was only the Australian Cricket Board whose finances faced a significant threat from WSC. This was largely because of the number of Australian players who had signed up to WSC and that Australia was the base for WSC 'super tests'. There were also possible longer-term threats to both Australia and other countries if WSC expanded and developed into a more direct competitor by scheduling matches against official games or if new private promoters emerged. Slade J argued that, given the nature and extent of the threats, a far more limited prospective ban would have been easier to justify. As it was, Slade J found it 'impossible to see how resolutions in this extended and wider form can be adequately justified on any rational and objective grounds'.[57] As the custodians of the public interest in the game, the authorities also had to consider the effect on the public of the proposed bans, given that this was the interest that they sought to protect. Slade J observed that the bans would result in 'the certain detriment to the world public interested in cricket'. It had been accepted that, if the ICC ban amounted to an unlawful restraint of trade, then the TCCB proposal would similarly fall. The success of both the players and WSC against the TCCB and the ICC led to two seasons of competition between WSC and official test matches. Eventually an agreement was reached between the ACB and Packer: 'A 10-year agreement has been signed by Mr Kerry Packer and the Australian Cricket Board ... Packer will cease to promote his own matches and will pay off the 68 players under contract to him.'[58]

The post-Packer landscape of international cricket is very different from the one he parachuted into in 1977. Many of the innovative features that appeared in WSC have now been accepted into the official game. The camera techniques and marketing of the game have followed the leads provided by WSC and the game has been dragged from its conservative past. The most important result has been the furtherance of the one-day format, which has many more commercial advantages and now dominates the schedule of international tours. However, professional cricketers in England are still restricted in their ability to change employers and find a new county club freely.

The ECB, which is the successor to the TCCB, operates a fairly strict regime. Counties may register a maximum of only 30 cricketers and only one of these may be an unqualified player. This latter category is a non-EU national, effectively the overseas stars from the test-playing nations.[59] Players may be registered for only one county at a time and not move during the course of the season;[60] this provision prevents transfers occurring mid season. At the end of the summer, before 30 September, each county must provide a list of players who have a contract for the forthcoming season or whose contracts have expired and have been offered a new one. In essence, this List I contains the players the county wishes to contract for the forthcoming season. The second list, List II, is of the other cricketers who were contracted or registered by the county. A player who refuses the offer of a contract should not be placed on List I unless a new offer has been made to him before the lists are sent to the ECB. Once the ECB has the lists it may move a player from one list to another or remove him completely. Counties are forbidden from signing players on List I without the authority of the ECB:

> The ECB will not register that Cricketer for the applicant County for at least 21 days after the receipt of such a notice and, in any event, will not, except in the most exceptional circumstances, register the Cricketer for the applicant County if the ECB is satisfied that the Cricketer has entered into a contract in writing to play for that other County for the whole or part of the next season.[61]

Contracted players cannot ordinarily be registered for another county by the ECB, though the question remains as to what amounts to 'exceptional circumstances'. Either the county or the player may make representations to the ECB and, if the new registration is granted, it is treated as an 'Extraordinary Registration'.[62] In deciding whether or not to grant an extraordinary registration the ECB will consider whether the offer of terms made to the cricketer was 'fair and reasonable'. Thus even contracted players may move between counties with ECB approval, but counties are limited in the number of such registrations that are permitted: 'Save in exceptional circumstances which, in the opinion of the ECB, are exceptional, no County shall be permitted to effect more than *two* Extraordinary Registrations in any period of twelve months or more than three Extraordinary Registrations in any period of five years.'[63]

In one sense, players do have freedom of movement after the end of any contractual period, but a player who is under contract has a limited right to request any move. More than this counties are unable to create a freer market in players owing to the restrictions on Extraordinary Registrations. The authorities have always sought to restrict the development of a transfer market in players and they have been assisted in this by the lack of funds within the county game. A greater degree of flexibility has begun to emerge, particularly with respect to younger players, though the sanctity of contracts in cricket is treated very differently in comparison with association football.

Professional Boxing

While sportsmen, particularly in contact sports, may at any stage develop a career threatening injury this is most obvious with full contact sports such as boxing. This uncertainty, coupled with the continual need to perform at the highest level and the discipline of a rigorous training regime, means that a professional boxer's career is likely to be short.[64] The dangers of boxing were gruesomely spelled out in *Watson* v. *BBBC*:

> The primary injury happens through a very familiar mechanism. The boxer's head jerks under the impact of the blow and the brain moves abruptly in its space within the skull, striking itself against the unyielding bone. The risk of secondary injury is that the veins passing through the dura are unable to accommodate the sudden stretching to which they are subjected and tear. The subdural haemorrhage follows from that tearing. This is the sequence which most often causes the death of a boxer, or, death apart, leaves him in a condition such as the claimant now exhibits.[65]

This chapter is not concerned with injury nor, indeed, the legality of such sports (see Chapter 3) but the on-going risk of a career-threatening injury means that the contractual arrangements must take account of this. Boxers need to maximize their limited opportunities and cannot afford to lose chances through poor contractual relationships. There is also the question of guidance and protection: a young inexperienced boxer may well need an experienced adviser to guide him through the minefield of professional boxing. One of the key points that has been raised in many entertainment cases has been the question of the sterilization of talent through contracts and this clearly has application in this profession.[66]

Professional boxing is organized and administered by the British Boxing Board of Control Ltd, originally as an unincorporated association since 1929, but as a limited company from 1989. It has an important licensing function for all participants in addition to its general administrative role.[67] The key relationships are those between boxer/manager and boxer/promoter. The BBBC provides standard form contracts to govern these relationships and the major problem that has faced the Board in this area has been the overlapping role of managers and promoters.[68] The important relationships have been examined through two influential cases; *Warren* v. *Mendy* and *Watson* v. *Prager*.[69]

The approved boxer/manager agreement is a relatively simple and straightforward one consisting of 17 clauses. There is an initial limitation that the manager must live within 50 miles of the boxer, unless he can persuade the BBBC that there is a suitable training regime in place. This is designed to ensure that the boxer receives the appropriate guidance and supervision which is part of the rationale for the agreement. The contract is an exclusive one on behalf of the boxer although the manager is free to act for other fighters. The manager has a number of obligations, the most important of which is to supervise and take all reasonable steps to preserve the health and safety of the boxer in his profession.[70] The manager is responsible for arranging a boxing programme and other suitable activities that extends, for instance, to media work, personal appearances and advertisements.[71] A major point is that if the boxer is not satisfied with the engagements arranged by the manager there is the right to refer the matter to the BBBC, and one potential remedy is the releasing of the boxer from the contract. The obligations of the boxer are essentially to keep himself in the 'best possible physical condition' and to fulfil the engagements arranged by the manager. Given the exclusive nature of the agreement, the boxer agrees not to arrange work within the compass of the manager. Given the extensive nature of the manager's scope, the last line of clause 3(iv) describing 'any other suitable activities whatsoever' will severely limit the rights of the boxer to arrange work independently.

The contract specifically recognizes the problem of the potential manager/promoter conflict. If a manager is intending to arrange an agreement for a boxer in which the manager is either the promoter or has some other interest or association with the promoter, the manager must inform the boxer by using a specific BBBC form (36A). This indicates to the boxer that at some stage of the contract – and the form lasts for the duration of the agreement – the manager intends to arrange events that may contain some conflict of interest with respect to the promotion. The manager can enter into such an engagement only unless and until:

1. The terms offered to the boxer are fair and reasonable and no less advantageous to the boxer than the terms (if any) which the boxer could reasonably have expected to obtain if the manager had been wholly independent of the relevant promoter or other persons.
2. A written copy of those terms has been provided to the boxer and they have been fully explained to him by the manager.
3. The boxer has been given a reasonable opportunity to consider those terms and to renegotiate them if he should so wish.
4. The boxer has accepted those terms or any renegotiated terms in writing.[72]

The crucial feature is the division of any television revenues that may be generated. Professional boxing is a sport that has encompassed the concept of pay-per-view and this may be a major source of income for the promoter. The concern is that this is an area where the potential conflict of interest could leave the boxer financially poorer. The standard promoter/manager agreement has a specific broadcasting income clause that keeps this money separate from other receipts:

> 10. In the event of an Agreement being entered into for the said contest to be broadcast or televised, whether BBC or any other person, film or corporation, either in Great Britain or elsewhere, the Promoter shall pay the Boxer 21¼ per cent of the fee or fees so received. In the event of the contest being filmed 21¼ per cent of the fee shall be paid to the Boxer, Fees in respect of Broadcast, Television or Film(s) shall be treated as being separate and apart from the purse money mentioned in Clause 9.[73]

Given that boxer/promoter contracts must generally be made by using the standard BBBC agreement this clause should be included. However, the boxer/manager contract envisages that clause 10 may be excluded, though it cannot be done so if there is the potential conflict of interest and the boxer has not been advised as required by the contract. In this case the boxer would be entitled to the benefit of clause 10 and this will be enforced by the Board.

The boxer/manager agreement has an initial period that cannot be longer than three years; there is though a provision to extend the contract in certain circumstances. If the boxer wins a title and there is less than two years of the initial period to run, the manager can serve a notice extending the contract by a maximum of 18 months from the point when the championship was won.[74] There is a provision for the boxer to object to any extension and the Board can determine whether the objection is reasonable.[75] The contract cannot be assigned and disputes have to be referred to arbitration within the BBBC's regulations.[76]

The form and content of the boxer/manager contract has been the subject of two cases that have provided significant legal scrutiny. It was the second of these, *Watson*, that considered the legality of the dual manager/promoter role in depth. At stake was the legal legitimacy of the boxer/manager agreement and whether it operated as an unreasonable restraint of trade. Scott J documented the history of dual licensing, as both promoters and managers, noting that it was only in the late 1950s, in response to the imposition of an entertainment tax, that the Board permitted an individual to hold both licences. In 1984, at the Board's AGM, dual licensing was again prohibited though this was then reversed at a special AGM later in the same year.[77] Following the decision in *Warren*, and specific comments by Nourse LJ, the Board altered its regulations to provide for a separation of the relationships. However, intervention from the Office of Fair Trading followed since there was concern that promotional opportunities would become limited and concentrated in only a few hands.[78] Accordingly the Board reverted to its original position that did not then address the comments made in *Warren*. The potential conflict of interest was most stark when the question of television income for bouts arose:

> The prescribed form of boxer–promoter agreement contains provision for the boxer to receive a percentage of television receipts. But this provision may be deleted from the agreement in a case where the purse is to be an all-in purse. In that case, the boxer will receive nothing extra on account of television receipts. The choice between the two alternatives would normally be expected to be a matter for negotiation between the boxer, acting by his manager, and the promoter. The manager would be expected to negotiate terms 'as advantageous as possible'. But where the manager and promoter is one and the same person, there can be no negotiation but simply a unilateral decision whereby the less the boxer receives, the more the manager–promoter will receive.[79]

It was this potential for a conflict of interest that was persuasive in Scott J determining that the contract was subject to the restraint of trade doctrine.

The defence had argued that the contract was one that regulated the normal commercial relations of professional boxing. Scott J thought that a contract that permitted such a conflict of interest was 'a very strange animal indeed'. It was capable of being enforced oppressively and therefore within the ambit of the doctrine.[80] The restrictions in the agreement were not, according to the judge, reasonable and therefore the contract was contrary to public policy and unenforceable.

There were two main issues arising out of *Watson,* the conflict of interest point and the ability of the manager to extend the agreement if the boxer won a relevant championship. At the time of *Watson,* the manager could extend the three-year initial period by a further three years from the end of the original period, and the judge suggested that an 18-months' extension would be more reasonable. Furthermore he thought that the conflict point might be lessened by allowing the boxer to reject the unilaterally determined terms and negotiate his own. The reaction of the BBBC has been to adapt its standard form agreements to take account of the decision. The permissible extension period is now reduced to 18 months, noted above, and the potential conflict problem is addressed by allowing the boxer to reject those terms negotiated when the manager is also the promoter.

However, there is still a serious problem with the form of the current arrangements. Permitting the removal of the television-income clause from the promoter/boxer agreement seems to be contrary to the Board's regulations which only permit deviance from the standard form contract for new contracts provided that the contract is not 'inconsistent with any provisions of these Rules and Regulations'. It would be strongly arguable that the removal of the requirement to pay a prescribed figure for television income is contrary to the rules of the BBBC. The whole point of the clause is to protect the boxer from a potential conflict of interest, and the removal of the protective clause leaves the boxer exposed. Indeed, the boxer/promoter contract specifically draws attention to the clause by the following notice at the bottom of the page: '*Note*: Promoters, Managers and Boxers should particularly note lines 4 and 5 of the first paragraph of Clause 10.'[81]

Lines 4 and 5 deal with the amount that a boxer should receive from broadcasting income. If it is so important that attention is drawn to it, its removal seems to be distinctly odd. The manager/boxer contract makes the position worse in that it requires that, where a conflict of interest exists, the manager must take the steps noted above to inform the boxer and allow him to renegotiate the terms. This latter point itself raises another pertinent one given that the agreement is an exclusive one and that there is no provision for the boxer to obtain independent advice on engagements within the purview of the manager. Clearly, if the manager does not provide the necessary information this amounts to a breach and, given the conflict of interest, a fundamental breach that would allow the boxer to terminate. Yet clause 6.3 sets out that, if the manager does not inform the boxer, he will not arrange a promotion that excludes the infamous clause 10. This is a clear contractual obligation: to inform the boxer of a conflict of interest, which can be apparently mitigated by ensuring that the boxer obtains the required minimum percentage. The manager could argue that his default is then covered by another clause, which means that his failure to inform does not then amount to a breach of contract. Given judicial criticism of the manager/promoter conflict, this end result is rather surprising and probably unenforceable for the reasons given in *Watson*. The BBBC has had to adjust to the two cases but is constrained by the structure of professional boxing and the nature of the organization itself. The extension point is now within the guidelines suggested by Scott J, but the manager/promoter point is almost as confused as it was in 1984. The Board wants to allow dual licensing with appropriate safeguards but these are complicated and at times contradictory. It may take a further bout of litigation to have these clarified.

Conclusion

Sports contracts, indeed, entertainment contracts more generally, have several specific characteristics that render them markedly different from ordinary contracts for the supply of personal services. It is essentially the subject matter, the skill or talent of the artist, that leads to a flow of restrictions. The real problem is that this talent may well be ephemeral, more so in some sports, especially where a risk of career-threatening injury is inherent. Even those sports that do not require the highest degree of physical fitness, such as snooker, may not lead to a vastly prolonged career, given that intense mental concentration may be needed. There is always a new generation of players waiting in the wings and snooker is an example where young players may quickly overtake older players. The number of years at the top may be few which means players will want to maximize their earnings while their bargaining power is at its greatest. The employer will want to keep the performer in a contented state, especially within team sports since the individual player can have an effect, either positive or negative, on the team ethos.[82] In one sense this is an unknown quantity, when players are bought, how they will fit into a new club with different group dynamics. So while the contract is to purchase the ability, or rather the delivery of that ability, there are numerous factors that may affect performance, not least mental elements.[83] The contractual product can, therefore, be extremely uncertain and often a great gamble. This is but one point that makes the use of rigorous legal principles inapplicable, what level of performance is required to fulfil the obligation on behalf of the player? While some individual sports have 'non-trying' regulations, it is more difficult to see how this principle might be applied to individuals within team sports.[84] Given that the contractual performance obligations, on behalf of the player, are uncertain, enforcement becomes similarly difficult to determine. Clearly, as a contract for personal services it is not open to enforcement through specific performance.[85] Thus we have an informal regime that generally works without legal interference, though there are examples of disputes over terminations being subject to litigation; see, for example, *Macari* v. *Celtic Football and Athletic Co Ltd*.[86] These are more likely to be concerned with non-players, given the few occasions when players' contracts are likely to be terminated. For footballers with a transfer market for in-contract players, a player who is unwanted will either be sold, given a free transfer on the expiry of his term or, in rarer circumstances, have the remainder of the contractual period bought out.[87] Contracts may also be renegotiated during the course of the agreement to preserve continuity. The whole picture is that of obligations that may be difficult to deliver, without any fault on behalf of the performer and without any prospect of enforcement by the employer. The absence or inapplicability of the legal regulation of the relationship is also demonstrated by the use of internal adjudication such as the Football League Appeals Committee.

This absence of formal legal regulation is not in itself unique and the non-use of legal sanctions to enforce agreements has been observed by a number of writers.[88] The market in sports talent does not lend itself to formal regulation, given the customs that have emerged. While practices, such as 'tapping-up' players to see whether they are interested in moving clubs (legally inducing a breach of contract), may be formally outlawed by the rules, they clearly occur and are occasionally internally punished. Recourse to legal sanctions rarely takes place given that they will inevitably end up as a dispute over the level of compensation due. Legal action has occurred to challenge the administrative regimes that have been set up and this represents a failure of the collective bargaining process and a breakdown in industrial relations. In all three examples examined above, football, cricket and boxing, individual cases have advanced the contractual terms and conditions of all the players who fall under the collective regimes. The law has been a progressive and useful tool for sportsmen to strengthen their position against employers. That said, contracts of dubious legality undoubtedly still exist and are being signed by players who are less concerned with the form than the dream.

NOTES

1. J. Guthrie, *Soccer Rebel*, London, 1976, preface.
2. D. Birley, *Land of Sport and Glory*, Manchester, 1995, describes an historical (the Edwardian era) example of this phenomenon: 'For the urban masses football was often the supreme social experience, and the success of their team a vicarious glory nothing else in life could supply' (229).
3. Some information as to total player salaries can be gleaned from company reports, along with the typical chairman's warning as to rising wage bills. Directors' remuneration is revealed and the Tottenham Hotspur accounts show that the Director of Football, David Pleat, was paid £326,372 in the year ending 31 July 1999. It is not only reports of salaries that need to be viewed sceptically: an interview with a leading Football League manager unveiled the fact that clubs will manipulate reported transfer fees for public relations purposes.
4. *Union Royale Belge de Sociétés de football (ASBL)* v. *Jean-Marc Bosman* [1996] ALL ER (EC) 97
5. *Eastham* v. *Newcastle United* [1964] Ch.413.
6. For the history and development of the PFA see J. Harding, *For the Good of the Game*, London, 1991.
7. The PFA supported the challenge by L.J. Kingaby to his employing club, Aston Villa, in 1912, and as a consequence incurred legal costs of £725. See D. Dougan and P. Young, *On the Spot*, London, 1975.
8. M. Marqusee, *Anyone but England*, London, 1994, 102.
9. The PCA voted to ban the players who had contracted to Packer.
10. T. Mason, *Sport in Britain*, London, 1988.
11. There is neither the space nor the expertise to explore this point in great detail. Fortunately there has been some excellent work by a number of sports historians who have charted the development of several sports and assessed the impact of the factors upon them.
12. It was the attempt to deal with differences in local rules and particularly the question of 'hacking' and 'carrying' that proved controversial. The move to adopt the more civilized 'Cambridge' rules led to the withdrawal of those favouring the original 'Rugby' rules and the formation of the Rugby Football Union in 1871 see P. Young, *A History of British Football*, London, 1969 and G. Williams, *The Code War*, Middlesex, 1994.
13. Scottish clubs had developed a passing game, as opposed to the dribbling game adopted in the south.
14. Young, 117.
15. The FA altered its rules in 1882: 'Any member of a club receiving remuneration or consideration of any sort above his actual expenses and any wages actually lost by any such player taking part in any match, shall be debarred from taking part in either cup, inter-Association contests, and any club employing such a player shall be excluded from this Association', B. Butler, *The Official History of the Football Association*, London, 1991, 29. The Lancashire FA outlawed the signing on of Scottish players in 1881.Young.
16. See Young, 117.
17. The acceptance of professionalism certainly took place but problems over definition remained. The Chester Report commented: 'In its evidence the FA said: "Drawing a strict line between amateurism and professionalism becomes very difficult, therefore, and is open to a number of interpretations".' Chester Report, London, 1968, 69.
18. T. Collins, *Rugby's Great Split*, London, 1998, 34–5.
19. J. Snow, *Cricket Rebel*, London, 1976, 23.
20. C. Brookes, *English Cricket: The Game and Its Players through the Ages*, London, 1978.

21. Young, 120–1 details the terms on which professionalism was conceded by the FA in 1885:

    'professionals shall be allowed to compete in all Cups, County and Inter-Association matches, provided they be qualified as follows:

    (a) in Cup matches by birth or residence for two (2) years last past within six (6) miles of the ground or headquarters of the Club for which they play.

    (b) In County matches as defined in Rule XI, which applies equally to all players whether amateur or professional.

    (c) In Inter-Association matches by bona fide membership for the two (2) years last past of some Club belonging to one of the competing Associations.

    No professional shall be allowed to serve on any Association Committee or represent his own or any other club at any meeting of the Football Association.

    No professional shall be allowed to play for more than one Club in any one season without special permission of the Committee of the Football Association.

    All professionals shall be annually registered in a book to be kept by the Committee of the Football Association, and no professional shall be allowed to play unless he has been so registered.

22. See generally I. Smith and G. Thomas, *Smith and Wood's Industrial Law*, London, 2000.

23. Partial restraints may apply over a reasonable geographical area and for a limited duration while a general restraint is wider in terms of coverage.

24. *Esso Petroleum Co. Ltd* v. *Harper's Garage (Stourport) Ltd.* [1968 AC 269] at 295F.

25. *Kingaby* v. *Aston Villa, The Times*, 28 March 1912; *Aldershot Football Club* v. *Banks* unreported, see E. Grayson, *Sport and the Law*, London, 1994.

26. Harding, 100.

27. Guthrie notes that one example was that of Frank Brennan who was in dispute with Newcastle United, although he left football and did not pursue his claim, 74–5.

28. See Grayson, 295.

29. Guthrie suggests that the action by Aldershot was 'perhaps under guidance or orders'.

30. J. Hill, *Striking for Soccer*, London, 1961, 29.

31. Harding, 281.

32. Wilberforce noted that between 1956 and 1963 out of 2,232 players on the transfer list there were 499 appeals in which 259 were given free transfers and 123 were given a reduced fee. (*Eastham* 148).

33. *Eastham* 149.

34. *Warner Brothers Pictures Inc.* v. *Nelson* [1936] 3 All ER 160.

35. In particular, publishing and recording contracts which have traditionally used option periods to extend duration. These are exercisable by the company and do not require, indeed permit, any assent from the artist. See S. Greenfield and G. Osborn, *Contract and Control in the Entertainment Industry*, Aldershot, 1998.

36. Guthrie, 110.

37. The terms of reference were: 'To enquire into the state of Association Football at all levels, including the organisation, management, finance and administration, and the means by which the game may be developed for the public good; and to make recommendations.' Chester Report, iv.

38. The figures from the Chester Report were as follows:

Year	Fee Required	Free Transfer
1962	192	296
1963	179	317
1964	214	355
1965	86	489
1966	70	480
1967	55	410

39. Chester Report, 81.

40. See G. Wright, *Betrayal*, London, 1994.
41. See J. Bannister, 'The Cricketers' Association', 49 *The Cricketer* (1968) no.7, 30.
42. M. Edwards, 'Cricketers' Association', 52 *The Cricketer* (1971) no.11, 9.
43. There are a number of practical and legal reasons why a union will want a certificate of independence within the Trade Union and Labour Relations (Consolidation) Act 1992. See Smith and Thomas, 40–3.
44. M. Baldwin, 'The Graveney Train', *The Cricketer* (January 1995).
45. In September 1977 the PCA voted at an extraordinary meeting to call upon the ICC and the TCCB to open negotiations with Packer but also by 91 votes to 77 that county cricketers playing in the WSC should be banned by the TCCB. (*The Cricketer* (1977), Oct., 3.)
46. According to *The Cricketer*, there were 35 players of whom five were South African: Eddie Barlow, Denys Hobson, Barry Richards, Graeme Pollock and Mike Procter. According to Slade, J there were 34 players signed to the WSC including only four South Africans. Ultimately neither Pollock nor Hobson played, though the eventual contingent was five South Africans with the addition of Clive Rice and Garth Le Roux. The South African Kepler Wessels played for the Australian side, see G. Haigh, *The Cricket War*, Victoria, Australia, 1993.
47. *The Cricketer* (July 1977), 9.
48. The ICC was founded in 1909 as the Imperial Cricket Conference, comprising Australia, England and South Africa. It had a period as the International Cricket Conference before being renamed the International Cricket Council in 1989. G. Wright, *Betrayal*, London, 1994.
49. The three players were Tony Greig, John Snow and Mike Procter.
50. *Greig* v. *Insole* [1978] 1WLR 302.
51. E. Swanton, *The Cricketer* (1977), August 6. He also noted 'the mentality that cricket is dealing with. Who but a ruthless tycoon could have supposed that a body of sportsmen would have sold down the river organisations such as the Australian Broadcasting Commission to whom they have been contracted since the dawn of broadcasting?'
52. Jeff Stollmeyer, President of the West Indies Board, commented: 'I don't see how anyone can condemn the players. After all their careers are not that permanent.' *The Cricketer* (July 1977), 7.
53. *Greig*, 307.
54. Slade indicated that he considered that there were nine principal questions:
    (A) Are the contracts between World Series Cricket and its players void?
    (B) Has World Series Cricket established that as at 3 August 1977, and subject to any statutory immunity conferred by the Act of 1974, it has a good cause of action in tort against the ICC, based on inducement of breach of contract?
    (C) Has World Series Cricket established that as at 3 August 1977, and subject as aforesaid, it has a good cause of action in tort against the TCCB based on the same grounds?
    (D) Subject to the provisions of the Act of 1974, are the new rules of the ICC void as being in restraint of trade?
    (E) Subject as aforesaid, are the proposed new rules of the TCCB void as being in restraint of trade?
    (F) Is the ICC an 'employers' association' within the meaning of the Act of 1974?
    (G) Is the TCCB an 'employers' association' within the meaning of the Act?
    (H) If either or both of the ICC and the TCCB be 'employers' associations' does this itself bar any cause of action that would otherwise exist?
    (I) In the light of the answers to the eight preceding questions, what relief (if any) should be given to: (i) the individual plaintiffs and (ii) World Series Cricket?
55. The position was not the same in all the test-playing countries. For example, cricket in the West Indies relied upon the money made from home series against England and

Australia and overseas tours to England. Matches played against Pakistan, India and New Zealand did not contribute in the same way (*Greig*, 315).

56. Slade noted that £3,500 for the season seemed to be typical of a county player's remuneration (*Greig*, 315).

57. *Greig*, 352.

58. *The Cricketer* (July 1979), 4.

59. There is a long history of overseas involvement at both professional and semi-professional level and this is a contentious issue, see A. McLellan, *The Enemy Within*, London, 1994 and D. Lemmon, *Cricket Mercenaries*, London, 1987. It is also an increasing phenomenon in the amateur game; see S. Greenfield and G. Osborn, 2 *Social Identities* (1996) no.2.

60. There are provisions for minor county players to transfer; see ECB (2000) Regulations and Playing Condition, 4.32.

61. Ibid., 4.7.

62. Any of the parties, including the ECB, may request that the matter be referred to an investigating tribunal. Under Regulation 9, this consists of a chairman nominated by the ECB and approved by the PCA and a member from both parties.

63. ECB (2000) Regulations and Playing Condition, 4.11. There are stricter rules on extraordinary registrations if the player is under 25.

64. In *Watson*, 283 Scott noted the short duration of the career of a professional boxer, with few 'who can, safely and successfully, continue boxing far into their thirties'. But there are some contemporary examples of boxers, notably heavyweights such as George Foreman, boxing to a much later age.

65. *Watson* v. *BBBC* 1999 (unreported) transcript, 9.

66. See S. Greenfield and G. Osborn, *Contract and Control in the Entertainment Industry*, Aldershot, 1998.

67. The categories requiring licences are: promoter, manager, boxer, trainer/second, agent, matchmaker, referee, timekeeper, second, ringmaster/whip and master of ceremonies (BBBC, *Rules and Regulations*, 2000).

68. Most recently the BBBC has had to deal with two significant pieces of legal action. First, the claim brought by Michael Watson for the injuries he suffered in his fight against Chris Eubank. Secondly, the industrial tribunal claim by Jane Couch over the refusal to grant her a professional licence. In both cases the BBBC was unsuccessful in its defence.

69. *Warren* v. *Mendy* [1989] 1WLR 678 and *Watson* v. *Prager* [1993] EMLR 275.

70. BBBC (2000), *Rules and Regulations*, 59.

71. Frank Bruno is a good example of the variety of work that could be obtained for the right boxer; his television work extended well beyond commenting on boxing and included HP Sauce advertisements.

72. BBBC (2000), *Rules and Regulations*, 60.

73. Ibid., 69.

74. Relevant championships are: 'a British Championship or European, Commonwealth or World Championship organised by a controlling body to which the Board is affiliated'; clause 12.1(i).

75. There are procedural requirements imposed on both the manager and the boxer with respect to the extension notice. The manager must file the notice within 60 days of the winning of the championship and any objection must be served, by the boxer, within 30 days of the serving of the extension notice; clause 12.3, 12.4.

76. Regulations 24, 26, 28, BBBC (2000), *Rules and Regulations*.

77. This was due to pressure from regional managers and, as Scott noted, 'It is I think, relevant to notice that all members of the Board are entitled to vote at general meetings, that resolutions may in general be passed by a simple majority and that the members of the Board include all holders of licences issued by the Board, whether managers, boxers, promoters or others. It would, given the Board's constitution, be

possible for a well organized clique of licence holders to obtain the passage of a resolution at a general meeting, even if the independent members of the Board – by which I mean the stewards and others with no financial interest in professional boxing – were opposed to the resolution' (*Watson*, 284).

78. One of the most astonishing aspects of the organization of professional boxing promotion was that four of the leading promoters (Duff, Astaire, Barrett and Lawless) had an agreement which pooled their promotional interests and then shared the income. This was found by the BBBC not to be contrary to its regulations (*Watson*, 287).

79. *Watson*, 292.

80. Scott noted that the duty owed by the manager to the boxer was not only contractual but also fiduciary, which raised serious points about such potential conflicts.

81. BBBC (2000), *Rules and Regulations*, 69.

82. The idea of using psychology to build teamwork and performance is gaining increasing significance; see S. Bull *et al.*, *The Mental Game Plan*, Cheltenham, 1996.

83. Supporters of all clubs will be able to recite the great failures, players of whom there were great expectations who for one reason or another failed miserably.

84. See, for example, BBBC (2000), *Rules and Regulations*, 9; 'not trying' is classed as an act not permitted under the rules. Jockeys have a similar provision and there is an obvious link to gambling.

85. The statutory provision is now to be found within s.236 of the Trade Union and Labour Relations (Consolidation) Act 1992.

86. [1999] Scot CS 121

87. This latter point is only likely to happen when there is no potential buyer for the unwanted player who is on high enough wages to make the buying-out economic. A recent example is that of the Swedish player Thomas Brolin, whose contract was reportedly bought out by Leeds United.

88. For example, see Macaulay 1963, Collins, H. 1999.

PART 3

Statutory Intervention

9

Resisting the Pressures of 'Americanization': The Influence of European Community Law on the 'European Sport Model'

Stephen Weatherill

Introduction

Legal systems all over the world are increasingly confronted by the need to grapple with their impact on sport. Its accelerating commercialization has generated incentives to litigate. This in turn prompts questions about the extent to which the business of sport is properly treated as special and deserving of full or partial immunity from the application of normal legal rules. The European Community (EC) legal order is no different from others in its need to address these complex questions. But the purpose of this chapter is to enquire into the distinctive elements of the EC system of regulation. EC trade law is built around the pursuit of market integration and this conditions the application of the law of free movement and competition law to sport. Moreover, the institutional and constitutional characteristics of the EC system, relating in particular to the watchdog role allocated to the European Commission and the capacity of the individual to pursue violations before national courts, contribute to shaping a distinctive system. The European Court's *Bosman* ruling provides a high-profile illustration of the vigorous potential of EC law in driving change in the practices of sporting organizations, and the decision has brought to the fore many more intriguing issues, which will be discussed here. The chapter proceeds from the assumption that it is realistic to suppose that European sport, particularly football, will become ever more lucrative in the next few years in the wake of the media revolution, perhaps eventually to the extent that it compares financially with the dominant sports in North America, but that there are aspects of the American model that will prove unpalatable in Europe. It is significant in this context that the Commission has recently tentatively put forward a 'European Sport Model' and, in the light of the Commission's Helsinki Report on Sport of December 1999, this chapter assesses the viability of maintaining key aspects of the European tradition. Although the *Bosman* ruling has frequently been criticized as damaging to the fabric of European football, it is argued that the European Court in *Bosman* was, in fact, generous to sport's appeals for special treatment under the law. A series of legal issues, including the sale of broadcasting rights and transfers, is discussed. The chapter concludes with observations on how special sport should be taken to be as an industry, arguing that the mutual interdependence of clubs in a league demands a much deeper commitment to wealth distribution between clubs than has been visible in recent years, but that pleas to be allowed a form of renovated transfer system should be rejected as irrelevant to the true needs of restructured organized sport. The conclusion is that 'Americanization' of the European game is by no means inevitable, and that EC law, too often misleadingly portrayed as a motor for change in circumstances where it is, in fact, the financial interest of clubs which is driving departures from traditional European preferences, in truth allows sport considerable autonomy to make the relevant key decisions about the shape of the game.

The Appeal for Self-regulation in Sport

As EC intervention in sport has increased in recent years, so too expressions of resistance by international sporting bodies as to what they perceive as inappropriate external interference in their affairs by ill-suited legal systems have become increasingly prominent. A selection of recent examples must suffice. Marcel Benz, a legal adviser to UEFA, is reported to have observed: 'We have our rules and our traditions. We are asking: Why should the EU interfere? The interests of sport are not necessarily best served by EU rules.'[1] Keith Cooper, FIFA's director of communications, commented that 'Football has always been remarkably successful at looking after its own affairs. It is difficult to understand why regulatory authorities feel they now have to become involved.'[2] The FIA, the governing body of grand prix racing, responding to the threatened application of EC competition law, stated that 'The Commission is being naive... The bottom line is that the FIA is not a European organization and if the EU tries in this unsubtle way to impose its regulations it will accentuate the trend to have more races elsewhere in the world.'[3] In a similar vein the International Rugby Board sees itself as 'a governing body for the whole of world rugby and not simply the Unions within the jurisdictional area of the European Union'.[4]

Sport, then, seeks to maintain a pattern of self-regulation, perceiving its special character as being in danger of being misunderstood by 'normal' lawmakers; and as the third of these four quotations suggests, it is not afraid to allude in its own unsubtle way to its capacity to skip beyond the jurisdictional reach of interventionist regulators. Thus far the business of sport has failed to provide an intellectually convincing account of why it should be allowed a partial or total immunity from the application of legal rules to which normal industries are subject. The simple assertion of the adequacy and coherence of self-regulation cannot on its own suffice, for it is hard to imagine any industry which would not seek to make such a claim. The suggestion made in the third and the fourth of the extracts cited touches on the case that sport is a transnational, in some instances global, activity which should accordingly not be subject to the confining grip of national or regional laws. But, one might respond, a global cartel may be more, not less, pernicious than a domestic or regional cartel and may require supervision in the public interest by any and every available regulator. Sport possesses a number of unusual characteristics which set it apart from normal industries, but its accelerating commercialization has brought with it a sharpening of legal intervention and as yet its ruling bodies grope falteringly towards a framework which would legitimize their case for special treatment at law. As already observed, the EC legal order is no different from others in its need to address these complex questions. But this chapter will, first, explore the distinctive elements of the EC system and, secondly, test the extent to which European sport's adaptability and autonomy are conditioned by subjection to the rules of the EC legal order. As already suggested, the chapter develops the thesis that in so far as the 'European sport model' is being beckoned down the path of a form of 'Americanization', it is not EC law but rather the choices taken within sport that will be decisive. This case will be made by examining, first, the position of the European Court and then that of the Commission.

Bosman – the Road to Luxembourg

The European Court's dramatic ruling in *Bosman* is the unavoidable starting point in tracking the current pattern of EC law applied to sport. The facts of the case are now well known, but they deserve recapitulation not least, for the purposes of this chapter, to identify the elements of the judgment which underpin the subsequent rethinking about the viability of traditional regulatory structures within sport.

Jean-Marc Bosman was a Belgian national, born in 1964. He had earned a reputation in his youth as a footballer of some promise and he was sufficiently skilled to play at first-division level in Belgium. He had been employed by RC Liège on a contract expiring at the end of June 1990 on an average salary of BFR120,000 per month, including bonuses. In April 1990 the club offered him a new one-year contract at a quarter of his previous salary. Bosman refused RC Liège's unattractive offer and was transfer-listed at a 'compensation fee' of BFR11,743,000 fixed according to indicators based, in particular, on age and salary.

The transfer system then operating in football had a bewildering number of nuances, varying country by country and adjusted periodically over time.

However, it operated by virtue of the hierarchical structure within the game. Football clubs wishing to participate in official competitions must affiliate to national football associations. National associations are in turn members of FIFA, the world organizing body, which is based in Switzerland. FIFA is split into confederations for each continent. The European confederation is UEFA, also based in Switzerland, and the national associations in the EU member states are members of UEFA and as such undertake to comply with its rules. No club is an island.

The rules which most intimately affected Bosman were those applicable to the transfer system. Players were unable simply to move freely between clubs once their employment contract had come to an end. A club was only able to field a player in an official match once it had secured the player's registration, held by the previous employer. That registration would be released only when the previous club was satisfied with the terms offered by the new club, typically involving payment of a fee. A club which chose simply to field a player without complying with the requirements of the transfer system would find itself subject to heavy and immediate penalties imposed by national and transnational organizations. Footballers, then, were not treated like ordinary employees. They were traded.

US Dunkerque, a French second-division club, contracted with Bosman to pay him a monthly salary of some BFR100,000 plus a signing-on fee of some BFR900,000. In July 1990 RC Liège and Dunkerque agreed a contract for the transfer of Bosman for one year only, at a price of BFR1,200,000, plus an option allowing Dunkerque to buy the player subsequently. Both contracts, RC Liège/Dunkerque and Bosman/Dunkerque, were conditional on the sending of a transfer certificate by the Belgian association to the FFF, the French association, in line with the rules governing the transfer system. It was worthless to Dunkerque to conclude a contract with Bosman without compliance with these transfer requirements, for they would have been unable to play him in official matches. It emerges from the Court's summary of the background that RC Liège came to doubt Dunkerque's solvency. It did not ask the Belgian association to send the certificate to the FFF. So neither contract took effect.

In accordance with the rules prevailing in Belgium, RC Liège suspended Bosman so that he could not play in the 1990/91 season. This prompted him to pursue redress before the Belgian courts. He based his case on the alleged violation of Articles 48, 85 and 86 of the EC Treaty, which concern free movement of workers, control of anti-competitive agreements and prohibition of the abuse of a dominant position, respectively.[5] The matter ultimately reached the European Court in Luxembourg by way of the preliminary reference procedure.

Bosman – What Did the European Court Decide?

In a damning judgment,[6] the European Court rejected a series of submissions presented by the football industry in defence of its system and concluded that Article 48 governing worker mobility had been infringed (although it declined to examine the matter in the light of the EC Treaty's competition rules). The transfer system to which Bosman had fallen victim was incompatible with EC law. The Court added that the system of nationality-based discrimination applying to European club competition, which limited the scope of clubs to select players eligible for national sides other than that of the association of which the club was a member, also violated the principles of EC law. Bosman himself was finally compensated three years after the judgment and eight-and-a-half years after his transfer to Dunkerque had fallen through,[7] but his name will long remain associated with the renovation of football.

The Court's finding that the transfer system operated in violation of the EC Treaty liberated professional footballers from their peculiar status as employees *not* entitled to sell their labour to the highest bidder once their contract of employment comes to an end. Wage bills have increased overall, although distribution has doubtless not been even across all players in all divisions. If clubs want to retain their players, they must now use contracts not cartels. Players move into an especially strong position as they run into the final few months of a contract. Hence the prevalence of long contracts lately struck between big-name clubs and big-name players. Keeping a group of players together over an extended period may involve drafting contracts with generous loyalty bonuses payable in the later stages. None of these features are novel in a 'normal' industry. This is standard fare for employers seeking to retain the services of valued employees. Contract negotiation rules.

This has doubtless caused dismay among footballing traditionalists. It obliterates the caricature of the player whose loyalty is the greater, the tighter the legal tie to the club; whose toil is the more honest, the lower the wage. Yet this is to do more than to place footballers on a par with any other type of employee.

Bosman and the Vigour of EC Law

Bosman is a strong statement of individual rights deployed to challenge collective arrangements. The European Commission had been strikingly reluctant to intervene in sport, even declining to challenge the maintenance of nationality-based discrimination in club football. But individual suits based on EC law are not subject to Commission control. It cannot lock the floodgates. In this sense Bosman the litigant broke open, not simply a cartel within football, but also a cartel between the football authorities and the Community's regulatory authorities, thereby emphasizing the two routes to securing observance of EC law via, not only the European Commission, but also the vigilance of private parties concerned to assert their rights before national courts.

Moreover, the very existence of EC law as an 'extra' regulator diminishes the room for manoeuvre for national regulators. The basic constitutional principles of EC law dictate that it prevails over national law in the event of conflict. This conditions one's appreciation of the limited value of the exemption recently allowed under German cartel law to the central marketing of broadcasting rights for sports events[8] and of the July 1999 judgment of the British Restrictive Practices Court that the collective selling of rights to televised football was not contrary to the public interest under domestic competition law.[9] In so far as such agreements exert an effect on interstate trade patterns, they must comply with Article 81 EC and, if they fail that test, the concessions made at national level cannot save them.

More generally, the Court's ruling in *Bosman* emphasizes how readily EC law spreads into areas apparently out of its bounds. This in turn sharpens awareness of the difficulty of persuading the European authorities that they should leave sport alone. Although the EC may lack explicit competence to regulate a sector, or else enjoy only very limited competence, none the less the cross-cutting effect of its rules, especially the Treaty's economic freedoms which were at stake in *Bosman*, may greatly influence the conduct of actors in that sector.[10] The EC's competence under its Treaty to act as a regulator in the fields of, for example, culture or education is closely circumscribed. It is allowed no explicit competence in the sports sector. But rules in those sectors must comply with EC rules encroaching from elsewhere, most prominently from the realms of free movement. So the football industry in *Bosman* enjoyed no success in keeping EC law at bay by the argument that sport is not economic in nature. It is, subject only to an exception for amateur events where no economic motivation is at stake.[11] Nor can the impact of EC law be displaced by appeals to the principle of subsidiarity. The Court was not persuaded to allow football an immunity from the application of the principles of Community trade law by the German government's submission that the subsidiarity principle dictated that the intervention of public authorities in private commercial affairs should be limited to what is strictly necessary. According to the Court, this could not be accepted as a basis for permitting private associations to adopt rules which restrict the exercise of Treaty rights conferred on individuals. Moreover, the Court brushed aside the submission that the EC lacked jurisdiction as a matter of law over practices in the (transnational, global) sporting industry. The rather crude argument presented frequently by UEFA and FIFA, that they are based in Switzerland and therefore lie beyond the EC's jurisdiction, is as a matter of EC law plainly wrong.[12] Their rules are implemented on the EC's territory.

It seems highly implausible that the Court will ever be prepared to grant sport a blanket exemption from the application of the rules of the EC Treaty. It is very rare that matters with a transnational impact are treated as 'non-economic' for the purposes of the application of EC law. Activity in the industry of sport must comply with basic Treaty provisions such as those concerning the free movement of goods, persons and services and competition policy. This is *not* to say that EC law will necessarily condemn the rules of sporting bodies. Justifications in different form may be advanced, as explained below, but such justification falls to be assessed according to the standards recognized by EC law. These may be based on assumptions which differ from those of sport.

The Declaration on Sport attached to the Amsterdam Treaty, which entered into force in 1999, offers a powerful example of the way in which vague notions about the desire to protect sport are difficult to convert into operational norms in the face of the clear-cut vigour of the basic EC Treaty freedoms. The Declaration asserts that:

> The Conference emphasizes the social significance of sport, in particular its role in forging identity and bringing people together. The Conference therefore calls on the bodies of the European Union to listen to sports associations when important questions affecting sport are at issue. In this connection, special consideration should be given to the particular characteristics of amateur sport.

This is frankly rather feeble and far distant from the murmurs in the immediate aftermath of *Bosman* that a Treaty amendment might be drafted to set aside the impact of the ruling on sport. Assembling unanimous support for such a revision, which would have undermined the basic principles of EC law in one particular sector, proved infeasible. And it is important to appreciate that the setting aside of decisions of the Court via Treaty revision, though occasionally discussed as a live prospect, is in fact exceedingly rare, for several very good legal and political reasons, not least the requirement of unanimity for Treaty revision, the difficulty of attaining which tends to lend powerful support to the 'default setting' of the status quo under the Treaty as already interpreted by the European Court. The result at Amsterdam was the anodyne Declaration. It has, however, bred initiatives at the political level, as sports ministers have subsequently met. One cannot entirely rule out the possibility of unanimously agreed Treaty revision setting aside aspects of the *Bosman* ruling in future, but it would require an unusually high degree of political consensus about the special status of sport.

Why Sport Is Different

The *Bosman* ruling has been widely, and perhaps deliberately, misread. Contrary to much of the misconceived criticism levelled at the European Court, the Court did *not* treat football as an industry like any other. True, it insisted that sport is an economic activity and therefore subject to EC law, and it applied the rules of free movement to the industry accordingly. But the Court did acknowledge that sport is different. Justification for its peculiar practices is possible – albeit on EC law's terms. With reference to the transfer system, the Court was willing in principle to allow the football industry to present two particular justifications that might not be tolerated elsewhere:

> In view of the considerable social importance of sporting activities and in particular football in the Community, the aims of maintaining a balance between clubs by preserving a certain degree of equality and uncertainty as to results and of encouraging the recruitment and training of young players must be accepted as legitimate (para.106 of the ruling).

However, it is well established in EC trade law that both the ends pursued and the means employed by a restrictive measure must be justified. The Court regarded the means employed in the current football industry as inapt to achieve ends which might be capable of justification in principle. The Court did not consider that the transfer system acted as an adequate method of maintaining balance between clubs. The rules neither precluded richer clubs from buying the best players nor prevented the 'availability of financial resources from being a decisive factor in competitive sport thus considerably altering the balance between clubs'. The Court agreed that a transfer fee system might act as an incentive to clubs to recruit and train new and young players, but it observed that, because only a handful of young players will repay the investment by making the professional grade, it is impossible to predict the fees that will be obtained. In any event such fees will be unrelated to the actual cost of training all players. The system was hit-and-miss, rather than a carefully constructed, distributive mechanism. The Court concluded that 'the same aims can be achieved at least as efficiently by other means which do not impede freedom of movement for workers' (para.110 of the judgment).

It is of major significance that the Court has built a justification test into the application of EC rules. Moreover, it allows recognition of the perceived special concerns of the football industry. The Court, and especially Advocate General Lenz, went so far as to comment on the types of internal regulation that might be allowed in football, though not in a normal industry, in recognition of its peculiar features. Mr Lenz accepted that a system stopping rich clubs from becoming ever richer and the poor ever poorer could be justified. He mentioned two particular methods for preserving the financial and sporting balance between participating clubs that is vital to a healthy professional sports league. His first suggestion was for a collective wage agreement capping the salaries to be paid to the players by the clubs. His second – and apparently preferred – route involved the distribution of receipts from, for example, the sale of broadcasting rights and ticket sales among the clubs. Such internal taxation would probably be regarded as unlawful in a 'normal' industry; indeed, there would rarely be an incentive to institute such a system. But participants in a sports league are interdependent. The clubs do not have the aim of driving their competitors from the market. They need credible rivals. Neither Mr Lenz nor the Court specifies exactly what may lawfully be done in sport in order to attend to the special demands of the industry; but they open the door to arrangements designed to reflect the unusual competitive relationship that prevails between football clubs. The industry, post-*Bosman*, was left to select its own processes of internal regulation. In line with the thesis of this chapter, EC law has admittedly foreclosed the option of the brutal transfer system under which Bosman himself suffered; but the autonomy of the industry to provide structures apt to realize its unique aspiration to maintain 'a balance between clubs by preserving a certain degree of equality and uncertainty as to results' has not been called into question. Quite the reverse. One might shrewdly note that since the *Bosman* ruling conspicuously little has been done in football to address by other routes the need for wealth distribution among clubs upon which such emphasis was placed in the pleadings of the football authorities in the case aimed at defending the transfer system.

I entirely agree that in sport the clubs are mutually interdependent and that, needing credible rivals, they properly support each other. But I am much less persuaded by the second of the perceived special concerns of organized sport: the need to encourage the recruitment of young players. The key paragraph of Mr Lenz's Opinion is 239, in which he suggests that an adjusted transfer system could be justified if, first, fees were limited to the costs incurred in training the player by the previous club (or previous clubs) and, secondly, provided the fee was payable only in the case of a first change of club where the previous club had trained the player. This would exclude the multimillion euro deal. There would also have to be a proportionate reduction for every year the player had spent with that club after being trained, since during that period the training club will have had an opportunity to benefit from its investment in the player. Even Mr Lenz cautiously concedes that such a system might not be sustainable in the light of the counter-argument that its objectives 'could also be attained by a system of redistribution of a proportion of income, without the players' right to freedom of movement having to be restricted for that purpose'. The associations, he noted, had not submitted anything to refute that objection. Nothing in the Court's judgment seems to support Mr Lenz's tentative embrace of a revamped transfer system. Para.114 of the ruling seems to exclude it. It states firmly that Article 48 of the EC Treaty 'precludes the application of rules laid down by sporting associations, under which a professional footballer who is a national of one member state may not, on the expiry of his contract with a club, be employed by a club of another member state, unless the latter club has paid to the former one a transfer, training or development fee'. I find the whole notion that clubs need financial support when players move in order to sustain an incentive to train young players wholly unconvincing. I cannot see any compelling reason for supposing that a football club is any less likely to train young employees because they might subsequently quit the company than a supermarket or a university would be. Naturally, clubs assert the need to claw back costs and protest that they would abandon youth training were they not allowed to do so. No empirical nor economic evidence suggests any plausible basis for such claims. Quite the reverse; all employers need to train employees in order to take the benefit of their skills for as long as they are able to attract them to stay with the company. Football is no different. A club which neglected youth training would simply perform poorly. I would not exclude the possibility that it could be regarded as legally permissible for football to devise an internal taxation system to transfer money into the hands of nursery clubs, as part of a scheme for sustaining a larger number of clubs than would survive in 'pure' market conditions and to diminish gaps in economic strength between clubs.[13] But this should be regarded as part of the wider mission to maintain a degree of competitive equality and organizational solidarity within the sport, which may also embrace the anxiety to preserve viable national leagues even in smaller European countries. It should not be defended as a device that is necessary to induce clubs to invest in training. And, in line with the Court's strong assertion of free movement rights in its *Bosman* ruling, any such system must be wholly disassociated from residual restrictions on the ability of players to contract with their preferred employer. That is to say; the economics of football are special when it comes to preserving competitive equality between clubs; the economics are much less obviously special when it comes to compensating and thereby encouraging the training of young players.

In fact I would go even further. The *Bosman* ruling was explicitly directed at the status of players whose contract had come to an end. But I submit that a violation of EC law may also be established when transfers of players are blocked where those players have unilaterally terminated their contract and fulfilled relevant obligations under local employment law.[14] This would further slice into the persisting viability of what remains of the transfer system post-*Bosman*. The law of free movement forbids collectively-imposed sanctions on players wishing to escape agreed contractual obligations and pushes the consequences of such 'player power' into the realms of national private law, giving a privileged status to astute contract negotiation with star players by an employer.[15] This is normal in most industries, and, in my submission, the essence of the Court's approach in *Bosman* was that the football labour market should be organized in much the same way as any other labour market.[16] The special demands of organized sport must be reflected other than through the imposition of extra burdens on players. Football may be different; footballers should not be.

Commission Thinking in 1999

In February 1999 the European Commission published preliminary conclusions on the application of EC law to sport. This took the form of a press release summarizing a confidential (but widely leaked) Commission draft communication.[17] The breadth of interest in sport was emphasized by the fact that the release appeared under the name of three of the 15 Commissioners, representing competition policy (Van Miert), culture (Oreja) and social affairs (Flynn). Four main topics were to be addressed by the Commission: (i) the application of the competition rules, (ii) the development of a European sport model, (iii) sport as an instrument of social and employment policies, and (iv) the fight against doping.

This chapter is mainly concerned to examine the first of these topics, the application of the Treaty competition rules, but with special reference to its spill-over into the shaping of the European sport model. It is accepted in the February 1999 confidential draft that, following *Bosman*, sport's inter-dependence of competitors and the need for uncertainty in results might justify special arrangements, in particular, in the markets for the production and the sale of sports events. But this does not warrant automatic exemption from the EC Treaty's competition rules of any economic activities generated by sport. It is conceded that Commission practice is not yet sufficiently well developed to answer all the important issues on the agenda. Cited as pending issues are the principle that sports be organized on a national territorial basis, the creation of new sporting organizations, club relocation, the ban on organizing competitions outside a given territory, the regulatory role of sporting event organizers, the transfer systems applying to team-game players, nationality clauses, selection criteria for athletes, ticket distribution for the 1998 World Cup,[18] broadcasting rights, sponsorship, and the prohibition on clubs belonging to the same owner taking part in the same competition.

By way of preliminary conclusion the Commission identified four categories of practice which should be kept separate for the purposes of applying the EC Treaty's competition rules:

> 1. Rules to which Article 81(1) (ex 85(1)) does not in principle apply, given that such rules are inherent to sport and/or necessary for its organization.
> 2. Rules which are in principle prohibited if they have a significant effect on trade between member states.
> 3. Rules which restrict competition but which are in principle eligible for exemption, in particular rules which do not affect a sportsman's [*sic*] freedom of movement within the EU and whose aim is to maintain the balance between clubs in a proportionate way by preserving both a certain equality of opportunities and the uncertainty of results, and by encouraging the recruitment and training of young players.
> 4. Rules which are abusive within the meaning of Article 82 (ex 86). The draft communication declares that it is not the power to regulate a given sporting activity as such which might constitute an abuse but rather the way in which an organization exercises such power. It would violate Article 82 (ex 86) to exclude from the market without objective reason any competing organizer or, indeed, any market player who, even meeting justified quality or safety standards, failed to obtain from the organizer a certificate of quality or of product safety.

This intriguing agenda attempts to provide a framework for analysis within which EC law will apply while showing sensitivity to sport's peculiarities. After discussion with the sports world in line with the Amsterdam Treaty's Declaration on Sport, the Commission planned to draw up final conclusions. For the purposes of discussion, a 'European Union Conference on Sport' was organized in Olympia, Greece, in May 1999 and attracted representatives from, *inter alia*, governing bodies in sport, public authorities and the media. This forum generated a set of conclusions.[19] The features of the European Sport Model agreed at the conference include the need for sport 'to keep its operational autonomy safe from any political or economic manipulation', which should involve preservation from 'over-commercialization' tending to distort its values. Systems of sport governance in Europe, spanning clubs and national and international federations, ensure solidarity between different levels, which is taken to mean both horizontal solidarity, meaning a balance between participants in the same competition, and vertical solidarity, whereby profits from major competitions should be reinvested in the promotion of sport, especially among young people. The system of promotion and relegation is 'another identifying feature of European sport'. It promotes equal opportunities for all participants, increasing the appeal of participation in competition. The balance that this has brought has allowed sport to flourish in Europe, but would be upset by clubs' choosing to break away from the established structure. The conclusions also warn that links between sport and television should not be used as a lever for damaging the way in which sports competitions are organized in pursuit of financial gain, and it is mentioned in this context that doubts or even outright opposition have been expressed about acquisition of clubs by broadcasters.[20] The role of sport in protecting young people is emphasized; so too, yet more ambitiously, its contribution to promoting democratic values, the integration of minorities and tolerance and fair play in society.

The European sports model, like its cousin the European social model, provides an exciting though slightly unstable springboard for debate, and a number of participants at Olympia were resistant to the Commission's perceived tendency to downplay differences between individual sports in its quest for a broadly applicable model. It should be noted that the model is not an attack on commercialism *per se*, for money has always played a significant role in professional sport even if income generation is more vigorously pursued today than in the past, but rather it is a quest to foster an environment within which commercialism will not undermine core sporting values such as uncertainty of result, integrity of competition and achievement based on merit. The Commission's European model is to an extent defined by what it is not: it is not an American model. The preference for promotion and relegation in Europe is explicitly contrasted with the closed league typical of North American sport, in which the autonomy of clubs from the league is typically less pronounced and investment doubtless more safely protected because of the absence of risk of loss of status.

It will be immediately apparent that several of these features of the European Sport Model have lately been called into question in Europe. The pressures are conveniently grouped under the rubric 'Americanization' because of the increasing perception that European sport, and most of all football, is steadily increasing its income generation by learning some lessons from North America. This does not mean that all aspects of North American sport are likely to be embraced in Europe. The draft pick, for example, is culturally wholly alien to the leading sports in Europe. In fact, it is a system which reflects the deeper commitment of North American sports leagues to managing competitive equality and uncertainty of results. However, some other typically American trends are plainly finding their way on to the agenda of some actors on the European stage – most of all, the richest football clubs. The removal of the 'uncertainty' of relegation and the elimination of the criterion of merit as the basis for qualification for the competition were at the heart of plots in 1998 by 14 leading European football clubs to create a league independent of the less lucrative structure offered by UEFA, the governing body. The mooted breakaway league would have been based on guaranteed membership for the elite group. It would have generated more revenue in absolute terms but, in addition, a much higher percentage of proceeds would have been retained by the participant clubs than under UEFA's schemes, which involved wealth distribution within the game.[21] The plans never came to fruition largely because of concessions made by UEFA. Its own most prestigious club competition, the Champions' League (formerly the European Cup), was expanded,[22] allowing increased revenue generation by the leading clubs at the cost of, *inter alia*, damage to traditional structures of national club competition.[23] UEFA's precarious hold over the governance of European club football leaves it vulnerable to further pressure from this group of 14 clubs to relax its traditional sporting rules. Rumours persist of, for example, attempts to broaden the elite group's eligibility for the major club competitions beyond qualification via placement in national leagues and to secure greater financial compensation for the release of players participating in international matches.[24]

By late 1999 it seemed that the Commission's ambitions to publish a final version of its February 1999 confidential draft communication had been put on hold, at least for the medium term, amid speculation about the high level of controversy the draft had aroused. The Commission now seems likely to pursue a clutch of *ad hoc* individual decisions in the sports sector, predominantly concerning EC competition law, before returning to the quest for an overall policy framework. It did, however, produce a less ambitious policy paper than its February draft in December 1999, when it published 'The Helsinki Report on Sport', designed for the consideration of the European Council held that month in the city.[25] The paper is strikingly less detailed in its treatment of the outstanding legal issues than that of February 1999. Instead, the focus of the Helsinki Report is on safeguarding current sports structures and on maintaining the social function of sport within the Community framework, which were areas on which the Commission had been invited to report by the Vienna European Council of December 1998. The report begins with the ambitious assertion that it 'gives pointers for reconciling the economic dimension of sport with its popular, educational, social and cultural dimensions'. It maintains the Commission's identification of 'a European approach to sport based on common concepts and principles', which includes sport's role as 'an instrument of social cohesion and education'. It is suggested that tensions have emerged between this function and the economic motivations for sport which have increased in recent years. One example cited is

> the temptation for certain sporting operators and certain large clubs to leave the federations in order to derive the maximum benefit from the economic potential of sport for themselves alone. This tendency may jeopardize the principle of financial solidarity between professional

and amateur sport and the system of promotion and relegation common to most federations.

The Commission contents itself with a relatively brief summary of the legal environment, repeating the orthodox constitutional point that, although the EC lacks explicit competence in sport under its Treaty, nevertheless sports bodies must comply with Community law. Pending disputes are merely mentioned with negligible elaboration. The pattern according to which the Treaty competition rules are likely to apply is summarized in terms familiar from the February 1999 confidential draft, but less fully explained than in it. 'The rules of the game' will escape the scope of the competition rules. Other rules are in principle impermissible; for example, restrictions on parallel imports of sports products, ticket sales which discriminate according to the residence of buyers,[26] and the exclusion from the market by a sporting body, for no objective reason, of any economic operator who complies with justified quality or safety standards yet has been denied a certification document by the body. In between lie practices that are likely to be exempted from the competition rules, including exclusive rights to broadcast sporting events that are limited in duration and scope, and agreements within the game designed to achieve the two objectives recognized in *Bosman* as special to sport, namely preservation of competitive balance and inducement to develop young players.

The Commission asserts the value in preserving 'the social function of sport and therefore the current structures of the organization of sport in Europe', while assimilating a changing legal and commercial environment. This requires consultation between interested levels of governance – sports bodies, member states and European institutions. A partnership is presented as the way forward.

Some Outstanding Questions

Increasingly visible subjection to EC law flows naturally from the rising economic significance of sport. The February 1999 confidential draft, the Helsinki Report of December 1999 and a small collection of individual Decisions begin to reveal the Commission's concern to put flesh on the bones of the Court's acceptance in *Bosman* that the special characteristics of sport should be taken into account while subjecting it in principle to the rules of EC law. Several comments about the Commission's thinking are appropriate.

The use of the law of free movement in *Bosman* appears increasingly anomalous. It was always surprising that the Court in *Bosman* chose to decide the case exclusively on the basis of Article 39 (ex 48), neglecting entirely the impact of the Treaty competition rules. This was perhaps a hint that the Court realized the complexity associated with the application of Articles 81 and 82 (ex 85 and 86) to sport and that, by focusing on violation of the free movement rules alone, it preferred to leave consideration of competition law to another day and, perhaps better still from its perspective, to another institution. The Commission has now picked up the baton, and it seems plain that, *Bosman* notwithstanding, it is competition policy that will be the major battleground in the future elaboration of the application of EC law to sport. The appreciation that Articles 81 and 82 (ex 85 and 86) were the dogs that didn't bark in *Bosman* and that Article 39 (ex 48) has now been relegated in the Commission's thinking should not detract from the realization that Article 39 (ex 48) remains relevant in the shaping of EC law in this sector. It affects the flexibility allowed to the Commission in applying Articles 81 and 82. Specifically, any concession granted to the industry must also comply with Article 39 (ex 48)[27] and, in so far as a revised system violates free movement rights, it may be challenged by a private litigant relying on the directly effective right contained in Article 39 (ex 48) even where the Commission is satisfied that the competition rules have not been infringed. It is explained above that this may be pertinent in the shaping of an adjusted system of transfer fees, where I submit that Article 39 (ex 48) injects a powerful strain of hostility to restrictions on labour mobility. This insistence on individual economic freedoms fatally damages attempts to resuscitate a transfer system claimed to serve the collective interests of the game in so far as it involves burdens imposed on players direct.

The willingness to exclude some arrangements from Article 81(1) (ex 85(1)) altogether on the basis that they are inherent to sport and/or necessary for its organization represents the most malleable tool available to the Commission. This offers a method for reflecting the special nature of sport, but the debate about which rules are properly treated as inherent to sport and necessary for its organization, and which, by contrast, constitute supplementary restrictions of an essentially economic nature falling within Article 81 (ex 85), promises to reveal much about the perceived peculiar nature of the industry of sport and its subjection to EC law. What really are the 'rules of the game'? The supposed divide between a socially and culturally important core sporting agenda and other 'normal' economic interests and activities generated by sport is hard to fix and remains intellectually and commercially elusive. The most widely cited example of a rule which may seem restrictive yet is treated as part of the sporting context within which competition is organized and therefore beyond the reach of EC law is provided by selection policies for national representative teams. The German national team may comprise only Germans without violating Article 12 (ex 6). This has always been taken as the consequence of the Court's notion of rules of 'purely sporting interest' adopted in the first of its sports law rulings, *Walrave and Koch* v. *UCI*.[28] The Court in *Bosman* seemed anxious not to kick wide open this concession to sporting bodies, for it showed itself completely unpersuaded that reasons of sporting interest could dictate an enforced link between the location of a club and the origins of individual players. The nationality of individual players is disassociated from the sporting identity of clubs, in contrast to that of national representative sides, and it was therefore necessary in law immediately to treat all EU nationals playing club football in the same way, irrespective of nationality.

It is submitted that the Court was correct in this finding, but it is plain that elusive distinctions are apt to present themselves in future. Rules that limit the number of clubs in a league to, say, 18 would not be open to challenge on the basis that 20 would allow wider access. These are 'the rules of the game' and they lie within the autonomous decision-making competence of sport's governing bodies. But once a practice is identified as lying within the scope of EC law – that is, because it possesses a sufficient economic element to constitute more than something which defines the core identity of the sport – it must be justified in accordance with the rules of EC law, albeit that sport's recognized special characteristics would at this stage be taken into account. In formal legal terms, exemption of a restrictive practice under Article 81(3) currently remains the exclusive preserve of the European Commission (although this may alter).[29] In fixing the margin between rules that escape the scope of EC law and rules that fall foul of it unless they can be shown to be justified, the EC's institutions – the Commission, supervised by the Court, and the Court itself in receipt of preliminary references from national courts[30] – are placed in a powerful position to shape the practical scope of decision-making autonomy allowed to sport. Many issues remain unresolved at the margin and there is an obvious peril that, in addressing them, the Commission will, in practice, stray close to assuming the function of sports regulator, which it conscientiously denies it could or should perform.

Examples of the problem abound in connection with rules designed to maintain 'balance between clubs by preserving a certain degree of equality and uncertainty as to results', which the Court in *Bosman* conceded as a legitimate objective in sport. Systems of internal wealth distribution, designed to reflect the interdependence of clubs which is the peculiar hallmark of a sports league, might be treated as inherent to sport (and therefore outside the reach of the competition rules) or as economically motivated and therefore requiring exemption. An uncertainty of outcome may be regarded as a means of improving the quality of the product, but, more than that, it may be treated as essential to the very conduct of sport in the first place. The latter view might lead to the conclusion that the establishment of a solidarity fund within a sport, to which wealthier clubs are required to contribute from the proceeds of, *inter alia*, the sale of broadcasting rights and ticket income and on which poorer clubs may draw for financial support, may escape supervision under EC competition law. I concede that this system may be attacked as an inapt and inefficient route to achieving the objective of workable, competitive equality between clubs. This is an issue demanding analysis; removing the rewards of success and muffling the pain of failure by compulsory wealth distribution may damage the competitive edge, although this fear should not neglect the point that in organized sport it is much more than financial success alone that provides incentives to strive for supremacy.[31] But if such wealth distribution is treated as inherent to sport's need for a truly competitive base, then the relevant arrangements do not even need to run the gauntlet of EC competition law.

This tricky issue is relevant to legal treatment of the sale of broadcasting rights. The acquisition of rights to cover popular sporting events by media companies forms a central plank of strategy for the exploitation of new markets in the rapidly restructuring broadcasting sector. It is a major reason for the recent increase in the 'commercialization' of sport. In turn, these trends explain the Commission's own interest in sport, for acquisition of rights by media companies may imperil sustained flexibility in the broadcasting industry. As the revolution of media convergence gathers technological pace,[32] mergers between media groups and sports clubs may eventually come to be the subject of scrutiny at the European level as they already have at the national level,[33] but thus far such anxieties have emerged at the European level in connection with the sale of television rights. Article 81(1) and (3) may be used to control the reach of exclusive rights which, as is well known, may have ambiguous implications for the competitive structure of the market.[34] The Commission's 1999 documentation on sport properly accepts that a degree of exclusivity may be granted; but the Commission will carefully scrutinize the duration of the grant of exclusivity lest it cause unacceptable market foreclosure. Typically, the more speculative the investment (which might be the case if untried technology is involved), the longer the protection of exclusivity that is likely to be sanctioned. Questions of the collective selling of rights are still more complex. Clubs have an interest in acting collectively to sell rights to broadcast matches, rather than in making individual deals with separate broadcasters. This will typically be presented as a means of selling a coherent package covering an entire league programme and it also doubtless serves to simplify the task of sharing the proceeds from the central pool to all the participant clubs, which, in pursuit of competitive equality, typically involves some degree of support for the less successful or less attractive clubs. However, by reducing competition it will enable the clubs to keep prices (artificially) high. Broadcasters could complain that this is simply a price-fixing cartel which serves sport's internal requirement of 'organizational solidarity' through wealth distribution, but at a cost represented by the suppression of a market for rights involving many clubs and many potential buyers. This forces up prices and reduces consumer choice. A robust response would be to insist on the dismantling of collective selling, releasing a competitive market for purchase of rights to the advantage of third-party buyers, but to allow the sport in question, should it so choose, to adopt internal rules designed to underpin organizational solidarity requiring clubs able to extract high fees to share part of the income with clubs less favoured in the market place. It would need to be determined whether this alternative device for securing wealth distribution and competitive equality based on a type of internal taxation could, in practice, be reliably maintained once collective selling was ended.[35]

The Commission remains understandably cautious in this area but has left space for the possible exemption of arrangements for the collective selling of rights. In the Helsinki Report the Commission insists that any exemption would have to take account of the benefits for consumers and the proportionate nature of the restrictions in relation to the end in view. It is observed that it is therefore appropriate 'to examine the extent to which a link can be established between the joint sale of rights and financial solidarity between professional and amateur sport, the objectives of the training of young sportsmen and women and those of promoting sporting activities among the population'. This hints intriguingly at the use of the power to exempt restrictive practices as a lever for insisting that fostering the social and educational function of sport is a condition for giving a green light to collective selling. The cartel is permissible provided its proceeds are shared throughout the sport for the sake of its general health.[36] This suggests that collective selling designed solely as a tool of wealth maximization for the participants alone would not be exempted. So a 'breakaway' league of the type lately mooted in European football, may, by ridding itself of its roots in the wider organization of the sport, thereby surrender one commercially attractive opportunity, that of the collective sale of broadcasting rights. The 'European sports model' could in this way come to be defended by the Commission in deciding whether to grant exemption of restrictive practices under Article 81(3).

Rules designed to secure an uncertainty of outcome embrace not only general wealth distribution but may also be directed at maintaining the integrity of competition by excluding any whiff of match-fixing. The status of rules forbidding multiple ownership of clubs could fall within the notion of 'rules needed to ensure uncertainty as to results' which fall outwith legal control. UEFA's rules restricting multiple ownership of clubs participating in European competition have been examined by the Court for Arbitration in Sport (CAS), an arbitral body established by the industry and based in Lausanne. The CAS decided in July 1999 that such rules were lawful, examining the matter from the perspective of both EC law and Swiss law.[37] This judgment does not preclude the matter from emerging once again for decision by a tribunal within the EC, nor the possibility of a different conclusion on the matter being reached there. However, the commercial interests that brought the case before the CAS chose to adjust their shareholdings in order to comply with UEFA's requirements. And subsequently the Commission issued its preliminary conclusion that the rule could fall outwith the Treaty competition rules, although, in accordance with the orthodoxy of Community trade law, it requires further information to ensure that there are no less restrictive means of preserving the integrity of competitions where more than one club belongs to the same owner.[38]

Conclusion

Sport possesses unusual features which mark it out from 'normal' industry. It has an unusually well developed pattern of globalized regulation. It has its own adjudicative tribunals, such as the increasingly prominent Court of Arbitration in Sport. Sport has a need for healthy internal competition which is not the hallmark of 'normal' industry. There might be an intellectual case to be made that sport ought to be permitted to run its own affairs. One might contend that the 'law' of international sporting bodies be treated as an autonomous system worthy of protection from disruption by state law or the law of transnational entities such as the EC. After all, sport has already far transcended the rigidities of national political frontiers. Henri Delaunay was already far bolder than Jean Monnet; Jules Rimet a great globalizer more than half a century ago. This depiction of a system which responds to the special interests of sport, and which should not be invaded by differently motivated systems, begins to move towards an intellectually coherent version of the 'they don't understand, it's not their business' argument broached earlier in this chapter. To treat decisions of sporting associations as 'law' in their own right, rather than as private acts subordinate to 'real law', would argue for a differently conceived 'sports law' and would bring to mind questions surrounding the choice of which legal order to apply in case of conflict.

In the EC context, sporting bodies have shown little interest in making this case. They have largely been able to rely on the relatively short span of a player's career and the regularity of annual competition contrasted with the stately progress of legal proceedings to scare off most would-be litigants.[39] However, on the rare occasions that litigation has reached the final whistle – such as *Bosman* – the case that sport is special has not been enough to secure victory. This is in part because sport has been obliged to fight the battle on the EC system's own terms, as explained above. Perhaps, of course, one could in any event object to the characterization of sporting rules as 'law' with reference to the (relatively) unrepresentative, unaccountable processes of decision-making within the sector. In the United States bona fide arm's length negotiation operates as a precondition to the applicability of the non-statutory labour exemption, which is a judicial creation designed to immunize collective bargains struck between both sides of industry from anti-trust law.[40] In Europe rule-making remains predominantly based on a top-down model in which strong player unions are absent and so, for example, attempts to introduce a 'salary cap' in Europe by appealing to American precedents deserve scepticism for the European version would be no more than a horizontal price-fixing cartel among employers, with the effect of loading the 'blame' for high costs on players and protecting inefficiencies elsewhere in the industry.[41] A budget cap, rather than a salary cap, might be more promising, though still legally problematic; but there are other avenues than the capping of spending down which sport in Europe could constructively seek to move in order to secure protection for its distinctive characteristics without falling foul of EC law, most of all involving more vigorous wealth distribution.

In practice, sporting associations, subject to individual litigation and the scrutiny of the Commission, would now be better advised to abandon a confrontational attitude and to adapt their arguments in order to win autonomy for their role in fixing 'the rules of the game' while accepting subjection to the control of EC law in more obviously economic realms. This would, admittedly, leave space for debate about the precise location of the margin between the sporting and the economic category. It was discussed earlier that rules designed to maintain a degree of competitive equality and uncertainty of results cover a wide spectrum, and though some may count as inherent to the organization of sport, others seem to sit more comfortably in economically-motivated realms. But even in the latter instance, the fact that rules fall within the scope of EC law by no means inevitably deprives them of enforceability, for the Commission is clearly willing to consider exempting practices in recognition of the special characteristics of sport. The debate deserves to be entered into constructively on both sides. Both the Court's ruling in *Bosman* and evolving Commission practice, particularly in the generally conciliatory tones of the Helsinki Report, exhibit a readiness to acknowledge the special concerns of the sports sector, albeit not to the extent of conceding that its rules entirely escape the jurisdictional reach of the EC. Sporting bodies could improve their case by the more sophisticated use of empirical evidence about the needs of organized sport. Such submissions have been consistently absent from the plaintive cries of the industry in recent years. In its Helsinki Report on Sport, the Commission gently makes the fair point that sporting organizations could usefully clarify their missions and operate in a more transparent manner.

It is emphatically *not* the case that European sport is being propelled down the American road by the law of the Community. The Commission is keen to see the preservation of matters such as promotion and relegation. Nothing in the assumptions of EC law will necessarily disturb choices made in sport to protect vibrant competitive equality through arrangements for securing wealth distribution. *Bosman* explicitly allowed such planning, but conspicuously little advantage of this has been taken by the game since its preferred, but evidently flawed instrument, the transfer system, was ruled offside.[42] It is possible to wonder how committed to competitive equality clubs really are once they discover that they are unable to place associated burdens on the shoulders of their employees. But the EC is a regulator of sport in only a limited sense. It judges decisions taken by sporting bodies. It does not impose its own decisions. As the Commission's European Sport Model makes plain, there are distinctive features of European sport which may legitimately be pursued within a permissive framework established by EC law. But the Commission cannot demand compliance with the European Sports Model, except in so far as departure from it involves a breach of EC law. That (some) of its features appear to be under threat in Europe, as part of a trend which may be labelled 'Americanization' in recognition of the lurking desire to eliminate traditional rules of the game (such as promotion and relegation) which may inhibit wealth maximization on a North American scale, is not to be blamed on the incursion of EC law into the autonomy of sport. If governance of the game based on national associations affiliated to a continent-wide ruling body is abandoned in (some) European sports, it will be as a direct result of the choice made in the market by the small number of entrepreneurs who control the continent's major sports clubs, especially football clubs. The damage that this is capable of wreaking on the European Sports Model should make one think hard about whether, far from allowing sport an exemption from the EC Treaty, instead what is urgently needed is a powerful regulator acting in the public interest and which should operate at a European level in order to be effective. League rules requiring transfers of wealth between clubs would not be permissible, but mandatory. Smaller leagues could be protected. Criticism of EC law and of the *Bosman* ruling in particular, and talk of salary caps, intrusive player agents and a rejuvenated transfer system, obscures the central issues in today's organized sport, which do not concern the players but the short-sightedness of (some) clubs in pursuing commercialization without adequate respect for the nature and purpose of sport in society.

NOTES

1. *Financial Times*, 24 March 1998, 24.
2. Ibid., 23 January 1998, 2.
3. *Guardian*, 23 Dec. 1997, 21.
4. *Independent on Sunday*, 7 June 1998, Sports Section, 17.
5. Since the entry into force of the Amsterdam Treaty on 1 May 1999, these provisions are renumbered as Arts. 39, 81 and 82 EC, respectively.
6. Case C-415/93 *URBSFA* v. *Bosman* [1995] ECR I-4921. The decision has generated a substantial literature; see, for instance, at the time S. Weatherill, 'Annotation' 33 *Common Market Law Review* (1996) 991; D. O'Keeffe and P. Osborne, 'The European Court Scores a Goal' *International Journal of Comparative Labour Law and Industrial Relations* (1996) 111; J.-C. Seche, 'Quand les Juges tirent au but' 32 *CDE* (1996) 355; M. Hilf, 'Das Bosman-Urteil des EuGH' *NJW* (1996), 1169; R. Blanpain, *Droit et Sport, L'Affaire Bosman*, Leuven, 1996.
7. *Independent*, 23 Dec. 1998, 20; he received £312,000 in an out-of-court settlement by the Belgian football authorities.
8. s.31 Gesetz gegen Wettbewerbsbeschraenkungen, as amended with effect from 1 Jan. 1999.
9. *Re the Supply of Services Facilitating the Broadcasting on Television of Premier League Football Matches* judgment of 28 July 1999; currently available via <http://www.courtservice.gov.uk/highhome.htm>.
10. S. Weatherill, *Law and Integration in the EU*, Oxford, 1995, Chs.2, 7.
11. This confirmed the approach taken by the Court in the 1970s in its well-known pair of 'sports law' rulings, *Walrave and Koch* v. *UCI* (Case 36/74 [1974] ECR 1405) and *Donà* v. *Mantero* (Case 13/76 [1976] ECR 1333).
12. Cases C-89/85 *et al.*, *Ahlstrom* v. *Commission* [1988] ECR 5193.
13. On another level, it is not inconceivable that public authorities may choose to intervene to require income to be used in order to support the 'grassroots' of the game as part of a broader policy for tackling social exclusion.
14. Cf. Weatherill, n.6, 1028–31; M. Thill, 'L'arret Bosman et ses implications pour la libre circulation des sportifs a l'intérieur de l'U.E. dans des contextes factuels différents de ceux de l'affaire Bosman', *Revue du Marche Unique Européen* (1996), 89, 108–10.
15. It may even be argued that individual mobility would be unlawfully restricted by collective arrangements in the game even where local rules governing discharge of the employment relationship are not satisfied (that is, where the player is in breach of contract, in English law terms) and that the consequences of such action should be governed by national private law alone, not least because different jurisdictions in the EU adopt different approaches to such employee freedom.
16. Note also that, although *Bosman* concerned the transfer of an EU national between two member states, it is possible to argue, especially with reference to competition law (i) that non-EU nationals may be able to challenge the system and (ii) that a player involved in a transfer which is purely internal to a single member state (which would include one between England and Scotland) may also be able to present a challenge. The *Bosman* ruling clearly exerts an impact beyond its formal limits. See S. Weatherill, 'European Football Law', *Collected Courses of the 7th Session of the Academy of European Law*, The Hague, 1999, 339, 375–9; P. Spink, 'Blowing the Whistle on Football's Domestic Transfer Fee', *Juridical Review* (1999), 73; M. Beloff, T. Kerr and M. Demetriou, *Sports Law*, Oxford, 1999, Ch.4. Cf. also Case C-264/98 *Tibor Balogh* v. *Royal Charleroi Sporting Club* pending before the ECJ.
17. IP/99/133.
18. See now Dec. 2000/12 *1998 Football World Cup* OJ 2000 L5/55 (fine of EUR 1,000 imposed).

19. The conclusions are available via the Commission website <http://europa.eu.int/comm/dg10/sport>.
20. This provides an intriguing link with the treatment under British domestic law of the BSkyB/ Manchester United merger; see Ch.12.
21. See M. Bose, *Manchester Unlimited*, London, 1999, Ch.2. It might be noted that these financial motivations run parallel to those driving the establishment of the Premier League in England in 1992 as an organization separate from the Football League, although promotion/relegation between the two Leagues was not abandoned.
22. In 1998/99 the winner of the competition had to play a minimum of 11 matches; in 1999/2000, 17. The expansion was achieved partly by allowing more entrants; the tournament was conceived originally as open only to national champions, yet, entirely inconsistent with its renaming, some countries now contribute four entrants. The final in 1998/99 was between Bayern Munich and Manchester United, neither of which had qualified as national champion.
23. For instance, in 1999/2000 the dates of the English FA Cup were changed from those used for many decades and brought forward earlier in the season in order to make time for 'Champions League' matches which filled six of eight midweeks between early March and mid April 2000. In the event, one of the prime movers, Manchester United, did not participate in the 1999/2000 FA Cup, preferring instead to participate in a lucrative new tournament, the World Club Championship, staged in Brazil in January 2000.
24. For instance, *The Times*, 4 Feb. 2000.
25. COM (1999) 644 and /2. See S. Weatherill, 'The Helsinki Report on Sport' (2000) 25 *ELRev* 282.
26. Cf. *1998 Football World Cup* n.18.
27. This is plain from *Bosman*; see especially the Opinion of AG Lenz.
28. Case 36/74 [1974] ECR 1405. See Weatherill, n.16 above, 354–57.
29. See recent proposals for release of exclusivity in favour of a greater degree of national-level application by courts and competition authorities discussed in the White Paper on Modernization, OJ 1997 C132/1.
30. Case C-36/74 *Walrave and Koch*, n.11, and Case C-415/93 *Bosman*, n.6, were both preliminary rulings; see also Case C-51/96 *Deliege* and Case C-176/96 *Lehtonen*, pending before the Court.
31. For instance, P. Cairns, T. Jennett and P. Sloane, 'The Economics of Professional Team Sports: A Survey of Theory and Evidence', 13 *Journal of Economic Studies* (1986), 3. AG Lenz's Opinion in *Bosman* also considers the matter. For economic analysis from a US perspective, see J. Quirk and R. Fort, *Pay Dirt: the Business of Professional Team Sports*, Princeton, NJ, 1997.
32. See COM (1997) 623.
33. E.g. in the UK, BSkyB/Manchester United, n.20. The thresholds in Art.1 of the EC Merger Regulation, Reg.4064/89 amended by Reg.1310/97, are set at a level which makes it improbable that the Commission will ever be able to claim jurisdiction over such mergers, leaving them to national authorities to examine.
34. See H. Fleming, 'Exclusive Rights to Broadcast Sporting Events in Europe', [1999] ECLR 143 and, more generally, D. Brinckman and E. Vollebregt, 'The Marketing of Sport and its Relation to EC Competition Law', [1998] ECLR 281; Beloff *et al.*, Ch.6.
35. The perceived impracticality of alternatives in meeting the requirement of effective distribution of revenues was central to the UK's Restrictive Practices Court's finding that the system of collective selling in England be allowed to continue; see n.9.
36. In England the beneficial effects of distribution of revenues outside the Premier League was one element in the RPC's finding in favour of collective selling; see n.9 above, especially para.348 of the judgment.
37. CAS 98/200 *AEK Athens and Slavia Prague* v. *UEFA* 20 Aug. 1999.
38. OJ 1999 C363/2.

39. Consider the (probably disproportionately restrictive) ban on all English football clubs from European competition in the 1980s: A. Evans, 'Freedom of Trade under the Common Law and EC Law: the Case of the Football Bans' (1986) 102 *LQR* 510. In *Bosman* itself UEFA, apparently believing until very late that litigation would not be pursued to the bitter end, failed even to submit within the time limit evidence about the economic impact of the system; see paras.52–4 of the ruling.
40. See generally P. Weiler and G. Roberts, *Sports and the Law*, 2nd edn (St. Paul: Westlaw, 1998), especially Ch.3.
41. Cf para.275 of AG Lenz's Opinion in *Bosman*.
42. This has not escaped the Commission's notice. In the Helsinki Report, n.25 above, it is commented that 'sporting federations ... have not set up a new alternative system to the one condemned by the Court' in *Bosman*.

10

Legislating for the Football Hooligan: A Case for Reform

Geoff Pearson

Introduction

In 1991 a statute was introduced that was widely heralded as putting the finishing touches to a 15-year campaign of legislation intended to defeat the English football hooligan.[1] However, almost a decade after the introduction of the Football (Offences) Act 1991, it appears that legislative attempts to control football crowd disorder have not had their desired effect. Despite the successful hosting of the 1996 European Championships and a dramatic fall in football-related arrests inside stadiums during the 1990s, it has been claimed that English football is once more suffering from an 'outbreak' of football hooliganism. Internationally, widespread disorder, including a full-blown riot in Marseilles,[2] marred England's brief stay at the 1998 World Cup and was quickly followed by disorder at England's European Championship qualifiers in Sweden and Luxembourg.

In addition, serious trouble appears to be breaking out once again in the domestic game, although the reporting of this by the media – in sharp contrast to the 'moral panic' of the 1970s and the 1980s – has been sporadic.[3] The warning signs for another possible 'epidemic' of football-related disorder around football grounds were already in place by the time of the fatal stabbing of the Fulham fan Matthew Fox by Gillingham fans following a bad-tempered Derby in March 1998. In the opening months of the 1998/99 season, there was reportedly serious and highly organized crowd disorder before and after Manchester United's match with Liverpool and upon Manchester City's visit to Millwall. That autumn also saw attacks on Leeds United fans at White Hart Lane, running battles between Hartlepool fans and police during a match at Halifax, and violence involving a number of London and Manchester firms upon Millwall's visit to Maine Road.[4] More recently, organized violence in Glasgow, following the Scotland vs. England play-off, led to around 170 arrests, despite the biggest football security operation ever mounted in Britain.[5] Moreover, while the total number of football-related arrests continues to drop, concern has been raised that arrests for *serious violent offences* are sharply on the rise, having nearly doubled in the 1998/99 season.[6] There have also been claims that the increase in football-related violence was subject to a 'cover-up' in order to protect England's chances of hosting the 2006 World Cup.[7]

To suggest that such disturbances necessarily demonstrate the social-control failures of the legislative programme would, of course, be both premature and naive. Much of the legislation enacted was introduced to combat *specific problems* in and around football grounds and cannot solely bear the responsibility for any perceived 'return' of football-related disorder. Such a conclusion would also overlook the impact of other social-control policies, such as the sentencing of convicted 'football hooligans' and the role of the Football Intelligence Unit. In addition, it would deny the possibility that factors 'external' to the law may themselves be responsible for the problems still being faced. For example, it could be argued that changes in the *type* of football-disorder bear some responsibility for the apparent upsurge in serious violent football-related offences. Much of the serious violence is occurring further away from the grounds than it was in the 1970s and the 1980s.[8] This makes it more difficult both to predict and to police, and means that much of the 'football specific' legislation enacted against the hooligan (for instance, the Football (Offences) Act 1991) is powerless.

This chapter assesses the criminal-legal responses to 'football hooliganism' in terms of their own social-control aims and objectives. In particular, it will focus on three of the major pieces of legislation enacted in the fight against football crowd disorder, investigating whether these have made any serious impact on football hooliganism. This analysis will be carried out using a mixture of both the official statistics of football-related arrests and my own research,[9] drawn mainly – but not exclusively – from extensive participant and overt observation at football grounds and magistrates' courts in the north-west of England.

The three Acts analysed here are the Sporting Events (Control of Alcohol) Act 1985, the Football Spectators Act (Part II) 1989 and the 1991 Act.[10] As we shall see, although many provisions in these Acts are quite draconian, their effect has not been particularly dramatic. The tension between the provisions themselves and their *implementation* is a major, recurring theme, and, as Greenfield and Osborn have argued, 'The problem is essentially with the application of the law rather than the lack of it.'[11] Bearing this in mind, in the final section of the chapter the recent Football (Offences and Disorder) Act 1999 will be considered, as will proposals for new laws to deal with football-crowd disorder. These will be examined with respect to both their chances of preventing incidents of hooliganism and their impact upon the civil liberties of football fans.

The Sporting Events (Control of Alcohol etc.) Act 1985

This Act (hereafter called 'SECAA') was based on similar legislation in Scotland,[12] which the Scottish Football Association had cited as a contributory factor to a decrease in crowd violence in the 'Old Firm' games played since 1981.[13] SECAA was based on the premise that much disorder at football is related to alcohol intake,[14] making spectators more aggressive and less inhibited by deterrent social-control features such as a police presence and closed circuit television. This premise is not one that has been accepted without criticism. Indeed, the 1985 Act was implemented despite – rather than because of – the 1984 Report of the Official Working Group on Football Spectator Violence.[15] This argued that legislation preventing the consumption of alcohol at grounds or on football 'specials' was unnecessary, partly because the police had reported to them that alcohol was *not* a major factor for much football-related violence in England and Wales. My own research suggested that drinking in pubs around the ground and taking drink on the transport to the match was an integral part of many fans' trips to watch football, and evidence from the 'hooligans' themselves also points to the tendency of many fans to drink before and after matches.[16] However, this does not necessarily prove a *causal link* between the amount of alcohol consumed and the effect of this upon the levels of violence afterwards.

Moreover, even if we accept the link as proven, there are other serious criticisms of the social-control effectiveness of the Act. SECAA was introduced as a response to high-profile incidents of football-related violence towards the end of the 1984/85 season,[17] which had apparently been 'serious' enough to draw the attention of the Prime Minister.[18] The Act was seen as a 'rushed job' by many of the Members of Parliament involved in the debate as – despite the individual opposition of many of them to parts of the Bill – it did not receive the 'proper scrutiny'[19] of a Standing Committee (the intention was to have the Bill enacted before the beginning of the upcoming season). Furthermore, it was argued that to base the Act upon the pre-existing Scottish legislation – and its apparent 'success' – was a mistake since the Scottish situation before the 1981 Act was not comparable to the situation in England and Wales.[20]

Regardless of this opposition, the aim of SECAA was to reduce crowd disorder by restricting the availability of alcohol to spectators before, during and after a match. Its first two provisions were aimed at reducing the alcohol intake of spectators before they entered the ground. First, the Act prohibits the carrying of alcohol on so-called 'football specials'[21] and gives the police powers to stop and search such transport if they suspect that alcohol is on board. Secondly, the Act makes it an offence for an individual to attempt to enter a football ground while 'drunk'.[22] Prima facie, these two provisions appear in theory as quite rational attempts to fight disorder at matches, if we accept the link between alcohol and aggression as 'proven'.

Difficulties lie, however, in the practical enforcement of the provisions. As regards the first, my own research demonstrated that alcohol was allowed on many independent or affiliated supporters' coaches, with both the organizers and the consumers willing to risk the minimal chance of their being stopped and searched by police. In addition, the Act does not cover private vehicles used as transport to matches, although car-loads of drunken fans are presumably as undesirable as coach-loads. More importantly, as regards the second provision of the statute, there seems to be a reluctance by stewards on the turnstiles to attempt to prevent entry by those who are 'drunk'.[23] SECAA does not prohibit the consumption of any amount of alcohol, and thus stewards and police must be satisfied that the suspect is 'drunk', a term which relies upon a certain amount of subjectivity. Heavy drinkers, for example, may be able to consume many pints of beer, smell of alcohol and yet be quite sober, and to distinguish between rowdy and drunken behaviour at the turnstiles is also a difficulty. My research suggested that only in the most extreme cases would fans ever be arrested or even turned away for attempting to enter the ground while drunk.[24] If this scenario is repeated throughout the country, then it is likely that thousands of spectators pass through the turnstiles for matches every week who are heavily under the influence of alcohol, and would be many times over the limit to prohibit them from driving. Clearly, this has severely reduced this section of the Act's effectiveness.

Ironically, while the Act aims to increase controls on supporters entering the ground while drunk, decisions continue to be made that seriously undermine attempts to prevent drunken disorder inside grounds. A Second Division Derby between Preston and Blackpool in December 1996 that led to widespread disorder both during and after the match (and 78 arrests),[25] provides a classic case-study of the ineffectiveness of the Act. The game was classified as a high-risk match,[26] but, as a result of the intense local rivalry between the two clubs, *Sky Sports* decided to screen the match on a Friday night.[27] As a result, it appeared that many supporters simply saw the game as part of the usual Friday night 'pub crawl'. A large number of fans arrived for the game heavily under the influence of alcohol, and – following the match – both sets of supporters descended upon the town centre to continue drinking and fighting at the pubs and clubs of Preston.

It is noticeable that, of 17 Preston fans appearing before the magistrates' court on a single morning after this game, only two were arrested for trying to enter the ground while drunk (s.2(2)). However, the Crown Prosecution Service (CPS) solicitor noted that in many of the other cases where the offence occurred inside the stadium, the offender had been drinking heavily. Two of the offenders were charged with being drunk inside a football ground, one having entered despite his being warned outside and the other being arrested only after police caught him gesticulating threateningly at the visiting supporters. In addition, three defendants pleading guilty to public order offences inside the stadium, admitted being drunk and two of these even went as far as using the fact that they were drunk as excuses for their behaviour![28]

SECAA also aims to prevent the consumption of alcohol within football grounds by: (i) making it an offence to attempt to take alcohol into a football ground,[29] and (ii) prohibiting the consumption of alcohol within sight of the pitch.[30] In the enforcement of these two specific aims the Act appears – in the main – to have been highly successful, with clubs strictly enforcing the prohibition and few fans risking the smuggling of alcohol into grounds. Again, if we see the link between violence and alcohol as established, then to prevent fans from taking their own alcohol into a stadium seems a necessary social-control move (especially as alcohol consumed in bottles and cans also provides spectators with potential missiles).[31] However, even accepting this link, we need to examine the Act's second aim carefully. Does the prohibition of alcohol within sight of the pitch really reduce the amount drunk? It must be remembered that before the publication of the Taylor Report[32] it was impossible in many grounds to serve alcohol out of sight of the pitch, or licences for its sale were not granted, and SECAA does not actually prevent the consumption of alcohol before a match. Therefore many fans who wanted to mix alcohol with football tended to drink at pubs near the ground before a match. This was because they knew that alcohol would either not be available within the stadium or that it would be more expensive, of poorer quality and drunk in less comfortable surroundings, often with lengthy queues. There is still a tendency for fans, following this trend, to get 'tanked up' before a kick-off, with the poorly enforced provision against admitting drunken fans into stadiums acting as little or no deterrent. One problem caused by this is that fans tend to arrive at the ground later, causing long queues at turnstiles with drunken fans frustrated that they will miss the kick-off.

A more serious problem for public order is that drinking in pubs close to the ground provides an ideal opportunity for fans of both teams to meet before the match in a drink-charged atmosphere, usually without the deterrence provided by police presence or cctv. The Act may lead the visiting fans to arrive earlier and find a pub near the ground to drink in, where they may meet home fans with the same intent. Not only does this defeat the immediate purpose of the Act (in reducing alcohol consumption before a match), but it also makes incidents between rival fans drinking in the same establishment likely, with potential weaponry (glasses and bottles) to hand and a greater risk to the uninvolved public. The subsequent segregation of fans seems nearly pointless. For some supporters, entry into the home fans' pub is comparable to 'taking the home end',[33] and many supporters still 'scout' pubs in the locality of the ground in order to identify where rival fans are drinking in order to confront them.

The Taylor Report suggested the removal of the ban on the sale of alcohol at grounds, stating that it was having a detrimental effect because drunken fans were arriving late and causing congestion.[34] If more bars inside the ground were open, it was suggested that more fans would be likely to arrive earlier and therefore avoid trouble in pubs with rival fans. Furthermore, before the Act, controls on bars inside grounds already existed. Where there was evidence that bars in certain parts of a ground could potentially lead to disorder, the police could request that these bars should be closed by the club.[35] It seems that these 'requests' were regularly followed, especially as the police could insist on drafting in extra officers to oversee crowd disorder caused by the bar in question, with the club footing the bill.[36] Taylor's comments on the prohibition of alcohol at grounds appear well-founded. It would seem that the Act's restriction on alcohol at grounds is serving little purpose as regards social control, and could well be having a detrimental effect in the fight against crowd disorder.

While measures such as a complete alcohol ban in all grounds, combined with the stricter enforcement of the rules concerning the allowing of drunken fans into the ground and perhaps uniform 12 noon kick-offs, might be justifiable from a social-control point of view, the present system has few benefits and some serious drawbacks. SECAA is clearly not preventing drunken fans from entering football grounds owing to the non-enforcement of its provisions by match-day stewards and police. More seriously, in failing to prevent drunken fans from entering football grounds, the legislation itself in fact ignores trouble outside them. In attempting to exert more control over crowds within grounds, its provisions may even be pushing trouble out on to the streets and into nearby pubs. While it would be naive to suggest that the current resurgence in violence outside football grounds has been brought about as a direct result of SECAA's failings, the Act's impact on football-related violence has certainly been a far cry from that intended by the government in 1985.

The Football Spectators Act 1989 (Part II)

Part II of the Act introduced restriction orders,[37] intended to prevent those convicted of football-related offences from leaving the country whenever English teams are playing outside England or Wales,[38] for either two or five years after the commission of the offence. Instead, the individuals must attend certain police stations during the time of the match, to ensure that they are obeying the order.[39] Although in theory the Act appears valuable in preventing known hooligans from travelling abroad to cause trouble, in practice, the Act has failed in the main to achieve its objectives.

When English fans rioted in Dublin in February 1995, for example, only two 'hooligans' were subject to the restriction orders.[40] This was despite the fact that the Football Unit of the National Criminal Intelligence Service claimed that at least 30 'known hooligans' had travelled for the match. By the time of the disorder at the Italy vs. England World Cup qualifier in October 1997, this number had risen to just nine.[41] There seemed no obvious reason why the courts had not been willing to impose these orders on convicted hooligans (especially as at the time of the disorder in Rome, 400 fans were subject to domestic Exclusion Orders under s.30 of the Public Order Act 1986).[42] In response to this criticism, the Home Secretary issued guidelines in December 1997 that all persons convicted of football-related offences between then and the World Cup in 1998 should be placed under restriction orders.[43] By the time of the World Cup the number of orders issued had risen to above 70.[44]

However, the increasing numbers of orders issued – and an Anglo-French agreement in June 1998 whereby those convicted of football-related offences in France also had to appear before British magistrates on their return to have restriction orders imposed on them[45] – only served to demonstrate more fundamental problems inherent in the wording of the statute. More recently, questions have been asked as to the effectiveness of the 1989 Act in dealing with those convicted of offences which are considered 'football-related' by the government and the media but which do not actually fall within the definition of 'football-related' provided in the Act.[46]

The 1989 Act follows a strict statutory definition of what is 'football related'. As a result, offences which are carried out more than 2 hours before kick-off (but not on the journey to the match) were not classified as 'football-related' and therefore could not lead to the imposition of a restriction order. Such a narrow definition severely restricted the effectiveness of the Football Spectators Act. For matches abroad, many fans arrive days before the event, and are likely to remain in the area afterwards. This situation occurred in Marseilles during the World Cup, where it soon became embarrassingly clear that, despite the Anglo-French agreement, none of those arrested for rioting could have restriction orders imposed upon them.[47] Since then, the Football (Offences and Disorder) Act 1999 has extended the definition of 'football-related' for the purpose of the 1989 Act to include offences committed up to 24 hours before and after a game. But only time will tell whether the closing of this loop-hole will enable the 1989 Act finally to achieve its aims.

The Football (Offences) Act 1991

This Act[48] created three new statutory offences under which 'disorderly' fans could be convicted. Section 4 makes encroaching on to the pitch or the 'cinder track' surrounding it during a designated match a criminal offence. Section 3 makes racist or indecent chanting within a football stadium[49] an offence. Section 2, which is less problematic in terms of enforcement (and will not be covered in detail here), makes it an offence to throw any object within a football stadium. Before this Act, convictions could be obtained for these actions, but they relied upon legal ingenuity in twisting the definition of other offences (especially threatening behaviour under the Public Order Acts and the common-law offence of behaviour likely to cause a breach of the peace) to fit the specific action.[50] As a result, convictions were harder to obtain and court action was, to a certain extent, discouraged.[51] The 1991 Act, however, in making such actions specific criminal offences, intended to eliminate this problem. Furthermore, convictions under any section of the Football (Offences) Act can only be tried summarily,[52] which should encourage the police and the CPS to charge 'hooligans' under the legislation. Finally, the high publicity of the Act's provisions means that supporters are now clear that certain actions are criminal offences. Many football clubs discourage pitch 'invasions' by advertising in the stands that to invade the pitch is now a criminal offence, in much the same way as supermarkets have used posters stating that, 'Shoplifters will be prosecuted'.

Section 4 of the Act provides that: 'It is an offence for a person ... to go on to the playing area or any area adjacent to the playing area to which the spectators are not generally admitted ... without lawful excuse.' To criminalize 'going on to the pitch' as an offence in itself was born out of two motives. First, while many 'aggressive' pitch invasions could be 'dealt with' by means of the offence of threatening behaviour, other pitch invasions (in celebration or protest) were clearly not threatening. This was despite the fact that the mere presence of opposing fans on the pitch was often enough to provoke rival fans.[53] Instances of celebratory pitch invasions leading to trouble were high, as rival fans were already likely to be upset by the reason for the 'celebration', but the criminal law provided no fool-proof method of deterring such invasions.[54]

Prosecution depended upon charges made under either the Public Order Act 1986 (which, in turn, depended upon construing a celebratory pitch invasion as threatening or disorderly behaviour), or relying upon the common-law offence of behaviour likely to cause a breach of the peace. As Trivizas points out, 'prosecutions for common law offences are clearly avoided by the police ... Instead there is a clear preference for statutory offences'.[55] It is noticeable that only 136 out of 3,577 total arrests for football-related offences in 1996/97 were made for the common-law offence of behaviour likely to cause a breach of the peace. Secondly, the removal of perimeter fencing as a result of the Taylor Report[56] made access on to the pitch and the cinder track easier, and with no clear criminal deterrent existing to stop such behaviour, the Report recommended that an offence of running on to the pitch should be created.[57]

However, my own research demonstrated that the effect of the 1991 Act, even in terms of deterrence, is minimal. Many goals were greeted by minor pitch invasions from behind the goal and, on one occasion, I witnessed fans making 'sportsman's bets' with stewards on the gate that they would 'get past them' for the next goal. The typical response of the stewards on duty at nearly all of the matches attended was to try and catch fans who had invaded the pitch and then push them back to the terrace. During my participant observational research I witnessed few ejections and hardly any arrests for invasions of the pitch, and it was apparent that the majority of fans considered that the chances of their being ejected or arrested for invading the pitch were negligible.

Furthermore, at the end of the final game of the season it became common for fans of several clubs to invade the pitch – regardless of the result. At one match, for example, an announcement actually welcomed fans on to the pitch to celebrate with the players. At another game hundreds of visiting fans climbed over the perimeter fencing before the final whistle and stood on the cinder track, before invading the pitch and charging the home fans, who also invaded it from the other side of the ground. The police's response to the invasion at this game was to allow the game to finish first and then try and prevent confrontation with the home fans. However, there was no actual attempt to prevent the unlawful invasion itself. Attempts to arrest individuals from those attempting to invade the pitch may well have only inflamed the situation, and would certainly have reduced police manpower, allowing a pitch invasion before the final whistle and possible confrontation with the home fans.

In Bittner's ethnomethodological study of police officers patrolling in 'rough' inner-city areas in the United States,[58] it is argued that the police had two separate roles; that of law enforcement in individual cases and of 'peace-keeping' more generally. His participant observation suggested that officers were more concerned with the peace-keeping aspect of their work than with individual law enforcement and that the police tended only to arrest when the general peace was threatened.[59] Bittner also found that the police were much more likely to give informal warnings to those breaking 'minor' criminal laws than to arrest them, and made the distinction between *invoking* the law, and *enforcing* it.[60] The former was often used to prevent the latter and in this way the police attempted to keep the general peace and gain the trust and respect of those on 'skid row'. The policing of the football match in question, and of many other, similar matches attended during my own research, bears a clear resemblance to the types of situation Bittner described in his work in that the police's 'overall objective is to reduce the total amount of risk in the area. In this, practicality plays a considerably more important role than legal norms ...'[61]

However, experiences of invading the pitch *en masse* and of not experiencing or even witnessing arrests or ejections reinforce the fans' belief that invasions are acceptable. Although there were nearly 200 arrests under s.4 in the 1998/99 season, in comparison with the number of pitch invasions in a season this actually demonstrates that police and stewards are in the majority of instances not enforcing the provision. As a result, s.4 is serving little deterrent purpose.[62] Until this provision is enforced by the police and stewards to an extent to which it acts as a deterrent that makes even the most drunken and ecstatic fan think twice about running on to the pitch, its practical purpose is limited merely to the prosecution of a few unfortunate fans.

Section 3 of the Act prohibits 'racialist or indecent chanting' within a football ground. The synchronized chanting of fans to encourage their team or insult the opposition team or fans is a traditional and deep-rooted aspect of football support. Indeed, for many fans their 'duty' to their team resides in the vocal support they give, and, in turn, clubs actively encourage 'atmosphere' within grounds. However, observational research at football grounds in the North West demonstrated to me that many of the most popular terrace chants contain what may broadly be defined as 'swear words', and would be classed as 'indecent' under s.3.

The Act defined 'chanting' as 'the repeated uttering of any words or sounds in concert with one or more others'.[63] Therefore individual comments or even chants, were not included[64] until the Football (Offences and Disorder) Act 1999 closed this loophole. Therefore a fan who makes very audible attempts to start an indecent or racialist chant committed an offence under the Act only when others joined in. However, once a large crowd indulges in an illegal chant the police tend not to arrest, in part because of the impracticality of arresting all those involved. The fact that s.3 failed to make attempted indecent chanting an offence may, in fact, have prevented the only practical opportunity to prevent such chants 'breaking out', and it will be interesting to see whether the 1999 changes lead to an increase in the usage of this section.

My own research indicated that chants 'of a ... racialist nature',[65] were substantially outnumbered by the more common 'indecent' chants and as such were less of a problem in terms of s.3. However, there were several incidents of racist chanting, most noticeably by Blackpool fans at a televised Derby at Preston. These chants were sung quite clearly and on a large scale by fans at one end of the ground;[66] but despite a large police presence, no action was taken against any of the offenders. As we have seen, the problems of identifying an offender from a crowd for the purposes of the Football (Offences) Act (and providing evidence of guilt sufficient for a conviction) are particularly troublesome, especially for grounds that still have terracing.[67]

The result of this is that the police often consider the identification and punishment of offenders to be an issue for the club, rather than one for themselves. An example of this attitude with respect to identifying offenders under s.2 of the Act (throwing an object inside a football stadium) occurred following a highly publicized incident of bottle-throwing during Manchester United's visit to Everton in November 1998. On this occasion it was the club which announced that they would be taking action to identify and ban the offenders for breach of ground regulations, rather than the police's announcing they would be attempting to bring a prosecution under s.2.[68]

Even if successful action were being taken against offenders under s.3 of the 1991 Act, it could not succeed in wiping out all insulting or aggressive chanting from the terraces. This would require an exceptionally wide interpretation to be taken of the word 'indecent' to include threats that did not contain recognized swear-words (for instance, the word scum, which is a common terrace insult). Even chants that 'on paper' are not threatening or insulting may appear so when accompanied by aggressive pointing at the rival fans to, for example, 'rub in' the fact that their team had conceded a goal. The Act makes no attempt to cover these sorts of insulting or threatening chants, despite their potential to upset and provoke rival fans to the same extent as indecent chants. Instead, the prosecution of fans involved in these types of chants can only be carried out if the words are deemed as 'threatening' or 'insulting' under the Public Order Act (and it needs to be remembered that s.3 was drafted because this Act was considered to be inadequate in this respect). Therefore we can again see an inconsistency between the policy behind the Act and the construction of s.3 itself, with its emphasis on the exact wording of the chant rather than its intent or effect.

In conclusion, it may be argued that s.3 is even more impotent than s.4 in terms of achieving its social-control aims. Not only do the same problems of identification and mass arrest arise from police attempts to act, but the wording of the section excludes many chants, shouts and gestures which may be as threatening or insulting as those classified as racialist or 'indecent' chanting. Neither threatening or insulting chanting (which is not indecent), nor 'indecent' gestures carried out *en masse* or otherwise are included within the Act. It seems inconsistent to provide only a 'football specific' remedy for racialist or indecent chanting and yet to leave other types of abuse of fans, players and officials to the Public Order Act which was considered inadequate to deal with the former, often more clear-cut, forms of abuse.

The practicalities of enforcing the Football (Offences) Act are highly problematic throughout. Participant observation led me to the conclusion that the offences covered by the statute are often considered so minor that they rarely lead to police action, never mind arrest. So many offences occur during a football match that infringe one or more of the sections of the Act that, despite increased police powers, arrests are made in only exceptional circumstances. For actions infringing the Act which are generally considered 'non-harmful' (such as the throwing of ripped-up newspaper, the good-natured pitch invasion to mark the end of the season and the chanting of traditional football songs with abusive language) the police turn a blind eye. Usually arrests are made only when such actions are likely to break the general 'peace' with the possible result of more serious offences.[69] In addition, with football clubs relying increasingly on match-day stewards rather than police – and the emphasis being placed more on the observation of ground regulations than adherence to criminal legislation – there are likely to be even fewer arrests.

Although the police and stewarding policy of the general non-enforcement of the Football (Offences) Act may appear to be in line with the overall social-control policy of the statute, it does, in fact, dramatically reduce the effectiveness of the Act. Despite the threat of police action and the occasional arrest, the deterrent value of the Act is quite negligible. Statistics of arrest, when compared with data gathered from observational research, show that (with the possible exception of s.2), the number of arrests compared with that of the offences committed is exceptionally low. In the 1998/99 season 198 arrests were made nationally under s.4. And yet at only 34 matches attended during the 1995/96 season, there were over 20 pitch invasions involving between ten and 500 fans on each occasion. As regards racialist or indecent chanting, the number of arrests since the Act's coming into force has been as low as ten a season.[70] Again, observational research reveals that there are typically dozens of 'indecent' chants at the average league game, the largest of which may involve tens of thousands of spectators. Fans experience, week in, week out, the inactivity of police and stewards towards indecent chanting and (to a lesser extent) pitch invasions, and it is not surprising that the police's ambivalent attitude towards these offences is reflected in the behaviour of the fans. Again, we can see that, although the legislation in itself is quite draconian, the widespread failure to implement its provisions has severely weakened its impact.

Remedial Policies: the Problem with Pursuing a Strict 'Social-Control' Approach to Football Crowds

So far this chapter has measured the success of legislation targeted at 'football hooliganism' strictly against the social-control aims of the legislation itself. However, while this is a useful task in elucidating the several failings of many of the measures and their application, such a perspective tells us only part of the story. Indeed, the criticisms of the law's response to football hooliganism identified so far point towards remedial policies that would strengthen the state powers of social control on football fans. This could be carried out through the extension of s.3 of the Football (Offences) Act or s.15 of the Football Spectators Act, or through enforcing a 'unit limit' on alcohol intake of football fans by breathalysing spectators as they go through the turnstiles.[71]

However, accepting that the criminal law needs to prevent drunken fans from entering football grounds, or needs to prevent those with apparently 'football-related' convictions from travelling to matches, or needs to stop chants of 'You're gonna get your fucking heads kicked in' is a dangerous step. Football fans are already subject to all manner of highly restrictive, social-control measures. We have already considered some of the legislative restrictions, but the regulation of football fandom is by no means limited to these.

Further legislative measures arise from the imposition of Exclusion Orders under s.30 of the Public Order Act 1986, s.166 of the Criminal Justice and Public Order Act 1994 (ticket-touting),[72] and the recent Football (Offences and Disorder) Act 1999. In addition to these football-specific measures, other more general provisions have been applied to football fans in a highly restrictive sense. For example, 'threatening behaviour' under s.4 of the Public Order Act 1986 has been widely used to charge disorderly fans and s.60 of the 1994 Act could be used to legitimize the stopping and searching of all fans travelling to matches.[73]

In addition, these restrictions have been combined with deterrent sentencing, the admission of dubious evidence in the trials of alleged football hooligans[74] and extensive extra-judicial social-control policies. For example, the Football Intelligence Unit has the power to photograph and file the details of fans suspected of involvement in 'football-related' crime,[75] and these details have been used as a basis to prevent fans from leaving the country or to deport them back to Britain.[76] Other severe social-control provisions have also been used in this area, such as severe restrictions on the freedom of movement for supporters of a certain team[77] and the searching of fans as a condition of their entering a football ground.[78]

The point here is not just that such wide-ranging measures have failed to prevent continuing football-related disorder – although this criticism can easily be levelled. More importantly, these policies, both individually and in concert, expose further discrepancies between the 'promise' of the law and the lived reality for football fans. Those who introduce and apply law in the United Kingdom still claim that British law follows constitutional principles under the rule of law, such as equality before the law, the presumption of innocence and the requirement of due process,[79] all of which act to legitimize the law's interference in public life. Indeed, most of these principles have been incorporated into the legal system by way of the United Kingdom's ratification to the European Convention on Human Rights and the enactment of the Human Rights Act 1998.

Bearing in mind these supposed 'higher objectives' of United Kingdom law, it is clear that many of the measures used to fight football hooliganism already infringe the civil liberties of innocent fans.[80] For example, by preventing their leaving the country when England play abroad[81] if they are suspected of involvement in hooliganism – but without evidence sufficient to charge, never mind convict those fans of any offence – the principles of due process and the presumption of innocence are being clearly infringed.

An extension of restrictive social-control measures on fans to try and prevent hooliganism would run the risk of infringing the civil liberties of the innocent to an even greater extent. It was initially proposed that the Football (Offences and Disorder) Act 1999 should extend the courts' powers to impose 'international banning orders' upon those who are merely *suspected* of being hooligans, regardless of whether or not they had been convicted or even charged with a particular offence. Although this proposal was withdrawn from the Bill, Kate Hoey (then Under-Secretary of State for the Home Department) stated at the Committee stage that

> The power to make banning orders in respect of people without conviction is necessary... the Government will want to return to the matter, because from football intelligence we know that some people commit offences or are involved in organizing violence but cleverly manage not to be where they may be arrested. We need to find a way of dealing with those people.[82]

Should legislation to this effect become law, the most basic rights of football fans under the rule of law and the European Convention on Human Rights would be curtailed in the extreme.

Therefore before we start considering how best to increase the restrictions on fans, we need to ask whether this is absolutely necessary. Indeed, we need to consider whether the existing legislation and social-control policies can be justified in terms of the scale and scope of football-related disorder itself. Since incidents of such disorder first appeared in the national news, football hooliganism has been depicted as a particularly widespread and dangerous phenomenon, characterized by police, judges, politicians and the media as 'the English disease'.[83] In a case typical of the attitude towards the phenomenon during the 1980s, Lord Justice Russell remarked that an incident of violence involving football supporters on a cross-channel ferry was tantamount to piracy, and commented that: 'I know of my own knowledge that the foreign press call this particular form of mindless violence "the English sickness". It is a sickness and a scourge that threatens to destroy civilized life in our country ...'[84]

When football hooliganism is seen in this way, it is clear how governments have been able to impose such severe social-control sanctions upon fans. Indeed, it is arguable that the state is capable of severely infringing the civil liberties of fans without serious criticism precisely because it has *constructed* football hooliganism in such a way.[85] Armstrong and Young also question the reliability of such 'institutional truths'[86] about hooliganism, noting that 'partisan fanship' – as they define behaviour which may or may not be defined as 'football hooliganism' – has been 'largely misunderstood, misinterpreted and misrepresented, and this has led inexorably to vilification and a profound over-reaction'.[87]

Therefore, if we want a criminal-legal response to football hooliganism that is more 'appropriate' to the internal norms of the law and that takes into account the relative extent of the phenomenon, we should not look to merely increase the level of legal restrictions upon fans. Instead, we need to be more dispassionate when looking at how the law should respond to hooliganism. Does football crowd violence really 'threaten civilized life'? Is it so different from other forms of public disorder at – for example – extremist political rallies, drinking holidays in Ibiza or outside pubs at closing time? Should football fans be treated differently from those of other sports or those who attend such political rallies, drinking holidays or public houses?

If it could be argued that the enacted legislation and the social-control policies complementing it in the fight against hooliganism had been successful in reducing football-related disorder then there may be an argument, on the pragmatic grounds that 'the end justifies the means'. In that case, the losses in terms of the civil liberties of innocent football fans might be justifiable. However, as has been demonstrated here, the failings of the legislation in terms of both its drafting and its application are severe, even in its attempts to stamp out the most minor of public-order offences which may be described as purely traditional or ceremonial 'banter'.[88] Moreover, the exaggeration of the scale and the effect of football hooliganism means that such a pragmatic justification could not be taken seriously even if the legislation were achieving its specific objectives.

Conclusion

As the 1990s have come to a close, it is clear that the attempts to legislate the 'football hooligan' out of existence have not been successful. Even the most basic attempts of the Football (Offences) Act and the Sporting Events (Control of Alcohol) Act to prohibit specific actions within football stadiums have been thwarted by both over-ambitious drafting and the non-enforcement of their provisions by police and match-day stewards. In addition, the extent of the failure of these Acts is so manifest that their deterrent function is minimal.

Of more concern than this is the way in which the phenomenon of football-related disorder more generally appears to have sidestepped the legislative measures imposed upon football crowds as its resurgence continues to threaten England's bid for the 2006 World Cup. Serious violence within grounds does not occur as regularly as it did during the 1970s or the early 1980s; but since the relatively 'quiet' days of the early 1990s, violent disorder outside grounds appears to be as serious as ever, and is quite possibly on the increase.[89] The failure of legislation to address this problem competently is a serious issue. The Football (Offences) Act 1991 has been completely unable to achieve its own specific crowd-control objectives, and the Football Spectators Act 1989 has continually failed to prevent convicted hooligans from travelling abroad with England. Furthermore, once this failure is combined with the possible role of the Sporting Events (Control of Alcohol) Act 1985 in creating the opportunity for more violence outside football grounds, we can see that the legislation enacted against the hooligan has – at the very least – failed to prevent the current reported resurgence. In the worst-case scenario the legislation may well have actually contributed to the recorded growth in serious violent disorder.

However, the failures of the legislation to achieve its own social-control aims have been mirrored by a more general failure of the state, through its imposition of increasingly draconian policies and tactics, to live up to its own legitimating ideals in terms of the rule of law and human rights. The attitude that the independent regulation of football crowds is the best way to deal with hooliganism has led to the present spiral of legal measures, each of which increasingly attacks the civil liberties, not just of the 'hooligans', but also of innocent supporters. Certainly at present, the price being paid by the average fan cannot be justified by the extremely modest improvements in crowd behaviour in and around football grounds.

NOTES

1. See, for example, *Guardian*, 17 Feb. 1995.
2. 'The worst sustained violence involving England fans for a decade', according to the *Daily Express* (15 June 1998).
3. See 'Folk Devils and Moral Panics', in S. Cohen, *Images of Deviance*, Harmondsworth, 1970 and S. Hall, 'The Treatment of "Football Hooligans" in the Press', in R. Ingham *et al.*, *Football Hooliganism: The Wider Context*, London, 1978.
4. *Observer*, 4 Oct. 1998.
5. *Daily Telegraph*, 15 Nov. 1999.
6. National Criminal Intelligence Service press release 31 July 1999.
7. According to a spokesman from the Football Task Force (see *The Observer*, 4 Oct. 1998). This was strongly denied by Alec McGiven, chairman of England's 2006 World Cup bid-organizing committee (Football Research Unit Conference, Wembley Hilton, Jan. 1999).
8. According to the author's correspondence with the Football Unit of the National Criminal Intelligence Service.

9. An undergraduate dissertation and subsequent doctoral thesis on the law's response to football hooliganism, Lancaster University, 1995–98.

10. It needs to be recognized that these were not the only 'football-specific' legislative measures which have been introduced and have affected the control of football crowds (see below).

11. S. Greenfield and G. Osborn, 'Poor Laws', *When Saturday Comes* (Feb. 1999), no.144, 14.

12. The Criminal Justice (Scotland) Act 1980 which prohibited the consumption of alcohol at football grounds and on football 'specials'. This was based on the McElhone report, 1977 which said there was a strong link between football violence and alcohol intake.

13. This term refers to the Glasgow Derby between Celtic and Rangers. The legislation was also praised in the annual report of the Chief Constable of Strathclyde in 1983.

14. A link noted by the court in *R.* v. *Doncaster Justices ex parte Langfield* QBD 149 JP 26, 22 Oct. 1984, a case pre-empting the 1985 Act by confirming an alcohol ban within Doncaster Rovers' ground due to the 'link' with violence.

15. Especially para.5.

16. E.g., C. Ward, *Steaming In: Journal of a Football Fan*, London, 1989; D. Brimson and E. Brimson, *Everywhere We Go: Behind the Matchday Madness*, London, 1996 (especially Ch.7).

17. Luton Town v. Millwall, Birmingham City v. Leeds United and the European Cup Final at Heysel where a terrace 'charge' by Liverpool supporters led to the deaths of 39 spectators.

18. In 1981 a Bill similar to SECAA 1985 was blocked by the government.

19. D. Hogg, Commons Hansard, 3 July 1985, col.423.

20. Scottish football grounds were 'dry' before 1980 and the major problem regarding alcohol was fans taking their own alcohol into the stadiums (T. Pendry, Commons Hansard, 3 July 1985, col.358).

21. s.1.

22. s.2(2).

23. The switch away from direct policing to match-day stewarding at football matches may be one reason for the failure to implement this section. My own research at Preston Magistrates' Court in 1997 suggested that the police were far more likely to turn spectators away for being drunk than the stewards.

24. Although 1,113 fans were arrested in the 1998/99 season for drink-related offences, this includes offences outside the SECAA. Even though it is the highest reason for football-related arrests, the numbers still do not reflect the number of 'drunk' fans entering football grounds every week.

25. *Lancashire Evening Post* and *Blackpool Evening Gazette*, 14 Dec. 1996.

26. On the previous time that the teams had met in a competitive match there had been a major pitch invasion and fighting on the park outside the ground both before and after the match, and in 1992 Blackpool fans ambushed the Preston fans as they walked back to the train station, resulting in 20 arrests (*Blackpool Evening Gazette*, 12 Oct. 1992).

27. As a result of the disorder, the police have made the return games at Blackpool 12 noon kick-offs.

28. Preston Magistrates' Court, 14 Jan. 1997.

29. s.2(1)(b).

30. s.2(1)(a).

31. s.3 makes it an offence to possess any container 'of the kind usually discarded when empty' [s.2(3)(a)(iii)] for drink which could cause injury if thrown.

32. Hillsborough Stadium Disaster Inquiry Final Report, London, 1990.

33. The practice of visiting fans' infiltrating the home 'end' (i.e., the section of segregated terrace meant for home fans only) became prevalent in the 1970s. The tactic is reported widely in Ward's book (n.16) and more recently (1995) was dramatized in the BBC film *I.D.*.

34. Hillsborough Stadium Disaster Inquiry Report para.255.
35. And in *R.* v. *Doncaster Justices, ex parte Langfield* (QBD 149 JP 26, 22 Oct. 1984), a licensing application by Doncaster Rovers FC was rejected because of the supposed link between alcohol and football violence.
36. *Harris* v. *Sheffield United FC Ltd* [1987] 3 WLR 305. The Taylor Report also suggested that the sale of alcohol inside grounds might help to prevent drunkenness since the service is so slow at football ground bars that fans would not have the time to get drunk! (para.255).
37. Renamed International Banning Orders by the Football (Offences and Disorder) Act 1999.
38. s.15.
39. s.15(5); the Football (Offences and Disorder) Act 1999 now permits the confiscation of passports for those serving International Banning Orders.
40. *Guardian*, 27 Feb. 1995.
41. *Daily Mirror*, 13 Oct. 1997.
42. Ibid.
43. *Guardian*, 27 Dec. 1997.
44. *Daily Express*, 31 Aug. 1998.
45. *Independent*, 3 June 1998.
46. See *Daily Express*, 31 Aug. 1998.
47. Ibid.
48. A direct response to the request for specific legislation made in the 1990 Taylor Report (para.299).
49. Football grounds are 'designated' as such by a statutory instrument by order of the Secretary of State.
50. John Duncan argues that the 1991 Act has played an important part in 'winning' the battle against hooliganism (*Guardian*, 17 Feb. 1995).
51. In the debate before the passing of the Sporting Events (Control of Alcohol) Act 1985, an example was given of a Chelsea v. Sunderland game where, despite 80 fans' being arrested for football-related violence, many could not be brought to justice because there was not the sufficient legislation available at the time (J. Carlisle, Commons Hansard, 3 July 1985, col.376). The 1985 Act and the Football (Offences) Act 1991 would have meant that more of those arrested could have been 'brought to justice'.
52. s.5(2).
53. Hillsborough Stadium Disaster Inquiry Final Report, para.289.
54. G. Armstrong and D. Hobbs, however, claim that the law already provided police with sufficient powers in this area. 'Tackled from Behind', in R. Giulianotti *et al.*, *Football, Violence and Social Identity*, London, 1994, 225.
55. E. Trivizas, 'Disturbances Associated with Football Matches: Types of Incidents and Selection of Charges', *British Journal of Criminology* (1984), 377.
56. This identified perimeter fencing as a contributory factor to the crowd crush at Hillsborough.
57. Hillsborough Stadium Disaster Inquiry Final Report, para.299.
58. E. Bittner, 'The Police on Skid Row: A Study of Peacekeeping', 32 *American Sociological Review* (1967).
59. Ibid., 712.
60. Ibid., 710.
61. Ibid., 713.
62. At many games fans were quite willing to climb over signs advertising the criminal sanctions to celebrate a vital goal.
63. s.3(2)(a). Making note of every individual abusive or racist comment that I heard would be a practical impossibility.
64. Although they may be 'threatening' or 'insulting' enough to warrant prosecution under the Public Order Act.

65. s.3(1).
66. The chant at Preston was noted in a report by Football Against Racism in *When Saturday Comes* (Jan. 1997) no.119.
67. However, as more and more grounds become all-seater, the identification of fans should become easier, especially for season-ticket holders or those who have purchased tickets for numbered seats by credit card.
68. Ceefax, 3 Nov. 1998.
69. This policy may explain why five streakers who invaded the pitch at several Premiership matches on the final day of the 1996/97 season all avoided being charged by police (*Star*, 12 May 1997).
70. Thirteen arrests were made in the 1993/94 season, and this astonishingly fell to a mere ten in 1996/97, before a recent resurgence to 33 arrests in 1997/98 and 25 in 1989/99.
71. Such a move would probably be infeasible and dangerous, owing to the number of fans queuing to get through the turnstiles. It was for this reason that the Taylor report recommended that plans for an ID card scheme for all football spectators proposed under Part I of the Football Spectators Act 1989 should be abandoned.
72. See S. Greenfield and G. Osborn, 'After the Act: the (Re)Construction and Regulation of Football Fandom', 1 *Journal of Civil Liberties* (1996), 7–28.
73. Ibid.
74. See R. Giulianotti, 'Taking Liberties: Hibs Casuals and Scottish Law', in Giulianotti *et al.*, (note 54). G. Pearson, 'Legitimate Targets? The Civil Liberties of Football Fans', 4 *Journal of Civil Liberties* (1999), no.1, 37–40.
75. See Armstrong and Hobbs (note 54).
76. See Pearson (note 74).
77. Ibid., 41–4.
78. Ibid., 41.
79. Ibid.
80. Ibid.
81. Although there is no legal provision allowing this, the practice occurred at many English Channel ports during France '98 (see Pearson, note 74).
82. House of Commons, Standing Committee D, 5 May 1999.
83. See G. Pearson, 'The English Disease? The Socio-Legal Construction of Football Hooliganism', 60 *Youth and Policy: Journal of Critical Analysis* (1998), 1–15.
84. 11 Cr App R (S) 234, 1989, at 237.
85. This argument is pursued in Pearson, 'The English Disease?' (note 83).
86. G. Armstrong and M. Young, 'Legislators and Interpreters: the Law and "Football Hooligans"', in G. Armstrong and R. Giulianotti (eds), *Entering the Field – New Perspectives on Football*, Oxford, 1997, 184.
87. Ibid., 175.
88. Ibid., see also P. Marsh, *Aggro: the Illusion of Violence*, London, 1978.
89. See *The Observer*, 4 Oct. 1998, *Red Issue* (Nov. 1998).

11

Rethinking Sports Organizations' Responses to Workplace Concerns

David McArdle

Introduction

The purpose of this chapter is to discuss some of the practices that sports organizations would prefer the general public not to know about because they have failed to deal with them effectively. Concentrating on instances of harassment and discrimination, the chapter will commence with an exploration of sexual discrimination in sport and consider the circumstances in which the provisions of the Sex Discrimination Act 1975, s.44 (which legitimates discriminatory practices) are applicable. It will also discuss hostile environment sexual harassment (*Cummins* v. *Kingstonian Football Club*)[1] and instances of rape and sexual abuse perpetrated by those in positions of trust (*R.* v. *Hickson*).[2] Additionally, the chapter briefly considers the Lyme Bay canoe tragedy, where former employees of the leisure centre had informed the centre's management of their concerns but their warnings went unheeded. It will be argued that if proper provision had been made for employees to raise their concerns with individuals who did not have a vested interest in the running of the centre, the Lyme Bay tragedy could have been avoided.

While the emphasis is on the law of England and Wales and the practices of sports bodies within that jurisdiction, examples from the United States will be used to illustrate how recent Supreme Court rulings have obliged sports organizations there to take discrimination and harassment seriously. In an attempt to avoid liability for the discriminatory conduct of their employees, American sports organizations are making increased use of internal reporting mechanisms and employee codes of conduct. The steps that those organizations have taken in response to legal intervention provide an invaluable point of reference for bodies in the United Kingdom that wish to take these issues seriously too.

The theoretical basis of the chapter is located within the existing literature[3] concerning the expansion into sports organizations of the 'juridical field'.[4] It is concerned with how the juridical field's norms – its disciplinary codes and professional bodies – organized as they are around a body of internal protocols, characteristic behaviours and self-sustaining values[5] – are imposed upon social and cultural fields such as sport. The debate over whether the juridical field should extend into the field of sport (or whether law should 'stop at the touchline') is, in truth, a sterile and redundant one given that the ordinary law of the land has been intervening in sport for 200 years. Few branches of the entertainment industry (which includes sport, film, music and other forms of popular culture) have ever been self-regulating, notwithstanding the popular perception to the contrary.

What *is* worthy of comment, though, is the use that is increasingly being made of laws that are directed specifically and solely at sports organizations and their practices. The onset of the juridical tide could be slowed if the sport industry evinced both the ability and the willingness to regulate itself properly. But sport's failure to deal effectively with discriminatory conduct is but one example[6] of how this has not been the case hitherto. There are scant grounds for believing that this state of affairs will change in the absence of either legal intervention or coherent pressure for reform from central government or funding bodies such as Sport England. Sports organizations routinely adopt practices and policies that would be simply unacceptable in any other social, economic or cultural field.

Can the Judge Stop Me Playing?

In the United Kingdom the legislation that limits an employer's power to discriminate on the basis of sex or ethnicity has existed for over 25 years. The passing of the Sex Discrimination Act 1975 and the Race Relations Act 1976[7] had not been without controversy.[8] Although judicially implied terms into contracts of employment have a long history, the passing of these Acts represented a fundamental departure from the common law position. No longer was an individual entitled to enter, or not enter, into contractual relations with whomever he or she wanted, on whatever terms the parties agreed.[9] It was not for the law to enquire into the motives behind one's refusal to contract with another, and it was certainly not the law's role to interfere with the agreed terms and conditions of it. However, those Acts have provided for a modicum of substantive equality of opportunity in the workplace[10] and allowed aggrieved employees to seek remedies for discriminatory behaviour by employers or work colleagues.[11]

Professor Harry Street, the principal author of the 1967 Report,[12] was impressed by several aspects of American anti-discrimination law and recommended legislation that mirrored the Equal Pay Act 1963 and Title VII of the Civil Rights Act 1964.[13] However, he was critical of the Anti-Discrimination Commissions that enforced those Acts, for he thought that they were too willing to accept inadequate settlements offered by intransigent discriminators.[14] Although acknowledging the desirability of conciliation among the parties, he felt that aggrieved individuals should also be able to pursue remedies direct through the courts. Accordingly, individuals were given the right to take their complaints straight to an industrial tribunal, if they elected to do so. The proposed regulatory bodies (which became the Equal Opportunities Commission (EOC) and the Commission for Racial Equality (CRE)) became advisory and education services, with responsibility for monitoring the activities of institutions, firms or industries whose practices gave cause for concern.[15] Those bodies have provided advice and assistance to the complainants in the cases discussed below, most notably in *Hardwick* and *Hussaney*.

Direct Discrimination

Under the 1975 Act and the 1976 Act discrimination may be either direct or indirect in form.[16] The most straightforward examples of direct discrimination concern the use of racist or sexist language in the workplace, as peddled by the second defendant in *Hussaney* v. *Chester City Football Club and Ratcliffe*.[17] Kevin Ratcliffe, the manager of a professional club, called a 16-year-old schoolboy a 'black cunt' after the boy put the wrong studs into his boots.[18] Ratcliffe was forced into a grudging apology after being confronted by the claimant's parents and Chester City Football Club was obliged to instigate a travesty of an internal disciplinary procedure, which the industrial tribunal dismissed as 'inauthentic'.[19] The use of such racially-abusive words amounts to as clear an act of direct discrimination as can occur under anti-discrimination law, and in this case Ratcliffe's conduct was exacerbated by the way the club dealt with the case.[20]

Direct discrimination law covers far more than the use of hate speech by an employer. It seeks to prevent actions that are based on stereotypes of sex or race by rendering unlawful any decisions that emanate from the employer's reliance on them. It is no defence for an employer to argue that there was no malice or deliberate prejudice behind the discriminatory conduct. It would be direct discrimination for an employer to refuse to interview any woman who applied for a job that required heavy lifting (working in a gymnasium, for instance) by adopting the attitude that 'women are the weaker sex and I won't consider employing one'. The employer *can* reject the application of any woman who simply does not have the physical strength required for the task, just as he could reject a man for the same reason, but the employer has to consider the individual applicant, not the stereotype. A discriminatory act that resulted from an employer's introduction of 'quotas' or 'affirmative action' programmes would similarly be unlawful[21] even if the motives for introducing them were laudable.[22]

However, even though 'positive discrimination' and preferential treatment motivated by philanthropy are prohibited, the 1975 Act does not prevent the adoption of measures that do not involve preferential treatment but which aim to encourage a greater degree of equality of opportunity. Evidence that a firm has monitored its recruitment patterns and taken positive steps to remove barriers to the recruitment of women and ethnic minorities is invaluable evidence in a discrimination case, and the EOC and the CRE encourage their use by employers.[23]

Indirect Discrimination

The provisions on indirect discrimination were incorporated into the 1975 Act at the last possible moment, following the US Supreme Court's decision, in *Griggs* v. *Duke Power Co.*,[24] on the illegality of rules that are equally applied to both sexes but which have an unequal effect on them. Proving a discriminatory animus is not necessary under domestic law or EU law[25] for the purposes of indirect discrimination. Under s.1(1)(b) it is enough for the claimant to show the existence of a requirement or condition that is applied equally to all, but that the proportion of members of one sex who can comply with it is smaller than the proportion of members of the other. In addition, the fact that the applicant cannot comply with that requirement or condition must be to his or her detriment (emphasis added). It is a defence for the employer to show that his reasonable needs justified the application of the discriminatory provision.[26]

Sex Discrimination, Sport and s.44

In addition to the potential complexities offered by the law on direct and indirect discrimination, those concerned with advising parties alleging sex discrimination in sport have been obliged to consider the potential effects of the provisions of the 1975 Act, s.44.[27] This provision was put forward as a defence to discriminatory conduct in *Bennett* v. *The Football Association*,[28] *Greater London Council* v. *Farrer*,[29] *The British Judo Association* v. *Petty*,[30] and, bizarrely, in *Couch* v. *The British Boxing Board of Control*.[31] However, it was not raised as a defence in either *Hardwick* v. *The Football Association*[32] or *Cummins* v. *Kingstonian Football Club*.[33] This probably reflects the fact that the circumstances in which s.44 may be applied are so limited that it is, effectively, 'dead law'.[34] Except in cases where very unusual circumstances pertain, it is of no relevance – unless, like the British Boxing Board of Control – one will clutch at any straws that happen to blow past in a desperate bid to defend one's long-standing discriminatory practices.

Section 44 of the 1975 Act provides that:

> Nothing in Parts II to IV [of the Act] shall, in relation to any sport, game or other activity of a competitive nature where the physical

strength, stamina or physique of the average woman puts her at a disadvantage to the average man, render unlawful any act related to the participation of a person as a competitor in events involving that activity which are confined to competitors of one sex.

In *Bennett*, a schoolgirl (aged 11 at the time of the hearing) who played football with the boys at school wanted to join a boys' side that played in a local league. The rules of both the county Football Association and the national governing body did not permit mixed teams in league competitions, so they banned her from playing for the boys' side. The ban was upheld at first instance and Bennett appealed. The Court of Appeal heard medical evidence that the strength, stamina and physique of prepubescent girls is not markedly different from that of prepubescent boys,[35] and that there are at least as many physiological differences within the sexes as there are between them.[36] However, while accepting that the rest of the Act aimed to prevent the application of precisely these sex-based stereotypical assumptions,[37] the Court of Appeal ruled that s.44 had been drafted in a way that obliged it to take these generalizations into account. Football was a sport in which the strength of the *average* woman put her at a disadvantage to the *average* man and Bennett's individual attributes were irrelevant. Neither could s.44 be interpreted as meaning the Court should consider the attributes of the 'average female' at 11 years of age.

Lord Denning, MR accepted that Bennett 'used to run rings around the boys' and said that without the existence of s.44, the county FA would have had no defence to her claim. However, 'the average woman is at a disadvantage to the average man because [the average woman] has not got the physique to stand up to [the rigours of mixed football]'.[38] Allowing Bennett to play would require the Court to stretch the bounds of judicial creativity beyond breaking point,[39] and there were no grounds upon which her appeal could be upheld.

Section 44 was also discussed in *Greater London Council* v. *Farrer*,[40] which concerned a decision by the Council to issue entertainment licences to certain premises where the owners wished to hold wrestling bouts. The Council would issue licences only on condition that female wrestlers were not allowed to compete, regardless of whether they wrestled against men or against other women. A female wrestler who was denied the opportunity to compete as a consequence of that policy sought a declaration from the industrial tribunal that the Council had acted unlawfully by aiding an employer (namely, the bout's promoter) to discriminate against her on the ground of her sex. The Council contended that her application should be refused, arguing that the London Government Act 1963 allowed it to impose such conditions when granting licences and that the 1975 Act, s.51 permitted discrimination that was necessary to ensure compliance with earlier legislation.[41] The Council also mounted a s.44 defence, almost as an afterthought in case its first line of argument failed.

The industrial tribunal upheld the ban on s.51 grounds, and its decision was confirmed on appeal. However, in the Employment Appeal Tribunal, Slynn J (as he then was) said, *obiter*, that the way in which s.44 had been drafted meant that it could not be a defence in situations where all the competitors were female. Its ambit was limited to situations in which it was proposed that women and men should take part in the same event: 'It does not seem to us that this section is dealing with the situation where it is desired that a girl should play a game against a girl, or where teams of girls should play other teams of girls.'[42]

This brief consideration of s.44 was expanded upon in the subsequent case of *British Judo Association* v. *Petty*. A woman who was qualified as a coach and referee was banned from refereeing men's national tournaments, which were far more remunerative for referees than lower-level tournaments were. The Association argued that Petty would lack the physical strength to intervene and separate the competitors should the need to do so arise. It also argued that the elite-level males had made it clear that they did not want a woman to referee their bouts under any circumstances. It supported the men's stance and argued that s.44 allowed them to ban Petty from officiating if they wanted to, regardless of their motives for doing so.

The tribunal ruled that the Association's conduct contravened the 1975 Act and approved of Slynn J's dictum in *Greater London Council*. It went on to affirm that referees were not 'participants' for the purposes of s.44 and were entitled to the full protection of the anti-discrimination laws: 'We think that the words [of s.44] should be given their obvious meaning and not extended so as to cover any discrimination other than provisions designed to regulate who is to take part in the contest as a competitor.'[43]

So, as long ago as the early 1980s it appeared that s.44's relevance was limited to those very exceptional circumstances in which women wanted to actually *compete* with or against men. Indeed, so redundant did s.44 seem that it did not rear its head in legal argument for over 15 years – until the governing body of British boxing resurrected it in 1998, in *Couch* v. *British Boxing Board of Control*.[44]

Jane Couch was the holder of the World Women's Welterweight title. She had successfully defended her title in America on two occasions in 1997, but the British Boxing Board of Control (hereafter BBBC) had refused her application for a professional boxer's licence, which she needed before she could box professionally in Britain. Indeed, the BBBC had never granted a licence to any female boxer. Couch argued that the BBBC had failed to give proper consideration to her application and had therefore contravened the provisions of the 1975 Act, s.13 (which prohibits discriminatory treatment by a qualifying body).

At the tribunal hearing John Morris, the Secretary-General of the Board, stated that 'the British Board is very definitely not in favour of women's boxing at this time', and said that the particular danger that boxing posed to women's health was the sole reason for its stance. He confirmed that the BBBC had not even considered Couch's application because it was not willing to take any steps that could be seen as encouraging the spread of women's boxing. In defending its position, the Board argued that s.44 meant that its action was entirely lawful, regardless of the merits of the rationale behind it.[45]

The BBBC purported to rely on numerous medical arguments in support of its contention that boxing posed special dangers to women. In its Notice of Appearance, it claimed there was medical evidence that (*inter alia*):

- Hormonal changes occurring monthly can result in increased fluid retention prior to a period and that can result in a weight gain of anything up to 4 to 6lbs. This raises the difficulty of weight categories. Under no circumstances can any artificial means of weight reduction be adopted.
- Unfortunately, many women suffer pre-menstrual tension, when they are more prone to accidents. They are emotionally more labile[46] and this may also have relevance to a boxer's performance and tendency to injury.
- Dysmenorrhoea [painful periods] is not an uncommon occurrence and is treated with powerful painkillers. This would not be allowed in professional boxing.
- The taking of contraceptive pills to prevent pregnancy or to delay or avoid periods are strictly contra-indicated in professional boxing, as no drugs or medication whatsoever are allowed.[47]

Unfortunately for the BBBC, in *James* v. *Eastleigh Borough Council* the House of Lords had already established that neither chivalry nor paternalism justifies sex discrimination. Even if there were any truth to the medical arguments, a desire to protect women from the consequences of making an informed choice about consent to injury and the voluntary assumption of risk provided no defence to a sex-discrimination claim. In any event, the tribunal decided that the medical evidence was just a smokescreen for the BBBC to hide its double standards behind. It accepted that some of the rules of boxing pertaining to weight categories, banned substances and clothing might have to be changed for the purpose of women's boxing. However, those issues had already been dealt with in those countries where women's boxing was more widely accepted, which included the United States, Denmark, Germany, Belgium, Holland and Hungary. The inconvenience to a governing body of having to change its rules was no reason for allowing it to flout the law of the land:[48]

The Board has no medical evidence that it is more dangerous for women to box than men, or indeed vice versa. ... Her application was rejected allegedly on medical grounds although she was never medically examined. The real reason for her refusal was on the ground of sex. ... The 'medical grounds' are all gender-based stereotypical assumptions [and are] not capable of amounting to valid defences to a claim of discrimination.[49]

The failure to give Couch a medical also amounted to discriminatory treatment on the basis of her sex, because even the most hapless male applicant for a boxer's licence would have been given the medical.

So far as the BBBC's mounting of a s.44 defence was concerned, the tribunal confirmed Slynn J's dictum and said that s.44 'can only be relied upon where a female, if allowed to participate, would be involved in a game or sport where the other players were male. For example, a woman wanting to join a men's football or rugby team.' Of course, Couch was not seeking to fight against other men.[50] The tribunal concluded by saying that it was 'difficult to recall a more outrageous defence being proffered in a sex discrimination case'.[51] In September 1998, three months after the judgment, Jane Couch was granted a licence to box in Britain. She first fought in the United Kingdom, with little fuss, in November 1998 and at the time of writing is still World Champion.

Couch has removed any vestige of doubt that may have remained about the effect of s.44 and British sports organizations should now be fully aware of their obligations not to discriminate under the 1975 Act. On the basis of *Couch* and the other judgments, it is possible to formulate a three-stage test that one can use in order to determine whether sex discrimination is lawful:

• Is the applicant seeking to participate in a sport, game or physical activity?
• Is she seeking to participate as a competitor – as opposed to acting as a coach, referee or in some other capacity?
• Is she seeking to compete in the same event as (that is, by playing with or against) men?

Unless the answers to all three of these questions are 'yes', s.44 will have no application and will not provide a defence to discriminatory treatment. There are certainly no legal grounds for discriminating against women who apply for positions as managers, coaches, stewards or other non-playing roles because such people are not 'competitors' for the purposes of that section. Employers would be better advised to take adequate steps to safeguard the rights of their employees (and, by doing so, safeguard their own legal position), for the relevant case law has limited the applicability of s.44 to such an extent that it is now of historical interest only.

However, *Hardwick* v. *The Football Association*[52] shows there is still a long way to go before all governing bodies can claim to be rid of their discriminatory practices. Here, the Football Association compounded its obvious and systematic discriminatory conduct towards a female candidate for its highest level coaching qualification[53] by arguing, ridiculously, that she failed the course, not because she was a woman, but because she had sat it at the wrong time of the year. It appeared that one could pass the spring course with marks that would result in failure if one sat the summer course, as Hardwick did. Those responsible for running the Football Association's coaching courses had made the spring course easier to pass because most of the participants on it were retired professionals. Most of those who sat the summer course, like Hardwick, were schoolteachers.

Needless to say, this information was not passed on to the candidates and, in effect, the game's governing body was arguing that it was merely guilty of duplicity in offering preferential treatment to professional players, rather than being guilty of sex discrimination. Indeed, the Football Association's director of coaching confidently asserted that 'the fact that candidates passed in spring with inferior marks to the applicant was due to misdirection and mismanagement within our coaching scheme. It had absolutely nothing to do with sex discrimination'.[54] Unsurprisingly, the Association failed to convince the tribunal that a male candidate with the same results as Hardwick would have similarly failed the course.[55] Hardwick was awarded a total of £5,000 to compensate for injury to her feelings.

Reporting Workplace Concerns

The discriminatory practices of which Hardwick complained were so much a part of the Football Association's operations that it is difficult to believe they would ever have been changed had it not been for the intervention of the law.[56] Reporting mechanisms can do little to effect change in the face of well-established intransigence and the presence of systemic discriminatory practices. However, the potential benefits of ensuring that employees are aware of their rights and obligations, and of providing individuals with an opportunity to raise their concerns about workplace malpractice without going to law or involving organizations such as the EOC, were apparent in *Cummins* v. *Kingstonian Football Club*.[57] This case concerned a sex-discrimination claim by a woman who had started employment as an office administrator with the club in August 1997, initially on a two-month trial period. She worked under the supervision of two permanent members of staff and assisted a number of voluntary workers who helped at the club in various capacities. Kingstonian play in the Premier Division of the ICIS League and, as the tribunal chairman noted, they were 'a typical football club in the league to which it belongs' in that they depended on volunteer workers 'to oil the works of the machine'.[58]

The case arose out of alleged instances of sexual harassment by the club's finance director, who was one of the volunteer workers. The applicant gave evidence that the individual concerned had 'made verbal approaches towards her and on one occasion simply put his arm around her in a fashion which she found to be unacceptable'.[59] She had informally discussed the matter with a friend and with another volunteer worker, and was dismissed within a couple of days of mentioning the matter to the second volunteer. She claimed her treatment contravened the terms of the 1975 Act, s.1 and also alleged that the club had contravened s.4 by victimizing her through dismissal once she had made an allegation of harassment.

In response, the club made 'a blanket denial of all the applicant's main allegations'. It asserted that she had 'become extremely emotional and had appeared to overreact in an uncontrolled fashion' over the death of the Princess of Wales[60] and said the chief executive had decided to dismiss her on the ground that the standard of her typing was unsatisfactory. He had not discussed the possibility of dismissing her with the other employee nor with any of the volunteer workers. However, there were still three weeks left of the applicant's trial period when she was dismissed. While the tribunal accepted that there was certainly room for improvement so far as her typing was concerned, 'this is just the sort of thing that can easily be dealt with by a firm oral or written warning if it was a matter of concern'.[61] It did not amount to grounds for dismissing the applicant three weeks before the end of her trial period, especially as she had not even been given an oral or written warning of the need to improve beforehand.

The real reason for her dismissal was that, after the volunteer worker had taken the entirely proper step of informing the chief executive that the applicant felt that she was being harassed, he had taken a unilateral decision to sack her because she was a troublemaker. Indeed, the club's other permanent and salaried staff member (the finance director) 'only discovered the applicant's departure by chance, he thinking that she had apparently gone on holiday'.[62] The applicant had been the victim of sexual discrimination and had been victimized. The tribunal pointed out that had the matter been dealt with sensibly – by a properly drafted and implemented code of practice and reporting mechanism – 'it might never have been more than a distant memory for any of the parties. ... There was no actual physical sexual misbehaviour and although the language used was unacceptable it was by no means at the top of the bracket for that type of unacceptable language.'[63] She was awarded £3,500 damages for injury to feelings and compensation for loss of earnings of £7,200.

Individual clubs, governing bodies, trade unions and other interested organizations should be working together to create a viable reporting structure and a meaningful code of conduct which would avoid the need for individuals such as Cummins to seek recourse to the law in order to gain redress. At the very least, the creation of a written code of practice, disseminated to all staff regardless of the capacity in which they are employed and underpinned by a written guarantee that each signatory will adhere to the code's terms, would represent a worthwhile starting-point. The code should outline employees' rights and obligations in respect of, *inter alia*, equal opportunities, creating a workplace environment that is free from harassment and maintaining health and safety at work. The next step would be the provision of a framework through which employees can report their legitimate concerns; however, this framework must be formulated in a manner which allows the employee to bypass the individual who is the subject of their concerns – a provision which was noticeably absent in *Cummins*. The existence of such a scheme, and its proper implementation, could help to persuade an industrial tribunal that equal opportunities were being taken seriously in the particular workplace.[64] It would also reassure employees that their workplace rights are taken seriously.

There are two potential sources of information that sports organizations interested in supporting those who wish to raise concerns could look to for guidance. The first is the United Kingdom's own laws on whistleblowing, as contained in the Public Interest Disclosure Act 1998. The second is the practices of sports bodies in the United States, which are at present dealing with changes to the law that have had a fundamental impact on their potential liability for harassing behaviour. The next two sections will look at these developments in turn.

Blowing the Whistle

'Whistleblowing' is commonly understood to occur when workers express a concern externally about malpractices or wrongdoing within their organization because they do not feel able to raise the matter internally, or where they have already raised the matter internally but it has not been satisfactorily dealt with. Although there is still a tendency to view whistleblowers as disloyal troublemakers, an alternative management approach is to treat them as dedicated individuals who provide an alternative to legal intervention when management structures fail.[65] Whistleblowers – and, crucially, the implementation of a worthwhile internal reporting mechanism to support them – give employers the opportunity to address problems before matters escalate to the extent that they did in *Cummins* and *Hussaney*. If employees are not given the opportunity to have their concerns addressed internally, then the likelihood is that legal action will ensue – which invariably results in expense, adverse publicity and the irretrievable breakdown of the parties' working relationship. The alternative, of course, is that the matter will not be dealt with at all and the harm or wrong will continue unexposed. 'Whistleblowing is in the interests of wider society [and] proper protection must be provided for those who are driven to it.'[66]

Whistleblowers need the protection of the law and the security of internal codes of conduct and reporting mechanisms, because whistleblowing amounts to a prima facie breach of an employee's terms and conditions of employment. As such, blowing the whistle may result in dismissal or other disciplinary action. Ordinarily, there is an implied duty of fidelity that prevents an employee from disclosing information that has been acquired in confidence. Although since *Initial Services* v. *Putterill*[67] it has been possible for employees to argue that the alleged misconduct was so serious that disclosure was in the public interest, disclosure had to be to someone who had an interest in receiving it. In *Lion Laboratories* v. *Evans*[68] the Court of Appeal indicated that disclosure to the press might not always be appropriate. This meant that, before the 1998 Act came into force, the only external bodies to whom one could safely report one's concerns were those regulatory bodies which had been established specifically to investigate breaches of statutory duty. These would include the Inland Revenue and the Health and Safety Executive.[69] In fact, the 1974 Act places an express statutory duty on every employee 'to take reasonable care for the health and safety of himself and of other persons who may be affected by his acts or omissions'.[70] This obliges employees to report any concerns internally and, if their representations are ignored, to report them to the Health and Safety Executive regardless of any implied contractual duty of confidentiality they may owe to the employer.[71]

The 1998 Act amends the Employment Rights Act 1996 by inserting a new s.43 into that Act. It protects employees who disclose information which, *inter alia*, tends to show that a criminal offence has been committed; that a person has failed to comply with any legal obligation; that an individual's health and safety has been infringed or that the environment has been damaged.[72] It covers workers who raise genuine concerns about mistreatment, financial malpractice, dangers to health and safety or the environment and 'cover-ups' by protecting so-called 'public interest' whistleblowing to regulators, the media and Members of Parliament. It guarantees full compensation with the promise of penalty awards if the whistleblower is sacked. It applies whether or not the information is confidential and whether the malpractice is occurring in the United Kingdom or overseas. It covers trainees (such as James Hussaney), agency staff (which would include Agency stewards), contractors and those who work from home.[73] There are no restrictions on the basis of age and no minimum qualifying periods, but the Act does not cover the genuinely self-employed or volunteers – a crucial and regrettable omission, bearing in mind the extent to which most sports organizations rely on volunteer workers.

The Act provides that disclosure to a manager will be protected so long as the disclosure is made 'in good faith'.[74] Disclosure to a 'prescribed regulator'[75] will similarly be protected, as will disclosure to a 'responsible person', if disclosure to that person has been authorized by the employer.[76] However, disclosures to 'outsiders' (such as the police, the media and those who are not prescribed regulators) will be protected only if they are reasonable in all the circumstances. Such disclosures will never be protected if they have been made for personal gain.[77]

Unless the whistleblower reasonably believed that he would be victimized, the concern must have first been raised with the employer or with a prescribed regulator, if applicable. This provision does not apply if the matter is exceptionally serious, if there is no prescribed regulator *and* the whistleblower reasonably believed that evidence of the matter 'will be concealed or destroyed' if he first reported it internally.[78] If the whistleblower is victimized or dismissed in breach of the Act he can bring a claim to an employment tribunal for compensation and, if appropriate, may apply for an interim order prohibiting the employer from dismissing him.[79] Where the concern has been raised with the employer or a prescribed regulator, the tribunal will also consider the reasonableness of the response. Contractual duties of confidentiality, or 'gagging clauses', in employment contracts and severance agreements are void if they conflict with the Act.[80] Although the provisions of the 1998 Act have been broadly welcomed,[81] whistleblowers are still vulnerable. In any event, the ultimate goal should be to prevent the necessity for the juridical field to encroach on to the sports field at all, unless the involvement of the law is a necessary and appropriate response to the sports industry's inertia. In order to explore the most efficacious ways of achieving that, it is necessary to examine the alternatives to legal intervention that may exist and through which it may be possible to protect those who are involved in sport and who have concerns that they seek to raise.

The American Experience

As mentioned above, in the United States the law on sexual harassment in employment is governed by Title VII of the Civil Rights Act 1964.[82] Sexual harassment within the field of education is covered by Title IX of the Educational Amendments Act 1972,[83] which prohibits, *inter alia*, sexual harassment and discrimination in educational institutions that receive federal financial assistance.

There is a broad range of behaviours that amount to sexual harassment under US law,[84] but in the late 1990s three Supreme Court decisions substantially extended the ramifications for companies whose employees engaged in behaviour that contravened those provisions. The first case, *Oncale* v. *Sundowner Offshore Services*,[85] concerned a male employee who had been harassed by male co-workers and whose employer dismissed the incidents as horseplay. The Supreme Court ruled that the sexual harassment provisions of Title VII apply to same-sex harassment. In *Burlington Industries* v. *Ellerth*,[86] the Supreme Court held that an employee has a cause of action under the provisions of Title VII of the Civil Rights Act 1964, even if the harasser's threats had not been carried out. In this case, a sales representative who repeatedly rebuffed the amorous advances of a middle manager suffered no adverse consequences and was, in fact, promoted. She had been familiar with the company's sexual-harassment policy, but, rather than use that procedure, she went straight ahead and filed a lawsuit. The Supreme Court was asked to rule on whether the employer could be liable for the harasser's behaviour when there had been no detrimental effect on the claimant's employment status.

The Court held that the absence of tangible negative consequences did not prevent an employee from bringing a claim. However, it went on to say that employers can use the 'affirmative defence' and limit potential liability if they can show that they took reasonable steps to prevent and remedy sexual harassment. Employers may also avoid liability if they can show that an employee unreasonably failed to take advantage of corrective opportunities provided by the employer.

Finally, and most significantly, in *Faragher* v. *City of Boca Raton*[87] the claimant, a female lifeguard, had suffered sexual harassment by supervisors. Her supervisors had subjected her (and other female lifeguards) to uninvited and offensive touching and lewd remarks. Although she told another supervisor about the others' behaviour, the supervisor failed to report the misconduct to his superiors. The claimant had not taken steps to report the harassment to the city authorities and neither she nor her harassers had been aware of the council's written policy against sexual harassment. Shortly before the claimant resigned, another female lifeguard wrote to the council's personnel director and complained about the harassment. The claimant subsequently discovered that at least five other female lifeguards had made complaints about the conduct of the same supervisors. The council investigated the complaint and reprimanded the harassers. Subsequently, the claimant filed suit claiming that the city was liable for the harassment she had suffered. The case turned on whether, in the circumstances, the council could be held liable for a first-line supervisor's sexually-harassing behaviour.

The Supreme Court ruled in the affirmative: an employer will normally be liable for a pervasive, hostile environment of harassment – and is liable for the misconduct of its employees – regardless of whether it had been aware of the harassment. Its reasoning was based on the fact that employers have the opportunity to screen, train and monitor staff members who carry out supervisory roles. However, the Court also said that an employer would have a defence if it could establish that it exercised reasonable care to prevent and correct harassment; and that the complaining employee unreasonably failed to use the existing complaint procedures. In this case, the city's sexual-harassment policy had never been disseminated effectively among the beach employees and the internal complaint procedure did not provide a mechanism for bypassing the offending supervisors.

American Employers' Liability: The New Playing Field

Oncale, Ellerth and *Farragher* have substantially expanded American employers' liability for acts of sexual harassment by their employees,[88] especially in circumstances where the victim is a subordinate of the harasser.[89] These changes to the law have provoked consternation among employers, not least within organizations that are concerned with the provision of sports and recreation and within university athletics departments, both of which have well-documented case histories where sexual harassment and abuse have been dealt with ineffectually or not at all.[90] The most important development was that an employer is liable to an employee for a hostile environment created by a supervisor who has immediate (or successively higher) authority over the employee.[91] The employee need only prove that a direct line supervisor engaged in actionable harassment.[92] If the harassment culminated in a tangible employment action (for example, if the harassed employee were demoted, dismissed or otherwise sees the circumstances of her employment change), the employer has no defence and is liable for damages. The difficulty for employers is that a supervisor may engage in conduct that is so severe that a single incident amounts to sexual harassment (indecent assault or false imprisonment, for example). Consequently, all employers are now under pressure to maintain, and be able to prove that they disseminated, to all employees an anti-harassment policy that includes what the Court in *Farragher* termed 'a sensible complaint procedure'. An employer which (a) had no policy, (b) failed to disseminate its policy or (c) failed to include a means of bypassing the harassing supervisor to register the complaint would have no defence.

However, the Court also stressed that employers must take reasonable care to prevent, as well as correct, any sexually-harassing behaviour. Maintaining an anti-harassment policy alone is not enough to avoid liability, and prudent employers will put all their supervisory personnel through rigorous training on a continuing basis.[93] Other means of prevention can be addressed through the specific contents of the harassment policy itself and through the dissemination and reaffirmation of that policy.[94]

Learning from the American Experience

After *Farragher* the steps that sports bodies in the United States have been advised to take in order to comply with the law by preventing harassment or abuse in the workplace (and, failing that, to avoid liability should incidents occur) seem onerous. The recommended measures, which go far beyond the written equal-opportunities policies that one occasionally encounters in sports organizations within the United Kingdom, include the following:[95]

- Each company should carry out an immediate review of its sexual harassment and anti-retaliation policy to ensure that the company (*inter alia*):

    provides employees with convenient and reliable mechanisms for reporting incidents;

    posts the name, work location and telephone number of the person to whom employees may raise their concerns;

    encourages employees to report incidents promptly, either verbally or in writing;

    maintains a 24-hours complaint hotline.
- The company should identify all supervisors[96] and make them accountable for compliance with the company's anti-harassment and anti-retaliation policy.
- The company should train all supervisors on sexual-harassment prevention and make attendance at these sessions mandatory.[97]
- The company should make all its non-supervisory employees aware of the sexual harassment policy and the procedures to follow if they experience sexual harassment.
- To remove any doubt about dissemination of the sexual-harassment policy, the company should obtain signed receipts from all employees when distributing it.
- The company should redistribute the policy periodically – at least annually – and obtain new receipts.
- The company should instruct appropriate managers on the guidelines for conducting investigations into allegations of harassment.
- The company should incorporate the anti-harassment policy into its training programmes for new employees.
- The company should document the attempts it makes to prevent and correct harassment, and record any employee's failure to participate in the training programmes it provides.

However onerous these provisions may be, the reality is that for the most part[98] they represent little more than good practice from the point of view of risk management. Sports organizations in the United Kingdom would do well to consider whether there is anything they could learn from the United

States, for the Lyme Bay tragedy and the Paul Hickson case illustrate what may happen when people are unable or unwilling to speak out.

Reporting Concerns in Sport: from Theory to Necessity

Sexual Abuse in Sport

Paul Hickson was a swimming coach, working primarily with 13- and 14-year-old girls. In the early 1990s he was investigated in connection with allegations of indecent assault made by a number of girls whom he had coached in South Wales between 1983 and 1988. He was subsequently charged and was due to stand trial in 1992, but absconded before the trial started. However, publicity over his disappearance resulted in four other women, hitherto uninvolved in the case, coming forward to make complaints that they had been raped, buggered and sexually assaulted by Hickson when he worked in Norfolk between 1976 and 1981. Their evidence suggested that Hickson had used the same *modus operandi* in respect of all his victims over the whole period from 1976 to 1988. Consequently, when he finally stood trial he was confronted by new charges, including two of rape, that arose out of the allegations from that earlier period – allegations that would probably have never come to light had he not absconded. Hickson was duly convicted on 11 counts, including the rape charges, relating to young women aged between 13 and 20 (*The Times*, 28 Sept. 1995, 1). He was sentenced to 17 years' imprisonment.[99]

There is little quantitative evidence of the prevalence of sexual abuse in sport, and, given the sensitive nature of the topic and the fact that a lot of people involved in sport have a vested interest in denying its existence at all, this is of little surprise. Brackenridge has documentary evidence of 'almost 90' cases in the United Kingdom and research suggests that approximately one in four girls and one in nine boys experience abuse before the age of 16.[100] While there has been the inevitable tendency to make generalizations out of isolated incidents in a manner that merely serves to sensationalize a difficult and sensitive issue,[101] if these figures are accurate 'then it must be accepted that a large proportion of participants go through the traumatic experience of sexual abuse before their introduction to sport'.[102]

Given that the victims of abuse are quite likely to be victims on more than one occasion, one has to confront the likelihood that where abuse does occur in sport, abusers are probably building upon vulnerabilities that have already been established. The process of 'grooming' by an abuser – building trust, pushing back boundaries and making ever-increasing use of verbal and physical familiarity – is easier to achieve when the 'target' displays guilt, depression, low self-esteem or manifests the other forms of behaviour that are associated with abuse victims.[103]

In sports, abusers may come in the guise of 'coaches, instructors, chaperones, parent-helpers, bus drivers, other athletes', or anyone else who has access to persons who are potentially at risk.[104] The 'classic' sexual-abuse scenario often involves a period of grooming or coercion on the part of the abuser, and the dividing line between sexual abuse and sexual harassment is often blurred. Brackenridge[105] provides examples of the range of behaviour that amounts to harassment but which falls short of abuse, and her examples closely reflect what employers in the United States have come to understand as 'hostile environment' harassment in the wake of *Farragher* v. *Boca Raton*.[106] More controversially (but it is submitted correctly), she identifies 'exchange of reward or privilege for sexual favours' as *abuse* rather than 'mere' harassment. Such behaviour would probably have a sufficiently strong aura of consent to avoid attracting the attention of the criminal law (unless, of course, the victim is under age). Many of the other forms of abuse that Brackenridge mentions (rape, forced sexual activity, sexual assault and physical/sexual violence) are all criminal offences. But she recognizes that sports lend themselves particularly well to coercive behaviour where abusers may spend months, or even years, gaining the trust and adulation of their victims, culminating in the creation of an environment where the distinction between coercive sex and consensual relationships between adults becomes blurred. As Brackenridge says, 'abuse is abuse regardless of the age of the victim and abuser',[107] and this does not change simply because the abuse can be passed off as a consensual relationship.

Once again, much can be learned from the United States. In collegiate sport coaches' having sex with student-athletes is regarded as unacceptable conduct which strikes at the heart of the employment relationship, especially in the wake of *Farragher*. No university has attempted to impose a blanket prohibition on consensual sexual relationships between coaches and athletes, but the sexual-harassment policies at these institutions make it clear that in some circumstances even consensual relationships can lead to discipline or dismissal.[108] Most universities' harassment policies stress that the institution may refuse to support the coach if a student-athlete with whom he had a consensual relationship subsequently makes allegations of harassment against him.[109]

In the United Kingdom the view that sexual relationships between coaches and athletes are unprofessional is less widely held. Unless, of course, they attract the attention of the criminal law, as per *Hickson*,[110] they would not usually result in internal disciplinary action because employers do not prohibit them under the terms of an employee's contract of employment. One can envisage situations where discipline or dismissal would be an appropriate response to these relationships (if, for example, a coach's lover were selected ahead of better athletes). However, the view that these relationships are no concern of the club, governing body or other employing institution remains the norm. Organizations and individuals need to accept that having sex with athletes is not a 'perk of the job' and the question of whether the athlete is over the age of 15 should be irrelevant.[111] This is not to deny that athletes can and do genuinely fall in love with their coaches, but if this occurs the governing body should not implicitly condone the relationship by taking the view that it is not its concern. The proper response is for the governing body to stress to the coach that it would be appropriate for him or her to cease working with that particular athlete. So far as abusive relationships are concerned, the role of sports organizations rests in placing effective 'external inhibitors' in the path of potential abusers. Reporting mechanisms and codes of conduct go hand-in-hand with taking steps to help children in particular understand that it is acceptable to say 'no' and with providing a supportive environment in which participants, co-workers and others can express concerns about inappropriate behaviour.[112]

The Lyme Bay Tragedy

In the late 1980s and the early 1990s several disaster inquiries revealed situations where employees were aware of risks but did not say anything[113] or did not want to 'rock the boat'.[114] In other cases employees had voiced concern but either nothing was done[115] or they were victimized for speaking up.[116] Within the context of sport the Lyme Bay canoe disaster of March 1993 did much to raise an awareness of the difficulties facing those who have concerns about the industry.[117]

The four teenagers who died at Lyme Bay were in a party of 11[118] that had tried to canoe its way across Lyme Bay in Dorset. They died of hypothermia after heavy seas forced their canoes away from the coast and they capsized in strong winds. Their first aid and safety equipment was inadequate; some canoes were not equipped with spray decks, some life jackets had no whistles and no distress flares were carried. Although the weather forecast was for maximum temperatures of 10°C with a force five wind, the party had been told to wear only swimming costumes under their wet suits.[119]

Less than a year before the disaster two leisure centre employees had voiced their concerns about practices there and had resigned over the inadequate safety and levels of training that they and other staff members had received. The two had written to Peter Kite, the managing director of the company which ran the centre, complaining of the £50 per week wages paid to instructors and saying that 'not one person here is technically qualified to instruct children. ...We are walking a very fine line between getting away with it and having a serious incident.' Their letter concluded by recommending that 'you should have a very careful look at your standards of safety, otherwise you might find yourself trying to explain why someone's son or daughter will not be coming home'. Their concerns had been ignored.

Kite and the manager of the activity centre, Joseph Stoddart, MBE, were subsequently charged with four counts of unlawful killing. At the trial one of the instructors said that, although he had been canoeing since the age of 14, he had received no training in taking people out to sea. An official from the British Canoe Union said the training course the two instructors had attended was 'absolutely inappropriate' for sea-canoeing instructors.[120] The single biggest contributory factor to the tragedy was that neither the instructors nor the members of their party knew how to inflate their lifejackets properly. Kite[121] was convicted of corporate manslaughter after a three-week trial – the first successful prosecution for that offence in the United Kingdom. Sentencing him to three years' imprisonment (reduced to two on appeal), the judge commented that he was 'more interested in sales than in safety' and had ignored the 'chillingly clear' warning letter he had received from the two former employees.[122]

At the end of the trial Ognall J criticized the government for its approach towards outdoor activity centres and, in particular, its failure to introduce statutory registration of such centres and their mandatory accreditation and inspection. In January 1996 the government announced it would support a Bill[123] providing for the compulsory registration of activity centres and the introduction of a complaints procedure through which centre users (but not employees) could voice their concerns.[124] The Activity Centres (Young Persons' Safety) Act 1995 requires centres offering activity holidays in caving, climbing, trekking or watersports for persons under the age of 18 to register with the Adventure Activities Licensing Authority.[125] Centres which do not offer any of these activities are simply required to comply with the provisions of the Health and Safety at Work Act 1974,[126] although many of these participate in voluntary registration and inspection schemes. There is no obligation upon them to do so, however, and, in any event, neither those schemes nor the provisions of the 1995 Act provide a framework for employees and others to raise their concerns along the lines that are being advocated here.

Conclusions and Recommendations

To summarize, codes of practice should stress that reporting concerns internally (to one's employer) in the first instance is preferable to 'blowing the whistle' externally, which is likely to place an intolerable strain on the employment relationship.

The importance of communicating this policy to employees in writing, and in advance of any concerns arising, is that employees need to know beforehand what to expect. If an aggrieved employee attempts to raise an allegation of harassment with (for example) the governing body and is told that concerns should first be raised with their employer, there is a strong possibility that the employee will either keep silent or talk to the media. This is particularly the case if the employee has no confidence in the employer's taking the matter seriously.[127] Consequently, the code of practice should also clearly outline a recommended course of action for employees who feel unable to report their concerns internally or who are dissatisfied with the action that results from it. In order to comply with the 1998 Act, the code must stress that, although confidentiality will be respected, guarantees of anonymity can never be given. While the main argument in favour of anonymity is that it acknowledges whistleblowers' vulnerability and tries to accommodate it, the American experience shows that giving an undertaking of anonymity that should have never been given can prevent proper consideration of the issue. If an investigation results, the identity of the person concerned will quite possibly be revealed during that process.[128]

The code should emphasize that the subsequent victimization of employees who make a complaint of race or sex discrimination is an offence under the 1976 Act and the 1975 Act, respectively[129] and would, in addition, result in the governing body's taking appropriate disciplinary action. Indeed, the employment tribunal in *Hussaney*[130] came 'very close' to concluding that Chester City's failure to offer James Hussaney professional terms was an act of revenge rather than a decision based on his playing abilities. Similarly, victimizing employees who report concerns is unlawful under the 1998 Act.[131] Once again, the code should stress that such conduct, and seeking to deter employees from raising concerns in the first place, amounts to a serious breach of the code and will be treated accordingly – meaning that, if circumstances demand, the governing body will levy financial or other penalties. The code should also stress that the making of false allegations or allegations that are financially motivated also amounts to a serious breach. The rights and obligations it provides should apply to volunteer workers, who are the mainstay of so many sports bodies, as much as they do to salaried employees. If phrases such as 'malpractice', 'wrongdoing', 'reasonable' and 'in good faith' are used, they should be defined accurately but in terms that a lay person can understand.

The circumstances in which employees can refer their concern to the governing body rather than to their employer in the first instance should be stipulated. Likewise, provision should be made for employees to reveal their concerns to outside agencies, such as the police or the media, if such revelations would be 'in the public interest'. The code should also provide guidance on the meaning of 'in the public interest'. While this would undoubtedly present difficulties of definition, a satisfactory solution might be to state that the disclosing of unlawful acts or activities that would tend to bring the sport into disrepute would necessarily be 'in the public interest'.

To conclude, the necessity of sports bodies ensuring that they take up references[132] should also be emphasized. Failing to do lays the organization open to an action in negligence if participants suffer harm at the hands of an employee whose bona fides have not been established. Taking these steps also suggests that the organization is committed to best practice.[133]

Until recently, providing a reference that was unfavourable or inaccurate did not provide the employee with a course of action unless that reference was defamatory. But in *Spring* v. *Guardian Assurance*[134] the House of Lords ruled that an employer owes a duty of care to an employee in respect of the preparation of a reference and would be liable in damages for any economic loss suffered by the employee if the reference were negligently prepared. Careful employers have little to worry about, for *Spring* merely reinforces the necessity of following good practice by, for example, keeping proper employee records and using them when writing references. In the United States new employers have sued previous employers who have provided inaccurate references,[135] and British employers who fail to provide references properly could similarly find themselves on the receiving end of a negligence action.[136]

NOTES

1. Industrial Tribunal, unreported. Case no.2305384/97.
2. [1997] Crim LR 495.
3. S. Gardiner and A. Felix, 'Juridification of the Football Field: Strategies for Giving Law the Elbow', 5 *Marq. Sports LJ* (1995) no.2, 189.
4. P. Bourdieu, 'The Force of Law: Towards a Sociology of the Juridical Field', 38 *Hastings Law Journal* (1987), 814–53.
5. What has been termed the 'legal culture': Richard Terdiman, 'The Force of Law: Towards a Sociology of the Juridical Field' (translator's introduction), 38 *Hastings Law Journal* (1987), 805–13.
6. Football's governing bodies' unwillingness to contemplate the realities of European Union law pre-*Bosman* is another example; the confused and dishonest approach to the use of performance-enhancing drugs in athletics is a third.
7. Hereafter 'the 1975 Act'.
8. Lord Lester of Herne Hill, 'Discrimination: What Can Lawyers Learn from History?', *Public Law* (1994), 224–50.
9. 'An employer may...refuse to employ a man from the most mistaken, capricious, malicious or morally reprehensible motives that can be conceived, but the workman has no right of action against him.' *Allen* v. *Flood* [1898] AC 1, 178 per Lord Davey.
10. Race Relations Act 1975, s.37–42.
11. Ibid., s.62–76.
12. Professor Harry Street, Geoffrey Howe, QC and Geoffrey Bindman, *Report on Anti-discrimination Legislation*, London, 1967.
13. J. Martin, 'Scoring Points for Women', 8 *Ohio Northern Law Review* (1981), 481.
14. Lord Lester of Herne Hill, 224.
15. *Equality for Women*, London, 1974, Cmnd 5724.
16. The relevant provisions of the two acts are similar. What follows is an all-too-brief summary of a complex area of law. For a layman's introduction see D. McArdle, 'Can Legislation Stop Me from Playing?', 2 *Culture, Sport, Society* (1999) no.2, 44–58. For

something more sophisticated see, for example, I. Smith and G. Thomas, *Industrial Law*, London: Butterworths, 1996.

17. Industrial Tribunal, unreported. Case no.2102426/97.
18. Footballers use different studs in different weather conditions: generally, the harder the pitch, the shorter the stud. Changing the studs of senior players' boots is a traditional task of the young player.
19. In the words of the tribunal chairman, Chester City's response was 'not the action of an employer who has formed the view that a senior manager has gravely misconducted himself'; *Hussaney* v. *Chester City FC* Industrial Tribunal, unreported. Case no.2102426/97 at 4.
20. Hussaney was awarded £2,500 damages to compensate for race discrimination and injury to feelings. After the tribunal's decision was announced in November 1997, the Football Association said it was to hold an inquiry into the matter. No more was heard, so in the summer of 1998 the Association was contacted by the author and asked what was happening. Their Media Officer said the enquiry had already been held, but 'we want to avoid any bad publicity, so we've informed the club of our feelings and are leaving it at that. We won't be going public.'
21. Although EU law now makes provision for the introduction of such measures in areas of employment where women have traditionally been under-represented: EC Treaty, art.141(3).
22. M. Potter and E. Regan, *The Legal Limits of Affirmative Action in Redundancy Selection*, 147 *New Law Journal* (1997), 735. See also *James* v. *Eastleigh Borough Council* [1991] IRLR 288, HL. The Council allowed free admission to its swimming pools for women over the age of 60 and to men over the age of 65, and a 63-year-old male argued that this policy amounted to direct discrimination on the ground of sex. The House of Lords held that only charging an admission fee to the men was discriminatory: sex was the sole factor in determining who should pay and this amounted to direct discrimination. The Borough Council's admissions policy had been introduced before *Marshall* v. *Southampton and South West Hampshire Area Health Authority (Teaching)* [1986] IRLR 140, ECJ established that different retirement ages for women and men contravened EC law. However, the fact that the policy may once have been lawful did not mean that it continued to be so after the ramifications of Community law had become apparent. The policy should have been scrapped in November 1987 at the latest, when different mandatory retirement ages were abolished.
23. C. McCrudden, 'Rethinking Positive Action', 15 *Industrial Law Journal* (1986), 219. For a number of years Northampton Town were the only professional football club to possess such a policy, although one or two others have now followed suit.
24. 401 US 424 (1971). 'The technical and crabbed language of s.1(1)(b) [of the 1975 Act] was Parliamentary Council's version of the landmark judgment in *Griggs*': Lord Lester of Herne Hill, 227.
25. *Bilka-Kaufhaus GmbH* v. *Weber von Harz* [1986] ECR 1607, ECJ.
26. Although the burden of proof is a notoriously difficult one for the employer to discharge: *Bilka-Kaufhaus GmbH* v. *Weber von Harz.*
27. For a more detailed, though dated, discussion see D. Pannick, *Sex Discrimination in Sport*, London: EOC, 1983.
28. Unreported. Court of Appeal Transcript 1978, no.591.
29. [1980] ICR 266, EAT.
30. [1981] ICR 660, CA.
31. Industrial Tribunal, unreported. Case no.2304321/97.
32. Industrial Tribunal, unreported. Case no.220651/96.
33. Industrial Tribunal, unreported. Case no.2305384/97.
34. S. Redhead, *Unpopular Cultures: the Birth of Law and Popular Culture*, Manchester: Manchester University Press, 1995.

35. K. Dyer, *Catching up the Men*, Brisbane: University of Queensland, 1992.
36. B. Turner, *The Body and Social Theory*, London: Sage, 1984.
37. *Equality for Women*.
38. Unreported. Court of Appeal Transcript 1978, no.591 at 4.
39. Not normally an insurmountable barrier so far as Lord Denning was concerned. Following the growth of women's soccer in the UK over the past decade, a latter-day Theresa Bennett would have little difficulty finding a team. Mixed-sex soccer up to the age of 12 is the norm. Thereafter, girls can play for under 14s, under 16s or under 18s teams before moving on to adult women's teams.
40. [1980] ICR 266, EAT.
41. Since *Greater London Council*, the scope of s.51 has been significantly restricted. S.51 initially gave a blanket exemption for discriminatory acts that were necessary to comply with a statute that had been in force since before 1975. It was designed to avoid conflict with the provisions of the Factories Act 1961 and other industrial safety legislation that gave special protection to women (for example, by restricting night working or the number of hours they could work in a factory). Many of those restrictions had increasingly been regarded as unnecessary and were removed by the Sex Discrimination Act 1986. However, the EC believed that s.51 still breached Community law, and in particular the Equal Treatment Directive, EC 76/207. Accordingly, the Employment Act 1989, s.3(3) was passed in order to restrict s.51 still further: I. Smith and Sir J. Wood, *Industrial Law*, London: Butterworths, 1993, 191.
42. [1980] ICR 266 at 272, per Slynn J.
43. [1981] ICR 660 at 666, per Browne-Wilkinson J.
44. Industrial Tribunal, unreported. Case no.2304231/97.
45. *Couch, passim*.
46. *Labile*: 'prone to chemical change': *Collins's Concise Dictionary*, 1996.
47. Ibid., at 12.
48. Ibid., at 10–12.
49. Ibid., at 12.
50. Although mixed boxing does occur in the USA. Mohammed Ali's daughter has fought male boxers.
51. Industrial Tribunal, unreported. Case no.2304321/97 at 13.
52. Industrial Tribunal, unreported. Case no.2200651/96.
53. For a more detailed discussion of *Hardwick*, see D. McArdle, *Football, Society and the Law*, London: Cavendish, 2000.
54. Industrial Tribunal, unreported. Case no.220651/96 at 12.
55. Ibid., at 12–16.
56. While paying due respect to certain FA officials' personal commitment to equality of opportunity, one should not read too much into the considerable sums of money that the organization has spent on women's football in the recent past. FIFA President Sepp Blatter has made it known that the FA has to be seen to be taking the women's game seriously if England is ever to host the (men's) World Cup again; hence the FA's support for such initiatives as the women's Centre of Excellence. One should also add that women's football in this country continues to pay the price for years of mismanagement by the Women's Football Association before its merger with the FA: S. Lopez, *Women on the Ball*, London: Searlet Press, 1997.
57. Industrial Tribunal, unreported. Case no.2305384/97.
58. Industrial Tribunal, unreported. Case no.2305384/97 at 2.
59. Ibid.
60. Ibid., at 3.
61. Ibid., at 5.
62. Ibid.
63. Ibid., at 10.

64. S. Anderman, *Labour Law: Management Decisions and Workers' Rights*, London: Butterworths, 1993.
65. D. Lewis, 'Whistleblowers and Job Security', 58 *Modern Law Review* (1995), 208–21.
66. Ibid., 209.
67. [1968] 1 QB 396.
68. [1985] QB 526.
69. Lewis, 214.
70. Health and Safety at Work, etc. Act 1974, s.7.
71. This provision could be used, for example, by football club employees who have concerns about the inadequate training undertaken by many of the stewards who are hired from stewarding agencies but whom the clubs continue to use for want of an alternative. See D. McArdle, 'Full Yellow Jacket: Stadium Safety a Decade after Hillsborough', 6 *European Journal for Sport Management* (1999), 113–30.
72. Employment Rights Act 1996, s.43B.
73. Ibid., s.43K.
74. Ibid., s.43H(1)(a).
75. 'A person prescribed by an Order made by the Secretary of State': ibid., s.43F(1)(a).
76. Ibid., s.43C.
77. Ibid., s.43G.
78. Ibid., s.43G(2)(b).
79. The Public Interest Disclosure Act 1998, ss.4–16. In assessing whether a disclosure that has occurred under these circumstances was reasonable, the employment tribunal will consider the identity of the person it was made to, the seriousness of the concern, whether the risk or danger remains and whether it breached any duty of confidence the employer owed a third party.
80. Employment Rights Act 1996, s.43J.
81. <http://www.pcaw.demon.co.uk>
82. It is unlawful employment practice 'for an employer to discriminate against any individual with respect to his compensation, terms, conditions, or privileges of employment, because of such individual's race, colour, religion, sex or national origin.' [42 USCA s 2000e – 2(a)(1)].
83. 'No person in the United States shall, on the basis of sex, be excluded from participation in, be denied the benefits of, or be subjected to discrimination under any education program or activity receiving Federal financial assistance.' [901–905, 20 USC 1681 (1972)].
84. Unwelcome verbal banter or jokes of a sexual nature; unnecessary patting and touching; verbal harassment; subtle pressure for sex; constant 'invasion of personal space'; demanding sexual favours with explicit or implied threats about a person's employment status; offering preferential treatment in exchange for sexual activity; sexual assault.
85. 83 F. 3d 118 (1997).
86. 118 S. Ct. 2257 (1998).
87. 118 S. Ct. 2275 (1998)
88. B. Velasquez, 'Recent US Supreme Court Cases in Sexual Harassment May Provide Implications [*sic*] for Athletics Departments and Physical Education Programs', 9 *Journal of Legal Aspects of Sport* no.1 (1999), 26–34.
89. 'It's the liability of supervisory personnel, and of institutions for incidents of harassment that they weren't aware of, that frightens most people. Our legal counsel looked at last summer's cases and got highly anxious about our liability exposure, so we've had to revise our policy towards supervisors.' Interview with CU, an American university affirmative action officer, March 1999.
90. M. Messner and D. Sabo, *Sex, Violence and Power in Men's Sports*, Freedom, CA: The Crossing Press, 1994.
91. Although in some circumstances employers can avoid liability if they can show they

exercised reasonable care to prevent and correct promptly any sexually-harassing behaviour. The employer must also show that the claimant employee unreasonably failed to raise her concerns via a reporting mechanism that the employer had provided: *Farragher* v. *City of Boca Raton,* 118 S. Ct. 2275 (1998).

92. This ground-breaking 'theory of supervisory harassment' is based on the premise that supervisors' authority over others gives them greater opportunity to harass and employers should take all necessary steps to prevent harassment, whether through induction programmes, in-house training or codes of conduct. It means that unless the 'affirmative defence' applies, the employer will automatically be liable for any discriminatory conduct by an employee who has a supervisory role over the employee who is the victim of the discrimination: ibid.

93. 'Last summer's Supreme Court decisions have informed the current trend in training on harassment. They have influenced many institutions to do more training, and to publicise their policies far more widely.' Interview with DK, an American university affirmative action officer, March 1999.

94. 'New employees will get a full employee-orientation program. Existing staff members will have on-going training. We want to make sure that we are in the best legally defensible position, and I think that requires mandatory and ongoing training. ... That doesn't just mean lectures, it means role-play, providing brochures to all staff members and generally being as pro-active as possible.' Interview with DK, an American university affirmative action officer, March 1999.

95. Of course, this advice is not directed solely at employers in the sports sector.

96. 'When I am asked to provide mandatory training for people with a supervisory role, it can be hard to identify who the supervisors are. That's a logistics question that keeps me awake at night.' Interview with CU, an American university affirmative action officer, March 1999.

97. 'With mandatory training, there will always be people who tell you it is a waste of time. But I tell them that we have a College policy; if you follow that policy and someone makes an allegation against you, the College will indemnify you in any lawsuit that arises. However, if our investigations reveal you have not followed the College policy or have not attended the sessions, then you are on your own.' Interview with IC, an American university affirmative action officer, March 1999.

98. The benefits of employers operating a 24-hour hotline could be equally well achieved, and at markedly less expense, by proper implementation of the other reporting mechanisms. However, proper risk management would involve extending all aspects of the training programme to all employees, rather than limiting some aspects of it to those who operate in a supervisory capacity.

99. *R* v. *Hickson* [1997] Crim LR 495 is a fairly significant criminal evidence case. Hickson appealed against conviction on the grounds, *inter alia*, that in summing up the judge had failed to comment on the fact that the most serious counts – those concerning the allegations of rape – dated from 1976/77. No complaint had been made against Hickson at the time and the judge might have said that, given the absence of a complaint in 1976/77, Hickson could not be expected to provide alibi evidence for those dates nearly 20 years later. However, the appeal was dismissed. The Court of Appeal ruled that the absence of a direction on those issues had not rendered the verdict unsafe or unsatisfactory. It is unusual for a conviction to be upheld in the absence of direction on the difficulties the defence faces when there has been a delay in the making of allegations. However, in reaching its decision the Court of Appeal was particularly swayed by the striking similarities in the evidence of the two, entirely independent, groups of young women.

100. C. Brackenridge, '"He Owned Me, Basically ..." Women's Experience of Sexual Abuse in Sport', 32 *International Review for the Sociology of Sport* (1997) no.2, 115–30.

101. M. Burton-Nelson, *The Stronger Women Get, the More Men Love Football*, New York: Harcourt Brace, 1994.

102. Brackenridge, op. cit., 118.
103. National Coaching Foundation, *Protecting Children: A Guide for Sportspeople*, Leeds: NCF, 1998.
104. Brackenridge, 115.
105. Ibid.
106. See n.81.
107. Brackenridge, 117.
108. See, for example, the University of Nebraska's harassment policy at <http://www. uneb.edu/employees> and the University of Minnesota's at <http://www.fpd.finop. umn.edu>.
109. 'There has to be an understanding that, if you don't attend [our training courses] and a suit is filed against you, you are on your own. Also, part of your staff evaluation will concern whether you have attended these programs, and attendance could be tied in with pay rises.' Interview with IC, an American university affirmative action officer, March 1999.
110. [1997] Crim LR 495. Informed sources within the Amateur Swimming Association say some officials within the ASA are quite looking forward to having Hickson back once he has served his time and a post will be created for him.
111. The time when performers have reached a high standard but are performing just below elite level – the 'stage of imminent achievement' – may be when they are most vulnerable to abuse. They may be particularly vulnerable if that stage either precedes or coincides with their age of sexual maturity. See C. Brackenridge and S. Kirby, 'Playing Safe. Assessing the Risk of Sexual Abuse to Elite Child Athletes', 32 *International Review for the Sociology of Sport* (1997) no.3, 407–17.
112. Those working within sport might also like to consider whether more could be done in respect of the high incidence of disordered eating in 'appearance sports' such as diving, gymnastics and ice-skating. Brackenridge (1997) draws attention to the 'possible association' between disordered eating and sexual abuse and is able to provide anecdotal evidence of sports physicians in the United States treating athletes with eating disorders who subsequently reveal they have been sexually abused at some time. The link between disordered eating and sexual abuse may be as strong an indicator of which sports could be particularly susceptible to abuse as considering whether the sport involves lots of physical touching or whether peak performance occurs at a comparatively young age.
113. The Bingham Inquiry into the BCCI affair, London: HMSO, 1992, Cmnd 198.
114. The Hidden Inquiry into the Clapham rail crash, London: HMSO, 1988, Cmnd 820.
115. The Sheen Inquiry into the Zeebrugge ferry disaster, London: HMSO, 1987, Cmnd 8074.
116. The Blom-Cooper Inquiry into Ashworth Special Hospital, London: HMSO, 1992, Cmnd 2028.
117. In the same context, one could also discuss the Cullen Inquiry into the shootings at Dunblane Primary School, 13 March 1996, Scottish Office, 1986, Cmnd 3386. I have refrained from doing so because the tragedy of Dunblane and the lessons to be learned from it deserve far greater consideration than could be given here.
118. Eight children aged 14 or 15, a teacher and two hopelessly under-qualified supervisors in their early twenties.
119. A safety boat that was supposed to be in attendance was several miles away and the local coastguard had not been informed of the trip. Stoddart did not report the party's failure to return to the centre until three hours after their estimated time of arrival, and the children spent another three hours in the water before the coastguard spotted them.
120. He went on to say, 'I cannot believe anyone would contemplate taking a group of absolute and complete beginners on a trip like this', *Guardian*, 24 Nov. 1994, 13.
121. His company, OLL Ltd., was fined £60,000. The jury failed to reach a verdict in respect of Stoddart and he was formally acquitted.

122. In July 1996 a report by John Reeder QC absolved the coastguards from any responsibility for the youngsters' deaths, although he did say there had been 'some complacency' on the part of the coastguards who had been on duty that day: *Guardian*, 18 July 1996, 6.

123. A Private Member's Bill introduced by David Jamieson, MP.

124. *Guardian*, 25 Jan. 1995, 2.

125. 17 Lambourne Crescent, Cardiff CF4 5GG or <http://www.aala.org>.

126. Although many of these centres participate in voluntary registration schemes.

127. For an example of a code that falls far short of being taken seriously (not least because it does not commit signatories to taking effective disciplinary action against players or managers who engage in racist behaviour), see the Football Association's Anti-discrimination policy. This is reproduced in the Football Task Force, *Eliminating Racism from Football*, London: FTF Publication, 1998, at 53.

128. 'Once a report is made the machinery of the institution takes over... and we get complainants withdrawing their complaint once we make it known that we cannot guarantee confidentiality. ... I'm investigating a case right now in which a colleague gave a guarantee of confidentiality that should not have been given. Once the administration gave that guarantee, the College was in the loop of potential legal liability. So now we're trying to work out if there is a way to proceed while still maintaining this person's anonymity, and I don't think there is.' Interview with IC, an American university affirmative action officer, March 1999.

129. Sex Discrimination Act 1975, s.4(1) and the Race Relations Act 1976, s.2(1).

130. Industrial Tribunal, unreported. Case no.2102426/97.

131. Employment Rights Act 1996, s.47B.

132. Also, query gaps in CVs and ask to see the originals of any qualifications. As a general rule, a good coach will not object to the unobtrusive presence of bystanders at coaching sessions, will be reluctant to give lifts home (notwithstanding the potential insurance ramifications of doing so) and will try to avoid spending much time in the sole company of one particular child or athlete. Note that this is not an attempt to frighten parents or carers away from letting children do sports.

133. For reasons of brevity I have not considered the power of employers to carry out criminal conviction checks on potential employees. Of great significance here are the relevant criminal legal provisions (notably the Police Act 1997 and the 'certificate of criminal convictions') and the phenomenon of 'enforced subject access' which some employers used before the passing of the Data Protection Act 1998. On the 1997 Act, see S. Uglow, 'Criminal Records under the Police Act 1997', [1998] Crim LR 235–45.

134. [1994] 3 WLR 354, HL.

135. 'We advise those responsible for checking references to ask referees, "is there anything else we should know about the candidate?" We could have a harassment case proceeding against someone who, as a pre-emptive strike, succeeds in getting a job elsewhere. Now, unless you ask me the magic question, we are not going to volunteer that information. If somebody at another institution fails to answer that question when we ask it, that provides us with the opportunity to come after them, should we be sued for a negligent hiring.' Interview with IC, an American university affirmative action officer, March 1999.

136. Nii Lante Wallace-Bruce, 'Employers Beware! The Perils of Providing an Employment Reference', *Journal of Business Law* (1997), 456–64.

PART 4

Future Areas of Dispute

12

Ownership and Control of Sports Clubs: The Manchester United Football Club 'Buyout'

Nick Toms

In September 1998 Manchester United supporters everywhere were stunned by the news that their club was being bought by BSkyB, part of Rupert Murdoch's News International plc. It appeared inevitable that the club built by Sir Matt Busby into an national institution would become just a gilt-edged chip in the battle to corner the ever-widening television market.

Yet this did not happen. Almost uniquely, Murdoch's commercial ambitions were thwarted through determined opposition from Manchester United supporters and the Monopolies and Mergers Commission. This chapter examines how the campaign unfolded and looks at some of the wider issues that were raised by the proposed takeover.

The Commercialization of Football

Football has been transformed in the last 20 or so years. It was and remains a sport. However, at the professional level it is now also big business. A game which millions used to watch cheaply from the terraces has been turned into a commercial activity that can enable individual directors of clubs to make staggering returns on little or no investment.[1]

The game of football is part of our national heritage and culture – the people's game. In the words of the late Lord Justice Taylor in his report on the Hillsborough Disaster ('the Hillsborough Report'), 'Football is our national game. We gave it to the world.'[2] In 1990 it was estimated that half the population – 26 million people – watched England play West Germany in the World Cup semi-final.

Football clubs started off as local community organizations. Some clubs such as Everton, Aston Villa and Wolverhampton Wanderers originated from church teams. Others were old school teams, public house teams or works sides. Manchester United evolved from a team of railway workers from the carriage and wagon department of the Lancashire & Yorkshire Railway's engine shed at Newton Heath. It was not long, however, before these clubs became limited liability companies. The impetus for this change was the rise of professional players and the desire to purchase or rent better football grounds. Clubs have traditionally had a precarious position in

English law. Unincorporated associations have no legal personality and, with the exception of trade unions, cannot own property or be subject to legal rights and duties.[3] Limited liability companies were the obvious answer.

The creation of limited liability companies brought with it the danger of commercial exploitation. To prevent this, the Football Association imposed rules on football companies to protect and preserve their sporting natures. Directors were unpaid, dividends restricted and the grounds could not be sold off for profit. Some of these provisions remain in place today.[4] League football's communal character was maintained by the redistributing of money from gate receipts, sponsorship and television from the big clubs to the small.

The situation began to change in the early 1980s. In 1981 the FA allowed full-time directors to be paid and Martin Edwards almost immediately became chief executive at Old Trafford. The break-away of the Premier League, the ending of the redistribution of wealth in football, the public grants to redevelop grounds in the wake of Hillsborough[5] and the wealth provided through exclusive television contracts all combined to turn the major clubs into potentially lucrative investments.

The growing wealth in the top echelons of the game saw increasing numbers of businessmen involving themselves in football – not because of their support for their team – but for personal gain. They sought to turn football from being a sport into a business. The FA rules against profiteering in football were neatly sidestepped by the formation of public holding companies.[6]

Now about 20 clubs are quoted in the stock markets. The flotation of football clubs as public companies on the stock exchange has allowed club directors to gorge themselves on enormous profits.[7] Manchester United are a prime example of this process.

Louis Edwards took control of Manchester United for around £35,000 in the late 1950s and 1960s through the gradual purchase of individual shareholdings in the company. He had a meat firm which dominated the trade in the north of England, at least partly through bribing corrupt local authority officers in return for meat contracts in schools. Edwards' takeover of the club followed a similar pattern with his seeking to concentrate the ownership of the club in his own hands so that he could exploit it for his own gain.[8]

Edwards never reaped the rewards of his endeavours as he died from a heart attack shortly after his crooked business dealings were exposed on the BBC's *Panorama* programme. His son, Martin Edwards, inherited control of the club and it is he who has collected the jackpot. He has turned his inheritance into about £70 million in cash, annual dividends of £3 million and an annual salary of £500,000.

The evolution of clubs such as Manchester United into commercial 'brands' is reflected in the registration of trademarks. Since 1991 the club have registered 168 new trademarks, as compared to their having only the club crest registered as a trademark between 1970 and 1985.

The football authorities have been powerless in the face of these developments. The game has long been dogged by weak leadership. This problem was specifically identified in the Hillsborough Report.[9] The FA is supposed to be the game's regulatory body but, in reality, now largely acts as its spokesman. Lord Justice Taylor was particularly damning about the directors of individual clubs:

> As for the clubs, in some instances it is legitimate to wonder whether the directors are genuinely interested in the welfare of their grassroots supporters. Boardroom struggles for power, wheeler dealing in the buying and selling of shares, and indeed of whole clubs, sometimes suggest that those involved are more interested in the personal financial benefits or social status of being a director than of directing the club in the interests of its supporter customers.

The proposed takeover of Manchester United represented a further significant step in this trend. United's supporters and many others in football felt that it could see the end of the professional game as it currently exists in Britain. Instead of the media reporting and covering the sport, the sport would exist for the media.

Why Manchester United?

The £623.4 million bid for United certainly represented financial sense for BSkyB. Indeed, Greg Dyke, the current BBC Director General and then a United director, thought the club was worth over £1 billion given the growing opportunities in television.[10]

Manchester United, on all relevant measures, are the strongest English football club. Since the formation of the Premier League in 1992 they have won the championship on every occasion bar two, when they finished second. In the 1998/99 season they completed an unprecedented 'treble' of the Premier League championship, the FA cup and the European champions league. In the 1998 season, Manchester United attracted a total of 1.4 million spectators to home matches. They are estimated to enjoy the support of 18 per cent of all British fans.[11] A survey of 14 homes in the United Kingdom by the promotions group Team Marketing during 1996/97 showed ten per cent of the population (including those who do not regard themselves as 'fans') to support United.

United have over 200 supporters' clubs. Although these are mainly based in Britain (104) and Ireland (74), a significant number are to be found overseas (24) including in Australia, Canada, Germany, Hong Kong, Japan, Malaysia, Mauritius, New Zealand, South Africa, the USA and Scandinavia. In contrast, Arsenal has only 100 supporters' clubs. Furthermore, *United Monthly* is Britain's biggest selling monthly sports publication with average monthly sales of between 120,000 and 140,000. In contrast, Arsenal's equivalent magazine sells only around 50,000 copies. Moreover, around 40,000 copies of *United Monthly* are sold in Thailand (in Thai) each month and a Malay version is available in Malaysia.

Their success on the pitch has resulted in Manchester United's becoming, in financial terms, the largest English club by a substantial margin. According to the accountants Deloitte and Touche, Manchester United are the largest football club in the world.[12] In 1998 their turnover was 78 per cent more than that of the next English club, Newcastle United. The Deloitte and Touche report states: 'Manchester United dominated the financial performance of all clubs; their pre-tax profits exceed the whole turnover of Division Three, and the club's operating profit is about 30 per cent of all total Premier League operating profits.'[13]

The Importance of Football for BSkyB

Sport and football lie at the heart of BSkyB's control and dominance of the pay-TV market.

BSkyB are a publicly-quoted company, 40 per cent of which is owned by News Corporation of Australia through its British subsidiary News International. News Corporation's shareholding, while not giving it an absolute majority, is nevertheless sufficient to enable it to control BSkyB almost as if it were a wholly-owned subsidiary. Elizabeth Murdoch, daughter of Rupert Murdoch, formerly held a senior managerial position in BSkyB.

BSkyB dominates the pay-TV sector, as was confirmed in a report in 1996 by the Director General of Fair Trading ('the 1996 Report').[14] The effective monopoly over the provision of pay-TV by BSkyB is to a large extent maintained and enforced by several exclusive broadcasting rights that they have negotiated.

Exclusive rights to sports events have been a central part of this strategy. The 1996 Report underlined this, saying that BSkyB were 'dominant in the supply of sports channels in the UK Pay TV market and was at that time the only provider of premium sports channels with the exception of one specialist channel (The Racing Channel)'.[15]

Rupert Murdoch has explained the way he operates bluntly, 'We have the long-term rights in most countries to major sporting events and we will be doing in Asia what we intend to elsewhere in the world – that is, use sports as a battering ram and a lead offering in all our pay television operations.'[16]

Football and, especially, Premier League football, is of particular importance. BSkyB's expenditure on sporting rights in 1997/98 was £318 million of which £167.5 million (53 per cent) was used for the purchase of Premier League rights. It is not an exaggeration to say that BSkyB was saved from financial ruin by securing Premiership football on an exclusive basis in 1992.

The takeover bid for Manchester United was a further attempt by BSkyB to consolidate their control of live rights for Premiership football. They were also seeking to maintain their dominance in the event that the Restrictive Practices Court ordered an end to the collective negotiation of Premiership TV rights.[17] They wanted an important seat at the table in any future collective negotiations, including over a breakaway European super league. As Raymond Snoddy and Jason Nisse explained in an article on the merger,

> BSkyB's prime purpose in buying United is as an insurance policy to protect its exclusive live football… The Manchester United deal subject to approval by shareholders and regulators would at least give BSkyB the right to televised games at Old Trafford. The insurance policy could also work in the longer term. The BSkyB Premier League television deal runs out in 2001 and after that a number of clubs may be tempted to use digital television to create their own football channels.[18]

The Campaign against the Merger

It was clear that the BSkyB takeover of Manchester United heralded a radical departure both for the club and for professional football generally. Many United supporters were opposed to the merger; it would have marked the end of Manchester United as an independent entity. Until this point the football club was a largely self-contained operation. Even when it became a public limited company the football club remained the core of the business. This would not have been the case once Manchester United plc became just one small part of News Corporation's global media empire.

Despite the opposition, at first it seemed that the merger was a foregone conclusion. It was hard to see how ordinary United supporters could possibly take on the might of News Corporation and the Murdoch empire. However, gradually the campaign began to have an impact.

The fight against the merger was led by two organizations. The Independent Manchester United Supporters Association (IMUSA) represented the views of match-going supporters. Shareholders United Against Murdoch (SUAM) put forward the views of small shareholders opposed to the merger.

A highly effective campaign in the media was organized with numerous appearances on television and in newspaper articles. A rally in Manchester attracted nearly 2,000 United supporters opposed to the merger. Manchester United has approximately 30,000 shareholders and every one received a letter asking him to vote against the merger. Upwards of 120 Members of Parliament signed an Early Day Motion asking the government to intervene.

Ultimately, the merger was killed by the decision of the Secretary of State to uphold the findings of the Monopolies and Mergers Commission, that the merger was not in the public interest. However, the campaign against the merger played an essential part in paving the way for this decision. Above all, it underlined that this was not just a merger between company A and company B. Instead, it raised considerable matters of public importance concerning both competition and the future of football.

Reference to the Monopolies and Mergers Commission

Initially, the campaign was aimed at seeking a reference of the merger by the Secretary of State for Trade and Industry to the Monopolies and Mergers Commission. Such a reference may be made by him where it appears that two or more enterprises (one of which carries on business in the United Kingdom) will cease to be distinct enterprises and if the assets to be taken over exceed £70 million.[19] In deciding whether to make a reference the Secretary of State is advised by the Director General of Fair Trading. The Secretary of State potentially has a wide discretion as to whether to refer a merger for investigation. However, since 1984 government policy has focused on competition as the predominant matter to be considered when deciding whether or not to make a reference.[20]

The case under discussion appeared to be one where it was appropriate to take into account considerations in addition to any adverse effect on competition. It was very much a test case since it was clear that, if this merger went ahead, it would be followed by the take-over of other football clubs by media/communications companies. Already, at the time, Carlton had been linked to Arsenal and it had also been reported that Tottenham were negotiating with ENIC who have strong links with Time-Warner.

Reflecting this, IMUSA, SUAM and others submitted papers to the Office of Fair Trading that opposed the merger on two grounds. They claimed that the merger would have adverse effects on competition. They also pointed out the concerns of public interest; in particular, that football should not just stumble into what are potentially far-reaching changes without a full, detailed investigation about their impact on supporters and the future of the game.

Submissions by IMUSA

Competition

The paper submitted by IMUSA on competition detailed the dominance of BSkyB in a number of markets, including the coverage of Premiership football and pay-TV, which has been described earlier.

The paper argued that the relevant market for Manchester United was Premier League football. If BSkyB were to acquire United, the balance of power in negotiations for the Premiership rights would change in a way that could only reinforce BSkyB's position of strength. Other broadcasters would be at a significant competitive disadvantage if BSkyB controlled United.

The relevant market for BSkyB was pay-TV and the film and sports channels which are the main reasons why people subscribe to it. United's games accounted for a significant share of the total viewing of Premiership games. In the 1997/98 season 20 per cent of all Premiership games shown by BSkyB involved United and these accounted for 26.6 per cent of the total viewing of live Premiership games. The average viewing of United games was 33 per cent greater than that of Premiership games generally.

BSkyB already had the rights to most of the main sporting events under their control. Clearly, the merger could only strengthen this already dominant position.

Public Interest

The IMUSA public interest paper dealt with the potentially detrimental effects of the merger on football supporters, football clubs and football generally.

The Views of Supporters. The merger threatened to further marginalize the views of the supporters who are part of the lifeblood of the sport. Without the supporters to create the atmosphere the whole spectacle of professional football would be gravely diminished. Manchester United, like other clubs, enjoy loyal and dedicated support from large numbers of people. This support has been maintained both in times of success and failure on the football field.

The wealth of football clubs is generally largely generated through their supporters. They contribute through their payments at the turnstiles, the purchasing of items such as souvenirs and replica strips, and through revenue generated by their watching the game on television.

However, despite their importance, the views of football supporters have largely been ignored by those who run the game. This was expressly acknowledged in the Hillsborough Report:[21] 'In most commercial enterprises, including the entertainment industry, knowledge of the customer's needs, his tastes and his dislikes is essential information in deciding policy and planning. But, until recently, very few clubs consulted to any significant extent with the supporters or their organizations.'

Manchester United are no different from most clubs. Martin Edwards[22] refused to meet the supporters' organizations, including IMUSA, despite numerous requests. No supporters' representative sits on the board of either the football club or the public limited company. No attempts were made to consult supporters about the proposed merger or to obtain any guarantees on their behalf.

It was likely that supporters' views and interests would be even further marginalized if Manchester United became simply one part of the News Corporation empire. It was also probable that this would be repeated with the supporters of other clubs if they were taken over in this way.

The Exploitation of Supporters. Football is not just another commodity and football supporters cannot be seen as ordinary consumers. By and large, football supporters do not change 'brands' as shoppers might. Once you become committed you can never experience the same emotions for any other side. Only when watching your team will you feel the sense of anticipation before the match beginning, the elation when they score a goal and the despondency when they lose. Deep loyalties to clubs have often been built up in families over generations.

The possibilities in relation to Manchester United were spelt out by Tom Rubython as follows:

> Manchester United Football Club is an absolutely unique asset which can be leveraged as far as the directors' imaginations will allow. Sponsors, fans and TV companies are all locked in. There is nowhere else to go, even at treble the price, and anyone who won't pay can soon be replaced by someone who will.[23]

A report by the City analysts UBS says the following about football supporters:

> *The football fan as a captive customer.*
> As a business, football enjoys a particularly valuable and often brand-loyal customer base: the fans. Many fans inherit their clubs from parents or friends or by dint of locality, and as such become captive customers (it is unlikely they will change their colours).[24]

Football fans are ripe for exploitation. Recent years have shown that supporters will endure a great deal to continue to watch and be identified with their team. The disgraceful remarks of two of the directors of Newcastle United who were caught openly bragging about their exploitation of supporters has not dented the loyalty to that club. Manchester United's support is stronger than ever, despite the increasing commercial exploitation of supporters, including the introduction of 14 new strips since 1992.

The interests of Manchester United supporters were of a secondary, if any, importance to BSkyB. There was concern that this merger would lead to their facing even greater exploitation than was already the case.

Watching games at a stadium and on television are a partial substitute for each other. As a result of the merger, BSkyB would have obtained a monopoly over the watching of United home games in both media. All things being equal, the mere fact of the common ownership of these partial substitutes could have been expected to lead to price increases both for match tickets and for watching on television.

It was feared that supporters would face still greater exploitation through the costs of kit replicas and other souvenirs. Income from merchandizing now represents 28 per cent of Manchester United's total turnover.

Team selection could begin to be determined not for footballing reasons but to serve the commercial interests of News Corporation. Kick-off times faced possible further disruption should News Corporation have wanted to show live games in other parts of the world, including south-east Asia where they have extensive television interests.

The Heritage and Traditions of Manchester United. 'As for United, they stand for something more than any other person, any player, any supporter. They are – as was once written in the club programme of 1937 – the soul of a sporting organization which goes on from year to year, making history all the time. They remain a club with a rich vein of character and faith. Because of that they have no fear of the morrow.'[25]

There was concern at the impact of the merger on the culture and traditions of the club. Despite the commercialization of the game, Manchester United are not just a business. Like other football clubs, they remain an integral part of their local community and the heritage of the country generally. Particularly since the time of Sir Matt Busby's active involvement, Manchester United have become renowned the world over for their flair and tradition of attacking, entertaining football.

Football is a game of great drama and emotion which touches many lives. The tragedy of the Munich air disaster is indelibly written into the history of the club and football generally. It is the dying wish of many supporters that their ashes are scattered on the 'sacred turf' at Old Trafford.

Supporters feared that if Manchester United lost its independence and simply became part of the Murdoch empire then all this would be jeopardized. The interests of Manchester United could be sacrificed to the commercial concerns of News Corporation.

For instance, as seen above, News Corporation attach great importance to increasing their penetration of the Asian market. One strategy they might have adopted to achieve this goal would have been to ensure that United's first team included popular Asian players. Indeed, at the time there were press reports that representatives of BSkyB have been making enquiries about Hidetoshi Nakata, the Asian footballer of the year. Players could have been sold to suit the interests of News Corporation's global empire, despite the adverse effect this might have on the club.

It was questionable whether United would receive full value for their television rights if they were owned by BSkyB. There was no legal obligation for United to negotiate with more than one supplier in relation to broadcasting rights and it was unlikely that there would be any arm's length negotiations with BSkyB who would have been the effective monopoly broadcaster of United's games. Similarly, it was likely that United would have little choice but to be supplied by BSkyB with, for instance, hardware, and, consequently, it was again doubtful whether they would receive the full value for these products.

If a European super league comes to fruition it may be in United's best interests to join, but supporters questioned whether BSkyB would permit this if they did not have the television broadcasting rights.

There was even concern that the distinctive identity of the team, including the red and white strip, could be threatened if it conflicted with News Corporation's commercial interests.

The Impact of This Merger on Football Generally. The merger warranted closer investigation not just because of its impact on Manchester United but because of the wider implications for football generally. These concerns about the future of the game were not fanciful. In Australia, Rugby League was thrown into turmoil by the intervention of Rupert Murdoch through his cable TV company Foxtel. In 1994 attendances were at an all-time maximum and the sport dominated the television ratings. Foxtel wanted TV rights to attract subscribers to the company but they were contracted to a rival company. Foxtel therefore decided to try and establish a rival 'super league' by tempting more than 200 players to defect with huge salaries and cash bonuses. The game was deeply damaged with poor TV ratings and lower attendances becoming the norm in both leagues.[26]

In Mexico, two media conglomerates own four of the 18 first division clubs, all of which are linked to one of the two broadcasters that transmit every league and cup game. These teams regularly exchange players. They organize competitions and play a part in arranging kick-off times. They determine who will represent Mexico in international competitions. This is not based on the winning of domestic trophies but viewing figures.[27]

Matters of concern in relation to football included the impact on the game of the competition between the media corporations which own the major clubs. Sky Sports Managing Director Vic Wakeling had been reported as saying, 'What we don't want to happen in English football is perhaps what's happened in Scottish football. To take one example, where Rangers won nine titles in a row.'[28] The commercial interests of BSkyB in having a closed competitive league with different teams winning were not the same as Manchester United's, who would want to win all the time.

Smaller clubs would have faced further financial difficulties if media control of football led to the creation of a few super clubs. Already many are struggling to survive with the wealth in football being concentrated in fewer and fewer hands. The hopes of smaller teams rising to the top are already increasingly remote. They would become non-existent, and particularly if a European super league were established with no automatic promotion or relegation. This could harm much of the romance of football.

The kick-off times for matches are forever being changed to suit the schedules of media companies. The 3.00 p.m. Saturday kick-off time, which is the preference of most supporters, is increasingly becoming a thing of the past. The increasing ownership of clubs by television stations could see football becoming almost continuous with different companies seeking to avoid other big matches which might damage viewing figures. Already live televised football can be seen on nearly every night of the week.

None of the money paid by BSkyB for United would have gone into football. Instead, it would have gone to the directors and shareholders with Martin Edwards alone gaining a reputed £80 million in addition to the £33 million he had by then already obtained from the previous sale of shares.

Finally, FA rules currently prevent anyone owning more than one club. However, with football becoming big business this rule could constitute an illegal restraint of trade and be unenforceable. If so, BSkyB could buy further clubs, raising serious questions of conflict of interest and about the running of the game generally.

The Decision to Refer by the Secretary of State

The 1996 Report had not led to any action against BSkyB. The Director General of Fair Trading accepted undertakings from BSkyB regarding their conduct instead of referring the concerns about their dominance of pay-TV to the Monopolies and Mergers Commission for a full inquiry. It was also felt that the advent of digitalization might act to weaken BSkyB's position.

However, BSkyB's dominance of sports had continued. With the exception of the Racing Channel, their three sports channels remain the only premium sports channels on offer in the United Kingdom. Competitors such as On Digital continue to have to look to BSkyB for significant parts of their programming, particularly of sports.

On 29 October 1998 the Secretary of State referred the merger for investigation and report to the Monopolies and Mergers Commission. This, alone, was a significant achievement. From this moment the campaign against the merger intensified.

The Investigation by the Monopolies and Mergers Commission

The Commission has a broad remit when considering whether to allow mergers between companies. This was reflected in its terms of reference, which were to confirm whether a merger situation existed which qualified for investigation and, if so, 'whether the creation of that situation may be expected to operate or (if events so require) operates against the public interest'.[29]

In determining whether any particular matter operates, or may be expected to operate against the public interest, the Commission can take into account all matters which appear to it in the particular circumstances to be relevant.[30] Primarily the Commission focuses on matters affecting competition. It identifies the relevant markets that will be affected and carries out exhaustive investigations as to the impact the merger will have on them. In this instance, it also looked at wider issues affecting football, given the breadth of the opposition to BSkyB's plans.

The Commission heard evidence from a wide range of individuals and organizations in addition to BSkyB and Manchester United. It is significant to note that the only submissions aside from the two main parties to support the merger were from other Premier League clubs.[31] Opposition came from other media companies, non-Premier League clubs, the football authorities, the Professional Footballers' Association, supporters groups, local authorities and Members of Parliament. Over 300 individual members of the public contacted the Commission and all of them were opposed to the merger.

The Result of the Investigation

The Monopolies and Mergers Commission reported in April 1999. Its recommendation was that the merger should be prohibited as being contrary to the public interest. The Commission decided that the market Manchester United operated in was limited to Premier League football; the relevant market for BSkyB was premium sports TV channels. It found that, regardless of whether the existing collective arrangements continued or were superseded by individual selling, and whether the merger was the only one between a broadcaster and a Premier League club, or whether it precipitated other mergers, 'the merger may be expected to reduce competition for

Premier League rights with the consequential adverse effects we have identified in each case'.[32]

Importantly, the Commission did not limit its conclusions purely to matters of competition. It did not uphold all the concerns of supporters about the merger. However, it did state that it would adversely football in two ways.

> First, it would reinforce the existing trend towards greater inequality of wealth between clubs, thus weakening the smaller ones. Second, it would give BSkyB additional influence over Premier League decisions relating to the organization of football, leading to some decisions which did not reflect the long-term interests of football. On both counts the merger may be expected to have the adverse effect of damaging the quality of British football. This adverse effect would be more pronounced if the merger precipitated other mergers between broadcasters and Premier League clubs.

The final verdict of the Commission was damning, 'We were unable to identify any public interest benefits from the proposed merger. We, therefore conclude that the proposed merger between BSkyB and Manchester United may be expected to operate against the public interest.'[33]

The Future of Football

The rejection of BSkyB's bid was a victory for everyone who cares about the game of football. It has provided at least a temporary respite from the headlong charge towards the takeover of clubs by broadcasting companies. Most importantly, it showed that corporate barons such as Rupert Murdoch are not omnipotent. The individual supporter can make a difference.

However, many of the problems raised by the attempted merger remain to be solved. The media companies have not disappeared, but, instead, continue to chip away at the edges. BSkyB has changed its strategy from the takeover of one club to the purchase of shareholdings in a number of different ones.[34] As long as the shareholdings do not amount to ten per cent of a club's shares they are not in breach of Football Association rules. Clearly, though, this is a matter for concern as a nine per cent shareholding is going to give them considerable influence.

Rampant commercialization continues apace. Profits undoubtedly lie behind the expansion of European competitions and, in particular, the Champions League. The extra games are not welcomed by supporters, players or managers but are dictated by business interests. Manchester United's involvement in the so-called world club championship clearly put television and commercial interests above those of football which demanded the supporting of the FA Cup.

The governing bodies of the game remain powerless in the face of the demands by the big clubs. The game as a whole appears rudderless. It is likely legislation will be needed if any serious changes to return the game back to the supporters are to be made. The issues that are demanding of the most urgent attention are:

- The ownership of football clubs. It is wrong that the national game should be owned and controlled by often unscrupulous business men. Supporters need to be involved in the running of clubs and the 'plc' tide rolled back. Mutualization and other forms of fans' ownership need to be considered.
- The control and regulation of football. A unified body is needed to control the game and prevent further gross exploitation of supporters through higher ticket prices, merchandizing and television coverage.
- The control and regulation of television broadcasting in relation to sport. It is wrong that one company should be allowed to have a completely dominant position over the broadcasting of live sports. BSkyB's monopoly of premium sports channels needs to be broken up, with more sport being returned to terrestrial television.

The commercial juggernaut was temporarily derailed with the rejection of the BSkyB bid. However, it will be a brief respite. If reform does not take place soon then one thing is certain – Rupert Murdoch or some other media baron will be back and next time it may not be possible to stop him.

NOTES

1. Sir John Hall, for instance made around £100 million from his sale of Newcastle United which he had previously purchased with an investment of £2.4 million.
2. *The Hillsborough Stadium Disaster* (Cmnd Paper 962), para.10.
3. *Halsbury's Laws of England*, 4th edn, 1996 reissue, para.1.
4. See Rule 34 of the Football Association.
5. Manchester United was given £1.4 million.
6. The first of these was Tottenham Hotspur which became a plc in 1983.
7. See *The Football Business* by David Conn (Edinburgh, 1997) for an excellent account of the commercialization of the game.
8. See Michael Crick and David Smith, *Manchester United: the Betrayal of a Legend* (London, 1989) for a fascinating account of the Edwards' family's rise to power at Old Trafford.
9. *Hillsborough Stadium Disaster*, paras.51–8.
10. See *Business Age* (Oct. 1998), 68.
11. *Financial Times*, 18 Sept. 1998.
12. See *Annual Review of Football Finance*, Aug. 1998, 45.
13. Ibid., 18.

14. *Review of BSkyB's Position in the Wholesale Pay TV Market*, Dec. 1996, para.2.54.
15. Ibid., para.2.19.
16. *Guardian*, 7 Sept. 1998.
17. This, of course, did not happen.
18. *The Times*, 9 Sept. 1998.
19. Fair Trading Act 1973, s.64.
20. The so-called Tebbit guidelines have been regularly endorsed since 1984, including by the government elected in 1997.
21. *Hillsborough Stadium Disaster*, para.53.
22. The chairman of Manchester United Football Club Ltd.
23. *Business Age*.
24. *UK Football plc: The Winners Take It All*.
25. Geoffrey Green, *There's Only One United* (1978).
26. See Hiltzik, *Los Angeles Times*, 25 Aug. 1997.
27. See Downie and Twain, *Guardian*, 12 Sept. 1998.
28. Piccadilly Radio, 12 Sept. 1998.
29. Monopolies and Mergers Commission, *British Sky Broadcasting Group plc and Manchester United plc – A report on the proposal merger – April 1999*, Cm 4305, Appendix 1.
30. Fair Trading Act 1973, s.84.
31. Arsenal, Aston Villa, Leeds United, Newcastle United, Southampton and Tottenham Hotspurs made submissions supporting the merger.
32. Monopolies and Mergers Commission, *Report*, para.2.226.
33. Ibid., para.1.14.
34. Including a nine per cent interest in Manchester City.

13

Taken to Task: The Football Task Force, Government and the Regulation of the People's Game

Adam Brown

Introduction

This chapter will consider the Football Task Force as a means by which government has sought to influence the governance of the United Kingdom's most popular sport. It will outline how the Task Force came to be set up and the work which was undertaken, contrast the Task Force with other governmental interventions in professional football, and explain how the issue of the regulation of professional football became the key, and the dividing, issue for the body. The chapter will conclude with some comments about the body's likely influence on the governance of the sport. Although without legislative power, the Football Task Force was a unique initiative, aiming to combine consultation, representation and negotiation to arrive at a consensus of recommendations for the Minister of Sport on a range of issues, from racism to price control. The conflicts, contradictions and conclusions which this entailed make a fascinating study of the policy process, as well as of the divisions within football, particularly over the issue of government regulation.

I must, however, start by declaring an interest. I was a member of the Task Force Working Group from July 1997 to December 1999, when the Task Force was wound up, and was also 'elevated' to become a member of the full Task Force for the last year of its existence. I was involved in the majority of the Task Force's evidence sessions and heavily involved in drafting and commenting on some of its reports, most notably the split Final Report. This participation has undoubtedly given me a detailed knowledge of the Task Force's workings. However, as both author and researcher, this participation may raise more academic, methodological concerns for some. While I do not feel that this closeness to the subject affects my basic argument, this chapter should be read as an insider's view, with perhaps the concomitant loss of critical distance (although certainly not of criticism).

The Football Task Force was established by the in-coming Labour government in July 1997. Its roots lie in the Labour Party's *Charter for Football*,[1] one of a series of policy documents prepared in opposition. The *Charter* itself was the result of consultation between the then Shadow Sports

Minister, Tom Pendry, MP, and various bodies associated with the game, ranging from the Football Association (FA) to supporters' groups. It promised the establishment of a Task Force 'drawn primarily from bodies responsible for the national game', whose remit would be the restructuring of the Football Association; the investigating of links with television; the treatment of fans; football's finances; and a rather vague 'looking to the future'. It was, said the *Charter*, 'widely recognised that there was a need for change' and, most significantly, that the Task Force would be 'focusing specifically on the need for improved administration'.

Once in power, Labour chose to replace Pendry with someone considered to be a more dynamic and less risky option in the form of Tony Banks, MP, and it was he who established the Task Force. The body comprised representatives of 11 organizations in football: the FA, the Premier League, the Football League; the Professional Footballers' Association; the Football Trust; the Sports Council; the League Managers Association; the Association of Premier and Football League Referees and Linesmen; the Football Supporters' Association; the National Federation of Football Supporters' Clubs; and the Disabled Supporters' Association. Added to this were the Local Government Association, the Commission for Racial Equality and Liverpool University. The body was chaired by David Mellor, QC, the former Conservative Cabinet minister, with the former Football Trust Deputy Chair Richard Faulkner as the Vice-Chair and the Trust's Chief Executive Peter Lee as its Secretary.

Almost immediately, however, a quasi-Task Force sub-committee was established, known as the Football Task Force Core Working Group. The Working Group was established because key individuals, such as Mellor and David Davies at the FA, thought that the 'representative' nature of the Task Force itself would be a hindrance to progress, given the organizational loyalties and conflicts involved. These were being manifested at the time, not only in longstanding differences between organizations (fan groups and the FA, for instance), but also between different factions within some organizations – Davies, as head of the FA's public relations and considered a 'reforming' influence, was initially excluded from the main body as the FA's representative was the more conservative Graham Kelly.

The Working Group was designed to be the Task Force's engine – undertaking the evidence sessions, drafting reports, and, in Mellor's words, 'being able to think the unthinkable', free from organizational priorities. At first it was thought that the Group would produce recommendations and that the main Task Force would approve or amend reports. In truth, it rarely worked like that. Part of the reason was that the Working Group itself was an odd amalgam of those already on the main Task Force (such as Peter Leaver, former Chief Executive of the Premier League), different people from other bodies already on the Task Force (such as Davies) and some individuals. Thus many of the vested interests which the Group was set up to avoid inevitably came to the fore. This was never more true than with Peter Leaver who, before his disgrace and removal from post at the Premier League in the Chisholm and Chance scandal,[2] appeared at times to have the sole intention of obstructing Task Force business. Due to his Premier League role, Leaver used a variety of techniques to disrupt the body's workings, including calling for the dismissal of Mellor and Faulkner and using the League's leverage as trustees of the Football Trust to get its withdrawal of assistance to the Task Force. Conversely, Leaver was also able to use the Task Force for the benefit of the League, as when he got its support in the Restrictive Practices Court case (see below).

The full Working Group membership was: the executive of the full Task Force (Chair, Vice-Chair and Secretary); Sir Roland Smith (Chair Manchester United Plc); Peter Leaver, QC (Premier League); Sir John Smith (author of the FA's 'bung inquiry' and former Deputy Chief Constable, Metropolitan Police); the referee Uriah Rennie; Eleanor Oldroyd (Radio 5 Live); Robbie Earle; and myself. Later, and to complicate the picture yet further, some of the individuals from the Working Group were added to the main Task Force and given full voting rights (Sir John Smith, Oldroyd, and myself). Increasingly, and especially in the last year of the Task Force, the Working Group became largely redundant as the focus of deliberations shifted to issues of regulation and splits emerged on the main Task Force body.

The remit for the Task Force was divided into seven areas and its work was to be confined to football in England, reflecting the separate jurisdictions of Ministers for Sport for England and Scotland, as well as the separate football organization in each country. The seven areas were:

- to eliminate racism in football and encourage wider participation by ethnic minorities in both playing and watching;
- improve disabled access to the spectators' facilities;
- encourage greater supporter involvement in the running of clubs;
- encourage ticketing and pricing policies geared to reflect the needs of all, on an equitable basis, including for cup and international matches;
- encourage merchandizing policies to reflect the needs of supporters as well as commercial considerations;
- develop the opportunities for players to act as good role models in terms of behaviour and sportsmanship, and to become actively involved in community schemes;
- reconcile the potential conflict between the legitimate needs of shareholders, players and supporters where clubs had been floated on the Stock Exchange.

What was immediately apparent was that the wide ranging brief which the *Charter* had called for had been narrowed to more immediate social and consumer issues in the game. It should be noted that the Task Force was never given a brief to discuss the general administration of the game, as called for in the *Charter*, nor football's ever more crucial relationship with broadcasting, both of which perhaps made the Task Force's eventual leading role in public debates on the regulation of football somewhat surprising. It is vital to recognize, however, that the remit was a tool which could both restrict debate when necessary – such as preventing an examination of arguments to introduce safe standing areas when called for by fans[3] – and yet be flexible enough to encompass new issues in unlikely contexts – most notably to serve the powerful interests threatened by the Office of Fair Trading's Restrictive Practices Court (RPC) action, within a report ostensibly about players acting as role models. The *Investing in the Community* report, issued in January 1999, is indeed instructive: it embodied this widening of the remit to cover the community activities of clubs, yet also included what amounted to a 'behind-the-scenes' deal where the Premier League promised five per cent of future television income to the grassroots of football in return for the Task Force's support in the RPC.[4] Such support was somewhat surprising given the body's instruction not to consider broadcasting issues and given the ruling by the Department of Culture, Media and Sport that the body could not make an official statement on the BSkyB takeover of Manchester United which was being investigated by competition authorities at the time.[5]

The Task Force's work began in September 1997 with a series of evidence sessions held by the Working Group in London. These were followed by ten Regional Meetings staged around England, combining scheduled appointments in the day for local football organizations, fans' groups, clubs and local authorities, with open, public question-and-answer sessions in the evening. Whatever criticisms there may have been of the Task Force itself and the way it conducted its business, this exercise did amount to the biggest consultation exercise ever undertaken in English football and produced a vast body of evidence about the state of the game in the late 1990s.

The Task Force issued four reports: *Eliminating Racism* (March 1998), *Improving Disabled Access* (June 1998), *Investing in the Community* (January 1999) and *Commercial Issues* (December 1999).[6] These reports were intended to convey evidence and recommendations on the body's remit to the Minister for Sport, whose decision and responsibility it is to implement them. Of the reports, the government accepted in full the first three, which were backed unanimously by all parties. However, the fourth report, *Commercial Issues*, was a split one divided between Report One (backed by 11 members of the body, including fans' groups and all individual members) and Report Two (written and supported by the football authorities). At the time of writing (April 2000), the government has yet to make public its intentions and which document it supports, although there are some indications of the likely outcome, described below.

Government and Football

What is striking about the establishment of the Task Force is how it represents a marked shift in the attitude of government to professional football in some ways, yet incorporates established approaches in others. Whereas the 1980s were largely characterized by concern with football-related violence and the willingness to implement a series of legislative and other measures by the Thatcher government, the turn of the century under New Labour has brought a range of other issues into the political and regulatory agenda. Paradoxically, as I shall argue, these concerns are not associated with any discernible desire to impose intentions via legislation and reflect many of the traits of New Labour's policy process in other fields. Football had reached such a nadir in the public consciousness that at one point in 1988, Mrs Thatcher, the then Prime Minister, even suggested that the entire future of professional football was at stake.[7] The government's moral authoritarianism and concern to be 'tough' on law and order issues and a moral panic[8] in the media about 'hooliganism' meant that legislation was inevitable. This, together with the official inquiries by Lord Justice Popplewell and Lord Justice Taylor, 'amount,' as Redhead says, 'to a vast body of official stories about the control of soccer as a global business in the late 20th century. Further, the rhetorics of this official discourse, in the English scenario are, significantly, marked by a designation of football as disorder or violence.'[9]

Further, in the words of Murphy, Williams and Dunning: 'In the minds of many people, hooliganism and football are inexorably intertwined. Indeed, some see the problems that beset the game as almost entirely attributable to the "scourge of hooliganism".'[10] Such attitudes prompted the regulatory legislation described below and signalled that the government were prepared to make a special case of football under the law. Thus, the Sporting Events (Sale of Alcohol) Act 1985 restricted the sale to and consumption of alcohol by football supporters, both while travelling to a football match and while at the match itself, and was introduced in the belief that drunkenness and football-related violence were inextricably linked. Secondly, the Public Order Act 1986, although not being specific to football, did seek to define in law, in s.31, a 'football-related' offence. This meant that acts or threats of violence at, on the way to or when leaving an association football match were deemed to be 'football related' and as such made fans the subject of culturally-specific legislation.

Perhaps most controversial of all, the Football Spectators Act 1989 outlined the government's treatment of football supporters as a special case most graphically. Part I of the Act sought to impose a compulsory identity-card scheme for all football supporters, administered through the Football Membership Authority, meaning that supporters could not get into any Football League ground without a computerized card. Part II made provision for the restriction of the movement of convicted football offenders, as defined in the Public Order Act 1986. This was to stop offenders from travelling abroad and was to be exercised through the withdrawal of the identity cards of offenders, together with the requirement that they should report to a police station at times when English teams were playing abroad. Once again, football and football fans were given special legislative status and, in the light of the ID card scheme proposals, universally criminalized.

These measures were followed by the Football Offences Act 1991, which included a provision to criminalize 'indecent or racialist chanting'. Legislation was also supplemented by an agreement between government, police and clubs in 1987, which created a 'package of measures ranging from local plans for the vicinity of the grounds, right the way through to closed circuit television'.[11] Further to this, in 1989 a National Football Intelligence Unit was set up as part of the National Criminal Intelligence Service and the government agreed to a 'European Community Convention on Spectator Violence and Misbehaviour at Sports Events and in particular at football matches' in 1985, which sought a common code of practice towards football violence across Europe.

Further to these 'hooligan' measures were the inquiries into the Bradford fire (Lord Popplewell) and the events at Hillsborough (Lord Justice Taylor) with the subsequent rebuilding of many of the country's stadiums. Add to all these the Thatcher government's support of UEFA's ban on English teams playing in European competitions and the result was a considerable array of legislative and other measures which sought specifically to target football, and in particular football fans. Indeed, some of the legislation – and especially the all-seater requirement which followed the Taylor report – recognized that government intervention was necessary because self-regulation within the game had failed. Such an active approach was very different from that of the Labour government in relation to the Task Force.

Of course, the Labour administration has not abandoned a concern with law and order, far from it. Indeed, in some respects the Labour government's preparation for, and reaction to, violence at the World Cup in France in 1998 bore few dissimilarities from that of previous administrations and its Football (Disorder) Act (2000) is more draconian than any of the Thatcher legislation. In fact, it is one of the ironies of this discussion that the single piece of legislation enacted as a result of the Task Force's recommendations has been to amend the Football Offences Act to make it possible for an individual, rather than 'one or more people acting in concert', to be prosecuted for racial or indecent chanting.

New Labour and Football

However, that should not obscure the fact that the Football Task Force represented a new concern with football. While still in opposition Labour had responded to perceived crises in the game at a time (1995/96) when it seemed to be plagued by 'bungs', bribery, misbehaviour and bad leadership. The Premier League, all-seater stadiums and the flotation of several clubs on the stock market had brought with them new commercial priorities in football, reflected in more aggressive merchandizing policies and, most crucially to fans, huge increases in the cost of tickets. Concerns with this growing commercialization had been voiced by supporters' organizations for many years, but, crucially, in the mid-1990s, the media began to pick up on the changes and respond to them. Furthermore, and in sharp contrast to the 1980s, football became *de rigueur* and this was reflected in New Labour more than in any other political party.[12] For some, they were perfect partners:

> Football, like New Labour, is now 'cool', cosmopolitan and utterly modern. But both the game and the party have achieved this new found pre-eminence by moving away from their roots in local communities, by depending heavily on a media image to broaden their appeal, and by striking up unprecedented friendships with the movers and shakers of corporate business and high finance. The Football Task Force simply brings these parallel paths together.[13]

In addition to the *Charter*, therefore, were other indications that the incoming government would take on new issues in football in a way in which both the Thatcher and Major governments would not have contemplated. Pendry raised the prospect of a possible reintroduction of terracing, arguing that, given technological advances,[14] there was no justifiable reason against limited safe standing areas, something backed wholeheartedly by supporters' organizations; Labour promised to review the Hillsborough inquiry; and there were commitments to support the FA's bid for the 2006 World Cup following the success of Euro '96. Such a concern with the running of the national sport contrasted sharply with the hostile attitude and law and order agenda of previous administrations. However, a return to terracing – even allowing the Task Force to debate it – was ruled out, as was a new Hillsborough inquest. Also, the 2006 campaign became such an obsession for the FA and the government that they pressured Manchester United to withdraw from the 1999/2000 FA Cup competition for the somewhat spurious reason that to compete in the World Club Championships in Brazil would guarantee England's 2006 bid success. The furore which surrounded this decision was also to cost Tony Banks his job and his replacement by Kate Hoey. Add to this the Task Force's remit, which did not include broadcasting or the administration of the game, and the prospects of a whole new agenda to go with the whole new ball game seemed to be receding.

In some ways this was classic New Labour. Radical options and a wholesale reappraisal of the running of football seemed to be offered when in opposition, only to be withdrawn with the establishment of the Task Force. As such, it matches the party's attitude elsewhere – appearing conciliatory to powerful organizations (such as those that run football) and not wanting to offend the interests of big business, and of big broadcast business in particular.[15] Further, the remit for the Task Force focused on consumer issues and media-driven agendas such as players' acting as role models and merchandizing.

Indeed, the Task Force embodies, in many ways, the contradictions in Labour's interest in football: a new agenda for government intervention in football was set, but watered down considerably from the pre-election promises; consumer or 'coal face' issues took priority over the fundamental issues of football's governance, finance and organization; and the government made it fairly clear from the outset that they were interested in consensus agreements to bring about change rather than recommendations for them to legislate (particularly a statutory regulator). This is where the Task Force is quintessentially New Labour following a Third Way approach to politics:[16] it involved a former Tory cabinet minister as chairman; it invited 'all stakeholders' in the game to participate; it believed that the Task Force should produce a consensus on measures to improve the lot of supporters; and it involved probably one of the biggest quasi-focus groups yet undertaken in the form of the regional visits.

Furthermore, despite overwhelming support for a radical reorganization of football in England,[17] the Task Force was set up, not to alienate private business, but to attempt to engender enlightened self-interest. Given that this meant changing the practices of club chairmen and that certain interest groups in football (such as supporters' organizations) were vehemently opposed to the strategy pursued by others (for instance, the FA and the Premier League), this was perhaps fanciful. Further, encouraging self-reform and self-regulation in football failed to take account of the particular social make-up of the sport and the failures in the past of the game to 'put its own house in order', something Lord Justice Taylor deplored in the introduction to his report on the Hillsborough disaster.[18]

Indeed, Taylor appeared to give the government the prompt it needed in reassessing questions of governance and ownership:

> As for the clubs, in some instances it is legitimate to wonder whether the directors are genuinely interested in the welfare of their grass-roots supporters. Boardroom struggles for power, wheeler-dealing in the

buying and selling of shares and, indeed, whole clubs sometimes suggest that those involved are more interested in the personal financial benefits or social status of being a director than of directing the club in the interests of its supporters.[19]

Lord Justice Taylor made a number of recommendations about the running of the game as well as concerning the treatment of supporters as customers, including one that clubs should not use the introduction of all-seater stadiums to lift ticket prices.[20] At the time, for a government preoccupied with a law and order agenda as well as a dedication to the free market, the enforcement of price restrictions and an insistence on changes in club ownership structures and personnel were not going to be likely. However, for an incoming Labour government with a mandate to change the way football was run, there was an opportunity for legislation which even Taylor had highlighted: 'That football is a special case [in law] has been expressly recognized by the Government in promoting the Football Spectators Act 1989.'[21]

However, whereas successive governments have been fully prepared to initiate football-specific legislative attention, this has almost universally been concerned with regulating crowds – introducing safe arenas for them to sit in and special powers to police these. To date no legislation has regulated the owners and governors of football as a special case, and that did not change with the introduction of the Football Task Force. So, although the Task Force represented a new approach, some fundamentals remained the same.

The Regulator Debate

In many ways, then, it was surprising that the issue of the statutory regulation of football was able to gain so much currency during the life of the Task Force. Ironically, it was the government's own focus on consumer and 'coal face' issues – and above all ticket pricing – which led to this. The reports on racism and the disabled had achieved a good deal of agreement, although I would argue that without mandatory implementation their impact has been minimal. The 'community report' had seen benefits for all parties in the form of money for grass-roots football, success for the Premier League in the Restrictive Practices Court and a recommendation to give government backing to supporter–shareholder groups.[22] However, it was the 'commercial' areas of the remit – ticket policies, merchandizing, the role of the plcs and the involvement of fans – which were always likely to cause the most controversy.

During numerous evidence sessions, at all the regional meetings and during many internal Task Force debates the football authorities (the FA, the

Premier League and the Football League) insisted that they had no power or jurisdiction to influence the commercial policies of 92 private businesses. This was not in fact true: the Football League had once had a minimum price policy, ironically, to stop the bigger clubs from undercutting local competitors; Rule 34 of the FA restricted payments to directors and the payment of dividends to shareholders; and the competition rules of all three authorities make strict provision to prevent the dual ownership of clubs. Further, as governing bodies of membership organizations, the authorities do have the power to set conditions of membership: whether club chairmen would let it happen, however, is another matter. As such, there was precedent to have added criteria to safeguard access to football, to limit price increases or ensure that a minimum number of spaces in the stadiums were accessible to all income groups.

The facts that minimum pricing had long since disappeared (along with gate-revenue sharing); that Rule 34 was sidestepped and made redundant by the creation of holding companies, publicly-listed and wholly owning football clubs (so that they, rather than the club, paid directors and shareholders);[23] and that rules on dual ownership were not being enforced,[24] all signalled that the FA, in particular, had lost its historic role as the guardian of English football. As the doomed BSkyB takeover of Manchester United got under way in September 1998, it appeared that football was being governed increasingly by the City in the interests of corporate finance, rather than by the FA in the interests of football as a sport. For the Task Force this had major implications: the government wanted recommendations on ticket pricing to ensure that 'ticketing and pricing policies ... are geared to reflect the needs of all, on an equitable basis'; the football authorities were saying that there was nothing they could do to enforce this.

The authorities' reluctance to regulate the commercial activities of clubs also appeared in relation to other areas of the remit. Similar arguments were used in relation to supporters' representation at board level: 'It is for the shareholders of the club company to decide who shall sit on its board ...'; and whether clubs should be allowed to float on the Stock Exchange:

> The issue of whether or not to move to Plc status has to be a matter of judgement for individual clubs based on their own sense of what is best in the longer-term development of the club ... It would be wrong in our view for a new set of prescriptive rules to be devised to either prohibit or encourage flotation. Each club must be free to choose its own path.[25]

Such a position amounted to little more than an abdication of responsibility by football's governing bodies. They were not prepared to recognize that the form of ownership of football clubs and their governance principles fundamentally affect the priorities on which the game is run. Plc ownership of a football club meant that the shareholders, primarily institutional investors, determined the direction of the club with a legal obligation to maximize profit. That fact alone had already revolutionized English football, and the main beneficiaries of the new system of ownership – including many Premier League chairmen – were the ones now being represented on the Task Force. A commitment to regulate ownership or the participation of fans on club boards was hardly likely to get support from that quarter of the Task Force.

For supporters' groups and others on the Task Force, the reluctance of the FA in particular to govern was a motivation to look for alternatives. That the FA and the Premier League were in a state of crisis for much of the last 18 months of the Task Force's life did not help. Both had lost their chairman and chief executive in internal scandals and the much promised reform of the FA was and still is extremely slow in coming. Further, and perhaps most importantly, there was the crystallization of arguments calling for statutory regulation.

The premise of arguments on the Task Force for such regulation was largely developed in line with supporters' organizations' campaigns against the BSkyB takeover of Manchester United. That campaign (which resulted in the blocking of the bid by the Monopolies and Mergers Commission and the Secretary of State for Trade and Industry) had begun to look in some detail at the relationship of fans to clubs. Many submissions to the MMC argued that the supporter–club relationship was different from consumer–company relationships in other areas, which were based on the laws of supply and demand. What fans' groups and their allies were arguing was that supporters were effectively suffering because of a local monopoly: that is, that football support is 'a lifelong and unchanging emotional attachment' to a particular team.[26] As such, if a club charged the customers too much or if the customers were not getting value for money, they could not simply purchase the product elsewhere. The product, good or service therefore was to watch a *particular* football team and each club board was in a monopoly position to exploit fans' loyalties.

While all sections of the economy may have their own peculiarities, they share the fact that they are largely governed by the basic laws of supply and demand and competition between different suppliers of similar goods and services. That is, the consumer may shop around to find the supplier of the goods or service who offers the best value for money. The crucial difference in understanding the dynamics of the football industry is that, for the vast majority who pay to go to games as well as for most of those who buy televised football, the motivation is an emotional support for a particular team. Thus consumption, and competition between firms for it, is different in football from almost any other major sporting industry or other areas of the entertainment business.

Brand loyalty, rather than quality or value for money, is the determining factor in football 'consumption', an emotional commitment to the team which is above and beyond normal consumer choice. For the consumer of football, each company – football club – within the industry is itself the sole supplier of the product he/she wishes to purchase, competitive football played by 'his/her' team. As such, each club could be considered to be in a monopolistic position in its own right. This argument was recognized by the MMC Inquiry when they considered the peculiar characteristics of supply and demand in football: 'We have ... noted that all clubs have considerable independence in setting the ticket prices of their home games because many of their supporters have no substitute for these games. All football clubs with a strong supporter base will therefore have a degree of market power.'[27]

The fact that the football industry embodies this social and cultural aspect has been described as 'fan equity': 'fans are the customers in the sports business. And the relationship between a team and its supporters is exceptional in the sense that the customers do not need success ... fans can therefore constitute for some teams a real asset of truly intangible nature.'[28]

In this sense it is correct to argue that: 'Organised sport, and football in particular, draws on an emotional investment by the fan in the competitive proceedings which is highly unusual in the consumer/producer interaction relationship.'[29]

Those arguing against the football authorities on the Task Force also cited evidence that suggested that football was a different kind of business in other ways. The 'product' in football is a joint product and a match – whether consumed live or on television – which requires two companies to compete with each other. As such, football is a different kind of business because for the football 'product' to be meaningful it has, historically, been organized into leagues and cup tournaments which structure the competition between businesses/clubs. This structuring of the football industry has been underpinned by a regulated redistribution of income. The importance of this had, in fact, been recognized by all parties on the Task Force, when we argued that 'English football depends on the redistribution of income. It has been a feature of the game since it began ... English football's ability to reinvest in its own future is critically linked to there being no break up in the present collective bargaining arrangements.'[30]

Furthermore, research into other sports and in other countries supports this approach. For instance, in the United States, revenue sharing is a key feature of American football where 95 per cent of television revenue is shared equally between member clubs and where a draft system regulates the acquisition of new talent. It has been argued by some that the economic health of the industry as a whole is supported by this redistribution, and that unfettered competition – an absence of regulation – is damaging.

A key factor that determines the overall success of the league is *league balance* or *competitive balance*. If the gap between the dominant and lagging clubs in the league becomes too large then a significant number of league matches become too predictable and the absence of strong competition leads to unexciting games that attract less [*sic*] spectators. It is not difficult to see that in an unregulated league there is a tendency for imbalance to develop .... This inherent tendency to league imbalance results in one of the peculiar economic problems facing sports leagues, namely that while in most industries competitors are not adversely affected if their rivals go to the wall, in the case of a football league where the product supplied is the joint product of clubs that compete in a league, a certain number of competitors is required for the league to function at all.[31]

This may not have been directly related to any one of the Task Force's remit areas, but it had major implications for the philosophy of the football authorities, which was ardently non-interventionist in commercial matters. The case which was being put was that the regulation of private businesses – including questions of income – was an integral part of any sports league. Ironically, the Premier League found themselves defending the fact that they operated as a cartel, arguing the virtues of wealth redistribution and the regulation of sport as a business in the Restrictive Practices Court.

Another argument made on the Task Force was that football shared some characteristics of other regulated industries. This line was strengthened on the Task Force by the addition to the Working Group of Pamela Taylor, Chief Executive of Water UK, representing the privatized water companies and an advocate of regulation. First is the argument above, that football clubs are in a monopolistic position, like many of the privatized utility companies. Secondly, it was argued that football is a national and a local asset. Its social aspects and social benefits mean that it is an important source of civic pride and identity and, as the Task Force had already argued in *Investing in the Community*, 'football is the national sport and ... its interests are bound up with the national interest'. Thirdly, as with other industries such as the utilities, the game had undergone massive restructuring in recent years. Although progress had been made in many quarters, as with the privatized utilities, the regulatory function which safeguarded the industry from unfettered commercial pressures needed to be regenerated and renewed.

At the same time, the turnover of the game had been beyond all predictions. Some individuals – 'football's fat cats'[32] – made huge private profits from the restructuring of the industry, often with minimal investment in, and benefit to, the game. So, although some clubs had been models of good practice, in many quarters there was a failure to serve the game's main asset and source of income, its supporters. In a similar way to some sections of the previously nationalized industries, some clubs' abuse of their market power had been unjustifiable. There were also arguments that football needed proper, independent regulation because it had proved itself incapable of ensuring that the people left in charge of such important community assets as football clubs were 'fit and proper' ones to do so. The gaming and racing industries both regulate who is allowed to hold a significant interest, it was argued, and football needed to do the same.

The conclusion of a majority of the Task Force members was that, although traditionally the Football Association has been the regulatory body for English football, there were now good reasons for developing separate regulatory functions: one to do with the playing of the game and one to do with the running and corporate governance of it:

> The FA should continue as the body controlling the playing side of the game: enforcing rule changes within the global football governance structure of UEFA and FIFA, enforcing disciplinary codes, running its competitions and the national team. However, it should 'hand over' the regulatory functions concerned with the running of clubs, finance and codes of conduct for football clubs to a semi-independent body. Such separate regulatory functions would: ensure that the regulation of financial, legal and commercial activities of clubs is seen as independent from vested interests within the organisation; and ensure that there is a 'critical distance' between regulation and the FA's (and Leagues') own activities within the game, especially competition organisation, thus avoiding any potential conflict of interest.[33]

The strength of the arguments for regulation seemed to be growing when Banks spoke at the London regional Task Force meeting and said:

> You cannot treat football like any other product. It's a drug and clubs know that even if they continue to put up prices we will still go. Perhaps we should see it as a kind of national utility. As more clubs become public companies the whole area of financial accountability comes into play.

However, not only did the government indicate that they would be very unlikely to have parliamentary time for any further legislation (and that they were reluctant to provide it), but that deep divisions remained on the Task Force. Not only were the prescriptions within the various areas of remit causing conflict, but the issue of how they were to be enforced – the regulation of football as a whole – split the body.

The Final Split

In May 1999 the Task Force produced a first draft of its final report, to cover the four remaining areas of remit and the thorny question of how to enforce them. This report called for a Football Regulatory Authority at arm's length from the FA and had a series of measures which, on the whole, supported the fans' agenda, including restrictions on price increases and the provision of positions on club boards for supporters. The Premier League, followed by the FA and the Football League, rejected the proposals wholesale.

In turn, and with considerable delays, the authorities produced their response, in August 1999, somewhat arrogantly titled '*Football*'s Report to the Football Task Force' (author's italics). This offered little to fans in the shape of material guarantees. Where the first-draft Task Force report promised no increases for the lowest category of prices above the Retail Price Index, the authorities' report said that 'the differing economic realities between clubs must not be underestimated ... we do not believe that quotas should be imposed on the sale of match tickets', and the vague promise that 'clubs should be encouraged to promote inclusion'.[34] Where the first draft promised 'democratic forums through which all fans can be involved in decision making', the authorities said merely that 'we agree that clubs should be encouraged to consult more widely', failing to distinguish between involvement in decision making – as called for in the remit wording – and a glorified market research. Where the draft promised restrictions on clubs' floating on the Stock Exchange – such as clubs having to prove that it was in the wider interests of the club and football to do so – the authorities rejected that it was even a validly worded remit: 'The suggestion that club flotation produces a necessary conflict with the well-being of the football club and its supporters is, in our view, incorrect.'[35]

However, within a section on the general governance of football the authorities did propose an Independent Scrutiny Panel (ISP). While on the one hand they argued that 'in our view English football is not an under-governed sport ... English football does not need an additional set of imposed rules which prohibit and restrict the ability of clubs to make their own footballing and commercial decisions', on the other they called for an ISP which 'would perform a function not unlike that of the British Standards Institute [*sic*] or the Audit Commission'. While clearly there was some confusion here – the BSI and the Audit Commission perform different functions, and other discrepancies suggested that the Premier League was acting as a conservative brake on the FA[36] – there did appear to be a window of opportunity.

The FSA responded to the suggestion by outlining in a document to the Task Force what an Audit Commission for football would look like. Thus they proposed a body which would appoint external auditors to clubs to check for financial irregularity as well as act as an 'early warning system' to stop clubs from hitting a financial crisis; a 'balanced scorecard' model to report on the impact on society of clubs and the football authorities' policies; set criteria against which the clubs' performance would be judged; and 'real sanctions ... to cover failure to comply with the framework, including non-implementation of Task Force recommendations'.[37] It is worth quoting their conclusions at some length because they formed the basis of what became the majority Task Force report:

> One solution to the difficulties surrounding the regulation of the football industry is to adopt the recommendations of the football authorities for an Independent Scrutiny Panel. The idea has many advantages, not least the fact that it is supported by the football authorities who have themselves recognised the need to respond to the potential of clubs to find themselves in severe difficulties, and the need to investigate and develop best practice within the industry.
>
> For the idea to work, however, the Panel would need to be independent, and the Audit Commission model suggested by the football authorities could be the most appropriate. For the Panel to be effective it would need to take on some of the roles of the existing Audit Commission, particularly the auditing and publication of performance indicators. It would also need to have an inspection role in order to ensure that the impact on society of the activities of the industry is in accordance with public policy objectives.
>
> The framework must be real, however, and our support is dependent on an agreed set of sanctions, which would avoid the need for primary legislation, and a demonstrable commitment by all parties to the framework. Overall, we would assess the proposal of the football authorities to establish a Scrutiny Panel on the model of the Audit Commission against three criteria: firstly, the degree of its independence, secondly, the extent to which its remit covers the key issues of importance for the future of the game, thirdly, the effectiveness of its sanctions.[38]

It appeared, during the autumn of 1999, that agreement might be possible. For supporters' groups and others it was short of a statutory regulator – but the government had ruled out primary legislation anyway – yet offered independent, public accountability of football for the first time. What became obvious during the ensuing negotiations, however, was that the football authorities had not properly considered what an Audit Commission for football would mean to the governance of the game. This was true to the extent that when the incoming Premier League Chief Executive Richard Scudamore was asked how he proposed to ensure independence in the body's membership, he admitted he that he did not know. Although in a subsequent report the authorities did propose membership to be appointed on 'principles established by Lord Nolan', they seemed to back away from the Audit Commission model. The body would not scrutinize the performance of clubs, only the performance of the authorities in getting clubs to adhere to their vague code of practice, and it would be reliant on the authorities to provide aggregated evidence. Furthermore, the ISP which the authorities finally proposed was to sit only for a few weeks a year, would not be a standing body and would not have the power of sanction over either the clubs or the governing bodies.

As such it seemed that they had pulled back from what had been proposed before and it rapidly became clear that the hoped-for compromise had been a false dawn. What the authorities could not accept was the second two of the FSA's three criteria: a thorough remit to investigate the policies of clubs and sanctions to implement change. Without these there was to be no agreement and it was decided that the Football Task Force would issue a split report, one drafted by the football authorities and one by the Task Force executive, supporters' groups and individuals such as myself. The football authorities' report ('Report Two') was a simple combination of their two reports to the Task Force; Report One developed the drafts which had been the basis of discussion for the preceding eight months of the Task Force's life.

Within Report One were proposals for the establishment of a Football Audit Commission (FAC) based on the FSA's three principles of independence; robust remit to investigate and report to set performance criteria; and powers of sanction. Combined with this body, it was proposed that there should be an ombudsman for football, to investigate individual complaints on specific issues and reporting to the FAC. Such a proposal is consistent with Morris and Little's argument that self-regulatory sports systems need 'control mechanisms which are transparent, accountable and enjoy a measure of independence'. They argue that one solution which avoids the need for primary legislation and a constant recourse to the courts[39] is the appointment of an ombudsman as a form of alternative dispute resolution (ADR). Crucially for the Task Force model and the ombudsman's relationship with the FAC, Morris and Little argue that such a person 'can go beyond a narrow redress of individual grievance function by, in addition, using the individual complaint as a vehicle for raising standards of best practice within the organisations subject to his jurisdiction'.[40]

Such a development was not acceptable to the football authorities and was opposed, as were the majority of the other 60-plus recommendations made by the majority grouping. These included: a requirement for clubs to show evidence to the FAC on how they were using ticketing policies to increase access to football; for clubs to maintain the lowest prices in line with the RPI and to 'stretch' the range of prices in line with continental models; to extend concessionary prices and create flexible payment methods for season tickets; to have democratically-elected supporter representatives involved direct in the running of clubs; to further encourage supporter shareholding; and to force clubs that intended to float to offer at least 25 per cent of shares to fans. Such detailed policy proposals, to be overseen by the Football Audit Commission and the ombudsman, found little favour with a sport increasingly dominated by a free market philosophy and represented a sharp contrast with the vagueness of the football authorities' report. This was not surprising – the Premier League in particular, as representatives of the 20 club chairmen, wanted to minimize any restrictions on their activities. That the government ever thought that agreement could be found on commercial issues between such divided constituencies as fans and club chairmen, however, was.

The division of the Task Force was also one of the philosophy about what football is and should be – a business first and foremost, or a sport with too much cultural and social importance for it to be left to market forces. Given other developments, such as the increasing influence of media corporations in the ownership and future direction of the game,[41] the decision of the government on which report to support is even more crucial.

Further conflict in the process was to arise over whether members of the body 'signed' one report or the other. Given the government's overwhelming desire to avoid a split on the Task Force in the first place – majority and minority reports were not the 'Third Way' consensus which they had been looking for – and given the football authorities' desperation to avoid being seen as isolated, the two reports were issued together, unsigned. However, it quickly became clear that a large majority of the Task Force supported Report One. This included, unsurprisingly, the three supporter groups, but also the Chair and the Vice Chair, Sir Herman Ouseley from the Commission for Racial Equality, Chris Heinitz of the Local Government Association, and the private individuals Rogan Taylor, Eleanor Oldroyd, Sir John Smith and myself. This two-to-one majority represented the supporters and independent members on the Task Force – everyone, in other words, who did not have a current financial or organizational interest in the game. Those who backed the football authorities represented the football establishment: the FA, the Premier League, the Football League, referees, the Football Trust and managers. Allowing vested interests voting positions on the Task Force, which had appeared to be a problem at the start, had come home to roost.

The Task Force's final report was issued on 22 December 1999 and the body was wound up. The Minister for Sport, Kate Hoey, received the reports and promised a response 'in the new year'.

Conclusion

At the time of writing it is still unclear how the government will react to the split report. They have come under intense pressure from fans, MPs and others to back what has now been widely acknowledged as the 'majority report', through an Early Day Motion in the House of Commons which received well over a hundred signatures, a lobby of Parliament and a letter-writing campaign by fans to the Sports Minister. It is known that Hoey told the Football Association's in-coming Chief Executive Adam Crozier that she was 'minded' to support the majority report, although the government have been keen to distance themselves from such a suggestion and have played heavily on the fact that both reports called for some kind of independent public accountability. Such a stance barely recognizes the deep divisions of principle which lay between the two sides and the time and effort which went into attempting to reach an agreement; it smacks of a desperation for consensus when none is evident.

Having said that, Crozier, who was not part of any of the Task Force deliberations, did issue a document in March 2000 giving details of the Independent Scrutiny Panel which he proposed setting up. This moved some way from the FA's position in December – by not restricting the amount of time the body would meet for, for instance. However, the FA have not so far encompassed a remit based on the Task Force's majority recommendations, clear guidelines on what criteria clubs would be judged on, the ability to investigate individual clubs, nor clearly defined routes for the imposition of sanctions. As such, it is unlikely to get the support of supporters' organisations.

Currently (August 2000), negotiations are still in process over what kind of organization will be established. What is crystal clear about the government's role is that, quite differently from previous government attitudes toward law and order issues in football, they do not want to take firm legislative action. Indeed, the Minister for Sport and the Secretary of State for Culture, Media and Sport have both made it clear that they believe that the football authorities, and the FA in particular, should be given a period of two years to 'get it right'.

Although the Task Force process, the strength of the arguments on it and support for the majority report have certainly pushed all three football organizations further than they would have otherwise gone, it is a rather predictable response by the government in many ways. What it amounts to is a desire not to be seen as backing one 'side' against the other, much in line with Labour's Third Way approach. The desire to reach consensus has been overwhelming, even when the body which they created to make recommendations split, as many predicted it would. This reflects Labour's evidently mistaken belief that all stakeholders can be accommodated even in an industry which continues to fail to show many examples of enlightened self-interest. A desire not to regulate business, to let the market operate within certain guidelines and a belief in self-regulation make robust government intervention on the issues it sought answers to from the Task Force unlikely. Such an approach is in sharp contrast to the enthusiasm for legislative and other state action when the concern has been to regulate the behaviour of fans. The governance of the sport, and protection from exploitation for fans, however, are issues on which the government have proved unwilling to take decisive action. Such a reluctance, in the face of the dramatic and profit-motivated changes which have and still are revolutionizing football, is also, however, an abdication of responsibility for the future of the national sport.

NOTES

1. Labour Party, *Labour's Charter for Football*, London, 1996.
2. Sam Chisholm and David Chance were two former BSkyB employees contracted by Peter Leaver and John Quinton (Premier League Chair) to advise on the Premier League's next TV contract. The Premier League Chairmen, however, complained that they had never approved the contract and that the remuneration for Chisholm and Chance, reportedly in the region of £50 million, was excessive. Others were concerned about the possible additional advantage their appointment would give BSkyB and both Leaver and Quinton were forced to resign from their positions.
3. The Football Supporters Association led calls for a return to safe standing areas at football matches, based on technological developments as well as examples from Germany where stands were being rebuilt to comply with UEFA guidelines on all-seater stadiums, but allowing standing to continue in domestic matches. The Manchester Regional Task Force meeting, in particular, was totally dominated by calls from Manchester United supporters, and organized by the Independent Manchester United Supporters Association, for a return to terracing.
4. Football Task Force, *Investing in the Community*, London, 1999.
5. See A. Brown and A. Walsh, *Not for Sale! Manchester United, Murdoch and the Defeat of BSkyB*, Edinburgh, 1999.
6. Football Task Force, *Eliminating Racism*, London, 1998; *Improving Disabled Access*, London, 1998; *Investing in the Community*; *Football: Commercial Issues*, London, 1999.
7. P. Murphy, E. Dunning and J. Williams, *Football on Trial: Spectator Violence and Development in the Football World*, London, 1990.
8. S. Cohen, *Folk Devils and Moral Panics: the Creation of the Mods and Rockers*, London, 1973.
9. S. Redhead, *Football with Attitude*, Manchester, 1991.
10. Murphy *et al.*, 213.
11. C. Smyth, *Football Identity Cards: The beginning of the end for civil liberties?*, Belfast: University of Ulster, unpubd paper, 1990.
12. Brown and Walsh, Ch.4.
13. M. Brown, *Chelsea Independent*, London, 1998.
14. NNC in Sale, Cheshire, had developed a computerized crowd-monitoring system by 1990, just after the completion of the Taylor Inquiry. Although tested at Old Trafford and during New Year's Eve celebrations in Trafalgar Square, it has never been given the chance to be endorsed by football as a whole.
15. See S. Lee, 'The BSkyB Bid for Manchester United Plc', in S. Hamil, J. Michie and C. Oughton (eds), *A Game of Two Halves? The Business of Football*, Edinburgh, 1999.

16. A. Giddens, *The Third Way and Its Critics*, London, 1999; Barker, Byrne and Veall, *Ruling by Task Force: The Politicos Guide to Labour's New Elite*, London, 1999.
17. At all the Task Force's regional meetings there was much support for an independent regulatory body. This was backed up by the Task Force's own research, undertaken by Leicester University, which concluded that around 70 per cent of supporters wanted an independent regulatory body; J. Williams and S. Perkins, *Ticket Pricing, Football Business and 'Excluded' Football Fans*, Leicester, 1999.
18. Lord Justice Taylor, *The Hillsborough Stadium Disaster: Final Report*, London, 1990.
19. Ibid., para.53.
20. Ibid., para.72.
21. Ibid., para.15.
22. The Department of Culture, Media and Sport are currently negotiating over the establishment of a unit called Supporters Direct to give start-up grants and legal and financial assistance to groups of supporter-shareholders.
23. D. Conn, *The Football Business*, Edinburgh, 1997.
24. For several years, one man, Peter Johnson, had effectively owned both Tranmere Rovers and Everton. During 1999 and 2000 the media companies BSkyB and NTL took significant stakes in a number of clubs giving prima facie evidence that the dual ownership rules of the FA and Premier League were being broken; A. Brown, 'Sneaking in through the Back Door? Media Company Interests and Dual Ownership of Clubs', in S. Hamil, C. Oughton and J. Michie (eds), *Football in the Digital Age: Whose Game Is it Anyway?*, Edinburgh, 2000.
25. Football Association, Premier League and Football League, 'Football's Report to the Football Task Force', in Football Task Force, *Football: Commercial Issues*, 65, 74–5.
26. Football Supporters Association, *Submission to the Football Task Force*, Liverpool, 1998.
27. Monopolies and Mergers Commission, *Report into the Proposed Merger between Manchester United Plc and British Sky Broadcasting Plc*, London, 1999, 2.72.
28. Salomon Brothers, 'UK Football Clubs: Valuable Assets?', in *Global Equity Research: Leisure*, London, 1997, 9.
29. S. Hamil, 'A Whole New Ball Game? Why Football Needs a Regulator', in Hamil *et al.* (eds), *A Game of Two Halves?*.
30. Football Task Force, *Investing in the Community*.
31. J. Findlay, W. Holahan and C. Oughton, 'Revenue Sharing from Broadcasting Football: The Need for League Balance' in Hamil *et al.*, *A Game of Two Halves?*, 125.
32. Conn.
33. A. Brown, 'Notes on the Regulation of Football – Rationale and Outline', unpublished paper to the Football Task Force Working Group.
34. Football Association *et al.*, 12.
35. Ibid., 77.
36. The decision of the three authorities to respond to the Task Force *en bloc* may well prove to be an historic lost opportunity for the FA and the Football League to reassert their position in the face of the commercial might of the Premier League.
37. Football Supporters Association, *Modernising Football: How the Football Authorities' Proposal for a Football Audit Commission Could Work*, in Football Task Force, *Football: Commercial Issues*, App. B, 5.
38. Ibid., 7.
39. At the time of writing, Newcastle United fans are in the process of appealing a High Court decision which supported the club's removing fans from seats which they had 'purchased' with a £500 'bond'. Such civil actions may become more frequent without adequate governance of the sport.
40. P. Morris and G. Little, 'Challenging Sports Bodies' Determinations', *Civil Justice Quarterly* (1998) 128–48 at 146.
41. A. Brown, 'Sneaking in through the Back Door?'.

14

How Can Sport be Regulated?

Ken Foster

Introduction

How sport should be governed and regulated is a major topic of debate at present. This chapter presents a framework of analysis for this debate. There have been three streams of academic discussion flowing into it but with little evidence of intermingling. There has been an internal debate within sports law. This has considered the desirability of legal intervention, often posed as the question 'should the law stop at the touchline?'[1] One side of the debate presents non-intervention as an immunity from or exception to the ordinary law of the land; it argues that sport is different and that courts should recognize the difference. Legal intervention disrupts the good administration of sport. This position says that sport has its own 'internal constitutionalism' and operates a sporting 'rule of law'. It therefore already has a parallel legal system and this justifies its sporting autonomy. In this discussion legal intervention usually means judicial intervention,[2] but may include legislative intervention. The limitation of this debate in sports law is that it rarely progresses beyond a crude dichotomy between private internal autonomy and public external accountability.

A second stream of academic debate comes from public lawyers and economists, about the nature of 'regulation'.[3] This has asked whether particular industries should be self-regulating or whether there should be statutorily backed regulation. Much of the literature in this field has concentrated on the regulation of public utilities, where Britain has a well-developed system of independent regulators. As sport has not historically been treated as an 'industry', it is not surprising that 'regulation theory' has seldom addressed sport nor that sports lawyers have rarely ventured into these debates. The commercialization of sport in the past decade, especially of football, has made it easier to see sport as an industry.[4] This, in turn, has raised questions as to the suitability of governing bodies to regulate themselves and their ability to govern other than in their own narrow self-interest. The commercialization of football and a disregard for the interests of fans has led to a public debate about the need for regulation. This has culminated in the recommendations of the Football Task Force.[5]

The third stream comes mainly from management studies and centres on questions of corporate governance. Are football clubs financial institutions with profit as their purpose, or are they social institutions accountable to a wider public than the shareholders? This poses questions as to the ownership, legal form and accountability of sporting clubs. Governing bodies of sport are also captured within this debate and their competence and structure is questioned.

This chapter begins by presenting a typology of different models for regulating sport. It then asks the following questions: why regulate sport? Who is to be regulated? And what is the best strategy for regulation? It discusses the arguments for and against self-regulation in a sports setting and concludes by examining whether the independent regulation of sport can work.

Models of the Sports Market

The Pure Market Model

This model treats sport purely as a business. Money comes before sporting success and unregulated economic competition occurs. The prevailing ideology is 'competition is the best regulator'.[6] Governing bodies of sport have broad functions but mainly provide a loose regulatory framework in which profit maximization occurs. The public interest is ignored and supporters have limited power to resist their exploitation. There is a network of contracts between economic units with an individualistic ideology. The normal form of regulation is through the market and the predominant legal instrument is the contract.

The Defective Market Model

The limitations of the pure market model are manifest. The major one is that free markets tend to eliminate the weakest economic units. Sport cannot tolerate this market logic for too long because good competitions need teams or players of nearly equal ability. Monopoly of success is bad for sport; unpredictable outcomes are a key value. Governing bodies of sport, and the competitions they license, are often monopoly controllers of sport. They can use this power to restore the sporting balance by reallocating resources. The main legal method of regulation in a defective market is competition policy. If the market fails, competition law can be used to counterbalance the tendency to monopoly or to correct an abuse of a dominant position.

The Consumer Welfare Model

This model addresses the other main limitation of the pure market model.

Different interests may be linked through contracts, but there may be unequal economic power and bargaining power between contracting parties. The fan has only weak market power against the football club. Players historically had limited economic power against their clubs. Players and clubs may need protection against sporting federations which may take decisions over them with major economic consequences. The legal form of regulation is protective legislation to protect the weaker party or to allow a greater protection of the wider public interest.

The Natural Monopoly Model

One of the arguments to support statutorily-backed regulation is that the regulated industry is a natural monopoly and that therefore market competition is absent. A natural monopoly is said to be characterized by a single seller, a unique product and barriers to easy entry to the market. Sport, it is claimed, has these characteristics. It therefore needs a regulatory structure that assumes it is a private monopoly likely to ignore the public interest. Competition law is an inappropriate mechanism of regulation because the market cannot be freed if there is a natural monopoly. An alternative regulatory strategy is needed.

The Socio-cultural Model

This model argues that sporting values are dominant and that profit is ancillary. It also stresses the social and cultural significance of sport. It rejects all the assumptions behind the free market model. The importance of autonomy for sport is emphasized. The form of governance has historically been that of the private club, for example, the Jockey Club. Clubs are ideally not-for-profit organizations with limited scope for maximizing profits. Supporters are seen as stakeholders in 'their' clubs. The difficult question to answer is what form of regulation best suits this model. The private club, with amateur voluntary administrators, has been one solution with consensus regulation in the 'best interests of the sport'. But commercialism can and has undermined this voluntarism and autonomy. Nevertheless, the sporting judgement of governing bodies needs to be protected from commercial interests to preserve the best features of this model. The preferred regulatory strategy may be 'supervised self-government'. This allows governing bodies to be autonomous and to regulate their sports without external interference in sporting matters. But this autonomy must be matched by an internal constitutionalism, due process and good governance. This has links with the concept of 'enforced' or 'mandated' self-regulation. It shares with the pure market model a preference for 'non-intervention' but for diametrically opposed reasons. The pure market model argues for *laissez-faire* minimum interference to protect commercial interests. The socio-cultural model argues for autonomous self-government with 'constitutional' safeguards to protect sporting values.

These models may be represented in the accompanying table.

TABLE 1
MODELS OF THE SPORTS MARKET

Model	Values	Form of Regulation	Governing Bodies
pure market	profit/private interest (shareholders)	contract/intellectual property	maximize commercial opportunities
defective market	equal sporting competition (teams and players)	competition law	reallocate resources
consumer welfare	fans and viewers	protective legislation	widen democracy and accountability
natural monopoly	public interest	independent regulator	overcome rival organizations
socio-cultural (traditional)	private club	immunity/voluntarism	preserve sporting values
socio-cultural (modern)	fairness, internal constitutionalism and rule of law	supervised self-government	preserve sporting values with due process

Why Regulate?

The debate surrounding regulation has been handicapped by a failure to clarify these different models. Thus the answer to the question 'why regulate?' has itself sometimes been confused and contradictory.

Sport has traditionally been conducted by organizations, whether clubs or governing bodies, that have taken the legal form of unincorporated associations. This legal form gave them a degree of private autonomy because of the law's reluctance to interfere in the affairs of a private organization. They operate in 'civil society' outside the market.

The commercialization of sport, especially of football, has led to different legal forms, particularly the conversion of some clubs to public limited companies.[7] These changes reflect the tendency to treat football as a business like any other. The minimum form of regulation then becomes the normal contractual and company-law requirements that apply to any commercial enterprise, with a tendency to protect interests through contracts and intellectual property.[8] This moves towards a free market model.

But sport is not a free market. It arguably forms a natural monopoly. An initial problem is the way in which sports leagues, such as professional football in England, for example, are analysed. If the basic unit of football is the professional club, then a league is not itself a monopoly but a collection of individual units. If left unregulated except by the market the richest clubs may corner all the wealth and talent in the game.[9] However, if the league is treated as the unit then there is a co-operative, economic entity that can curtail or reverse any tendency to sporting monopoly by appropriate mechanisms of redistribution. So the sports league becomes an economic monopoly to counteract the drift to sporting monopoly.

Two sources of confusion for a regulatory strategy flow from this analysis. One is that economic monopoly, so often the target of competition policy and law, may be a necessary precondition for a successful sporting competition. Competition law has to recognize the unusual conditions of sport if it is not to give the clubs an unfair financial advantage as against the leagues. Second, to analyse football as being based on the individual clubs leads to a free market model. This implies that clubs may leave a league for an alternative or breakaway league without penalty. Conversely, to analyse football as a single-league entity is to give priority to wider sporting values that can only be administered by an overarching governing body with strong powers. It is a crucial prerequisite of analysis as to whether football is a single association of governance for its member clubs or whether it is an unregulated alliance of individual economic enterprises.[10]

Is sport a natural monopoly? This question is important because within the 'regulation' debate the existence of a natural monopoly is the chief justification for independent regulation. A natural monopoly is said to occur when three major criteria are satisfied: that there is only a single seller supplying the entire market; that there is a unique product that leaves the consumer with no substitute; and that there are substantial barriers to entry.

The football industry satisfies these criteria. Originally professional football was a product provided by a single supplier, the Football Association, which in turn approved the Football League. Since 1992 the position has changed and the Premier League, as a separate legal body, now runs the top league. But it faces no real competition. Professional football in reality has a single, joint provider. This occurs under an interlocking system of higher governance by UEFA and FIFA, as these governing bodies are, in turn, the sole regulators of European and world football, respectively.

On the second criterion, there is no real alternative for the consumer. There is an ambiguity in the concept of 'consumer' as applied to football; it may mean the fan who watches at the ground or the viewer who watches televised football. For the one who pays at the gate there are limited geographical and physical alternatives if he wishes to support another club. There is also a strong cultural attachment to a club that makes a transfer of allegiance to another club unthinkable to most fans. These have no alternative except to stop watching football. However, if the 'consumer' is the passive television viewer then there may be alternatives. Other national leagues may be viewed on television. The viewer has other options. He may be happy to watch other sports than football and could watch other types of televised entertainment altogether.[11]

Thirdly, a natural monopoly has barriers to entry. Professional football presents difficult economic hurdles to new clubs. They would have to climb the non-league pyramid and gain promotion to the Football League. This progress is not economically attractive. It could take many years, especially with the narrow bottleneck of a single entry into the League from the lower part of the pyramid of promotion and relegation.[12] The alternative is to allow a rich club with top-class talent direct entry into the elite. The suggestion that Glasgow Rangers and Celtic could join the English leagues had to surmount this problem. So far European football has abided by a model of advancement on sporting success via promotion and relegation. It has not embraced the American model of franchises awarded to teams because of their commercial potential.[13] The other route would be to challenge the monopoly of a single league by creating a new breakaway competition. The economic feasibility of such an enterprise is precarious. The history of sports where there have been rival governing bodies, such as boxing and darts, is not encouraging. Even in North America, where alternative leagues have occurred in most of the major sports, most have had a short history. They have ended in either total failure or enforced amalgamation with the existing league. As a natural monopoly, sporting organizations have considerable power to crush alternative leagues or rival federations. They can expel clubs, license new entrants and ban players.[14] They also control much of the revenue from broadcasting contracts and sponsorship deals. Few sports could bear the costs of a start-up from scratch of a new league.

The harmful consequence of a natural monopoly, and thus the justification for regulation, is sometimes said to flow from the failure of normal market mechanisms. In sport this mainly translates into the fact that there is inefficient economic competition between clubs. Weak economic enterprises that are not making a profit can continue to function. The captive supporter is likely to be exploited. This market failure also explains why some theorists consider that the regulation of a natural monopoly cannot be left to competition law. This assumes a free market and it intervenes to redress imbalances in the efficient working of the market. A natural monopoly is the antithesis of the free market. Regulation via competition law is inappropriate. Alternative forms of regulation are needed to protect the public interest.

If the analysis is that commercialized sports such as football tend to a natural monopoly, then the consumer has three possibilities to counteract excessive profits and prices. One, he can use his market power against football clubs. The most direct power is to refuse to buy the product. Fans could boycott games, refuse to buy season tickets or not buy merchandise such as replica kits. He could try to exercise indirect market power by weakening the sponsorship revenues of football, by boycotting sponsors. The weakness of such tactics is obvious and rests on the dual nature of the 'consumer'. He is both buyer and fan. To harm the club financially is to weaken the chance of sporting success for the club, which is just what most fans want. Football clubs have enormous brand loyalty. Fans who cease to go to games do not normally start supporting another club, even if there is one readily available geographically. For all these reasons the tactic of withdrawing from the market or transferring custom elsewhere is of limited efficiency in the football market.[15] Free market principles do not apply.

Second, the fan could rely on competition law to protect him as a consumer. The limits of this approach where there is a natural monopoly have already been mentioned. However, it is possible that some elements of undesirable economic concentration can be prevented to protect the football consumer. The refusal of the Monopolies and Mergers Commission to approve the proposed takeover of Manchester United by BSkyB is one example.

Third, if the market is inefficient in protecting the fan, it may be argued that corrective regulation is needed to redress the balance between club and fan in favour of the weaker party. This still begs the question as to the most effective form of such regulation. The other major problem with this approach is that it is limited to the economic relation between the club and the customer. It does not address the problems of weak accountability and the management of clubs or the poor governance of sport by governing bodies. This leads on the next question: who is to be regulated?

Who Is To Be Regulated?

If the theory of natural monopoly applies to sport then it also needs to be specified as to which is the monopoly. As argued above, this could be either the club or its governing body. If the focus of regulation is to be the clubs, then the real issues are the weakness of the fan as a consumer and the cultural monopoly that the club has over him. Because the relationship between the club and the fan is more than an economic one, regulation is needed to redress the uneven economic power, as with many other business–consumer relationships. Regulation is also necessary to manage the wider issues that are inherent in the monopoly influence of the club. This strategy of regulation has mixed motives. One ideology is that the fan is a stakeholder in the club. Football clubs should not be accountable solely to their shareholders. They should take into account wider interests such as their customers and even the local community. Sporting clubs are in 'social reality' clubs with members. Fans make an economic contribution to the club either directly through members' fees or indirectly as supporters who pay to watch. This gives them a 'moral right' to participation or consultation in the decision-making processes of the club or, at the very least, implies that the club should consider their interests.

Alternatively, the object of regulation might be the governing body of sport. In this case there could be three main motives. One, to use the governing bodies' power to control the clubs and modify their pursuit of profit or private interest. Two, to encourage the governing bodies to correct the 'internal sporting market' to prevent dominance by one team. Three, to improve the standards of governance within governing bodies.

The first of these is directed towards getting the governing bodies to use their economic and administrative power to control the clubs within their own association for the greater good of all and in the public interest. The governing body could use their monopoly control of entry into the sport to restrict the clubs' economic power and further other interests, especially those of the fans. They could impose conditions on the clubs' participation in their competitions, such as maximum ticket prices, specific forms of ticket allocation (allowing away supporters a fair allocation or insisting on fixed percentages for children, for example) and regulations on team colours to prevent frequent changes of kit. This is a form of indirect regulation that aims to force the system of private government to adopt wider aims than profit maximization for the clubs that it governs. It aims at making governing bodies act as the consumers' champion, rather like a professional trade association, and balance their interests against those of the clubs. Nevertheless, this assumes that governing bodies are independent and capable of acting neutrally. The governing structure of many sports remains undemocratic and excludes from formal representation fans, players and representatives of the community. In addition, as long as the elite clubs or players within a sport have a credible threat of breakaway, governing bodies are likely to be financially blackmailed into governing in favour of the few at the expense of the many.

A second motive for regulating governing bodies is better sporting competition. Many of the criticisms of the over-commercialization of football rest on the narrowing of sporting success and the domination of a few clubs. There appears now to be a close correlation between a club's financial health and its sporting success. The governing bodies are uniquely able to reallocate resources within the sport to counteract this undesirable concentration of money, players and trophies. Several tactics are available to them. They can aim for financial equality by ensuring the pooling of major revenue sources such as broadcasting rights, sponsorship money and gate receipts. These can then be redistributed with the weaker teams, both financially and in sporting terms, getting more money. Governing bodies have also historically tried to limit a free market in players, which is said to allow the rich clubs to consolidate their position by attracting the best players through higher wages or by paying higher transfer fees. The governing bodies could also try to govern access to new talent. The development and training of young players is a key element in sporting success. Governing bodies can prevent top clubs monopolizing all young talent and have mechanisms for compensating clubs who do develop it. All these tactics involve remedial intervention in the internal sporting market. This is difficult because it interferes with the clubs' autonomy. The justification nevertheless can be economic. The aim is a better overall 'product', with nearly equal teams producing close games and exciting championship races because they are 'handicapped' according to their economic strength.

A third motive for regulating governing bodies is to improve the standards of good governance. This covers many issues but in particular the standards of management, and the application of due process and fair procedures to the exercise of their considerable powers. Legitimate concerns include the potential for abuse in the exercise of private power. Sport can have enormous power of economic control and exclusion over the livelihood of competitors. To allow these powers to be exercised as if they were merely the running of a private members' club without any economic consequences is to ignore the reality of the situation and the rights of the players. Such power cannot be exercised unchecked or unsupervised without the danger of grave injustice or economic damage being caused to players by arbitrary or poor administration. Another concern is the protection of players. Sport often has a weak labour market and there is a need to prevent players from being exploited or abused. In all professional sports there is little collective bargaining by trade unions. Therefore it is left to the governing bodies to take responsibility for matters such as unfair contracts, inadequate health and safety, poor pension provisions and the sacking of staff who in other industries would be covered by collective bargaining. The post-*Bosman* situation in football may have improved for the top players who are able to negotiate their own terms, but for the benefit of the majority there could be more regulation of contracts and their terms and conditions. A final reason for improving the standards of governance is that the market cannot deliver sporting goals and values. Sport has a wider social and cultural dimension, and this can be protected by governing bodies interfering with the operation of the free market. The geographical distribution of teams is a good example. Rugby union has considered the awarding of franchises for the top division based on geographical considerations. If these things matter for the good of the sport it is only the governing bodies that can allocate such franchises rather than market principles.

What Kind of Regulation?

The two questions already posed – why regulate and who is to be regulated – are closely linked to the choice of the methods of regulation. The failure of the free market model in sport is patent. However, market-led solutions can only operate at the level of club and supporter; and even then somewhat ineffectively. At the level of rival organizations, whether leagues or governing bodies, there could, in theory, be market competition. North American sports have adopted the economic safety of closed leagues. In these, the exclusive rights to operate within the market of the sports league protect franchisees. Competition between rival leagues, since they are competing for the same audience, is fierce and has historically been short-lived and resulted in a single league. In general, sporting competition within the league has proved preferable to competition in the wider economic market. Market solutions and the related weakness of competition law in regulating the sports market can only have marginal effects on important aspects of the internal governance of sport. It already has a high degree of internal regulation; but the perceived failure of this has led to the demand for alternative strategies of regulation.

The debate in Britain has presented itself as self-regulation or autonomy versus external legally-enforced regulation. Although my analysis will use this dichotomy, it needs to be recognized that there are possible intermediate positions that combine elements of both. Many commentators have used the concept of 'enforced' self-regulation. Baldwin and Cave define it as 'self-regulation ... subject to a form of governmental structuring or oversight'.[16] It is often a form of blackmail by the state that threatens statutory regulation if better and stronger self-regulation is not implemented or fails. As a strategy, the government can implement it by appointing a body to supervise self-regulating organizations or by requiring self-generated rules to be approved by a government department or agency. It corresponds closely to the concept of supervised self-government used in the table, but there are important and subtle differences in sport that need to be recognized.

One is that if regulation of a natural monopoly is required in the public interest then what constitutes the public interest is a complex question. In the paradigm case of the regulation of public utilities the 'public interest' corresponds closely to the interests of the consumer. The 'public interest' in sport is wider and embraces more than just the fan as consumer. It may include, for example, the success of the national team.

Self-regulation is not non-regulation. Sport has rules; sport has an internal constitutionalism. Governing bodies are the apex of a governance structure. Rules are formulated and approved within a constitutional system. The powers to act are defined within rulebooks. Disciplinary procedures are now better drafted and usually show an awareness of the legal requirements of natural justice. There is something akin to an internal 'rule of law' in sporting bodies. This process must not be overemphasized. There is clear scope for improvement and a model code of conduct could be helpful.

Rules within institutions are often the result of a compromise between different interests within them. These can be delicate and fragile agreements that may easily be upset by external regulation. The divided jurisdiction in English football between the FA and the Premier League is the result of a compromise in 1992, caused by a threatened breakaway of the top clubs, resulting in a partial dismantling of the traditional structure of governing the game. There is a further problem that in many sports the national federations, which are the only possible target of external regulation, are often constrained in their powers of rule-making and executive action by the international federations of which they are members.

Another problem is the interaction between internal and external regulation. Where a public authority is charged with the regulation of a private group there is not necessarily a clear spilt between the two sides. Hancher and Moran have described the interlocking and shifting relationship between organizations involved in regulation so that they come to inhabit a 'shared regulatory space'.[17] Another form of interaction can be the process of 'juridification'. When this occurs external legal norms can be imposed upon an institution to produce changes within it. But a double process of alteration can occur. The external norms become modified, consciously or by misunderstanding, and are incorporated internally into the system of self-regulation in an altered state. Conversely, internal rules and procedures within sport may orientate themselves towards the external legal norms so that the internal rules become more legalistic.

A final preliminary point is the tendency to assume that 'regulation' means regulation by an independent administrative body exercising control or supervision. This use of 'regulation' seems to exclude regulation by the courts. Law and regulation appear to be mutually exclusive. Law is seen as adjudicating between different private interests and regulation as protecting the public interest against private self-interest. Law is reactive; regulation is proactive. These apparent differences help to explain why debates within sports law as to the desirability of legal intervention are conducted with little reference to debates on the need for regulation in sport, especially of football.

Self-Regulation or Not?

The supporters of self-regulation in sport advance several arguments. First, that expert and inside knowledge of sport is the best basis for effective regulation. There is a need to understand the context in which rules are made and enforced. In many sports administrators and referees are ex-players. Those who have played the sport are said to be best able to judge and govern it. They are well placed to detect breaches of the rules as they 'know the ropes'. They can understand the subtle distinction between acceptable and unacceptable infractions of the rules: what might be termed the 'it isn't cricket' test. It is also argued that internal regulators are better informed in making rules. They are similarly well placed to understand what will be accepted as reasonable by the participants. It follows that this can result in better compliance because the players will have a higher commitment to rules that they accept as sensible and legitimate. Rules imposed from outside by those who do not understand the game are less likely to be followed.

A second argument in favour of self-regulation is efficiency. Self-regulation is cheaper. The costs are borne by the sport and not by the public purse. The tradition of unpaid volunteers as administrators in many sports can lower the cost of regulation. Self-regulation can be more efficient because it is more flexible and responsive to change. It allows quick decisions to be made. Sport requires rapid decisions in many situations. The result of a game cannot remain contingent for very long if it is part of a wider competition.

Third, it is argued that self-regulation will produce better compliance because the governing bodies have a monopoly jurisdiction over their sport. They have available a wide range of sanctions, from persuasion to sporting penalties, such as expulsion. These are powerful disciplinary sanctions that external regulation may not be able to match. The need for compulsory submission to this sporting jurisdiction is a strong incentive to comply.

There are several counter-arguments against self-regulation. First, that self-governance of sport is non-democratic and that a private unregulated body is likely to be self-serving. This is a complex claim with several elements. It can be said that governing bodies are undemocratic in their internal governance in that they give insufficient representation in their constitutions to the players, teams and officials over whom they have economic power. In these circumstances the best interests of the game may be interpreted in a way that favours the administrators at the expense of the players or the clubs.[18] Wider interests, such as those of the fans, are also rarely represented within the self-regulating structures of sport. Clubs may also have undemocratic structures. Many professional football clubs are still effectively dominated by a single, large shareholder or a small group. Directors often have poor business skills and these have been exposed by the increases in legal accountability that have followed flotation on the stock exchange. The legal corporate form of most football clubs also gives no formal representation to the interests of fans. As Hamil has argued, 'there are other stakeholders in football than just the shareholders and employees'.[19]

The 'public interest' justification for regulation further assumes that sporting bodies could be forced by regulators to take decisions in the wider interest and thereby give unrepresented parties a voice. Regulation could tackle issues such as commercialization, for example, the price of merchandise, to protect the consumer; broadcasting contracts, to protect the viewer and his 'right' to view sport free on television; the distribution of revenues in the sport, to ensure, for example, the health of the grassroots of the game; or the exploitation of young players. These are all examples where self-regulation is currently failing because sporting bodies are unable, or unwilling, to recognize a wider public interest in the way in which sport is run.

A second major argument against self-regulation is that there is little or no accountability. As private entities, the accountability of sporting bodies is limited. This not only increases the possibility of abuse or arbitrary decisions but also means that public mistrust may be engendered. Many governing bodies are directly or indirectly, through tax concessions, receiving public money. This increases the pressure for public accountability.

A third argument is that sport has failed to develop good models of governance, especially in respect of due process and natural justice. It also offers inappropriate structures for managing conflict in sport. Most sporting federations do not operate a separation of powers. They legislate by making the rules. They administer the rules. They interpret the rules and decide when they have been broken. They also are the body that is responsible for policing the rules and detecting breaches of them. To keep all these functions under the same umbrella makes mistakes more likely. Governing bodies have become better at separating these different functions and ensuring that they are dealt with by separate parts of the organization. They have also introduced independent elements into their procedures by having outsiders chairing disciplinary enquiries or by agreeing to independent arbitration. There was an independent inquiry into financial irregularities in football recently[20] and athletics has independent laboratories for drug testing. But these independent procedures are still not widespread and they have sometimes been introduced only after expensive litigation. Sporting bodies can still appear to be unaware of the need for transparency, independence and procedural fairness.

Finally, if there is a wider public interest in effective regulation and good governance then self-regulation must command public confidence otherwise it will fail in one of its major objectives. There are several relevant benchmarks in sports. Are outside interests represented in the governing institutions? Is there consultation in the formation and implementation of rules? Are complaints or disciplinary procedures independent?

Making Regulation Work

The debate over the form and extent of regulation in sport also needs to incorporate questions of effectiveness. Ultimately effectiveness depends on the powers and the jurisdiction given to any regulatory body. But there are general problems of enforcement and effectiveness.

First, there is the question of independence. The underlying concept of regulation is that the regulator is distinct from the regulated. But, unless it is clear who the regulator is intended to represent, then his independence would be threatened. Is a football regulator to be the fans' champion, an ombudsman for complaints, or a substitute for inadequate self-governance? These are different functions and imply different approaches.

Second, there is a danger that the regulator will be 'captured'. The independence of a regulator can be compromised as he becomes more familiar with the industry and its key personnel. The knowledge and personal relations that develop may make the regulator more amenable to the interests of the regulated. The independence then becomes merely symbolic as the regulator is manipulated by the industry.

It has also been argued that there is a regulatory life-cycle. There is only a limited time before the regulator ceases to operate effectively. This seems to be especially true when the introduction of external regulation is not a fully developed strategy but a firefighting response to immediate abuses. Once these have been addressed, regulation can drift without clear direction or alternatively become too fussy.

Conclusion: The Football Task Force

I do not want to analyse in detail the report of the Football Task Force but, instead, use it to exemplify the themes of this chapter. It issued two reports in its submission to the government. The minority one broadly recommended a continuance of self-regulation. The majority report proposed an independent regulator. The intermediate position of 'enforced' self-regulation was not seriously considered. Similarly, the nature of the regulator's powers and the difficulties of enforcement were scarcely addressed.

The reports show some recognition of the different models of sport set out earlier. The failure of the 'free market' model is assumed. Football clubs are said to be failing their fans and exploiting them as consumers. The remedy therefore is consumer protection. There are recommendations such as a wider range of seat prices and a fairer merchandising policy for items such as replica kits. But there is no consideration of how these policies are to be enforced. Is it to be by a regulator who can sanction fines against the clubs, by the introduction of specific legislation, or by the governing bodies?

Other models of the sports market are hinted at in the majority report. It is proposed that clubs need better management. The issue of poor governance by the governing bodies is dealt with. A model of corporate governance is used and wider representation of stakeholders in football clubs is recommended. Thus there are proposals for greater consultation with fans and a proposal that 25 per cent of shares in a club should be reserved for them. The difficulties of implementing these proposals are disguised. Who, for example, counts as a 'fan'?

The Task Force seems to have been guided by the concept of consumer protection and improved corporate governance for clubs. There is little discussion of improved self-government for the football authorities, of greater powers for them over the clubs, nor of the role that the government could take in reforming these institutions. There is no extended discussion of the role and the limits of the law, of alternative legal forms for football clubs such as mutualization,[21] or of the scope for using competition law to address market failures. Above all there is no attempt to address the central issue – is sport a natural monopoly and if so what does this imply for a strategy of regulation?

NOTES

1. The phrase is Edward Grayson's.
2. The classic judicial statement of non-intervention is that of Browne-Wilkinson VC in *Cowley* v. *Heatley* (1986), *The Times*, 26 July, where he said, 'Sport would be better served if there was not running litigation at repeated intervals by people seeking to challenge the decisions of the regulating bodies.' Mrs Justice Ebsworth has recently put the opposite case in *Jones* v. *Welsh Rugby Union* (1997), *The Times*, 6 March, where she said, 'It would be naive to pretend that the modern world of sport could be conducted as it used to be not many years ago.'
3. There is a vast literature on 'regulation'. I found these sources most useful in preparing this chapter: R. Baldwin and M. Cave, *Understanding Regulation: Theory, Strategy and Practice*, Oxford, 1999; J. Black, *Rules and Regulators*, Oxford, 1997; I. Ayers and J. Braithwaite, *Responsive Regulation: Transcending the Regulation Debate*, Oxford, 1992; J. Black, 'Constitutionalising Self-regulation', 59 *Modern Law Review* (1996), 24; A. Ogus, 'Rethinking Self-regulation', 19 *Oxford Journal of Legal Studies* (1995), 97.
4. The landmark decision in *Bosman* depended on the court's recognizing that sport was an industry.
5. Football Task Force, *Football: Commercial Issues*, London, 1999.
6. Baldwin and Cave, 210.
7. B.R. Cheffins, 'UK Football Clubs and the Stock Market', 18 *Company Lawyer*

(1997), 66, 104; J. Michie, *New Mutualism: A Golden Goal? Uniting Supporters and Their Clubs*, London, 1999.

8. See D. Griffiths-Jones, *Law and the Business of Sport*, London, 1997, especially Ch.10. The explosion in professional lawyers' interest has been mainly in these areas.

9. See S. Szymanski and T. Kupyers, *Winners and Losers: The Business Strategy of Football*, London, 1999, Ch.7.

10. A parallel debate has occurred in the USA on the 'single entity' rule. See P.C. Wailer and G.R. Roberts, *Sports and the Law*, St. Paul, 2nd edn, 1993, 353 n.3. A good summary of the debate is L. Goldman, 'Sports, Antitrust and the Single Entity Theory', 63 *Tulane L. Rev.* (1989) 751.

11. This problem of the relevant market was discussed in *News Ltd* v. *Australian Rugby Football League* (1996) 139 ALR 193 and in the Monopolies and Mergers Commission report on BSkyB's bid for Manchester United, London, 1999, Cm 4305.

12. At present, only one club is promoted from the Conference, the top of the non-league pyramid, and only then if it meets particular conditions about finance and ground size.

13. Rugby league has experimented with franchises. See also 'The Development and Prospects for Community Action in the Field of Sport', Brussels: European Commission Staff Working Paper, DGX, 1998.

14. The legality of such tactics was discussed in *Greig* v. *Insole* [1978] 3 All ER 449.

15. It may not be so effective in other sports, such as cricket, where 'brand loyalty' is not so important for the customer.

16. Baldwin and Cave, 41.

17. L. Hancher and M. Moran (eds), *Capitalism, Culture and Regulation*, Oxford, 1989.

18. For an example, see J. Sugden and A. Tomlinson, *FIFA and the Contest for World Football: Who Rules the People's Game?*, Cambridge, 1998.

19. S. Hamil, J. Michie and C. Oughton (eds), *A Game of Two Halves? The Business of Football*, Edinburgh, 1999, 37.

20. J. Smith and M. LeJeune, *Football: Its Values, Finances and Reputation*, London, 1998.

21. See Michie.

Select Bibliography

Anderson, P., 'When Violence is not Part of the Game: Regulating Sports Violence in Professional Team Sports', 3 *Contemporary Issues in Law* (1998) no.4.

Armstrong, G., and Hobbs, D., 'Tackled from Behind', in R. Giulianotti *et al.* (eds), *Football, Violence and Social Identity* (London: Routledge, 1994).

Armstrong, G., and Young, M., 'Legislators and Interpreters: The Law and "Football Hooligans"', in G. Armstrong and R. Giulianotti (eds.), *Entering the Field: New Perspectives on Football* (Oxford: Berg, 1997).

Baldwin, R., and Cave, M., *Understanding Regulation: Theory, Strategy and Practice* (Oxford: Oxford University Press, 1999).

Beloff, M., 'The Court of Arbitration for Sport at the Olympics', 4 *Sport and the Law Journal* (1996) no.3.

Beloff, M., Kerr, T., and Demetriou, M., *Sports Law* (Oxford: Hart Publishing, 1999).

Benedict, J., *Public Heroes, Private Felons* (Boston, MA: Northeastern University Press, 1997).

Bibbings, L., and Alldridge, P., 'Sexual Expression, Body Alteration and the Defence of Consent', 20 *Journal of Law and Society* (1993) no.3.

Birley, D., *Land of Sport and Glory* (Manchester: Manchester University Press, 1995).

Black, J., *Rules and Regulators* (Oxford: Oxford University Press, 1997).

Blanpain, R., 'Droit et sport, L'affaire Bosman' (Leuven: Peeters, 1996).

Bose, M., *Manchester Unlimited* (London: Orion Business Books, 1999).

Bourdieu, P., 'The Force of Law: towards a Sociology of the Juridical Field', 38 *Hastings Law Journal* (1987).

Brackenridge, C., '"He Owned Me, Basically…" Women's experience of sexual abuse in sport', 32 *International Review for the Sociology of Sport* (1997) no.2.

Brackenridge, C., and Kirby, S., 'Playing Safe. Assessing the Risk of Sexual Abuse to Élite Child Athletes', 32 *International Review for the Sociology of Sport* (1997) no.3.

Brookes, C., *English Cricket: The Game and its Players through the Ages* (London: Weidenfeld & Nicolson, 1978).

Brown, A., and Walsh, A., *Not for Sale! Manchester United, Murdoch and the Defeat of BSkyB* (Edinburgh: Mainstream, 1999).

Cashmore, E., *Making Sense of Sports* (London: Routledge, 1996).

Cohen, S., *Folk Devils and Moral Panics: The Creation of Mod Rockers* (London: MacGibbon & Kee, 1972).

Collins, T., *Rugby's Great Split* (London and Portland, OR: Frank Cass, 1998).

Conn, D., *The Football Business* (Edinburgh: Mainstream, 1997).

Cornish, W., and Clark, G., *Law and Society in Modern England* (London: Sweet and Maxwell, 1989).

Cotton, D., and Wilde, T. (eds), *Sports Law for Sports Managers* (Dubuque, Iowa: Kendall/Hunt Publishing Co., 1997).

Craig, P.P., *Administrative Law* (4th edn, London: Sweet and Maxwell, 1999).

Crick, M., and Smith, D., *Manchester United: The Betrayal of a Legend* (London: Pelham Books, 1989).

Delves, A., 'Popular Recreation and Social Conflict in Derby, 1800–1850', in E. Yeo and J. Yeo, *Popular Culture and Class Conflict 1590-1914* (Sussex: Harvester, 1973).

Emery, C., 'The Vires Defence – Ultra Vires as Defence to Civil or Criminal Proceedings', *Criminal Law Journal* (1992).

Finnie, W., Himsworth, C., and Walker, N. (ed.), *Edinburgh Essays in Public Law* (Edinburgh: Edinburgh University Press, 1991).

Fiske, J., *Understanding Popular Culture* (London: Unwin Hyman, 1989).

Gardiner, S., and Felix, A., 'Juridification of the Football Field: Strategies for Giving Law the Elbow', 5 *Marquette Sports Law Journal* (1995) no.2.

Gardiner, S., 'The Law and the Sportsfield', *Criminal Law Review* (1994).

Gardiner, S., Felix, A., James, M., Welch, R., and O'Leary, J., *Sports Law* (London: Cavendish, 1998).

Giulianotti, R., 'Taking Liberties: Hibs Casuals and Scottish Law', in R. Giulianotti *et al.* (eds), *Football, Violence and Social Identity* (London: Routledge, 1994).

Grayson, E., *Sport and the Law* (3rd edn, London: Butterworths, 1999).

Greenfield, S., and Osborn, G., 'Aesthetics, Injury and Liability in Cricket', 13 *Professional Negligence* (1997).

Greenfield, S., and Osborn, G., 'Enough is Enough: Race, Cricket and Protest in the UK', 30 *Sociological Focus* (1997) no.4.

Greenfield, S., and Osborn, G., *Contract and Control in the Entertainment Industry* (Aldershot: Dartmouth, 1998).

Greenfield, S., and Osborn, G., 'Law's Colonisation of Cricket', 13 *Soundings* (1999).

Greenfield, S., and Osborn, G, 'After the Act: The (Re)Construction and Regulation of Football Fandom', 1 *Journal of Civil Liberties* (1996).

Gunn, M., 'Impact of the Law on Sport with Specific Reference to the Way Sport is Played', 3 *Contemporary Legal Issues* (1998) no.4.

Guttmann, A., *Sports Spectators* (New York: Columbia University Press, 1986).

Hall, S., 'The Treatment of "Football Hooligans" in the Press', in Ingham, R., *et al.*, *Football Hooliganism: The Wider Context* (London: Inter-Action Inprint, 1978).

Hamil, S., Michie, J., and Oughton, C. (eds), *A Game of Two Halves? The Business of Football* (Edinburgh: Mainstream, 1999).

Hamil, S., Oughton, C., and Michie, J. (eds), *Football in the Digital Age: Whose Game Is it Anyway?* (Edinburgh: Mainstream, 2000).

Harding, J., *For the Good of the Game* (London: Robson Books, 1991).

Hill, J., *Striking for Soccer* (London: Sportsman's Book Club, 1961).

Jackson, S., 'Beauty and the Beast: a Critical Look at Sports Violence', 26 *Journal of Physical Education of New Zealand* (1993) no.4.

Lemmon, D., *Cricket Mercenaries* (London: Pavilion, 1987).

Lester, Lord of Herne Hill, 'Discrimination: What can Lawyers Learn from History?', *Public Law* (1994).

Lewis, D., 'Whistleblowers and Job Security', 58 *Modern Law Review* (1995).

MacCabe, C., *The Eloquence of the Vulgar* (London: BFI, 1999).

McCutcheon, P., 'Sports Discipline, Natural Justice and Strict Liability', 28, *Anglo-American Law Review* (1999).

Malcomson, R., *Popular Recreations in English Society* (Cambridge: Cambridge University Press, 1973).

Marqusee, M., 'Sport and Stereotype: from Role Model to Muhammed Ali', 36 *Race and Class* (1995).

Mason, T., *Association Football and English Society 1863–1915* (Sussex: Harvester Press, 1980).

Messner, M., and Sabo, D., *Sex, Violence and Power in Men's Sports* (Freedom, CA: The Crossing Press, 1994).

Morris, P., and Little, G., 'Challenging Sports' Bodies Determinations', 17 *Civil Justice Quarterly* (1998).

Murphy, P., Dunning, E., and Williams, J., *Football on Trial: Spectator Violence and Development in the Football World* (London: 1990).

Ogus, A., 'Rethinking Self-regulation', 19 *Oxford Journal of Legal Studies* (1995).

Ormerod, D. and Gunn, M., 'Consent – a Second Bash', *Criminal Law Review* (1996).

Ormerod, D., 'Consent and Offences Against the Person', 57 *Modern Law Review* (1994).

Ostertag, T., 'From Shoeless Joe to Charley Hustle: Major League Baseball's Continuing Crusade Against Sports Gambling', 2 *Seton Hall Journal of Sport Law* (1992).

Pannick, D., 'Judicial Review of Sports Bodies', 2 *Judicial Review* (1997) no.3.

Pannick, D., *Sex Discrimination in Sport* (London: EOC, 1983).

Parpworth, N., 'Boxing and Prize Fighting: The Indistinguishable Distinguished', 2 *Sport and the Law Journal* (1994).

Pearson, G., 'The English Disease? The Socio-Legal Construction of Football Hooliganism', 60 *Youth and Policy: The Journal of Critical Analysis* (1998).

Pearson, G., 'Legitimate Targets? The Civil Liberties of Football Fans', 4 *Journal of Civil Liberties* (1999) no.1.

Poliakoff, M.B., *Combat Sports in the Ancient World* (New Haven: Yale University Press, 1987).

Quirk, J., and Fort, J., *Pay Dirt: The Business of Professional Team Sports* (Princeton: Princeton University Press, 1997).

Reeb, M. (ed.), *Digest of CAS Awards 1986-1998* (Berne: Editions Stæmpfli S.A., 1998).

Rippey, E., 'Contractual Freedom over Substance-related Issues in Major League Baseball', 1 *Sports Lawyers Journal* (1994).

Sisson, D., and Trexell, B., 'The National Football League's Substance Abuse Policy: Is Further Conflict between Players and Management Inevitable?' 1 *Marquette Sports Law Journal* (1991) no.1.

Strutt, J., *The Sports and Pastimes of the People of England* (1801; 1903 edition, edited by J. Charles Cox, London: Methuen).

Sugden, J., and Tomlinson, A., *FIFA and the Contest for World Football: Who Rules the People's Game?* (Cambridge: Polity Press, 1998).

Szymanski, S., and Kuypers, T., *Winners and Losers: the Business Strategy of Football* (London: Viking, 1999).

Tate, W., *The English Village Community and the Enclosure Movements* (London: Victor Gollancz, 1967).

Thompson, E., *The Making of the English Working Class* (1963; London: Penguin, 1991).

Trivizas, E., 'Disturbances Associated with Football Matches: Types of Incidents and Selection of Charges', 24 *British Journal of Criminology* (1984) no.4.

Turner, B., *The Body and Social Theory* (London: Sage, 1984).

Velasquez, B., 'Recent US Supreme Court Cases in Sexual Harassment may Provide Implications [*sic*] for Athletics Departments and Physical Education Programs', 9 *Journal of Legal Aspects of Sport* (1999) no.1.

Wallace-Bruce, N., 'Employers Beware! The perils of Providing an Employment Reference', 45 *Journal of Business Law* (1997) no.6.

Washburn, K., and Thornton, J. (eds), *Dumbing Down: Essays on the Strip-mining of American Culture* (New York: Norton Press, 1996).

Weatherill, S., *Law and Integration in the European Union* (Oxford: Oxford University Press, 1995).

Weiler, P., and Roberts, G., *Sports and the Law* (St Paul, USA: West Law,

1998).

Wigglesworth, N., *The Evolution of English Sport* (London and Portland, OR: Frank Cass, 1996).

Wolohan, J., 'Sports Injuries: Risk Management Developments in the United States', 1 *Sports Law Bulletin* (1998) no.6.

Young, K., 'Violence in the Workplace of Professional Sport', 26 *International Review for the Sociology of Sport* (1991).

Young, P., *A History of British Football* (London: Sportsman's Book Club, 1969).

Notes on Contributors

Adam Brown is a Research Fellow at the Manchester Institute for Popular Culture, Manchester Metropolitan University. He has researched issues of democratization and fans in football and the impact of commercialization. He is a member of the Football Task Force and its Core Working Group, and has also been involved in supporters' organizations. He is editor of *Fanatics! Power, Identity and Fandom in Football* (Routledge, 1998), and is co-author of *Not for Sale! Manchester United, Murdoch and the Defeat of BSkyB* (Mainstream, 1999).

Ken Foster teaches at the University of Warwick. He has taught a Sports Law undergraduate option on the LL.B course since 1987, and teaches on the MA Politics of Sport postgraduate programme. He is also currently developing an option in European and International Sports Law to be offered on the Law School's LL.M postgraduate courses in International Economic Law. Recent publications of his work include 'European Law and Football: Who's in Charge?', 1 *Soccer and Society* (2000) no.1.

Simon Gardiner is Director of the Sports Law Centre at Anglia Polytechnic University. He is currently researching areas of sports injury liability and legal issues surrounding European national identity and sport. He is co-author of *Sports Law* (Cavendish, 1998), and has published widely in the newly emerging discipline of sports law. His recent publications include 'The Law and Hate Speech: "Ooh Aah Cantona" and the Denomination of "the Other"', in A. Brown (ed.), *Fanatics! Power Identity & Fandom in Football* (Routledge, 1998).

Edward Grayson is Practising Barrister in Sport and the Law related cases, and Founding President of the British Association for Sport and the Law. He is the author of *Sport and the Law* (3rd edn, Butterworths, 2000) and *Ethics, Injuries and the Law in Sports Medicine* (Butterworth-Heinemann, 1999). He is also Visiting Professor of Sport and the Law, Anglia Law School.

Steve Greenfield is Co-Director of the Centre for the Study of Law, Society and Popular Culture in the School of Law at the University of

Westminster. He is the co-author of *Contract and Control in the Entertainment Industry: Dancing on the Edge of Heaven* (Dartmouth, 1998), and *Regulating Football: Commodification, Consumption and the Law* (Pluto, 2001). His works have been published in a broad range of both academic and more popular journals on various aspects of the relationship between law and popular culture.

Michael Gunn and David Ormerod Professor Michael Gunn is Head of the Department of Academic Legal Studies, Nottingham Law School, Nottingham Trent University. David Ormerod is Senior Lecturer in Law at the University of Nottingham. They have published widely in many fields, while their key works on sport and the law consist of two joint articles: 'The Legality of Boxing', 15 *Legal Studies* (1995) and 'The Second Law Commission Consultation Paper on Consent: Consent – A Second Bash', *Criminal Law Review* (1996). In addition, Professor Gunn has recently published 'The Impact of the Law on Sport with Specific Reference to the Way Sport is Played', 3 *Contemporary Issues in Law* (1998).

David McArdle is the Research Fellow in Sport, Law and Management at De Montfort University, Bedford. His current research is concerned with discrimination, health and safety and employment issues within the field of sport and leisure. His work has been published in various law, sociology and management journals, while his first book, *From Boot Money to Bosman: Football, Society and the Law*, has recently been published by Cavendish.

J. Paul McCutcheon is Associate Professor of Law at the University of Limerick and Visiting Fellow at the School of Law, Anglia Polytechnic University. He is author of *The Larceny Act 1916* (Round Hall Press, 1988), and co-author of *The Irish Legal System* (3rd edn, Butterworths, 1996) and *Criminal Liability* (Round Hall Sweet & Maxwell, 2000). He has published extensively in the areas of criminal law, criminal procedure and legal systems. His publications in the area of sports law include 'Sports Violence, Consent and the Criminal Law', 45 *Northern Ireland Legal Quarterly* (1994); 'Judicial Control of Sporting Bodies: Recent Irish Examples', 9 *Sport and the Law Journal* (1995) no.2; 'Negative Enforcement of Employment Contracts in the Sports Industries', 17 *Legal Studies* (1997); and 'Sports Discipline, Natural Justice and Strict Liability', 28 *Anglo-American Law Review* (1999).

Guy Osborn is Co-Director of the Centre for the Study of Law, Society and Popular Culture, and Course Leader of the LLM Entertainment Law at the University of Westminster. He has published widely in the areas of music, sport and media including *Contract and Control in the Entertainment Industry. Dancing on the Edge of Heaven* (Dartmouth, 1998), and *Regulating Football: Commodification, Consumption and the Law* (Pluto, 2001).

Neil Parpworth is Senior Lecturer in Law at De Montfort University, Leicester. His teaching and research interests lie in the fields of constitutional and administrative law, civil liberties, environmental law and sports law. He is the author of *Constitutional and Administrative Law* (Butterworths, 2000), and the joint or co-author of several other books with a public law or environmental law theme. He has had articles with a sports law theme published in several journals, including the *Sport and the Law Journal.*

Geoff Pearson presently lectures in Football and the Law at Liverpool University's Football Research Unit. Publications include 'The English Disease? The Socio-Legal Construction of Football Hooliganism', *Youth and Policy: The Journal of Critical Analysis*, 60 (Summer 1998) and 'Legitimate Targets? The Civil Liberties of Football Fans', *Journal of Civil Liberties* (March 1999).

Steve Redhead is Professor of Law and Popular Culture at Manchester Metropolitan University. He is the author of *Post-fandom and the Millennial Blues* (Routledge, 1997), *Subculture to Clubcultures* (Blackwell, 1997) and editor of *The Clubcultures Reader* (Blackwell, 1997). His latest book is *Repetitive Beat Generation* (Rebel Inc., 2000).

Nick Toms is a practising Barrister-at-Law. He advised the Independent Manchester United Supporters Association in relation to the proposed takeover by BSkyB and prepared submissions to the Office of Fair Trading on behalf of IMUSA opposing the merger. He attended the Monopolies and Mergers Commission hearing with the IMUSA delegation and made submissions opposing the merger.

Steve Weatherill is the Jacques Delors Professor of EC Law at the University of Oxford. He has written several books in the area of EC law, most recently the 3rd edition of *Weatherill and Beaumont's EC Law* (Penguin, 1999). In the area of sport, he wrote the 'Annotation of the *Bosman* Ruling', 33 *Common Market Law Review* (1996).

Index